THE RECORD OF A
FALLEN VAMPIRE

D0097331

Change always comes without warning. The sights you are accustomed to vanish before you notice. They say that everything changes, but it still gets me down... Vampires live thousands of years. What must they think of change? *-Yuri Kimura*

Artist Yuri Kimura debuted two short stories in Japan's *Gangan Powered* after winning the Enix Manga Award. Shortly thereafter, she began *The Record of a Fallen Vampire*, which was serialized in Japan's *Monthly Shonen Gangan* through March 2007.

Author Kyo Shirodaira is from Nara prefecture. In addition to *The Record of a Fallen Vampire*, Shirodaira has scripted the manga *Spiral~Suiri no Kizuna*. Shirodaira's novel *Meitantei ni Hana wo* was nominated for the 8th Annual Ayukawa Tetsuya Award in 1997.

THE RECORD OF A

FALLEN VAMPIRE

STORY BY: KYO SHIRODAIRA ART BY: YURI KIMURA

3

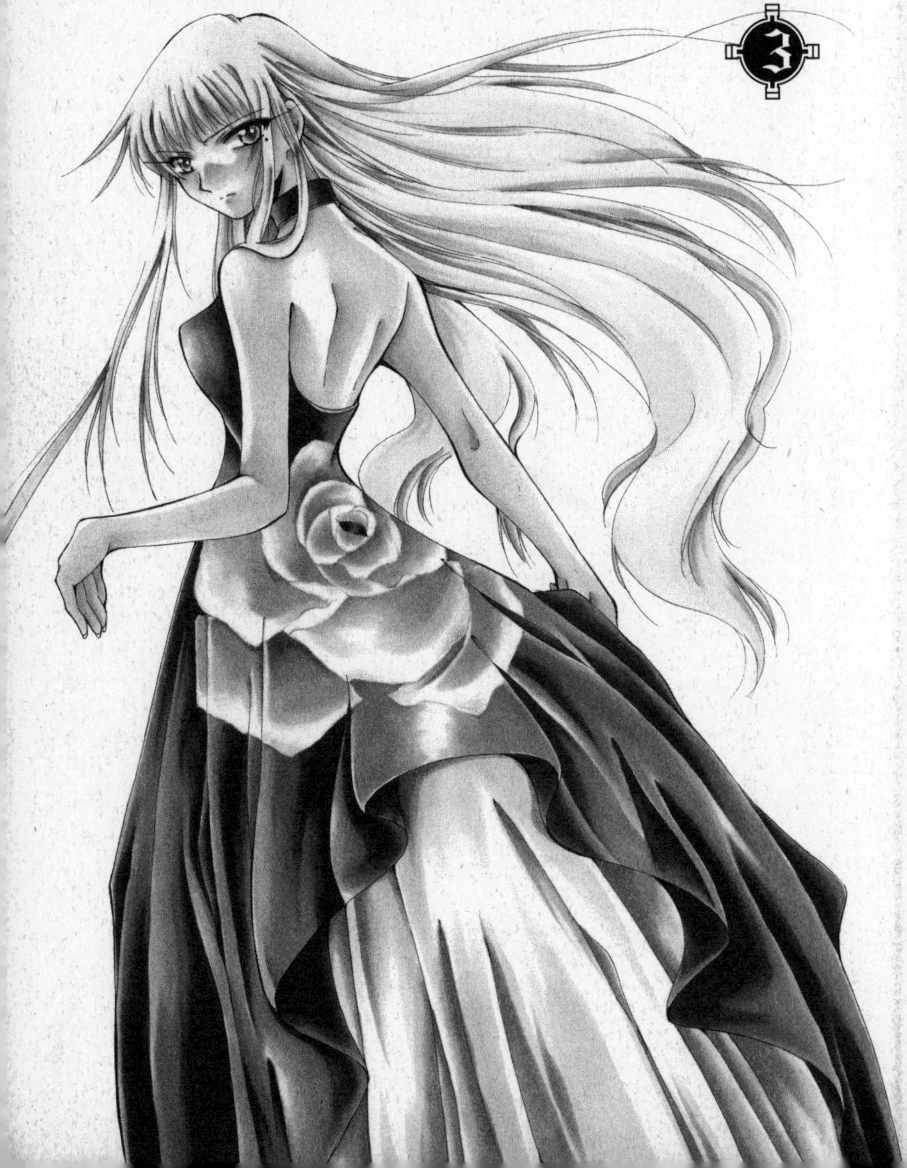

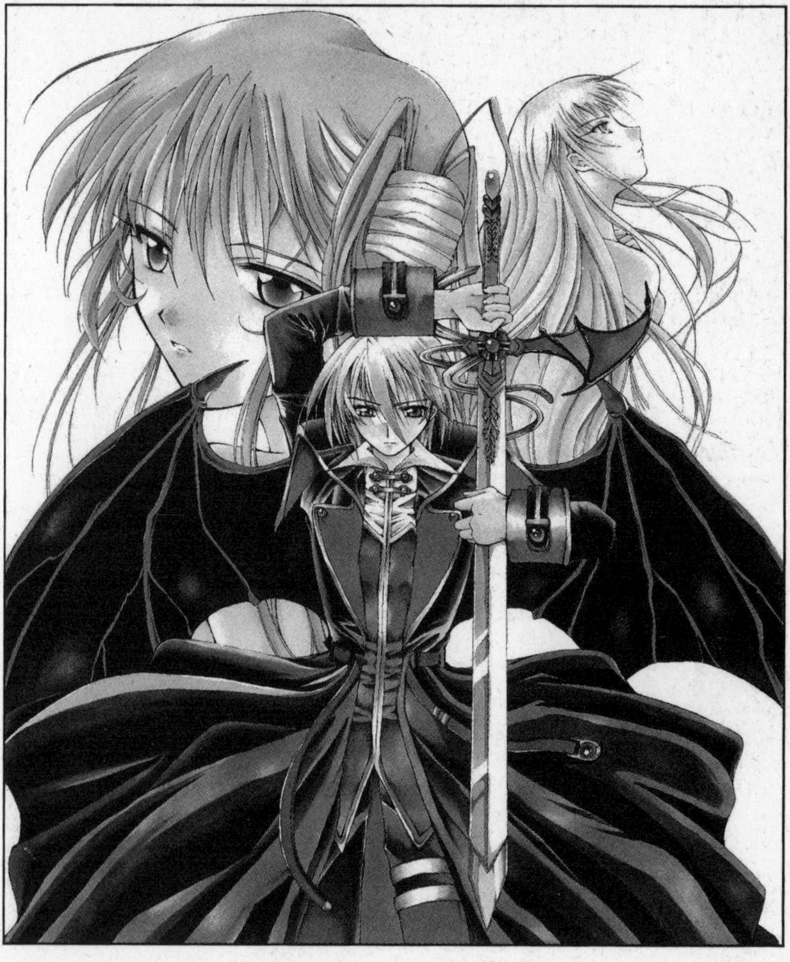

CONTENTS

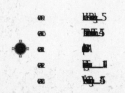

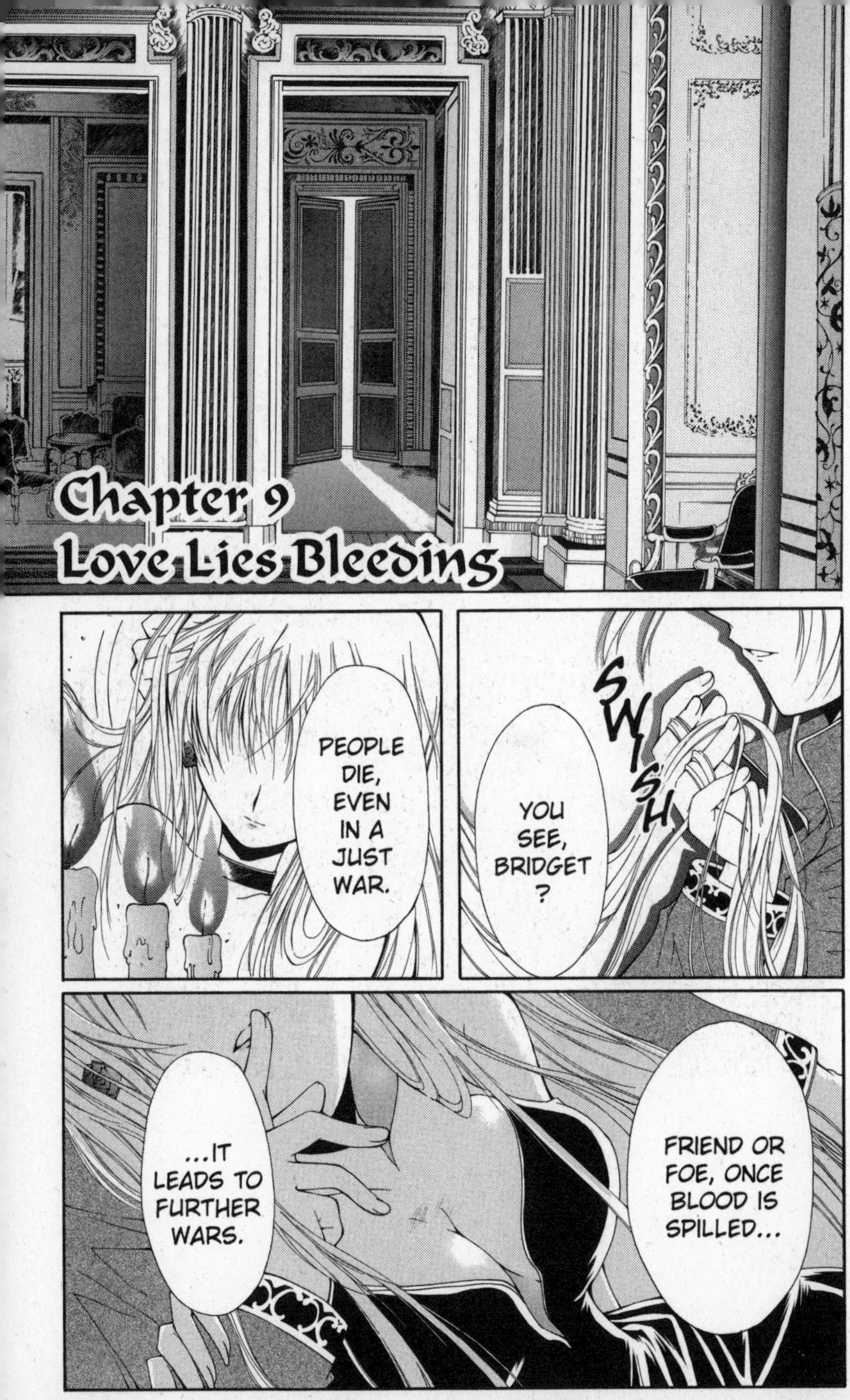
Chapter 9
Love Lies Bleeding
SWISH
YOU SEE, BRIDGET?
PEOPLE DIE, EVEN IN A JUST WAR.
FRIEND OR FOE, ONCE BLOOD IS SPILLED...
...IT LEADS TO FURTHER WARS.

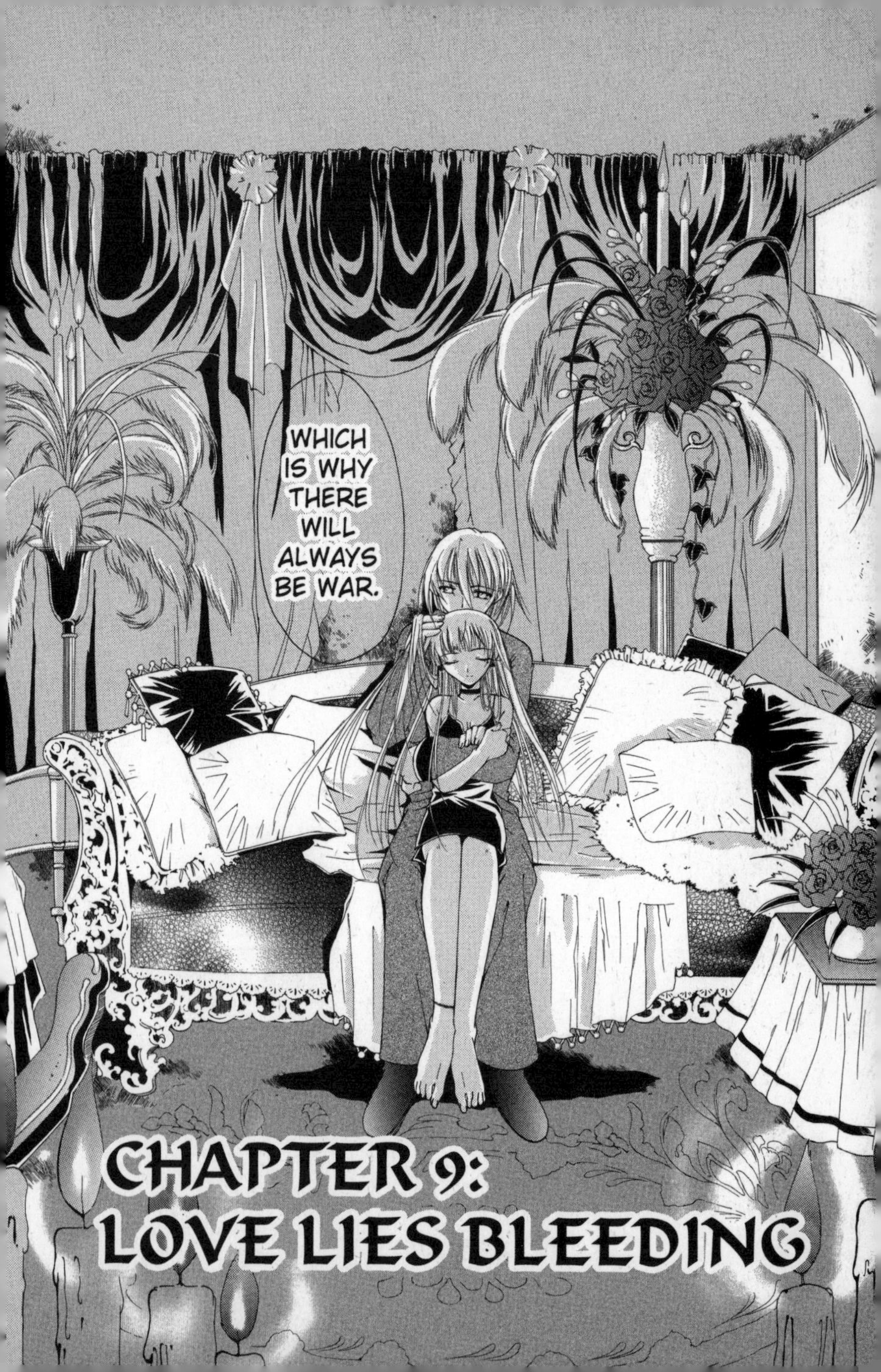
WHICH IS WHY THERE WILL ALWAYS BE WAR.
CHAPTER 9: LOVE LIES BLEEDING

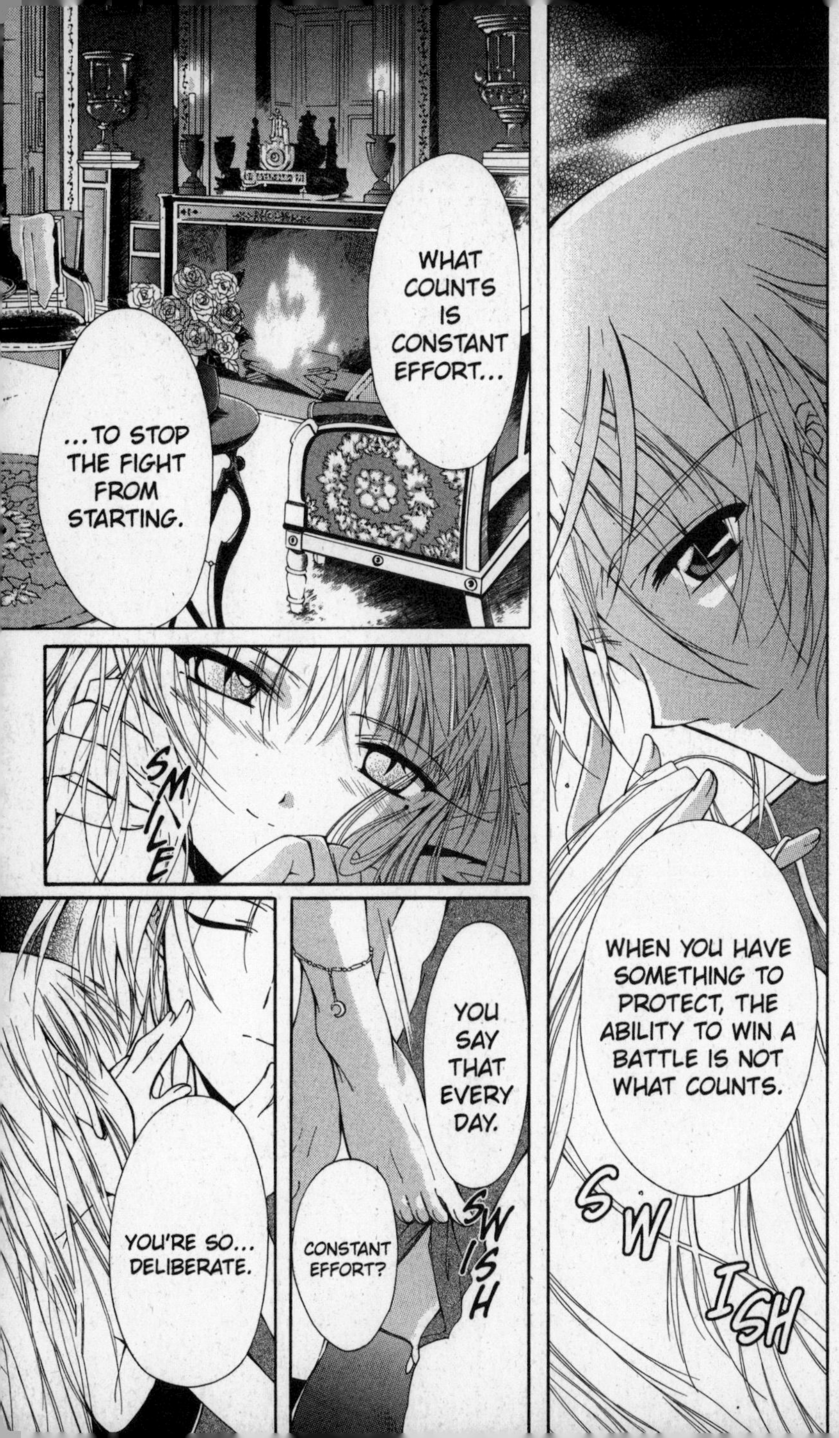
WHEN YOU HAVE SOMETHING TO PROTECT, THE ABILITY TO WIN A BATTLE IS NOT WHAT COUNTS.
SWISH
WHAT COUNTS IS CONSTANT EFFORT...
...TO STOP THE FIGHT FROM STARTING.
SMILE
YOU SAY THAT EVERY DAY.
CONSTANT EFFORT?
SWISH
YOU'RE SO... DELIBERATE.

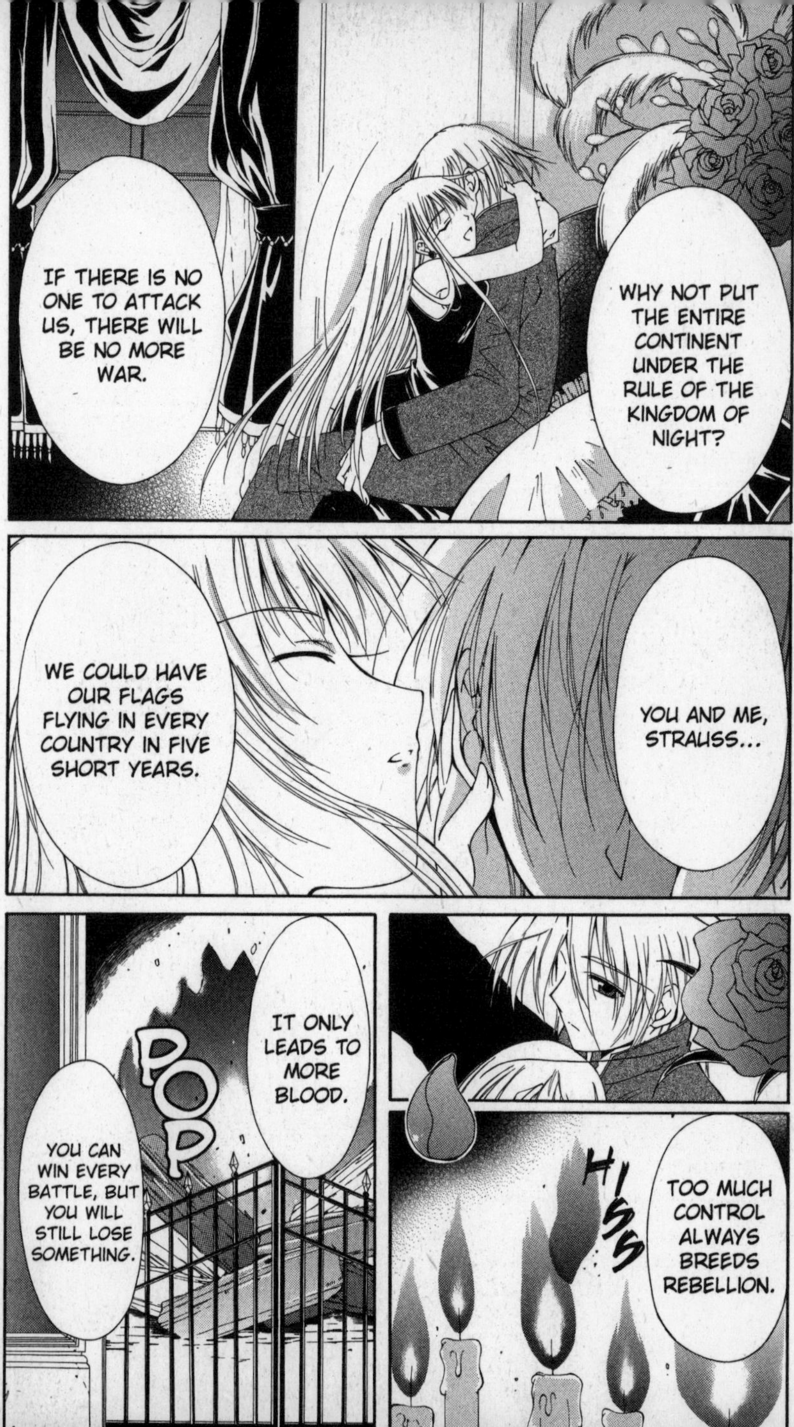
WHY NOT PUT THE ENTIRE CONTINENT UNDER THE RULE OF THE KINGDOM OF NIGHT?
IF THERE IS NO ONE TO ATTACK US, THERE WILL BE NO MORE WAR.
YOU AND ME, STRAUSS...
WE COULD HAVE OUR FLAGS FLYING IN EVERY COUNTRY IN FIVE SHORT YEARS.
HISS
TOO MUCH CONTROL ALWAYS BREEDS REBELLION.
IT ONLY LEADS TO MORE BLOOD.
POP
YOU CAN WIN EVERY BATTLE, BUT YOU WILL STILL LOSE SOMETHING.

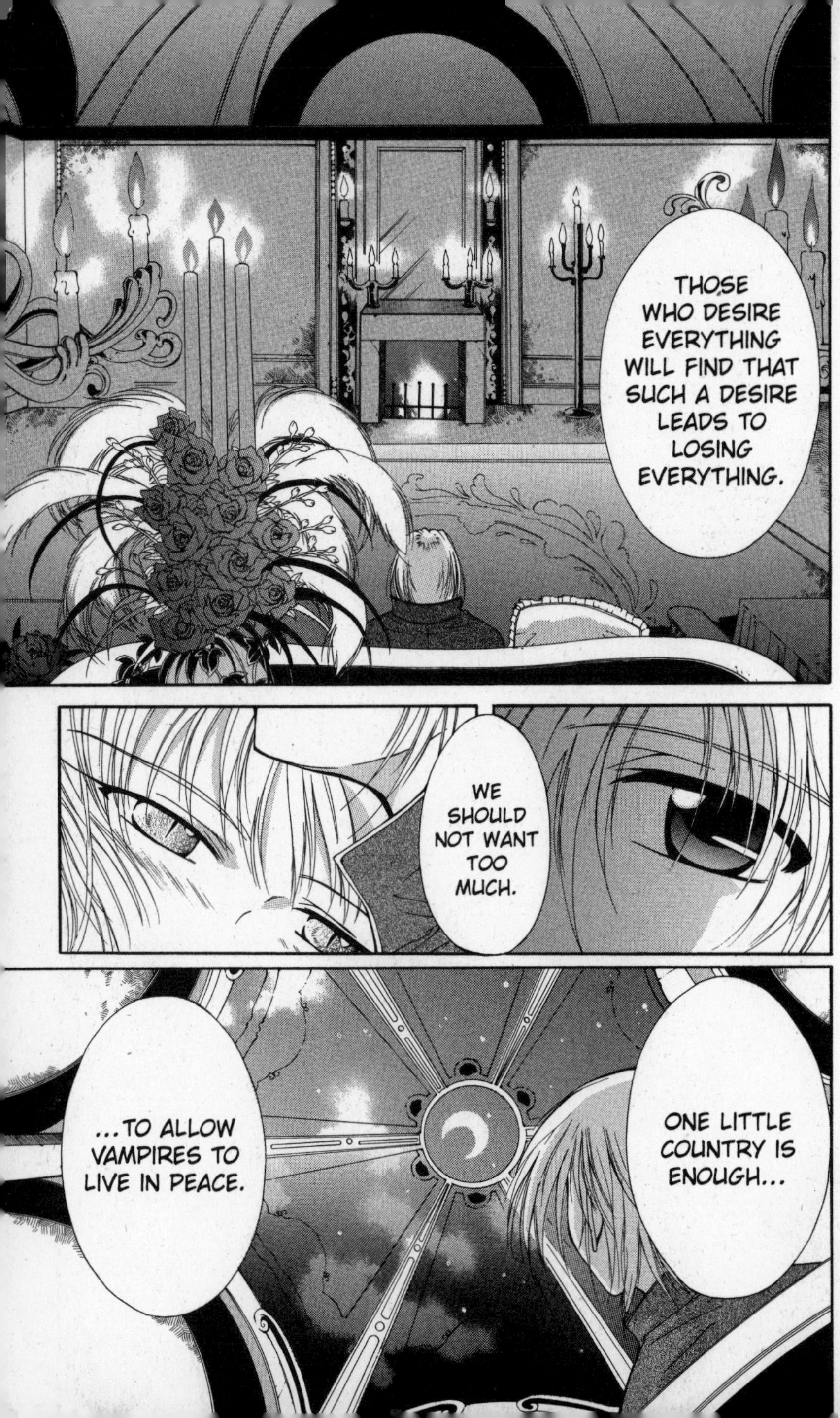
THOSE WHO DESIRE EVERYTHING WILL FIND THAT SUCH A DESIRE LEADS TO LOSING EVERYTHING.
WE SHOULD NOT WANT TOO MUCH.
ONE LITTLE COUNTRY IS ENOUGH...
...TO ALLOW VAMPIRES TO LIVE IN PEACE.

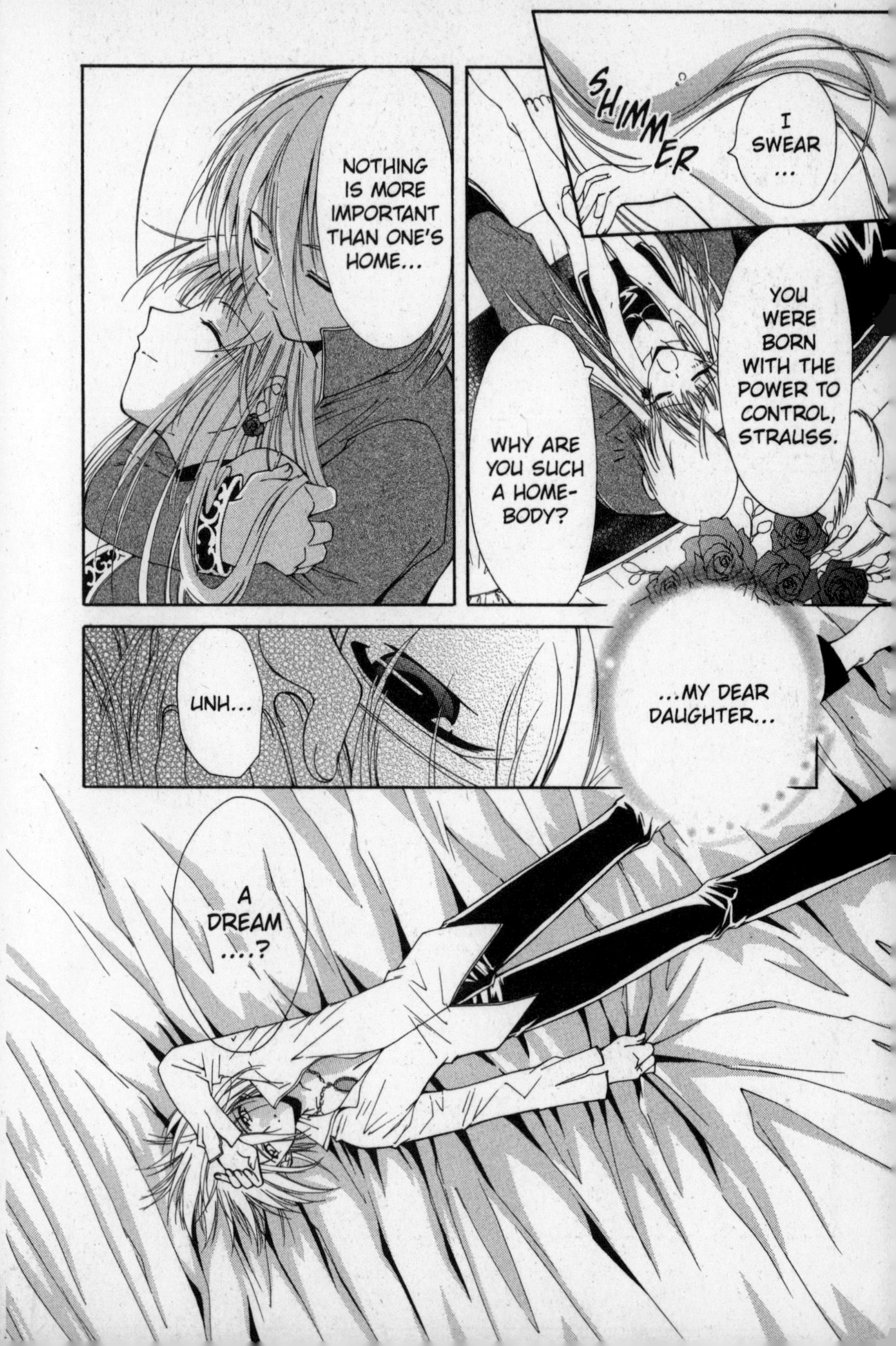
SHIMMER
I SWEAR ...
YOU WERE BORN WITH THE POWER TO CONTROL, STRAUSS.
WHY ARE YOU SUCH A HOME-BODY?
NOTHING IS MORE IMPORTANT THAN ONE'S HOME...
...MY DEAR DAUGHTER...
UNH...
A DREAM ....?

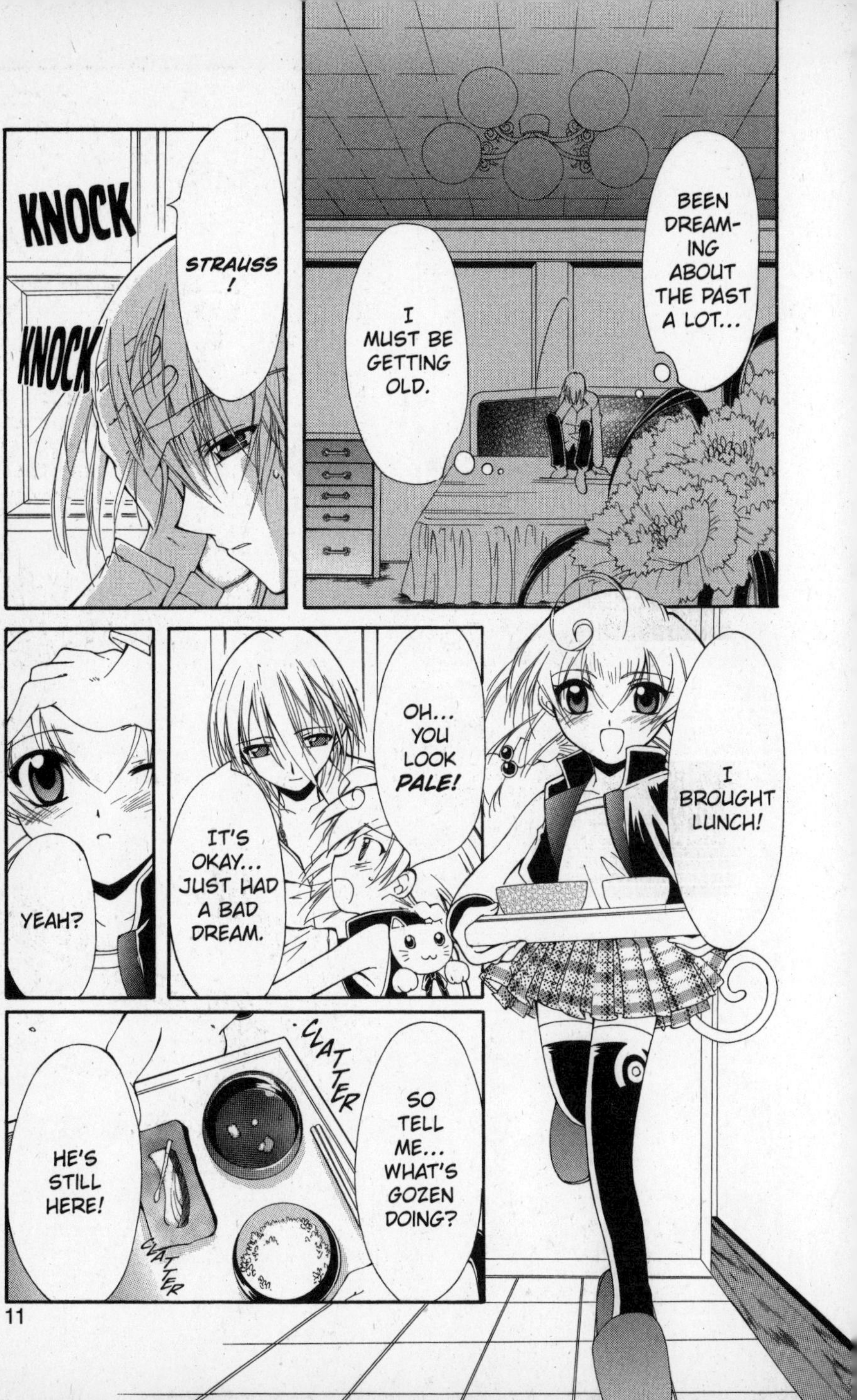
BEEN DREAMING-ING ABOUT THE PAST A LOT...
I MUST BE GETTING OLD.
KNOCK
KNOCK
STRAUSS!
I BROUGHT LUNCH!
OH... YOU LOOK PALE!
IT'S OKAY... JUST HAD A BAD DREAM.
YEAH?
CLATTER
SO TELL ME... WHAT'S GOZEN DOING?
HE'S STILL HERE!
CLATTER

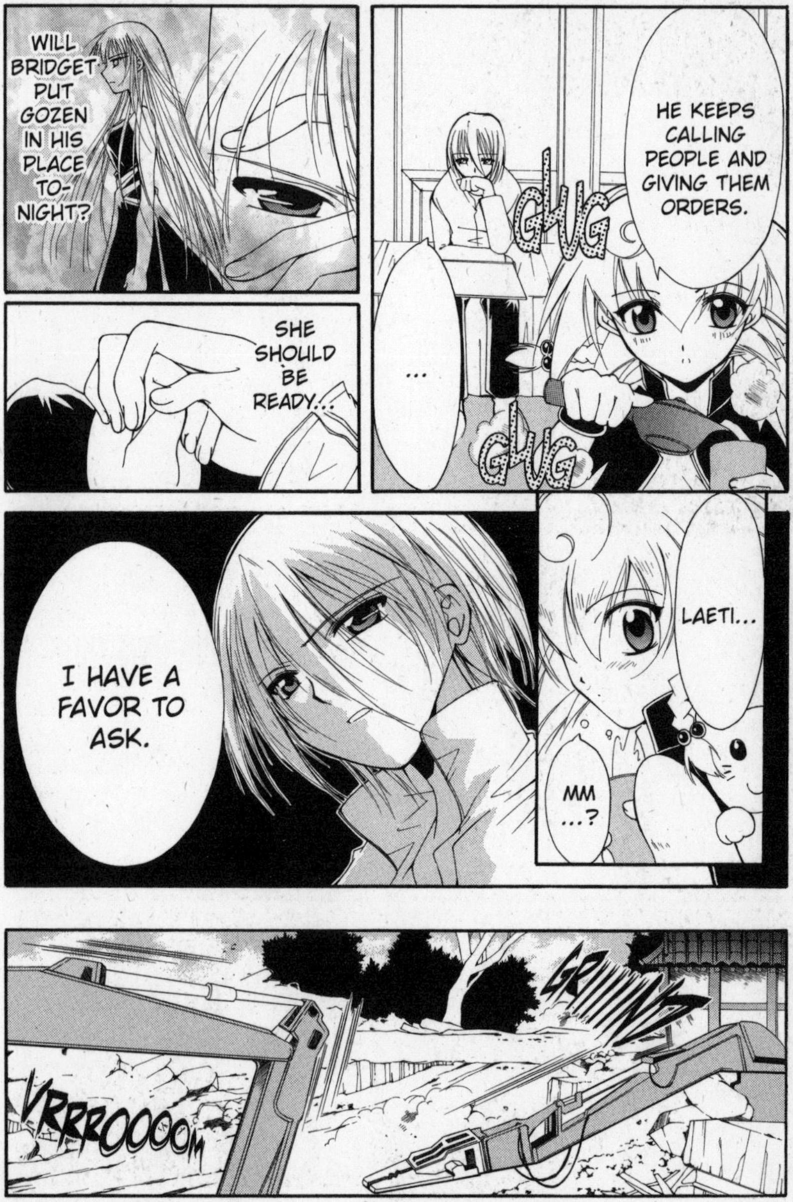
HE KEEPS CALLING PEOPLE AND GIVING THEM ORDERS.
GHUG
...
GHUG
WILL BRIDGET PUT GOZEN IN HIS PLACE TO-NIGHT?
SHE SHOULD BE READY...
LAETI...
MM ...?
I HAVE A FAVOR TO ASK.
VRRROOOOOM

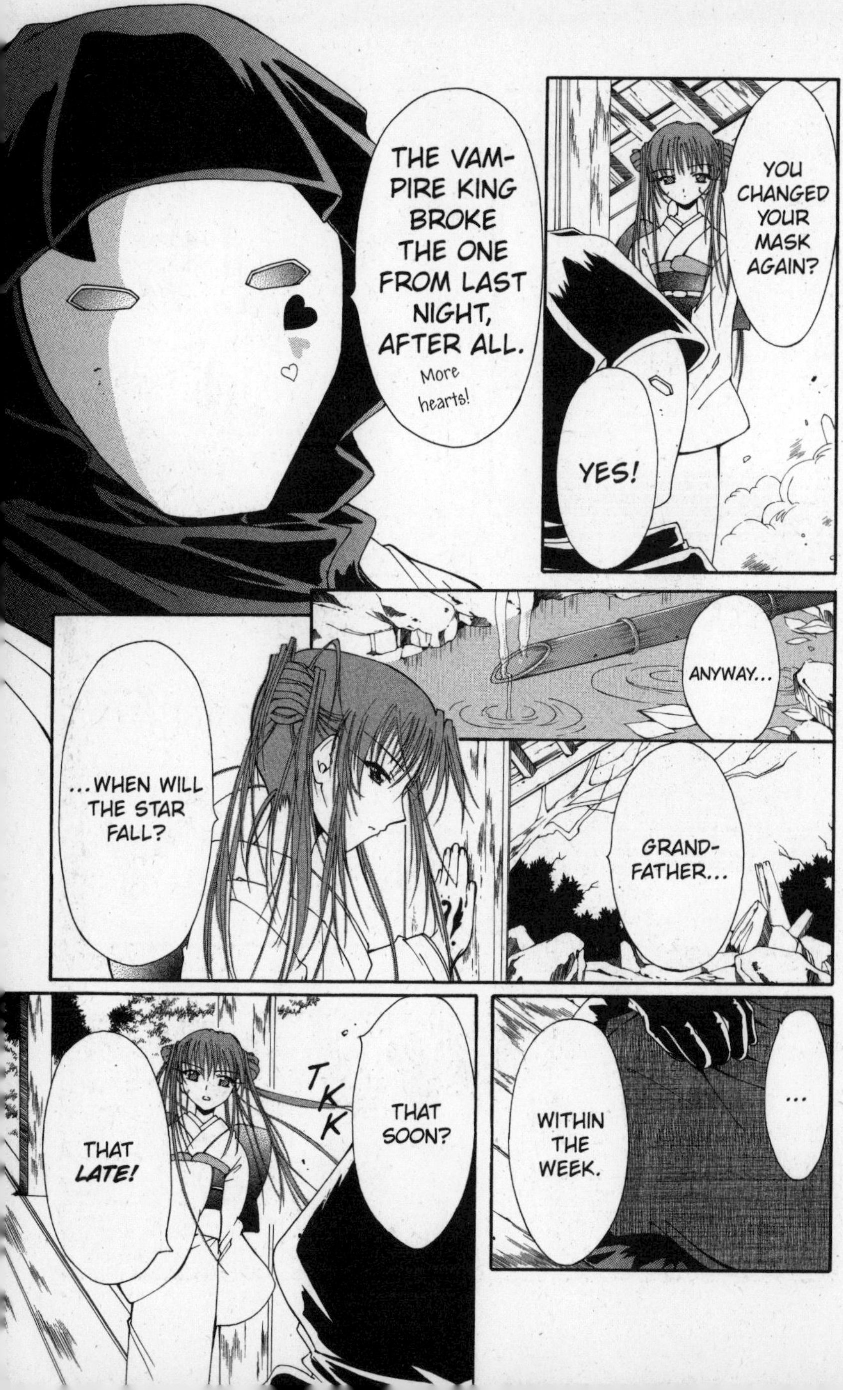
YOU CHANGED YOUR MASK AGAIN?
YES!
THE VAM-PIRE KING BROKE THE ONE FROM LAST NIGHT, AFTER ALL.
More hearts!
ANYWAY...
GRAND-FATHER...
...WHEN WILL THE STAR FALL?
...
WITHIN THE WEEK.
THAT SOON?
TKK
THAT *LATE!*

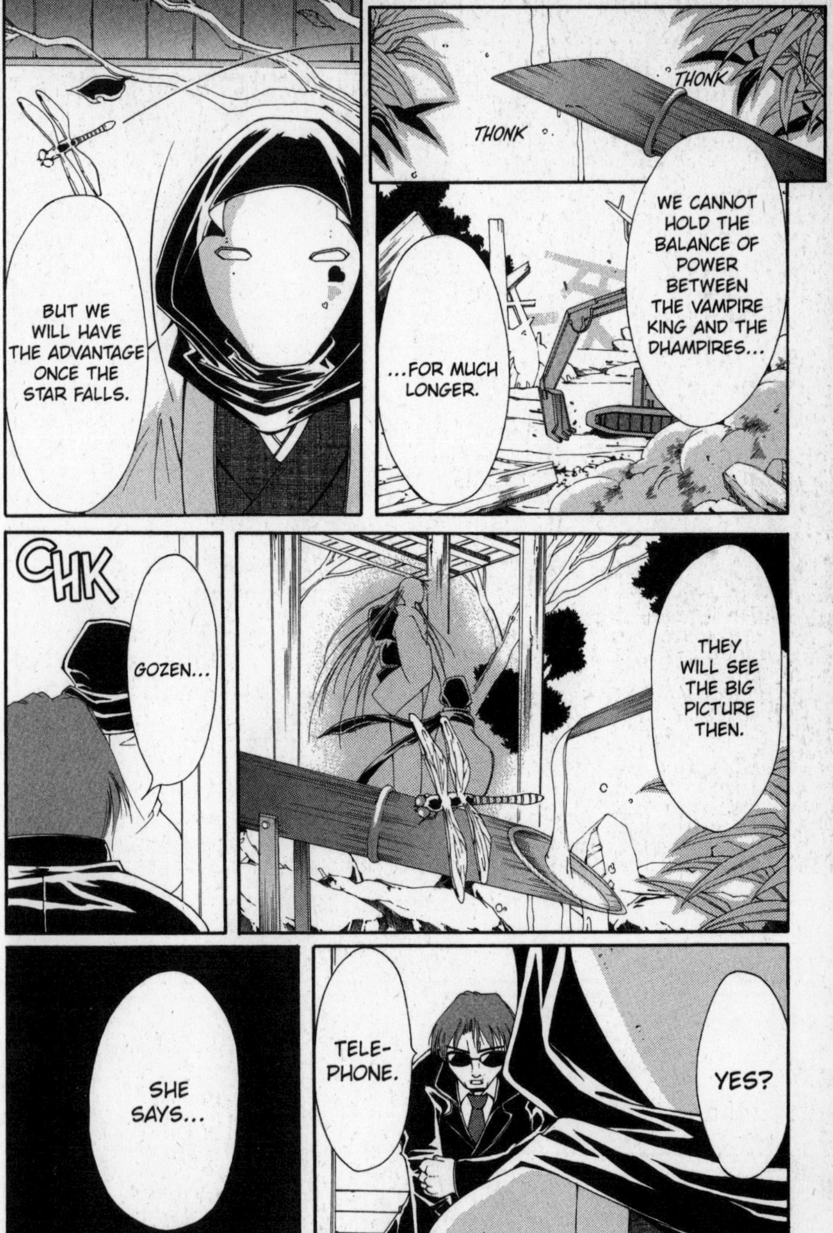
THONK
THONK
WE CANNOT HOLD THE BALANCE OF POWER BETWEEN THE VAMPIRE KING AND THE DHAMPIRES...
...FOR MUCH LONGER.
BUT WE WILL HAVE THE ADVANTAGE ONCE THE STAR FALLS.
THEY WILL SEE THE BIG PICTURE THEN.
CHK
GOZEN...
YES?
TELE-PHONE.
SHE SAYS...

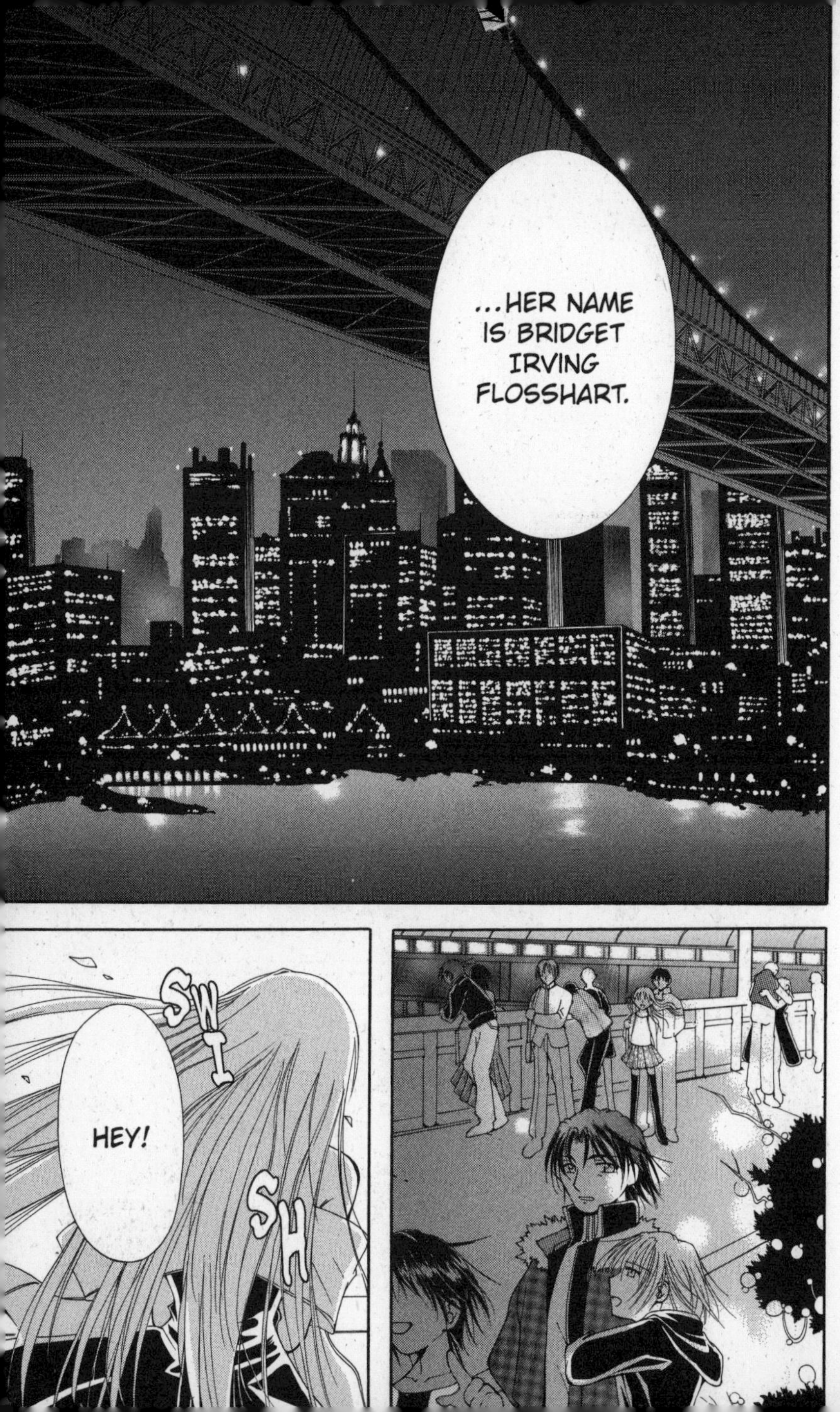
...HER NAME IS BRIDGET IRVING FLOSSHART.
SWISH
HEY!

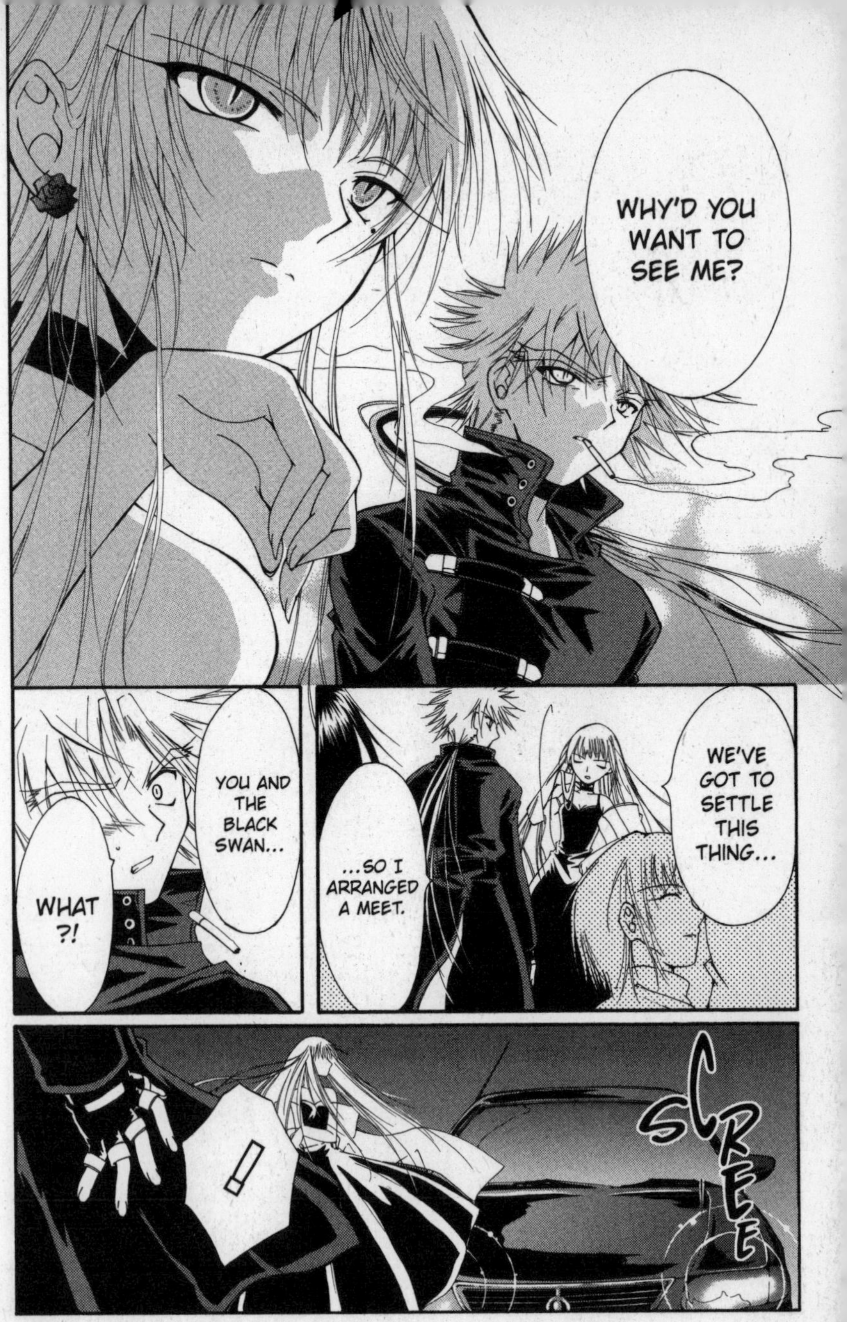
WHY'D YOU WANT TO SEE ME?
WE'VE GOT TO SETTLE THIS THING...
...SO I ARRANGED A MEET.
YOU AND THE BLACK SWAN...
WHAT?!
SCREEE
!

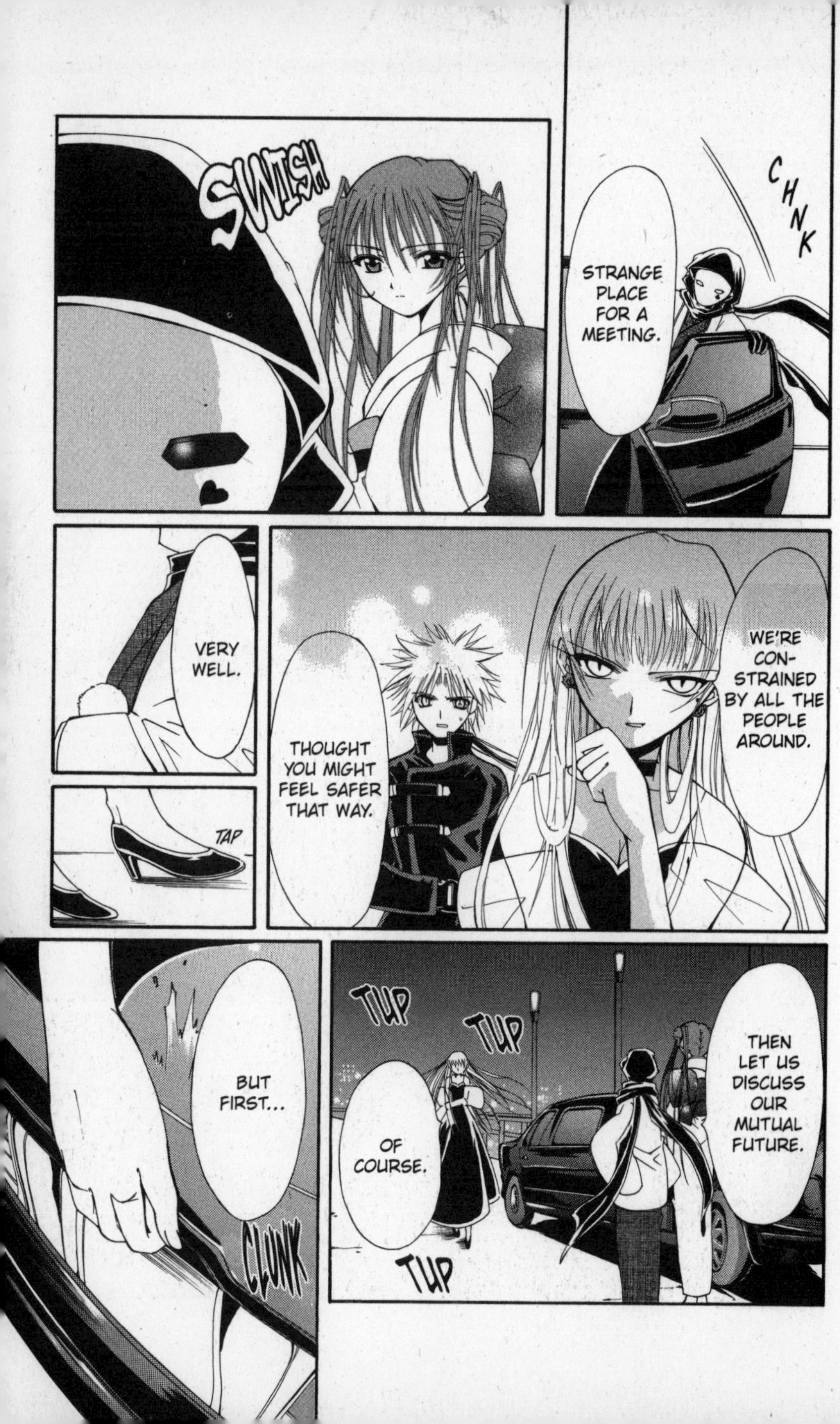
CHNK
STRANGE PLACE FOR A MEETING.
SWISH
WE'RE CON-STRAINED BY ALL THE PEOPLE AROUND.
THOUGHT YOU MIGHT FEEL SAFER THAT WAY.
VERY WELL.
TAP
THEN LET US DISCUSS OUR MUTUAL FUTURE.
TUP
TUP
OF COURSE.
TUP
BUT FIRST...
CLUNK

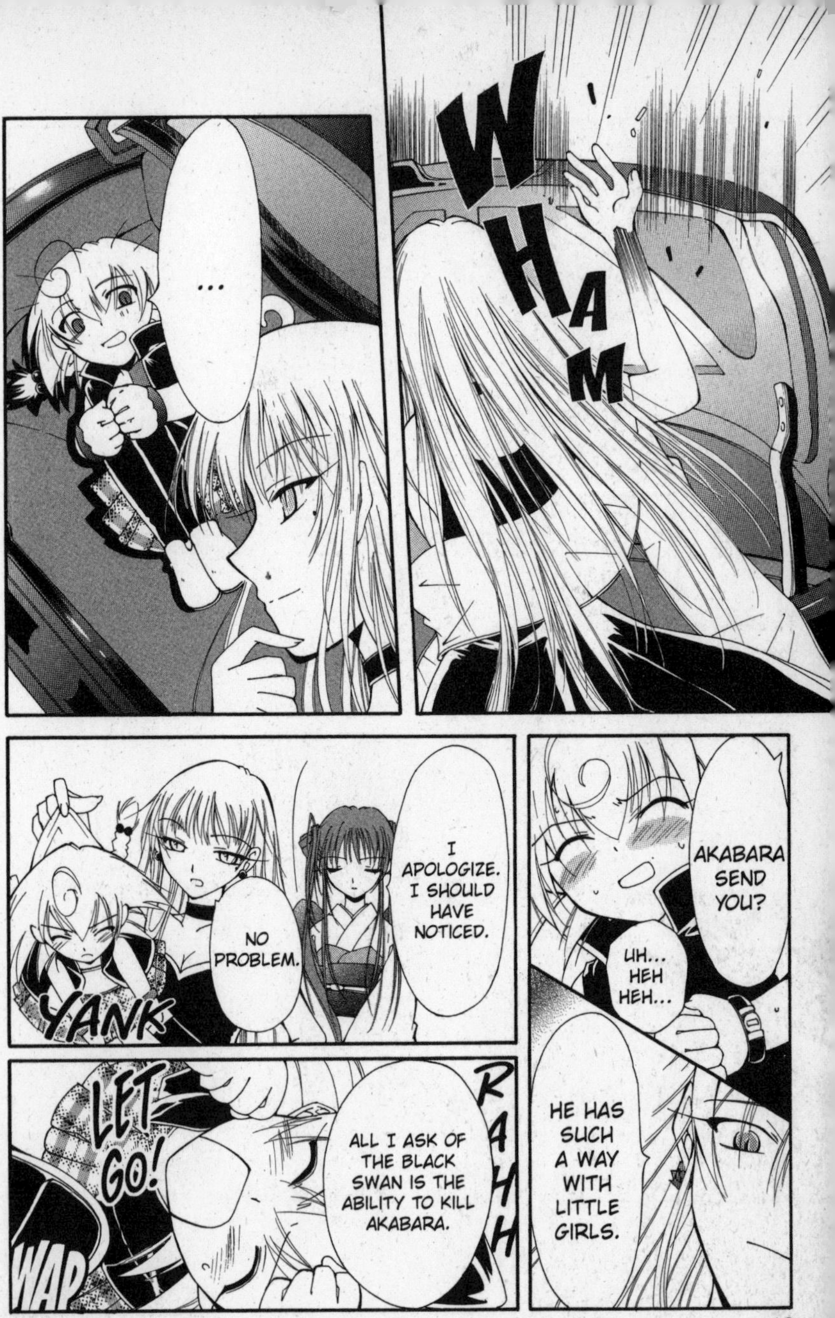
WHAM
...
AKABARA SEND YOU?
UH... HEH HEH...
HE HAS SUCH A WAY WITH LITTLE GIRLS.
I APOLOGIZE. I SHOULD HAVE NOTICED.
NO PROBLEM.
YANK
RAHHH
ALL I ASK OF THE BLACK SWAN IS THE ABILITY TO KILL AKABARA.
LET GO!
WAP

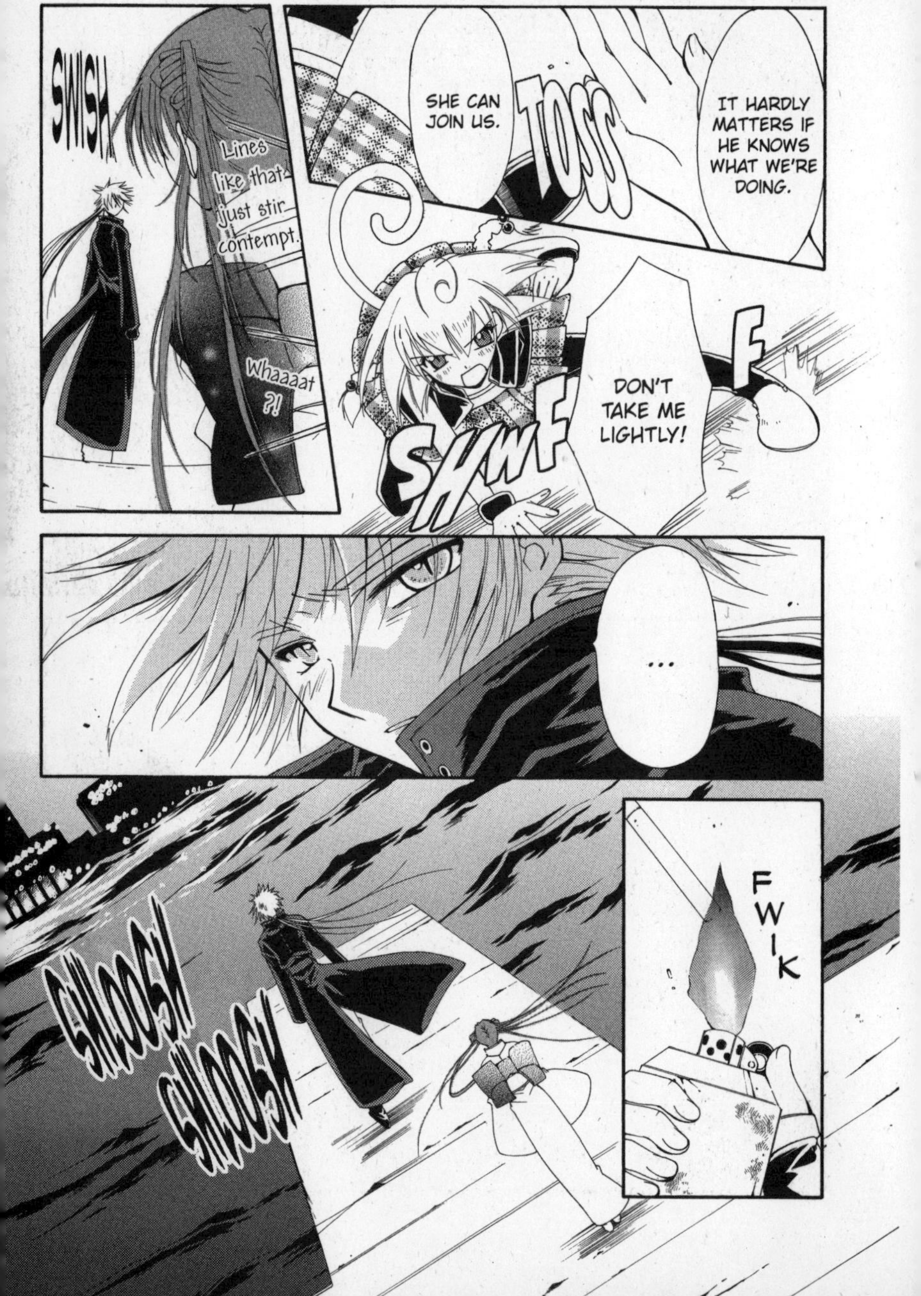
IT HARDLY MATTERS IF HE KNOWS WHAT WE'RE DOING.
TOSS
SHE CAN JOIN US.
F
DON'T TAKE ME LIGHTLY!
SHWF
SWISH
Lines like that just stir contempt.
Whaaaat?!
...
FWIK
SHOOSH
SHOOSH

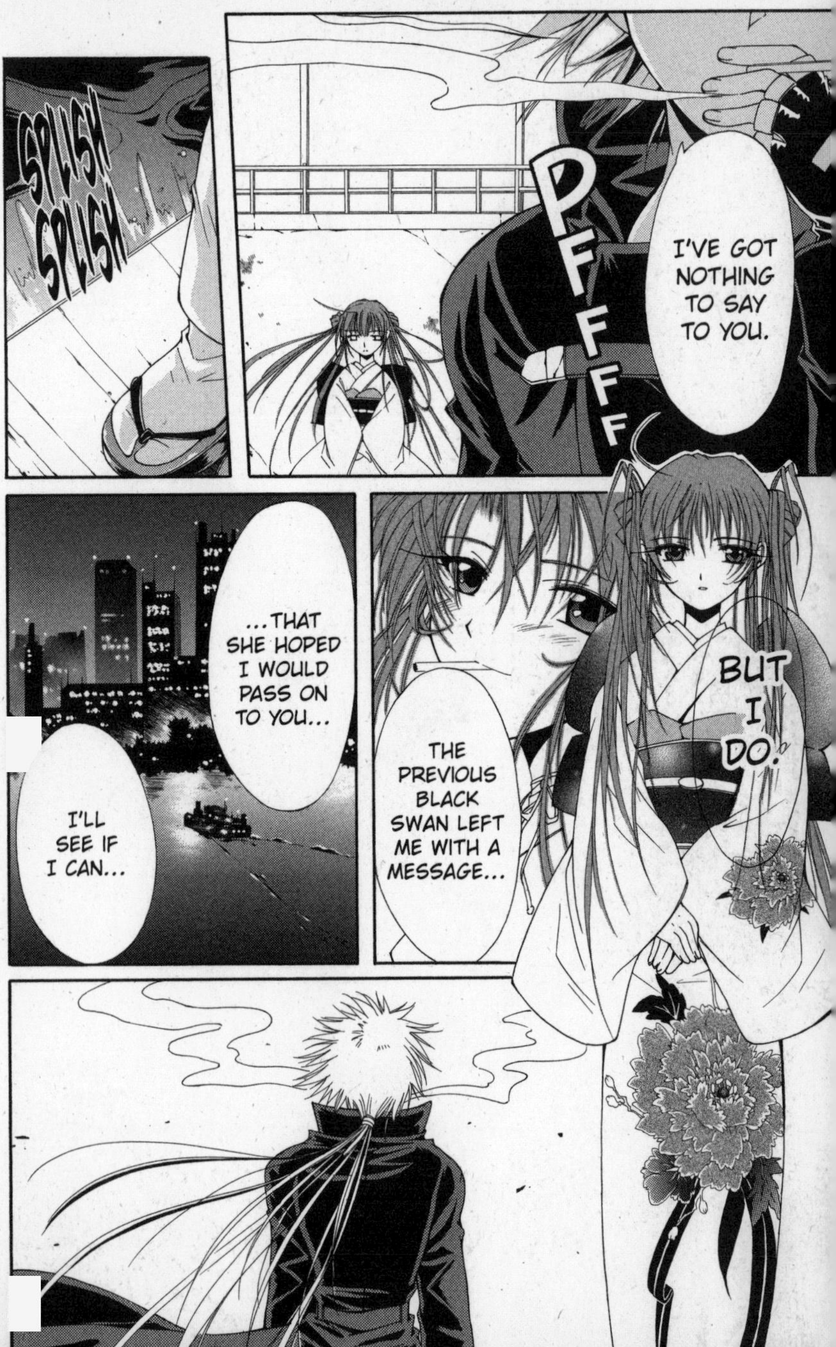
PFFF
I'VE GOT NOTHING TO SAY TO YOU.
SPLISH SPLISH
BUT I DO.
THE PREVIOUS BLACK SWAN LEFT ME WITH A MESSAGE...
...THAT SHE HOPED I WOULD PASS ON TO YOU...
I'LL SEE IF I CAN...

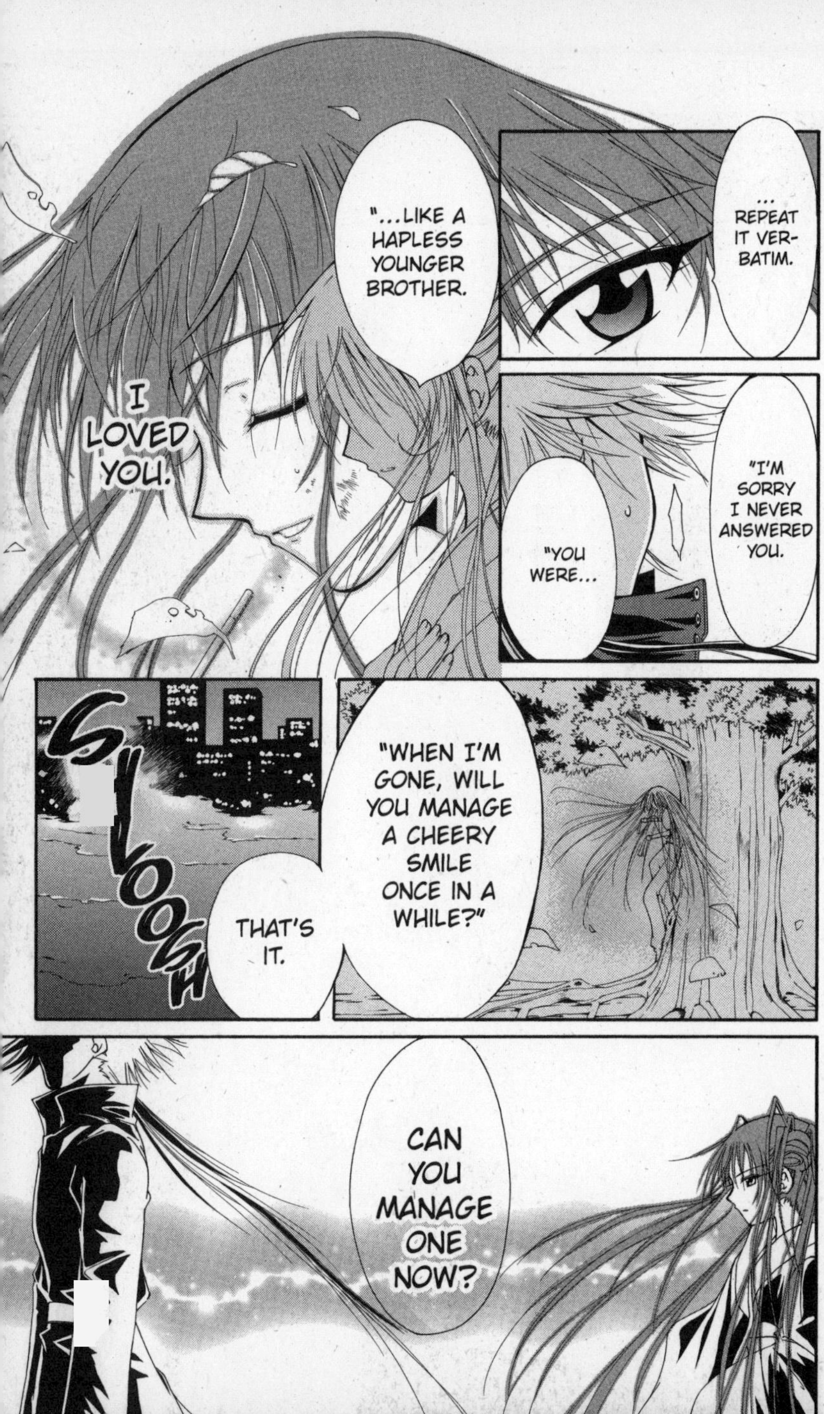
...REPEAT IT VERBATIM.
"I'M SORRY I NEVER ANSWERED YOU.
"YOU WERE...
"...LIKE A HAPLESS YOUNGER BROTHER.
I LOVED YOU.
"WHEN I'M GONE, WILL YOU MANAGE A CHEERY SMILE ONCE IN A WHILE?"
THAT'S IT.
SLOOSH
CAN YOU MANAGE ONE NOW?

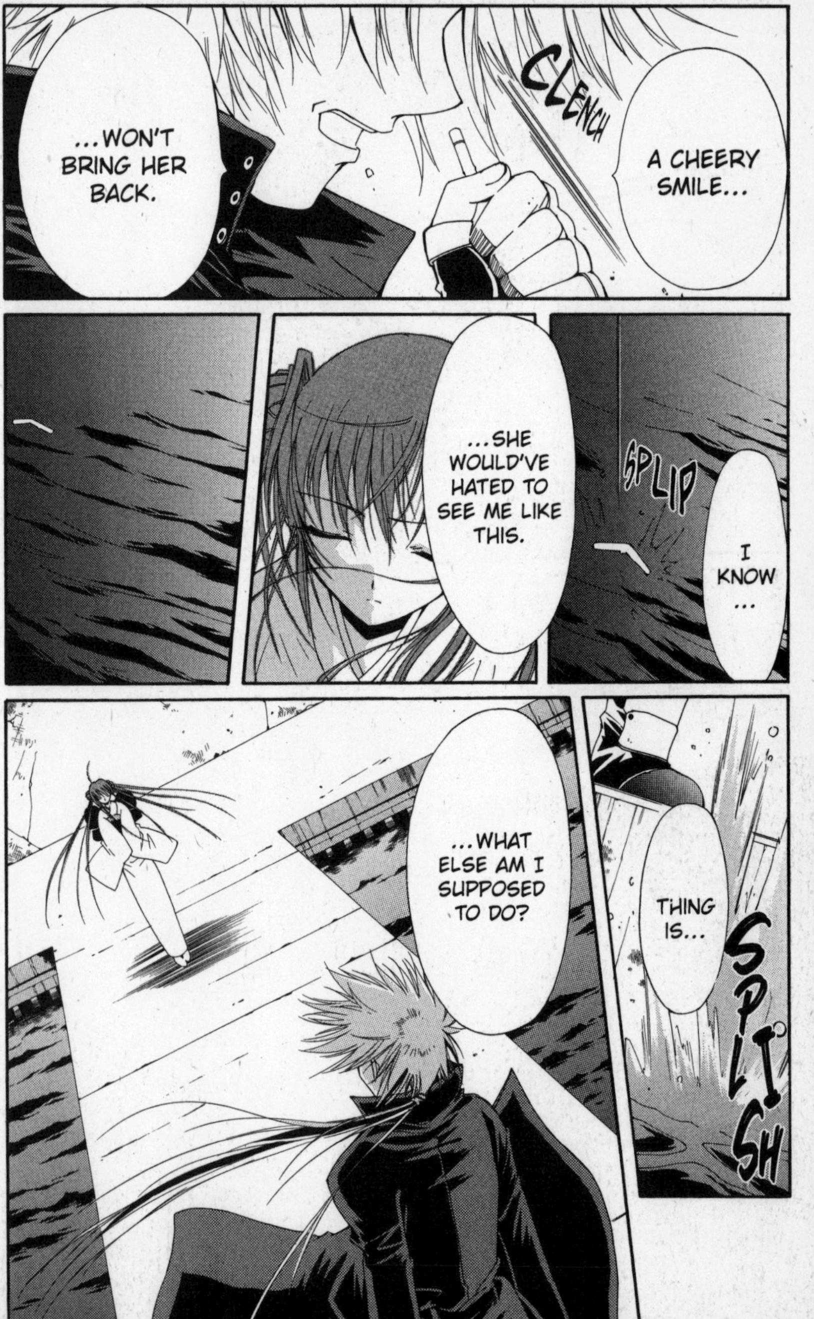
A CHEERY SMILE...
CLENCH
...WON'T BRING HER BACK.
SPLIP
I KNOW ...
...SHE WOULD'VE HATED TO SEE ME LIKE THIS.
THING IS...
SPLISH
...WHAT ELSE AM I SUPPOSED TO DO?

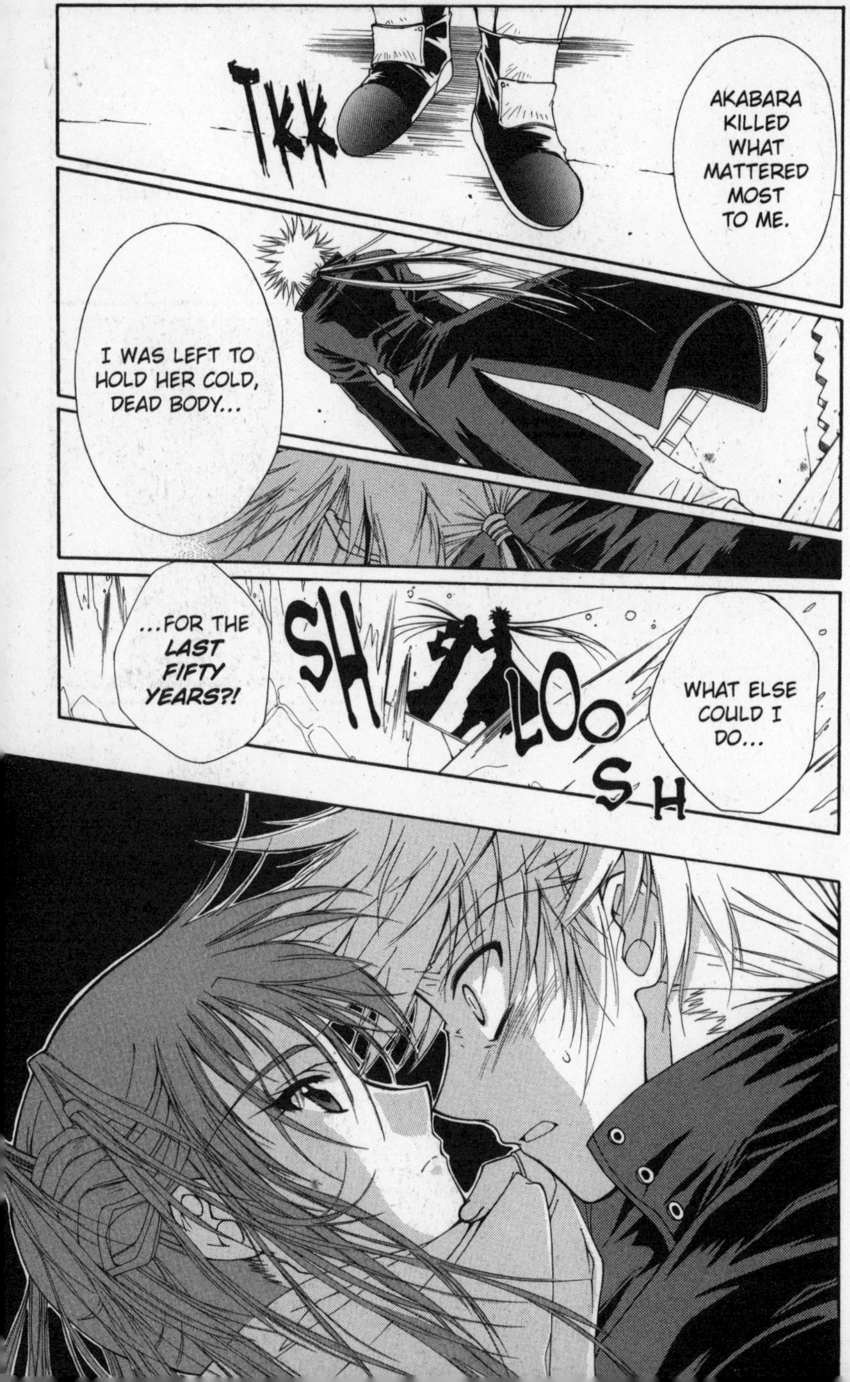
AKABARA KILLED WHAT MATTERED MOST TO ME.
TKK
I WAS LEFT TO HOLD HER COLD, DEAD BODY...
WHAT ELSE COULD I DO...
SHLOOSH
...FOR THE LAST FIFTY YEARS?!

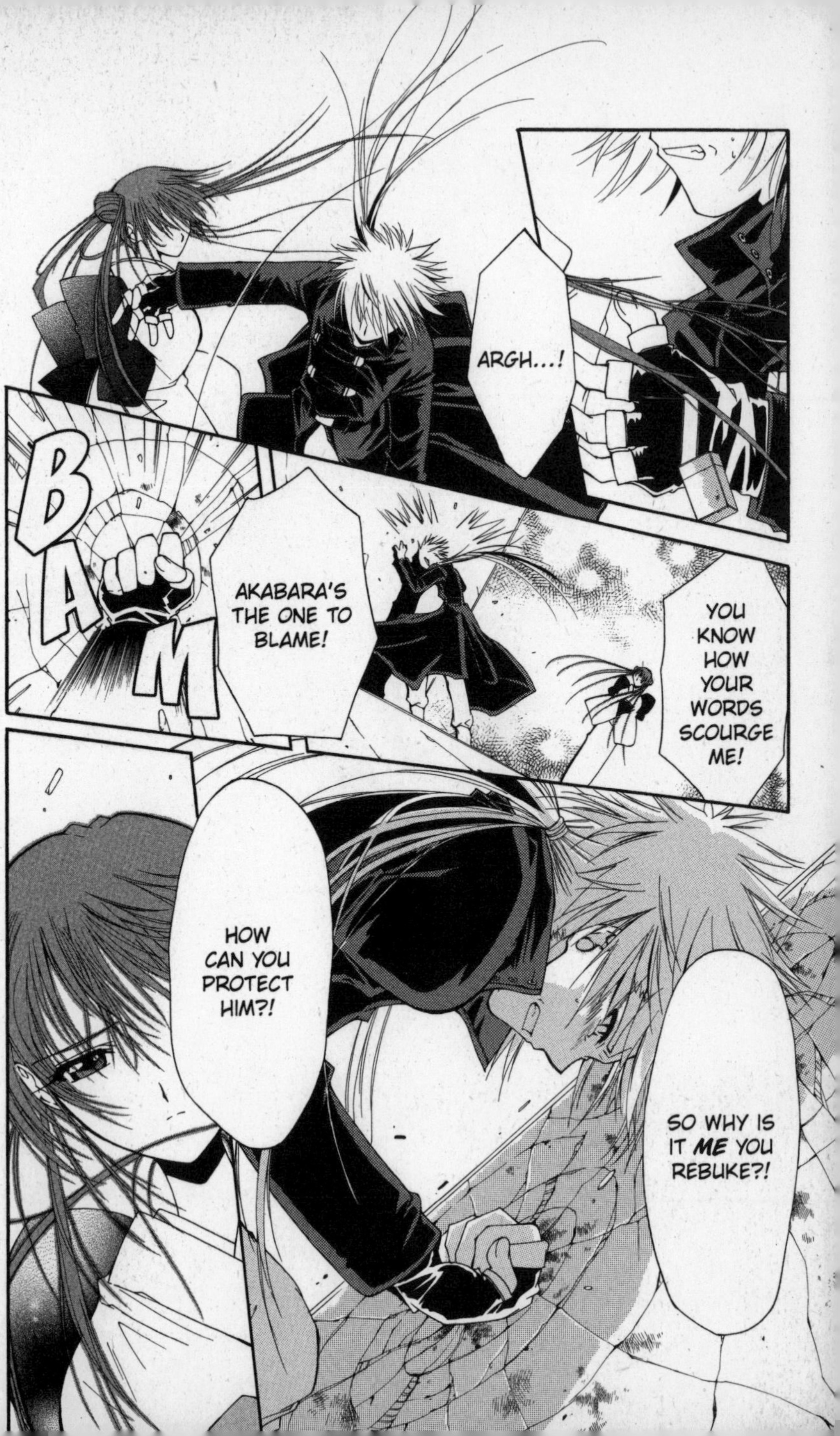
ARGH...!
YOU KNOW HOW YOUR WORDS SCOURGE ME!
AKABARA'S THE ONE TO BLAME!
BAM
SO WHY IS IT *ME* YOU REBUKE?!
HOW CAN YOU PROTECT HIM?!

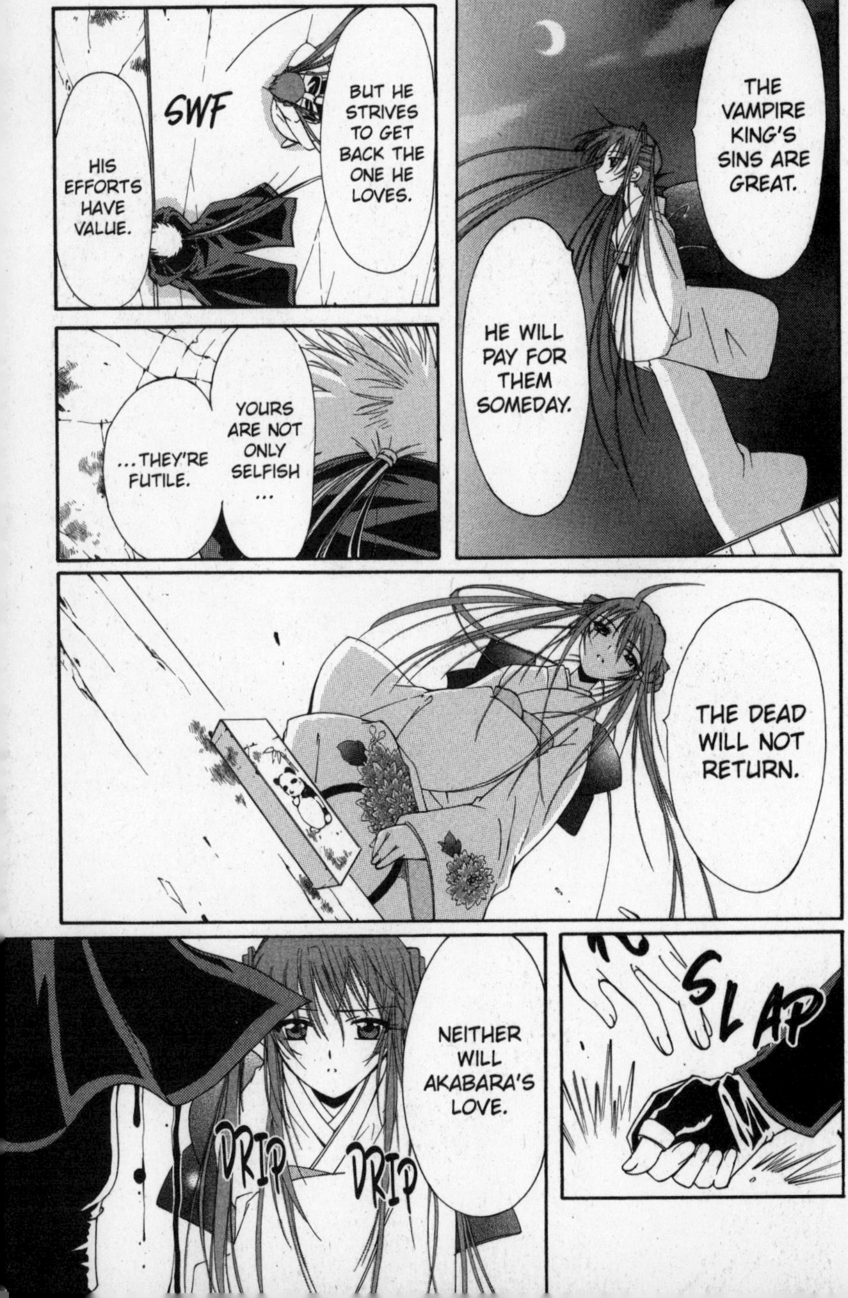
THE VAMPIRE KING'S SINS ARE GREAT.
HE WILL PAY FOR THEM SOMEDAY.
SWF
BUT HE STRIVES TO GET BACK THE ONE HE LOVES.
HIS EFFORTS HAVE VALUE.
YOURS ARE NOT ONLY SELFISH...
...THEY'RE FUTILE.
THE DEAD WILL NOT RETURN.
SLAP
NEITHER WILL AKABARA'S LOVE.
DRIP
DRIP

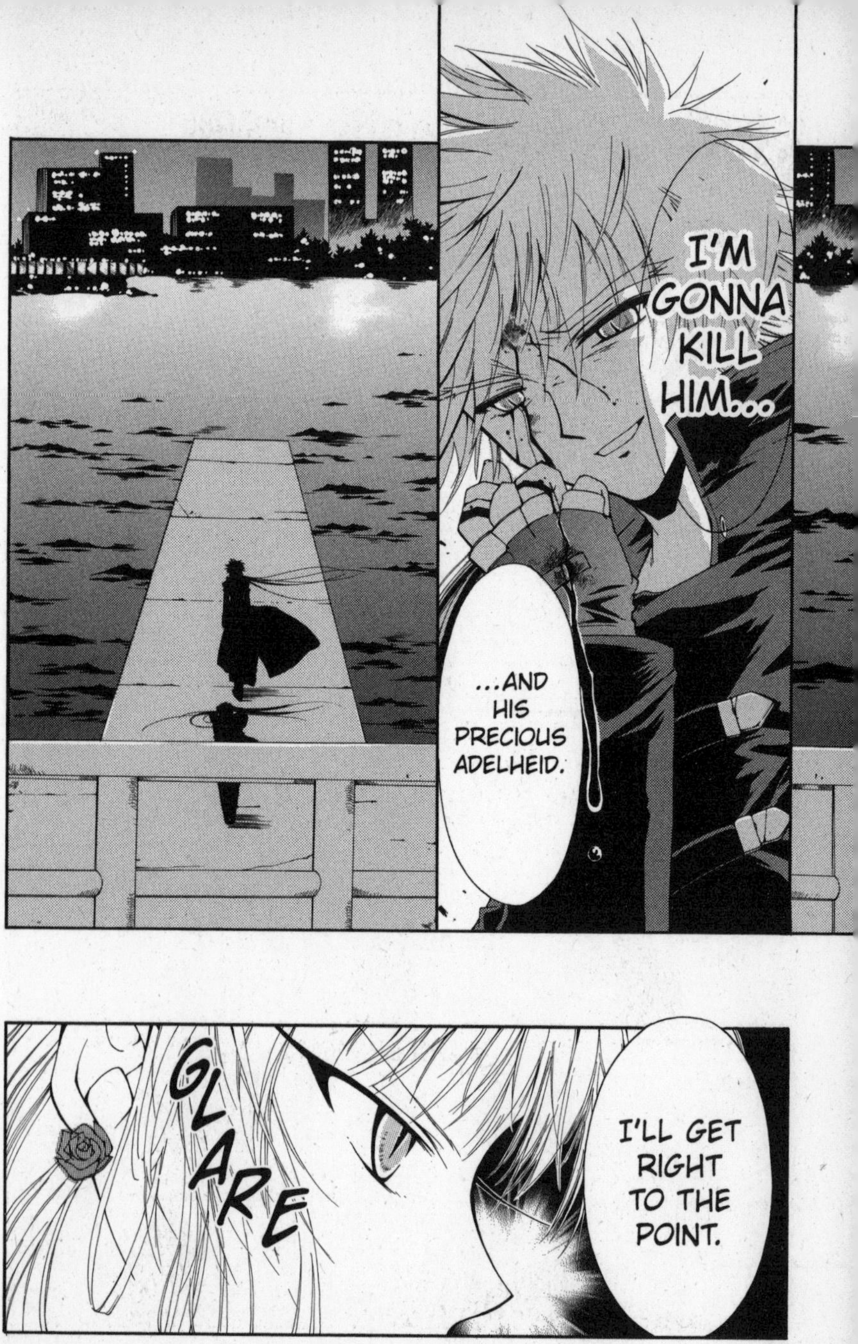
I'M GONNA KILL HIM...
...AND HIS PRECIOUS ADELHEID.
I'LL GET RIGHT TO THE POINT.
GLARE

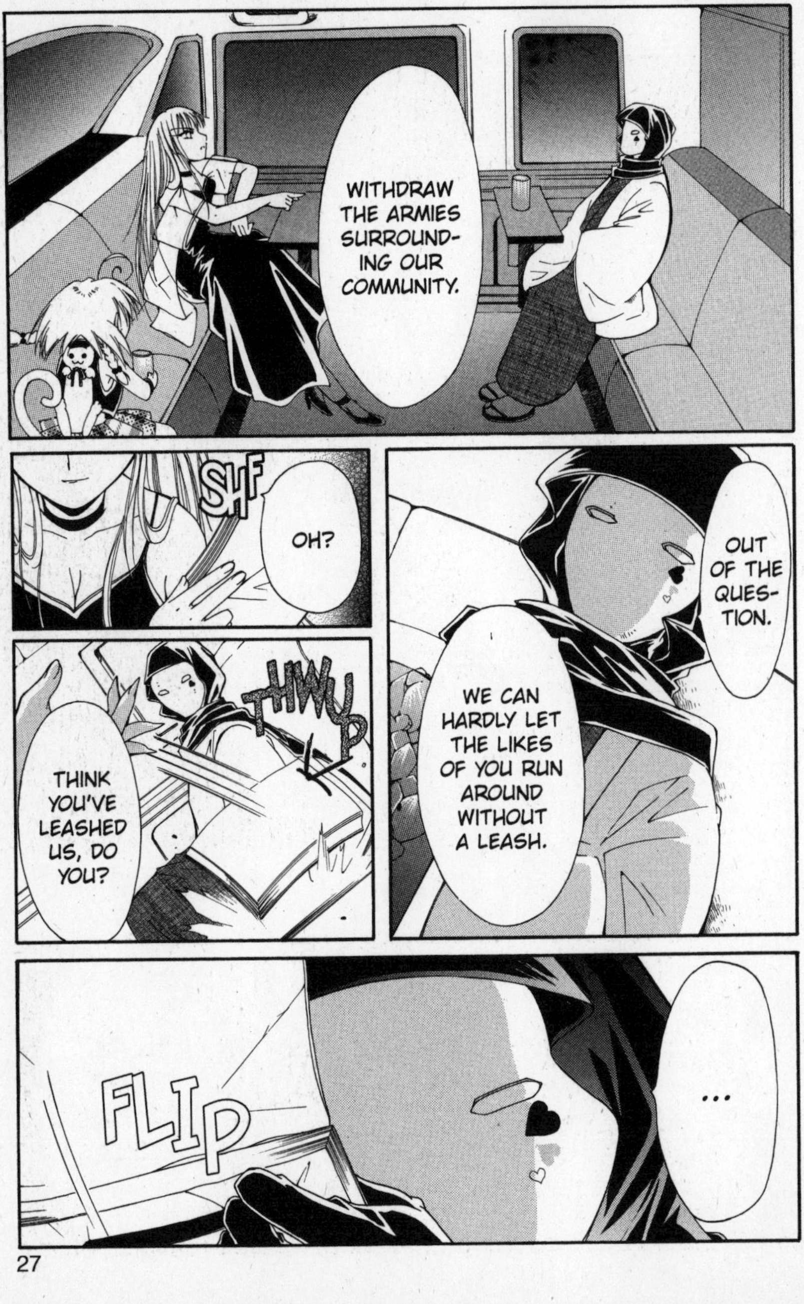
WITHDRAW THE ARMIES SURROUND-ING OUR COMMUNITY.
OUT OF THE QUES-TION.
WE CAN HARDLY LET THE LIKES OF YOU RUN AROUND WITHOUT A LEASH.
SHF
OH?
THWUP
THINK YOU'VE LEASHED US, DO YOU?
...
FLIP

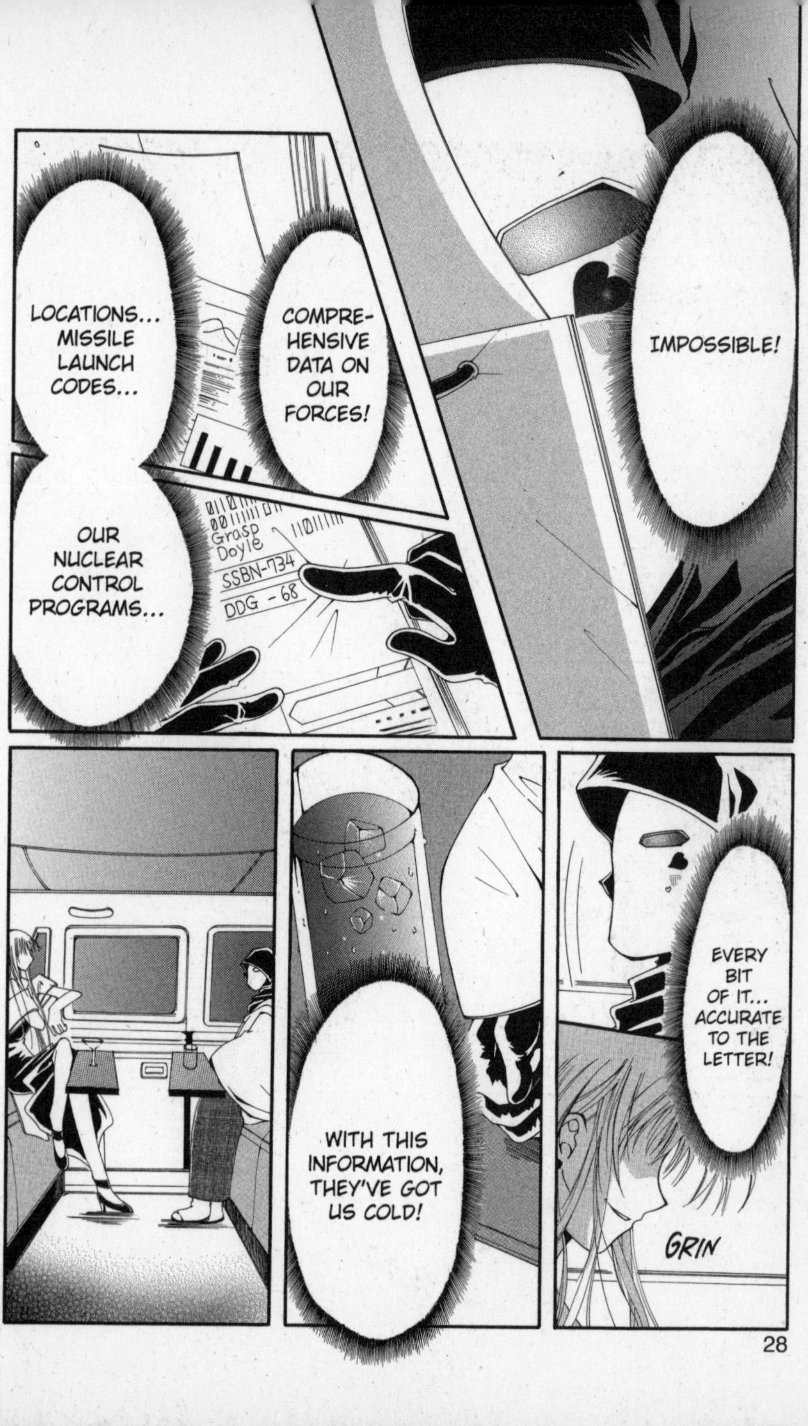
IMPOSSIBLE!
COMPRE-HENSIVE DATA ON OUR FORCES!
LOCATIONS... MISSILE LAUNCH CODES...
Grasp
Doyle
SSBN-734
DDG -68
OUR NUCLEAR CONTROL PROGRAMS...
EVERY BIT OF IT... ACCURATE TO THE LETTER!
GRIN
WITH THIS INFORMATION, THEY'VE GOT US COLD!

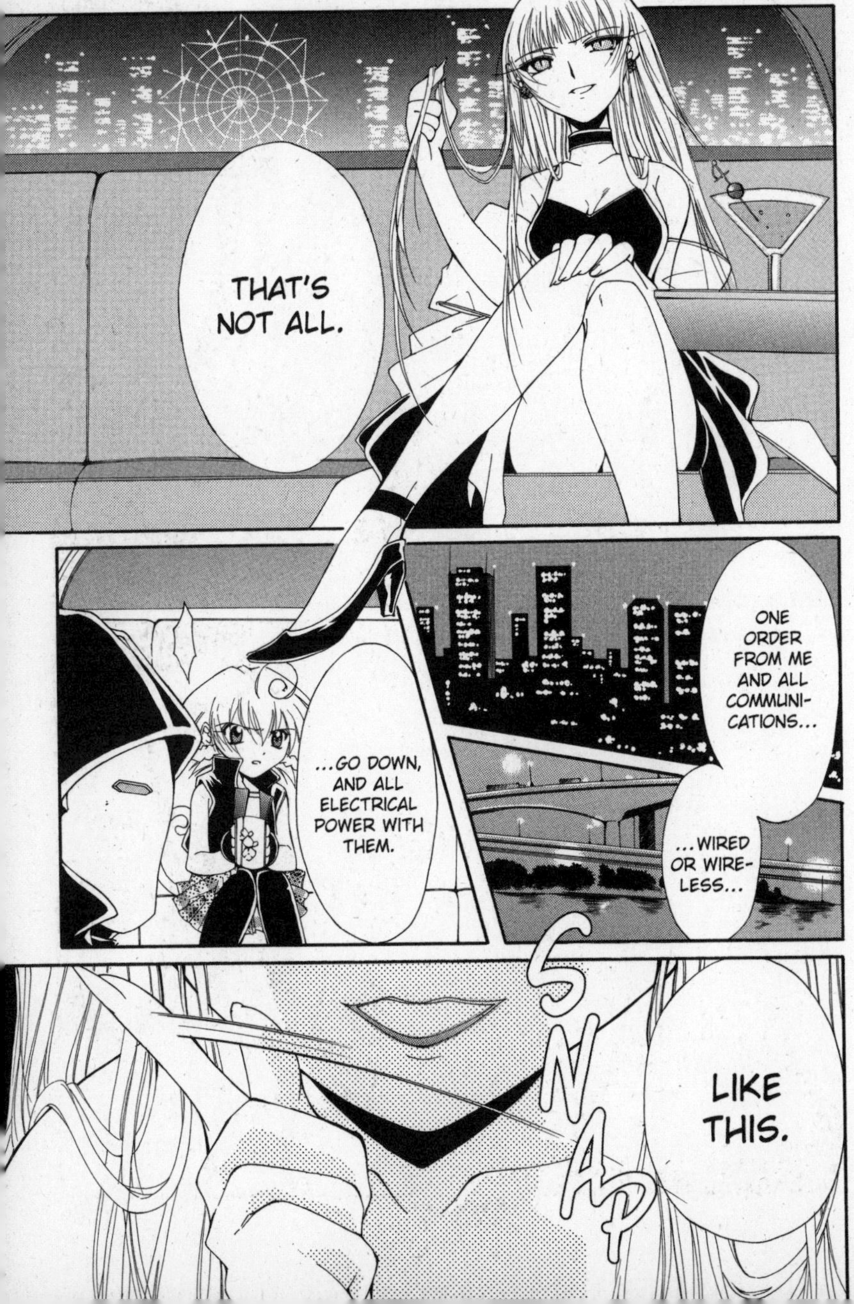
THAT'S NOT ALL.
ONE ORDER FROM ME AND ALL COMMUNICATIONS...
...WIRED OR WIRELESS...
...GO DOWN, AND ALL ELECTRICAL POWER WITH THEM.
LIKE THIS.
SNAP

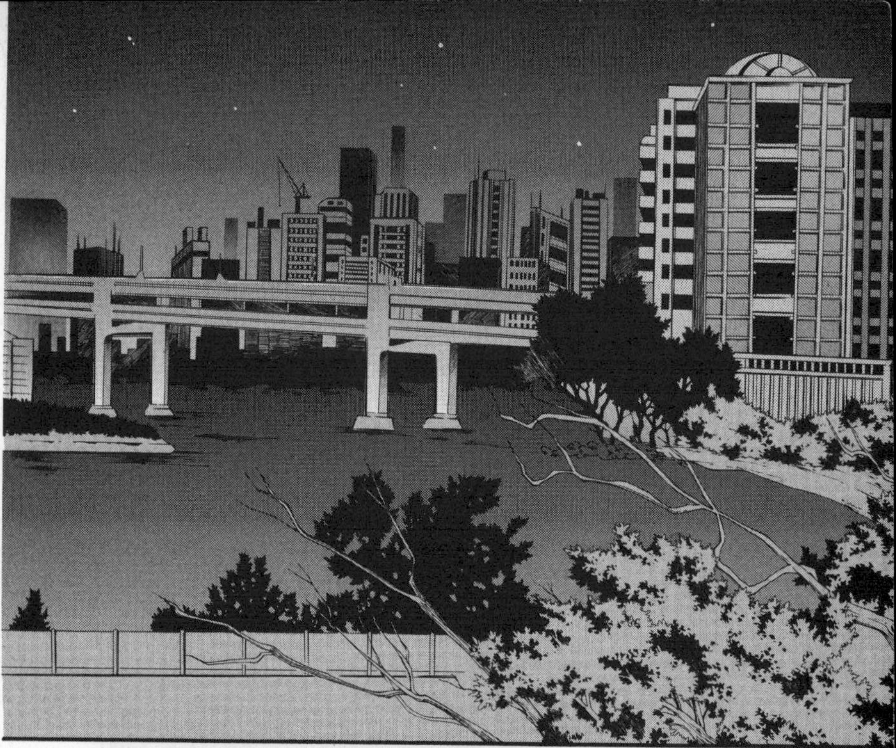
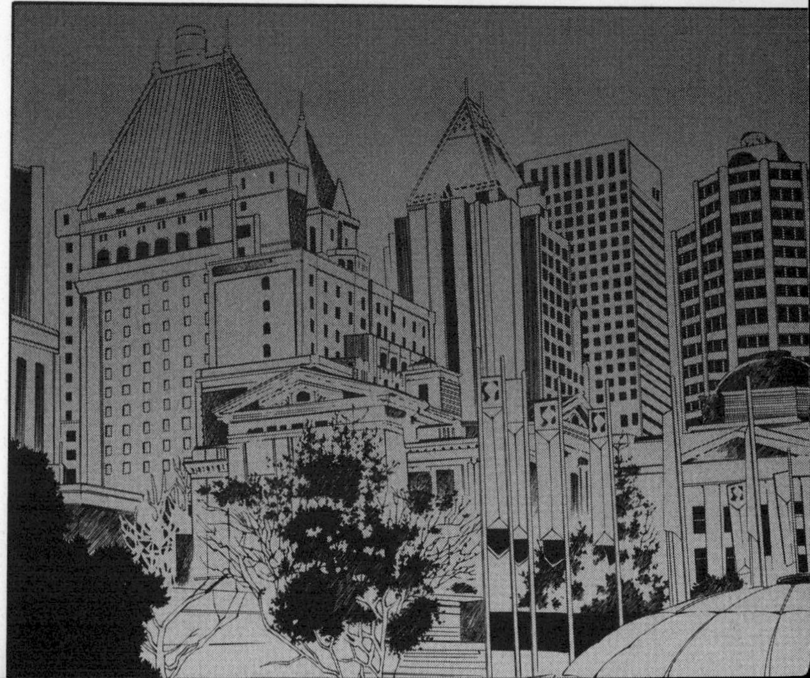

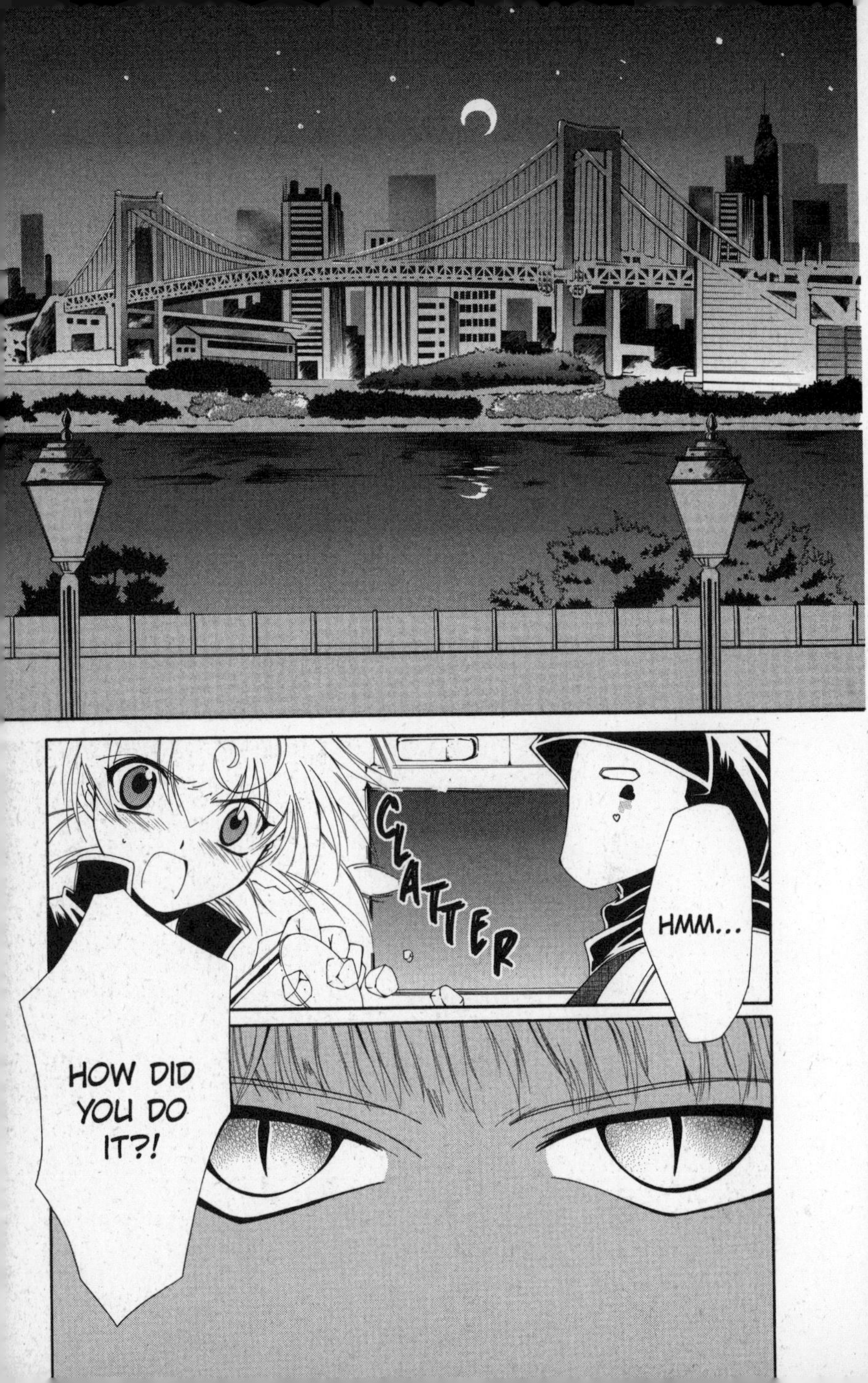
HMM...
CLATTER
HOW DID YOU DO IT?!

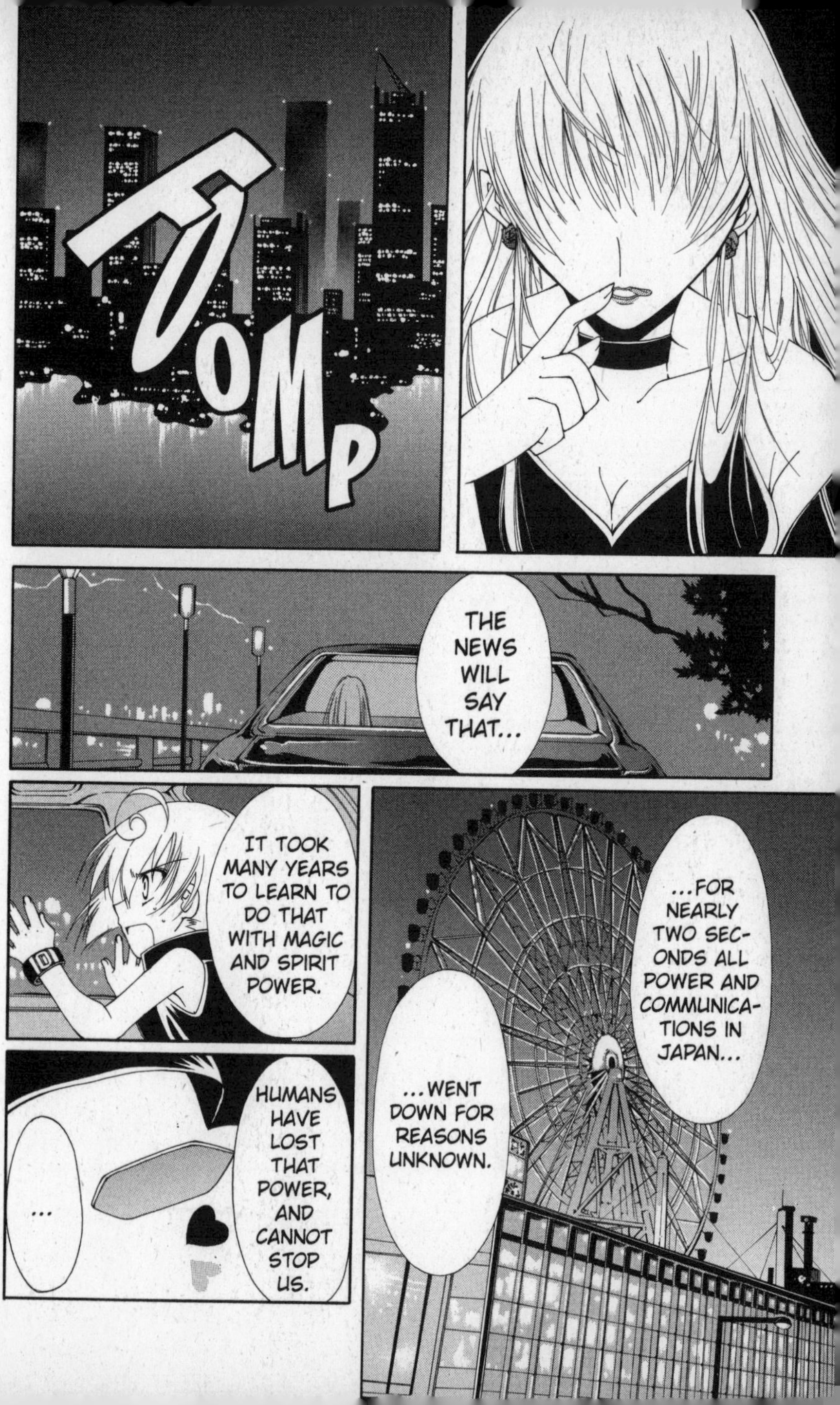
FOOMP
THE NEWS WILL SAY THAT...
...FOR NEARLY TWO SEC-ONDS ALL POWER AND COMMUNICA-TIONS IN JAPAN...
...WENT DOWN FOR REASONS UNKNOWN.
IT TOOK MANY YEARS TO LEARN TO DO THAT WITH MAGIC AND SPIRIT POWER.
HUMANS HAVE LOST THAT POWER, AND CANNOT STOP US.
...

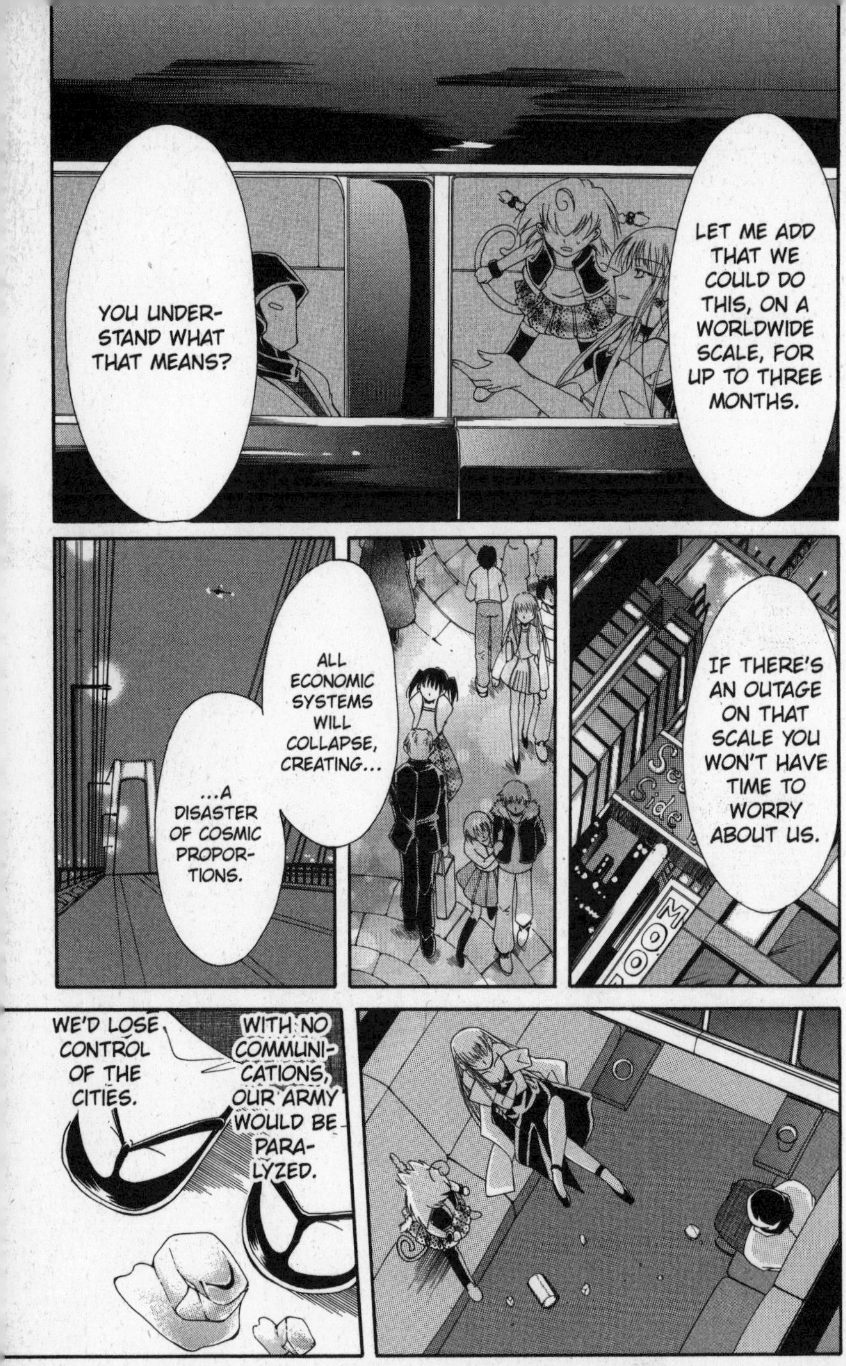
LET ME ADD THAT WE COULD DO THIS, ON A WORLDWIDE SCALE, FOR UP TO THREE MONTHS.
YOU UNDER-STAND WHAT THAT MEANS?
IF THERE'S AN OUTAGE ON THAT SCALE YOU WON'T HAVE TIME TO WORRY ABOUT US.
ALL ECONOMIC SYSTEMS WILL COLLAPSE, CREATING...
...A DISASTER OF COSMIC PROPOR-TIONS.
WITH NO COMMUNI-CATIONS, OUR ARMY WOULD BE PARA-LYZED.
WE'D LOSE CONTROL OF THE CITIES.

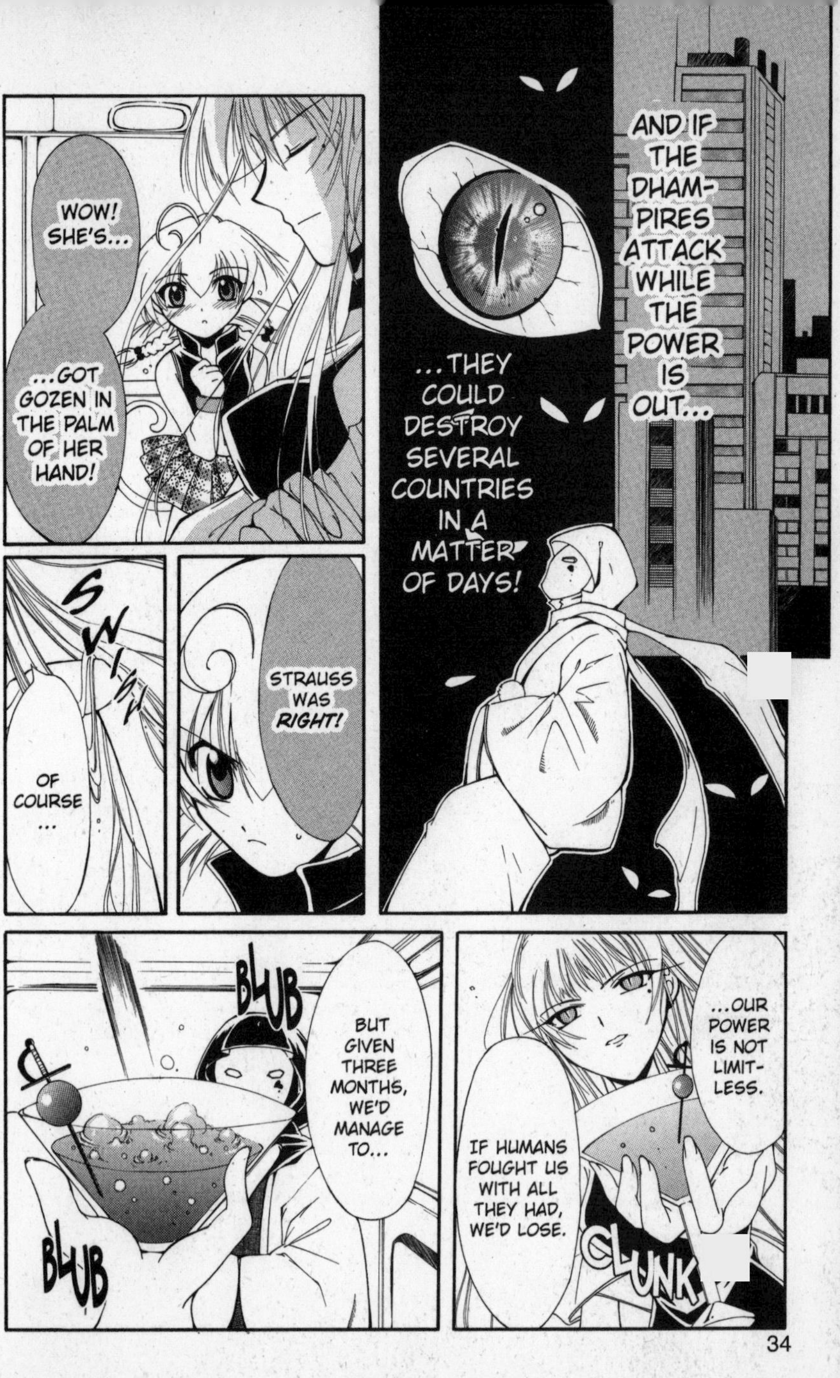
AND IF THE DHAMPIRES ATTACK WHILE THE POWER IS OUT...
...THEY COULD DESTROY SEVERAL COUNTRIES IN A MATTER OF DAYS!
WOW! SHE'S...
...GOT GOZEN IN THE PALM OF HER HAND!
STRAUSS WAS *RIGHT!*
SWISH
OF COURSE...
...OUR POWER IS NOT LIMITLESS.
IF HUMANS FOUGHT US WITH ALL THEY HAD, WE'D LOSE.
CLUNK
BLUB
BUT GIVEN THREE MONTHS, WE'D MANAGE TO...
BLUB

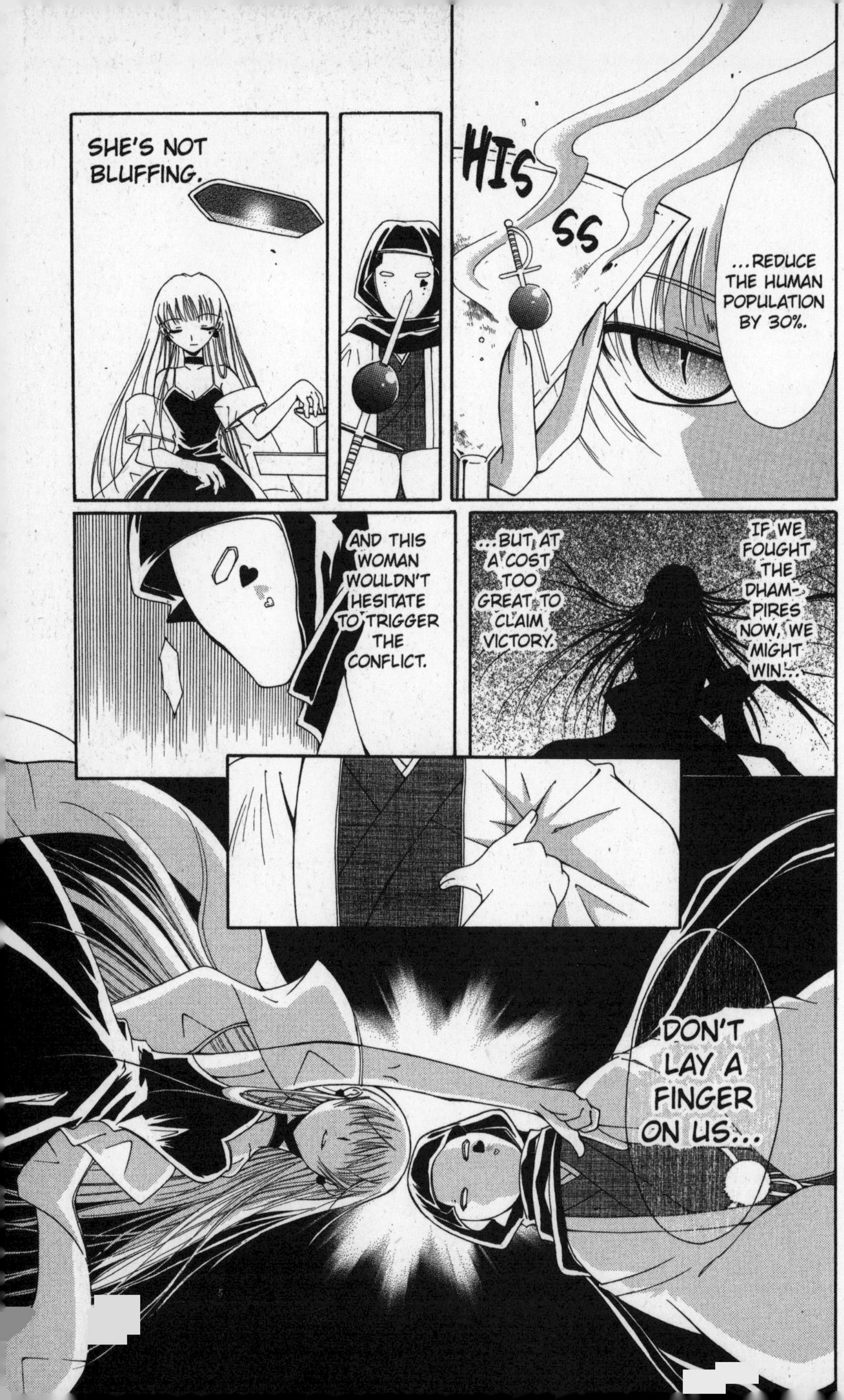
HISSS
...REDUCE THE HUMAN POPULATION BY 30%.
SHE'S NOT BLUFFING.
IF WE FOUGHT THE DHAM-PIRES NOW, WE MIGHT WIN...
...BUT AT A COST TOO GREAT TO CLAIM VICTORY.
AND THIS WOMAN WOULDN'T HESITATE TO TRIGGER THE CONFLICT.
DON'T LAY A FINGER ON US...

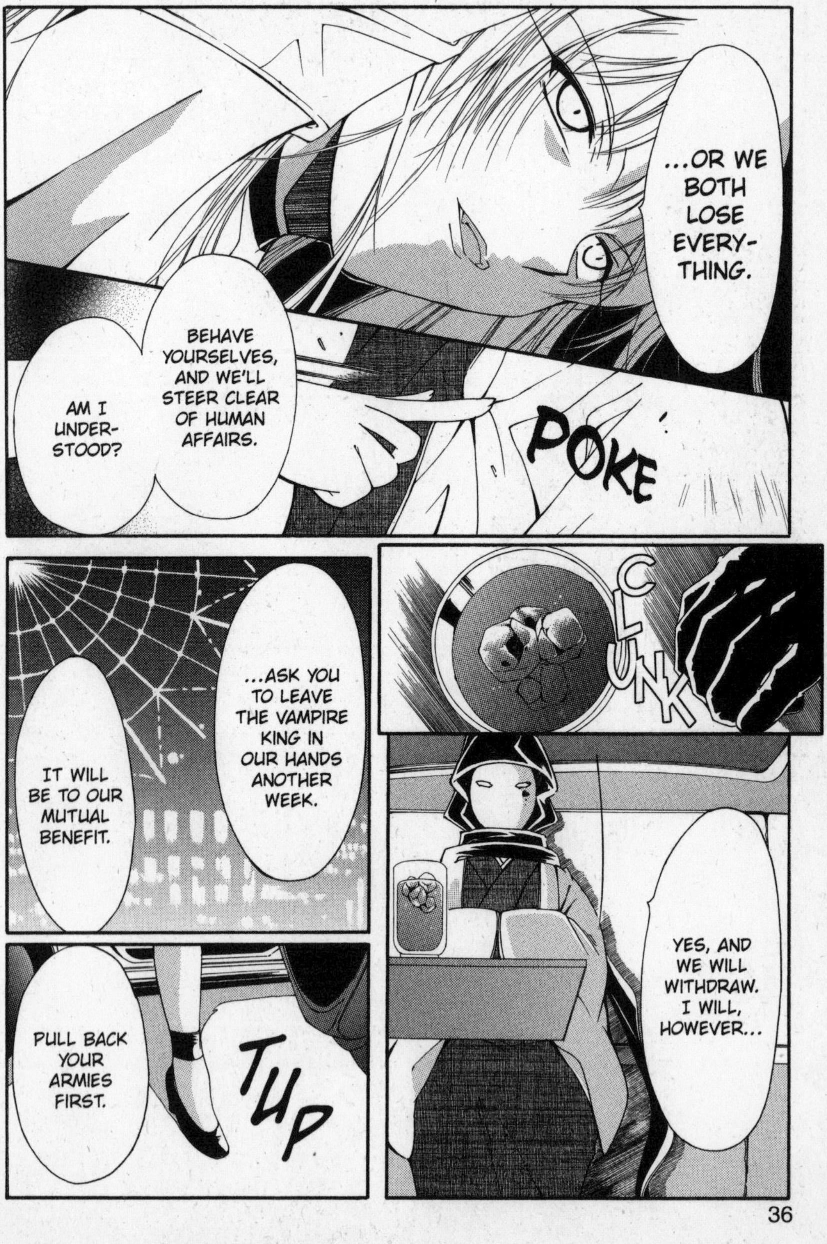
...OR WE BOTH LOSE EVERY-THING.
BEHAVE YOURSELVES, AND WE'LL STEER CLEAR OF HUMAN AFFAIRS.
AM I UNDER-STOOD?
POKE
CLUNK
PULL BACK YOUR ARMIES FIRST.
TUP
YES, AND WE WILL WITHDRAW. I WILL, HOWEVER...
...ASK YOU TO LEAVE THE VAMPIRE KING IN OUR HANDS ANOTHER WEEK.
IT WILL BE TO OUR MUTUAL BENEFIT.

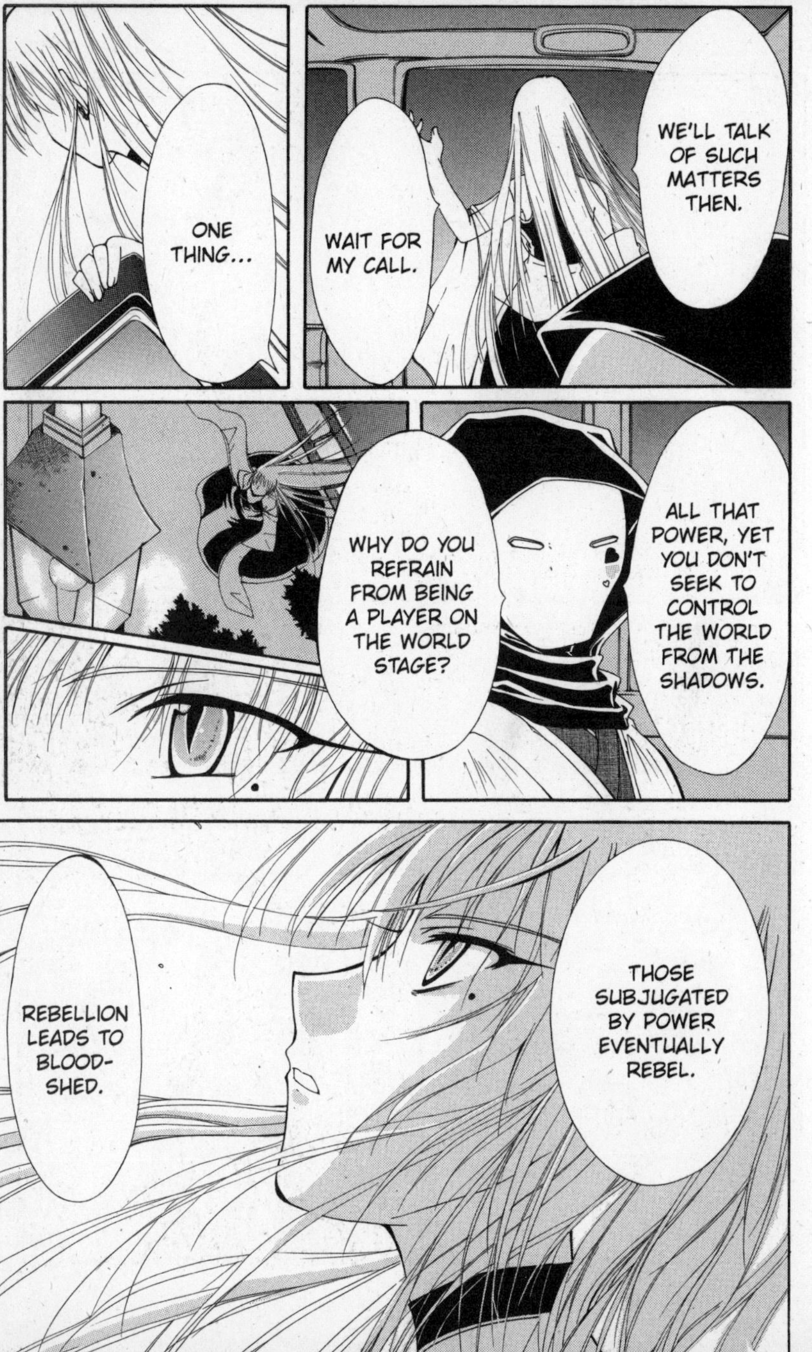
WE'LL TALK OF SUCH MATTERS THEN.
WAIT FOR MY CALL.
ONE THING...
ALL THAT POWER, YET YOU DON'T SEEK TO CONTROL THE WORLD FROM THE SHADOWS.
WHY DO YOU REFRAIN FROM BEING A PLAYER ON THE WORLD STAGE?
THOSE SUBJUGATED BY POWER EVENTUALLY REBEL.
REBELLION LEADS TO BLOOD-SHED.

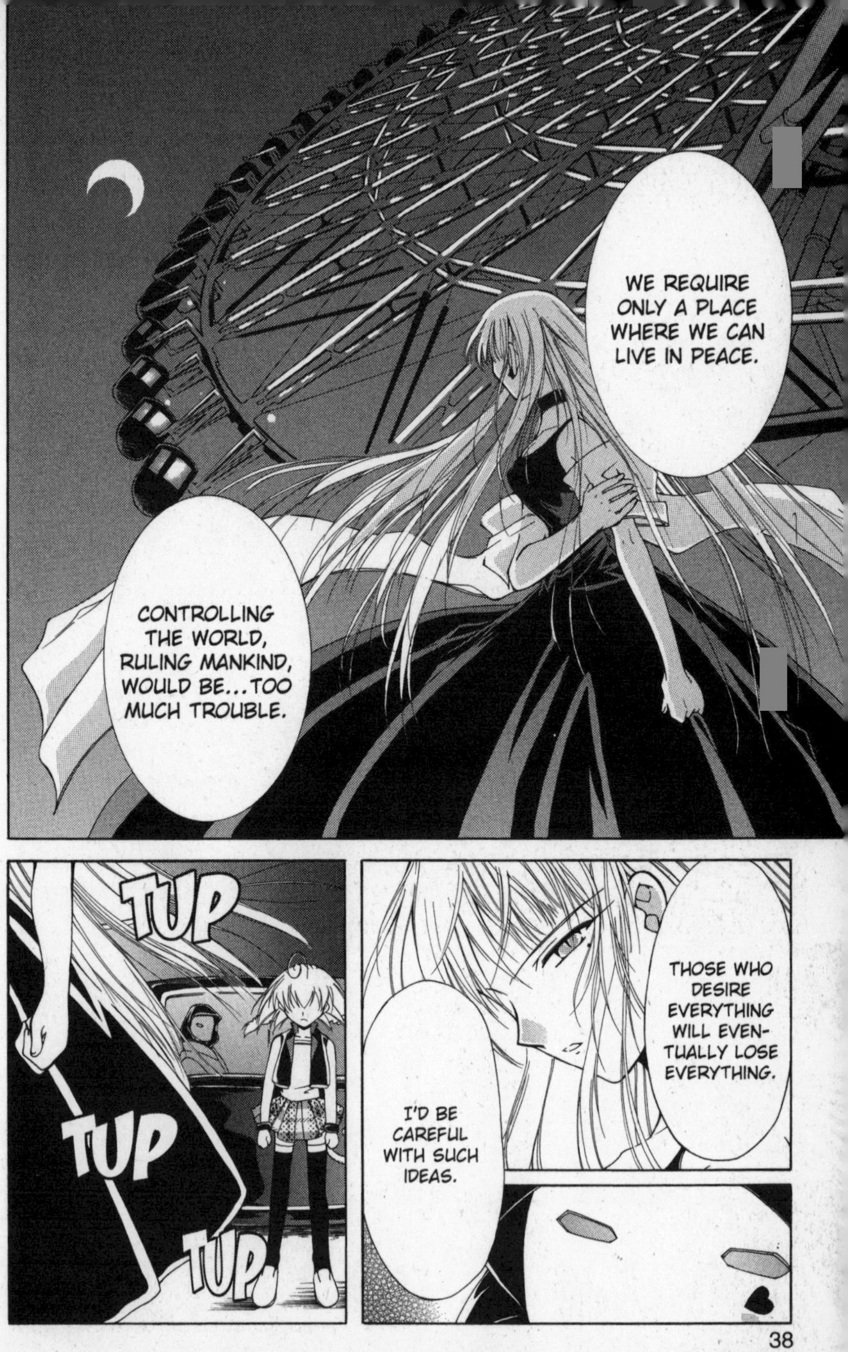
WE REQUIRE ONLY A PLACE WHERE WE CAN LIVE IN PEACE.
CONTROLLING THE WORLD, RULING MANKIND, WOULD BE...TOO MUCH TROUBLE.
THOSE WHO DESIRE EVERYTHING WILL EVEN-TUALLY LOSE EVERYTHING.
I'D BE CAREFUL WITH SUCH IDEAS.
TUP
TUP
TUP

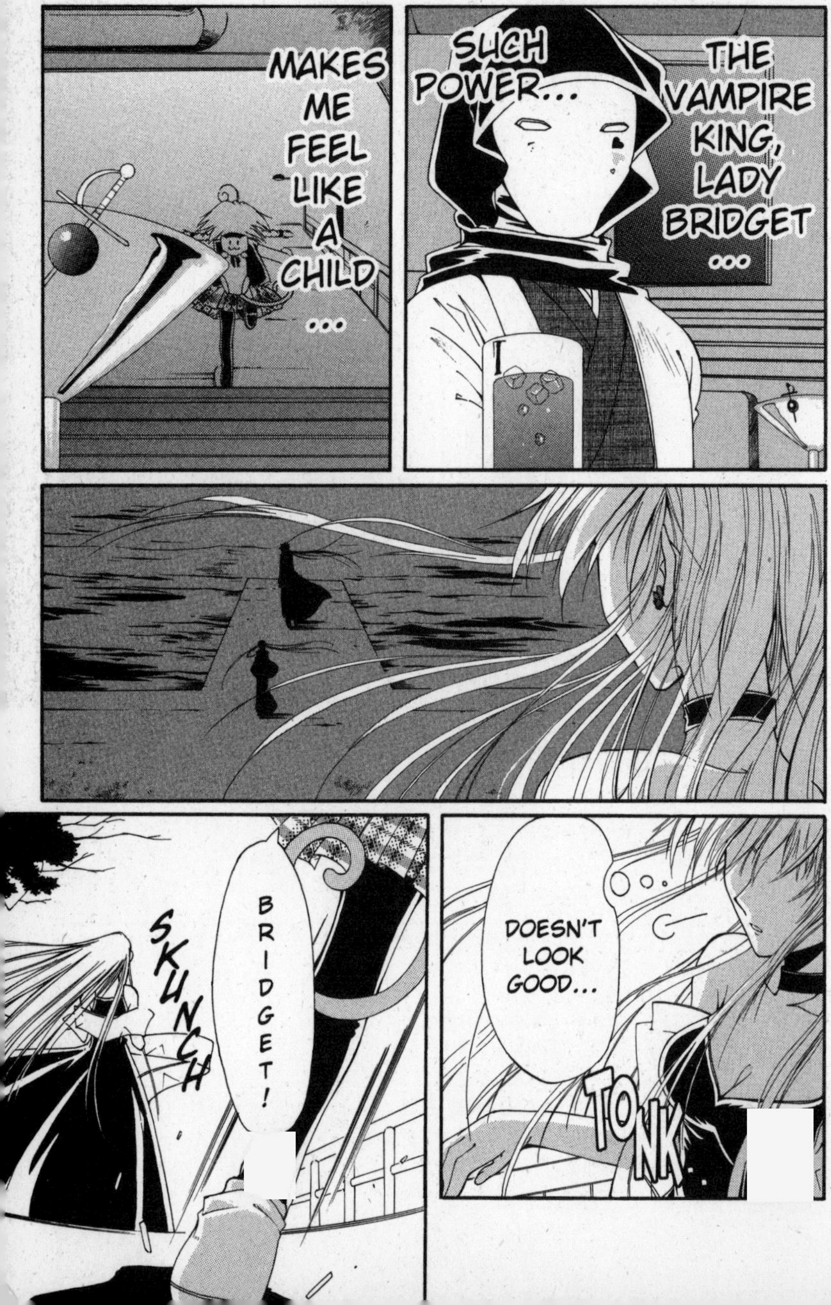
THE VAMPIRE KING, LADY BRIDGET...
SUCH POWER...
MAKES ME FEEL LIKE A CHILD...
DOESN'T LOOK GOOD...
TONK
BRIDGET!
SKUNCH

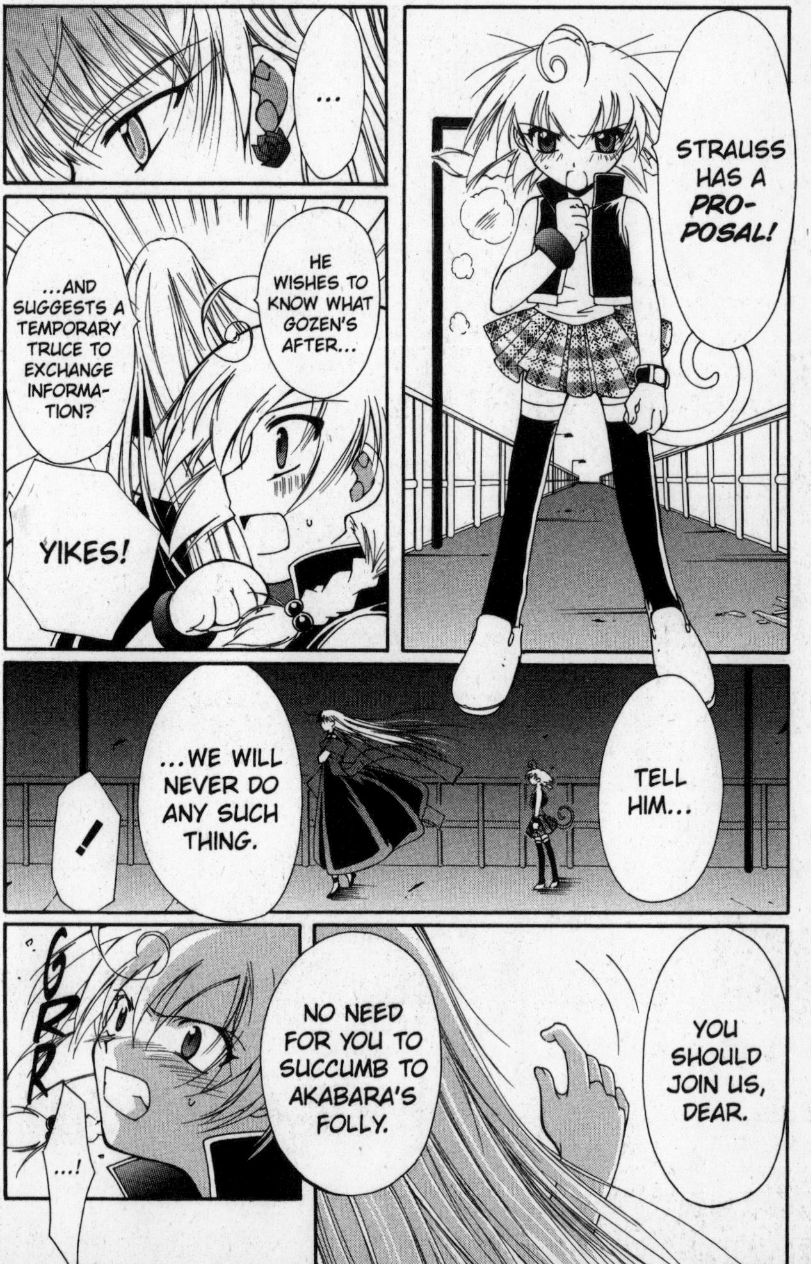

STRAUSS HAS A *PRO-POSAL!*
...
HE WISHES TO KNOW WHAT GOZEN'S AFTER...
...AND SUGGESTS A TEMPORARY TRUCE TO EXCHANGE INFORMA-TION?
YIKES!
TELL HIM...
...WE WILL NEVER DO ANY SUCH THING.
!
YOU SHOULD JOIN US, DEAR.
NO NEED FOR YOU TO SUCCUMB TO AKABARA'S FOLLY.
GRR
...!

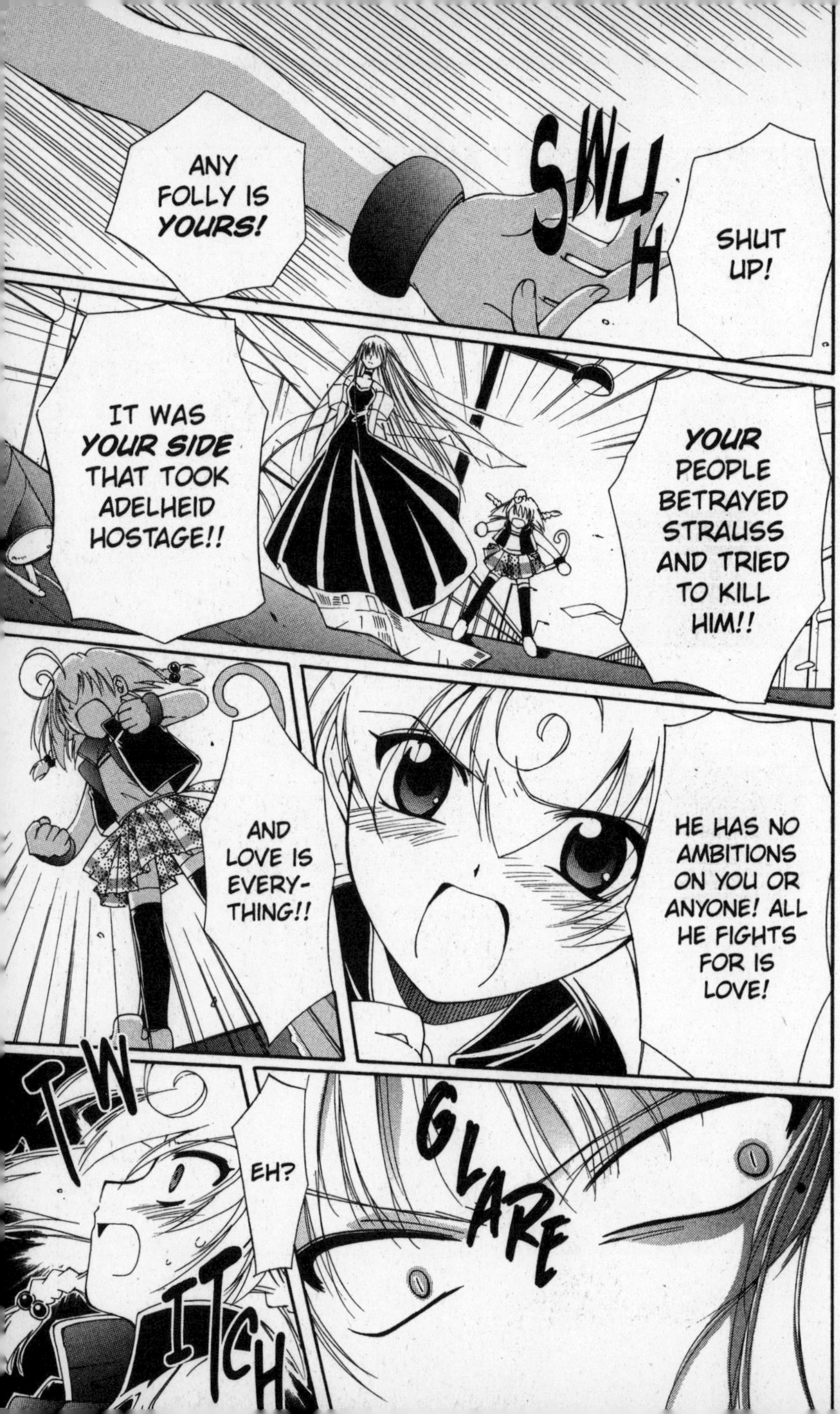
SHUT UP!
SWUSH
ANY FOLLY IS YOURS!
YOUR PEOPLE BETRAYED STRAUSS AND TRIED TO KILL HIM!!
IT WAS YOUR SIDE THAT TOOK ADELHEID HOSTAGE!!
HE HAS NO AMBITIONS ON YOU OR ANYONE! ALL HE FIGHTS FOR IS LOVE!
AND LOVE IS EVERY-THING!!
GLARE
EH?
TWITCH

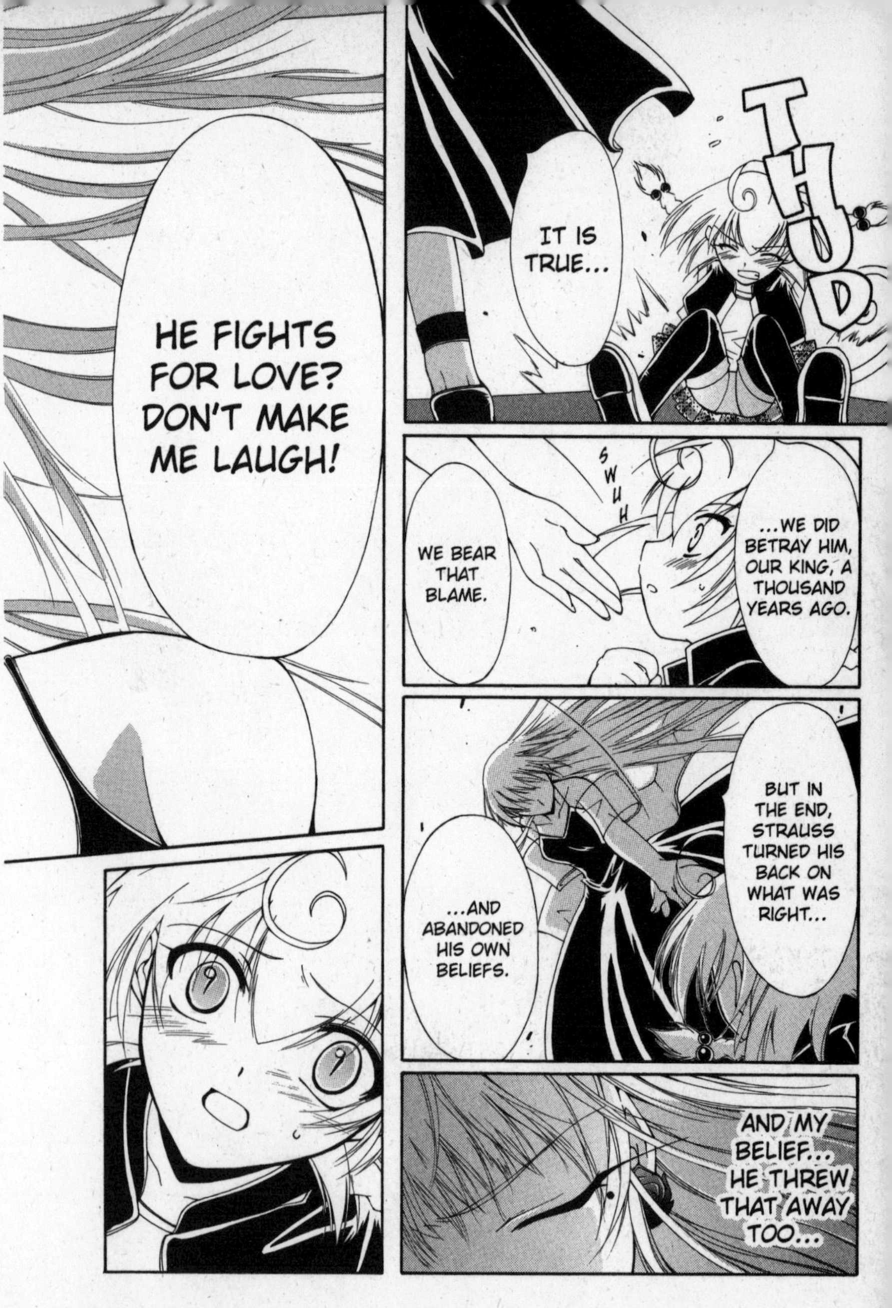
THUD
IT IS TRUE...
SWUH
...WE DID BETRAY HIM, OUR KING, A THOUSAND YEARS AGO.
WE BEAR THAT BLAME.
BUT IN THE END, STRAUSS TURNED HIS BACK ON WHAT WAS RIGHT...
...AND ABANDONED HIS OWN BELIEFS.
AND MY BELIEF... HE THREW THAT AWAY TOO...
HE FIGHTS FOR LOVE? DON'T MAKE ME LAUGH!

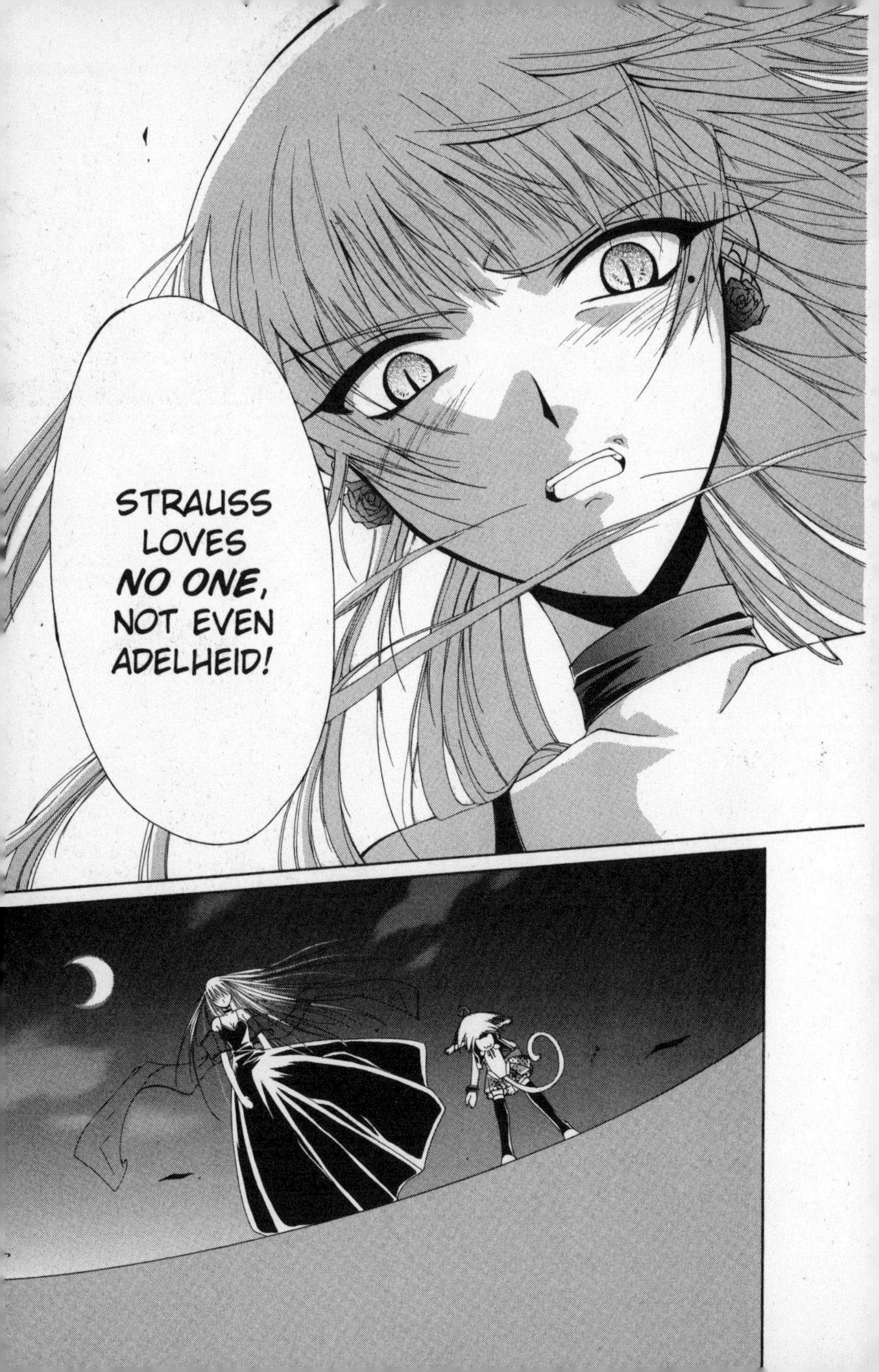
STRAUSS LOVES NO ONE, NOT EVEN ADELHEID!

THE RECORD OF A

FALLEN VAMPIRE

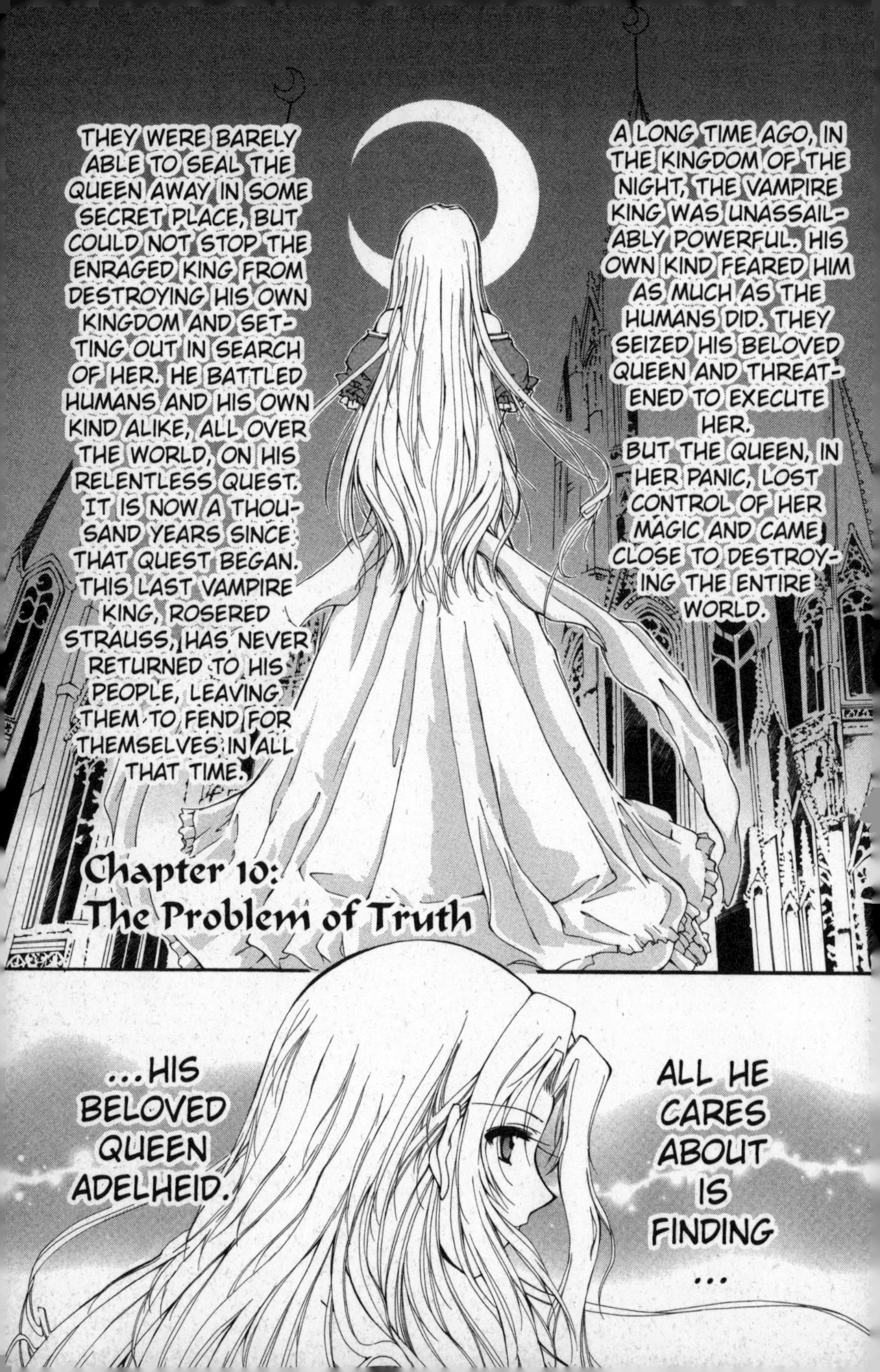
A LONG TIME AGO, IN THE KINGDOM OF THE NIGHT, THE VAMPIRE KING WAS UNASSAIL-ABLY POWERFUL. HIS OWN KIND FEARED HIM AS MUCH AS THE HUMANS DID. THEY SEIZED HIS BELOVED QUEEN AND THREAT-ENED TO EXECUTE HER.
BUT THE QUEEN, IN HER PANIC, LOST CONTROL OF HER MAGIC AND CAME CLOSE TO DESTROY-ING THE ENTIRE WORLD.
THEY WERE BARELY ABLE TO SEAL THE QUEEN AWAY IN SOME SECRET PLACE, BUT COULD NOT STOP THE ENRAGED KING FROM DESTROYING HIS OWN KINGDOM AND SET-TING OUT IN SEARCH OF HER. HE BATTLED HUMANS AND HIS OWN KIND ALIKE, ALL OVER THE WORLD, ON HIS RELENTLESS QUEST.
IT IS NOW A THOU-SAND YEARS SINCE THAT QUEST BEGAN. THIS LAST VAMPIRE KING, ROSERED STRAUSS, HAS NEVER RETURNED TO HIS PEOPLE, LEAVING THEM TO FEND FOR THEMSELVES IN ALL THAT TIME.
Chapter 10:
The Problem of Truth
ALL HE CARES ABOUT IS FINDING...
...HIS BELOVED QUEEN ADELHEID.

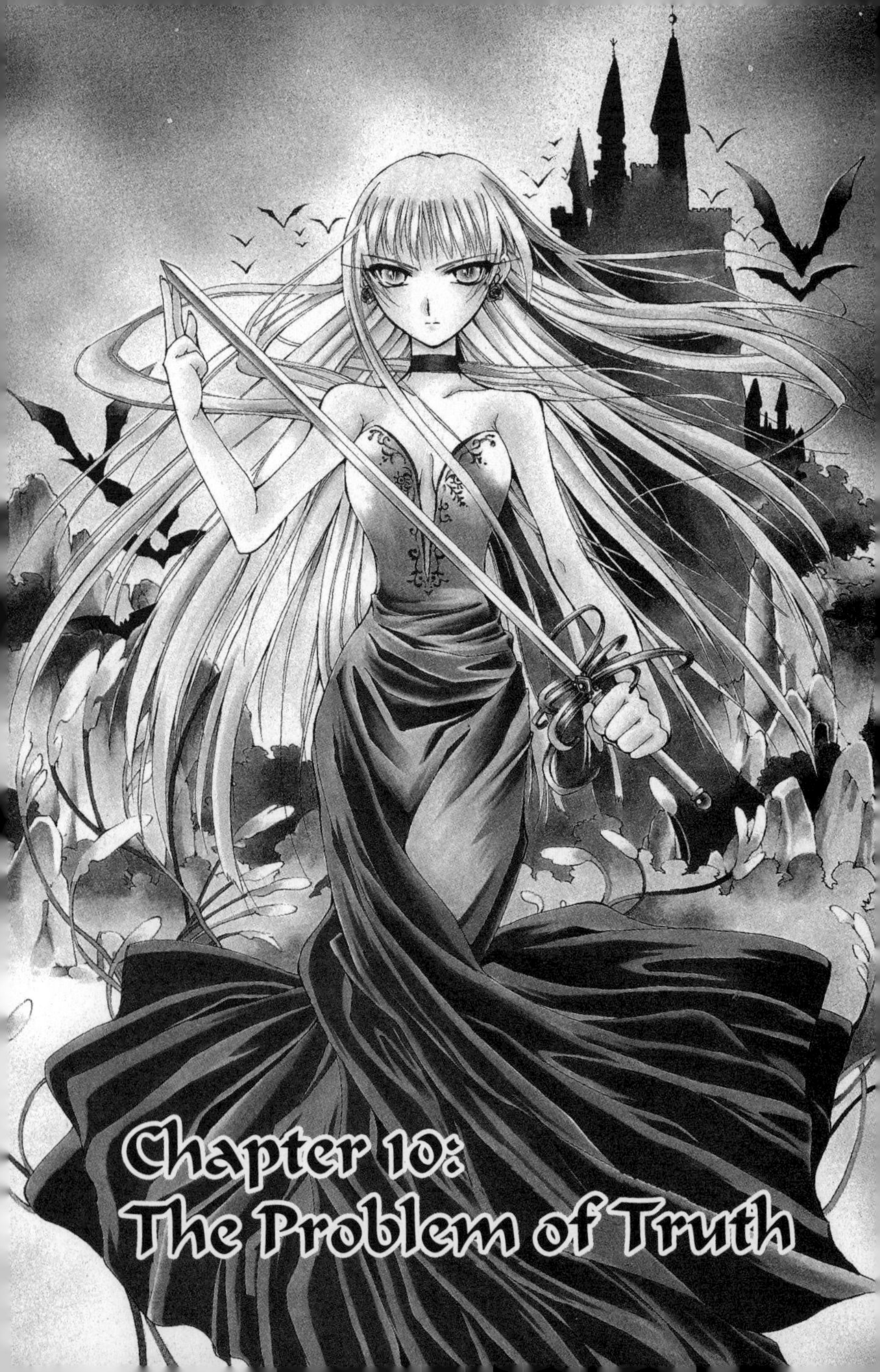
Chapter 10:
The Problem of Truth

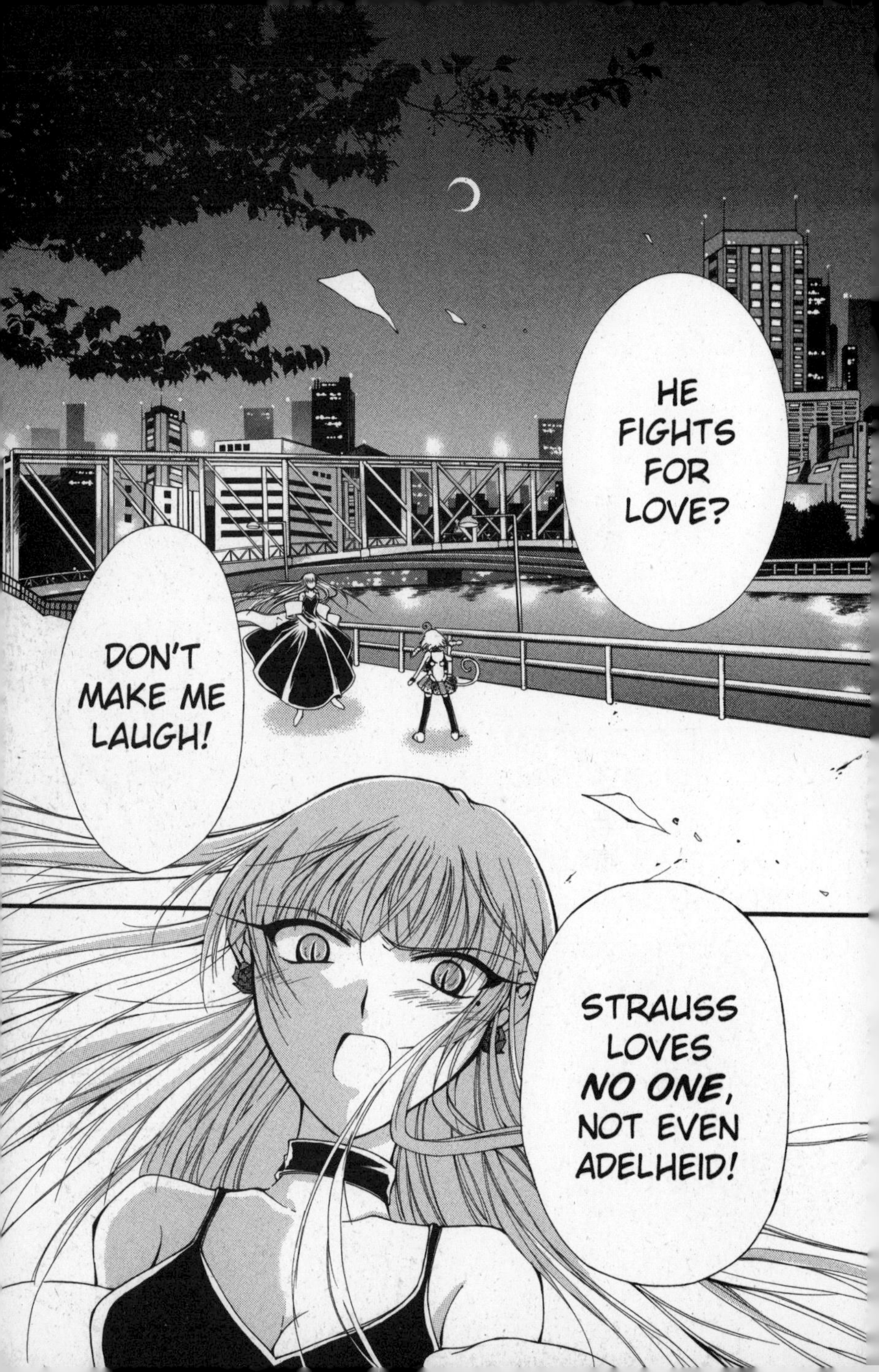
HE FIGHTS FOR LOVE?
DON'T MAKE ME LAUGH!
STRAUSS LOVES *NO ONE*, NOT EVEN ADELHEID!

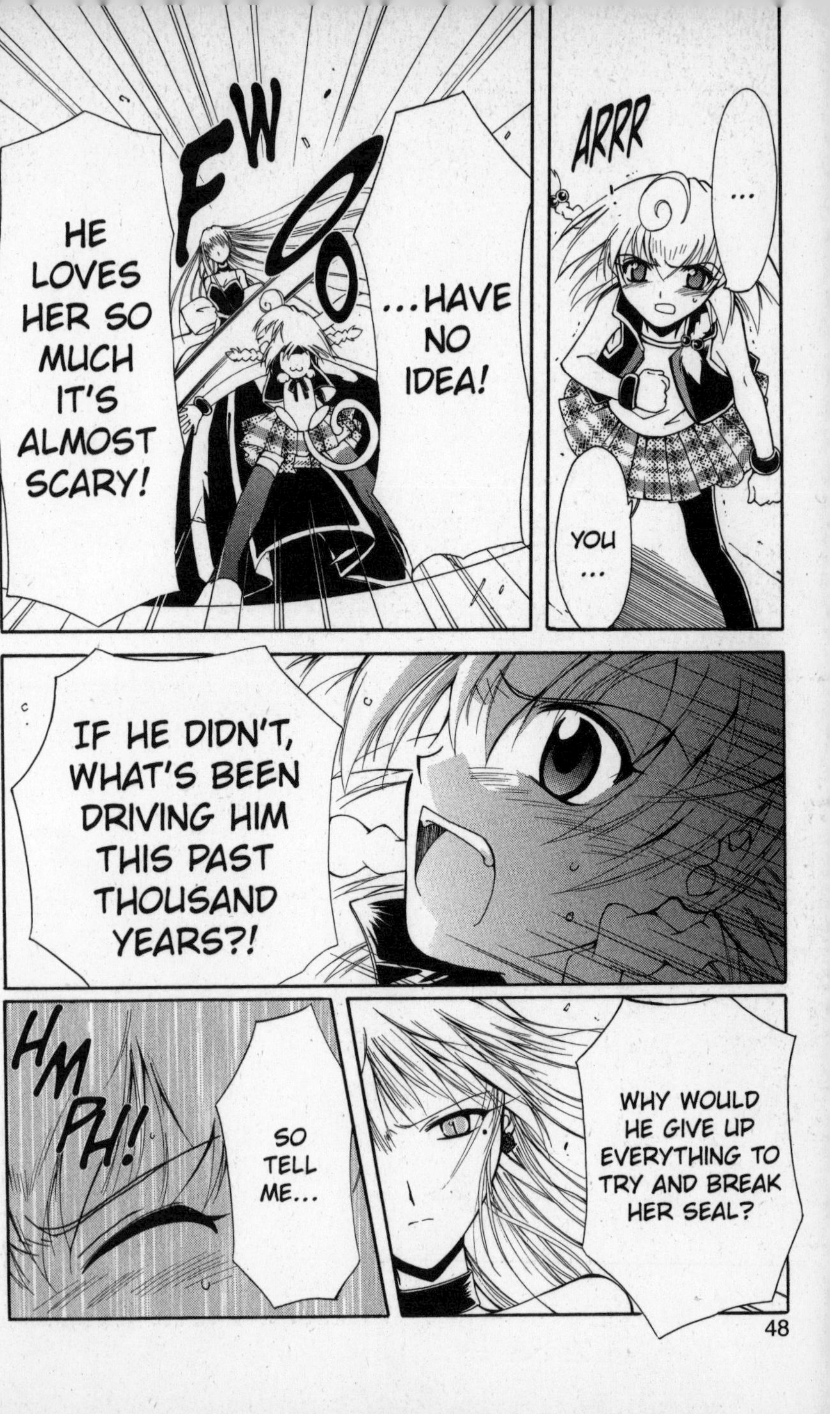
ARRR
...
YOU ...
FWOO
...HAVE NO IDEA!
HE LOVES HER SO MUCH IT'S ALMOST SCARY!
IF HE DIDN'T, WHAT'S BEEN DRIVING HIM THIS PAST THOUSAND YEARS?!
WHY WOULD HE GIVE UP EVERYTHING TO TRY AND BREAK HER SEAL?
SO TELL ME...
HMPH!

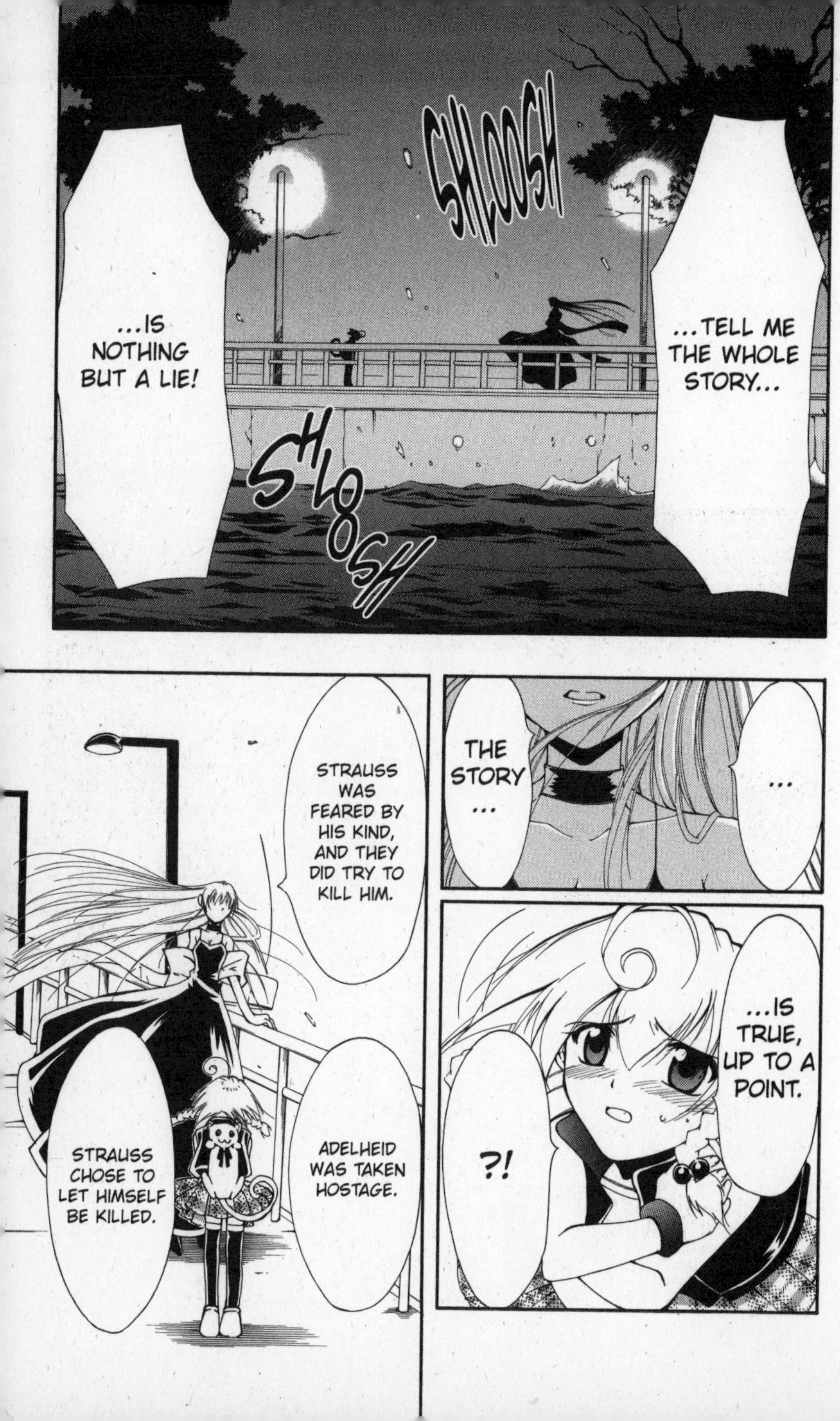
...TELL ME THE WHOLE STORY...
SHLOOSH
...IS NOTHING BUT A LIE!
SHLOOSH
...
THE STORY ...
...IS TRUE, UP TO A POINT.
?!
STRAUSS WAS FEARED BY HIS KIND, AND THEY DID TRY TO KILL HIM.
ADELHEID WAS TAKEN HOSTAGE.
STRAUSS CHOSE TO LET HIMSELF BE KILLED.

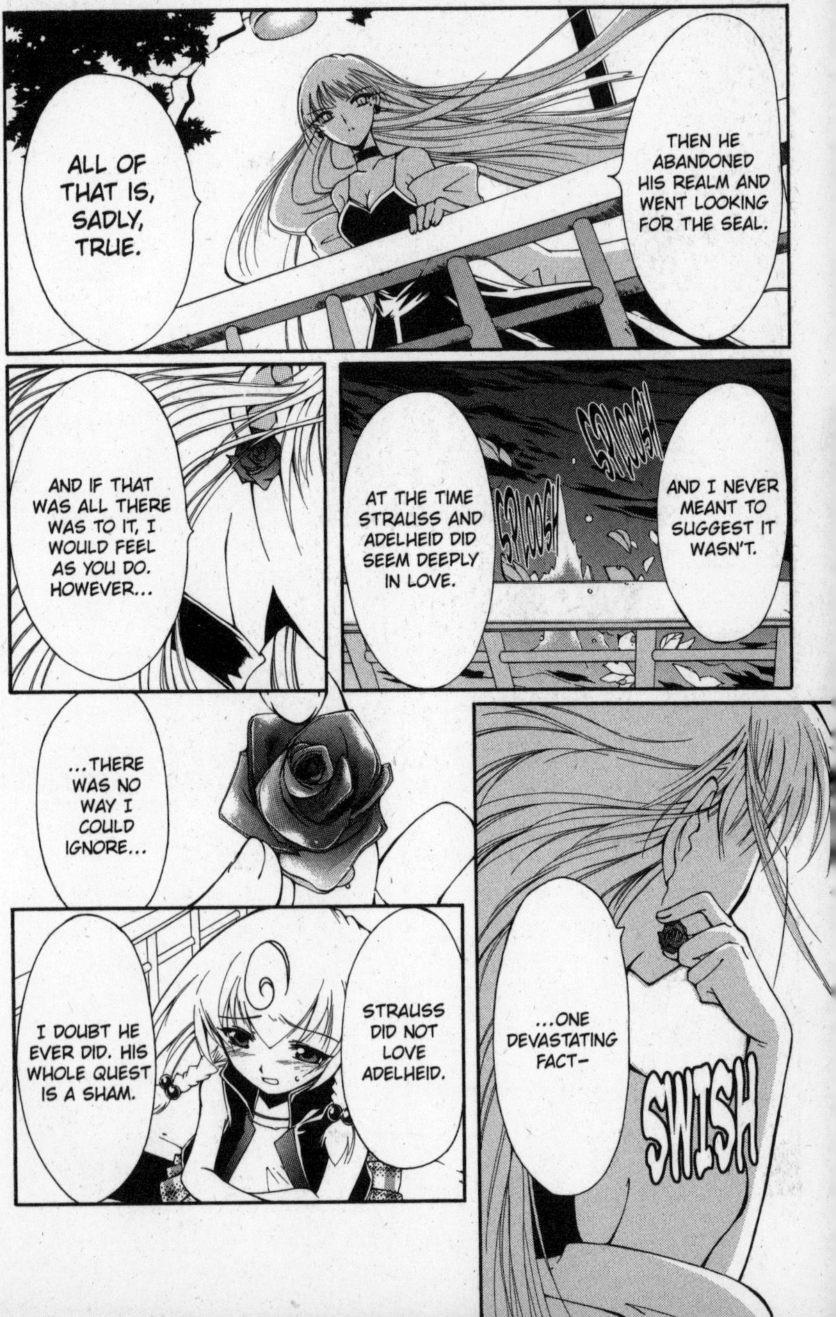
THEN HE ABANDONED HIS REALM AND WENT LOOKING FOR THE SEAL.
ALL OF THAT IS, SADLY, TRUE.
AND I NEVER MEANT TO SUGGEST IT WASN'T.
SPLOOSH
SPLOOSH
AT THE TIME STRAUSS AND ADELHEID DID SEEM DEEPLY IN LOVE.
AND IF THAT WAS ALL THERE WAS TO IT, I WOULD FEEL AS YOU DO. HOWEVER...
...THERE WAS NO WAY I COULD IGNORE...
...ONE DEVASTATING FACT—
SWISH
STRAUSS DID NOT LOVE ADELHEID.
I DOUBT HE EVER DID. HIS WHOLE QUEST IS A SHAM.

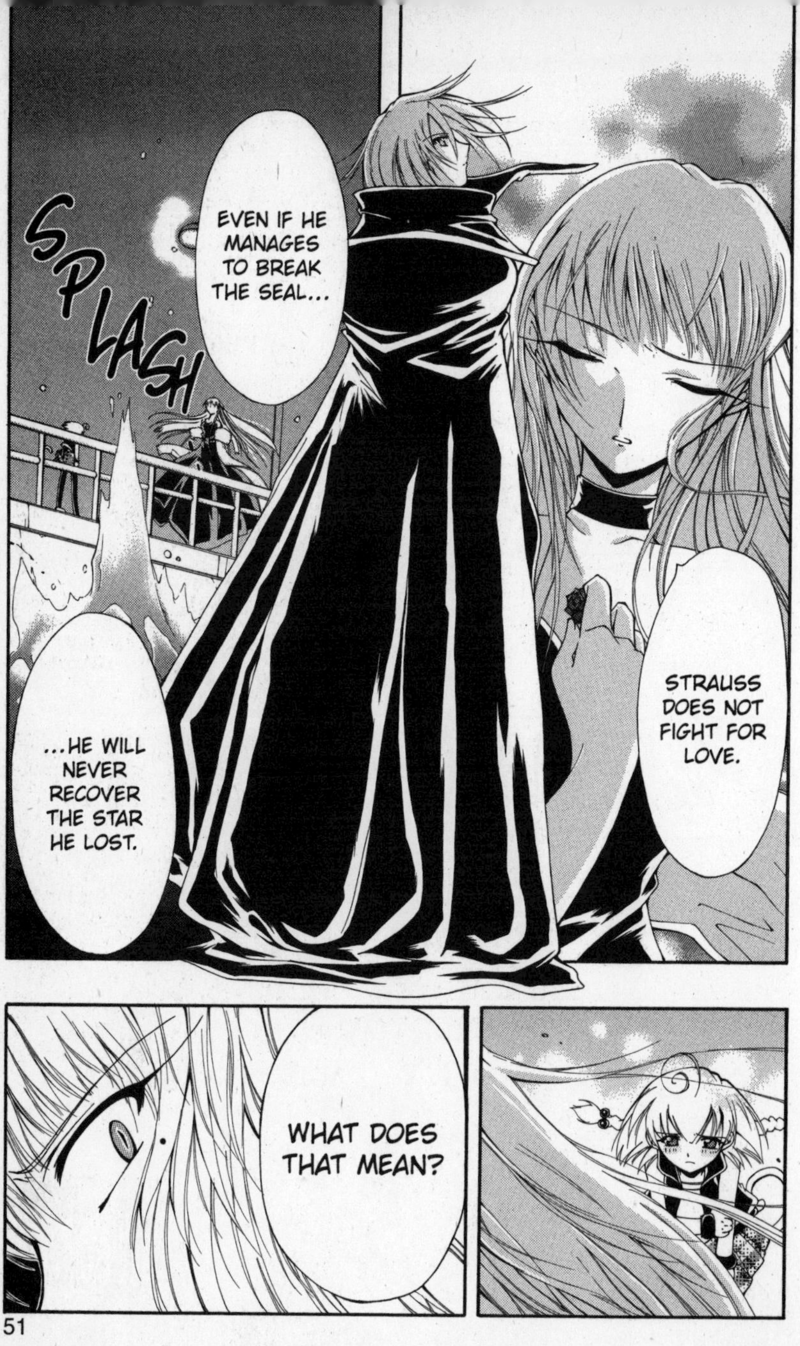
EVEN IF HE MANAGES TO BREAK THE SEAL...
SPLASH
STRAUSS DOES NOT FIGHT FOR LOVE.
...HE WILL NEVER RECOVER THE STAR HE LOST.
WHAT DOES THAT MEAN?

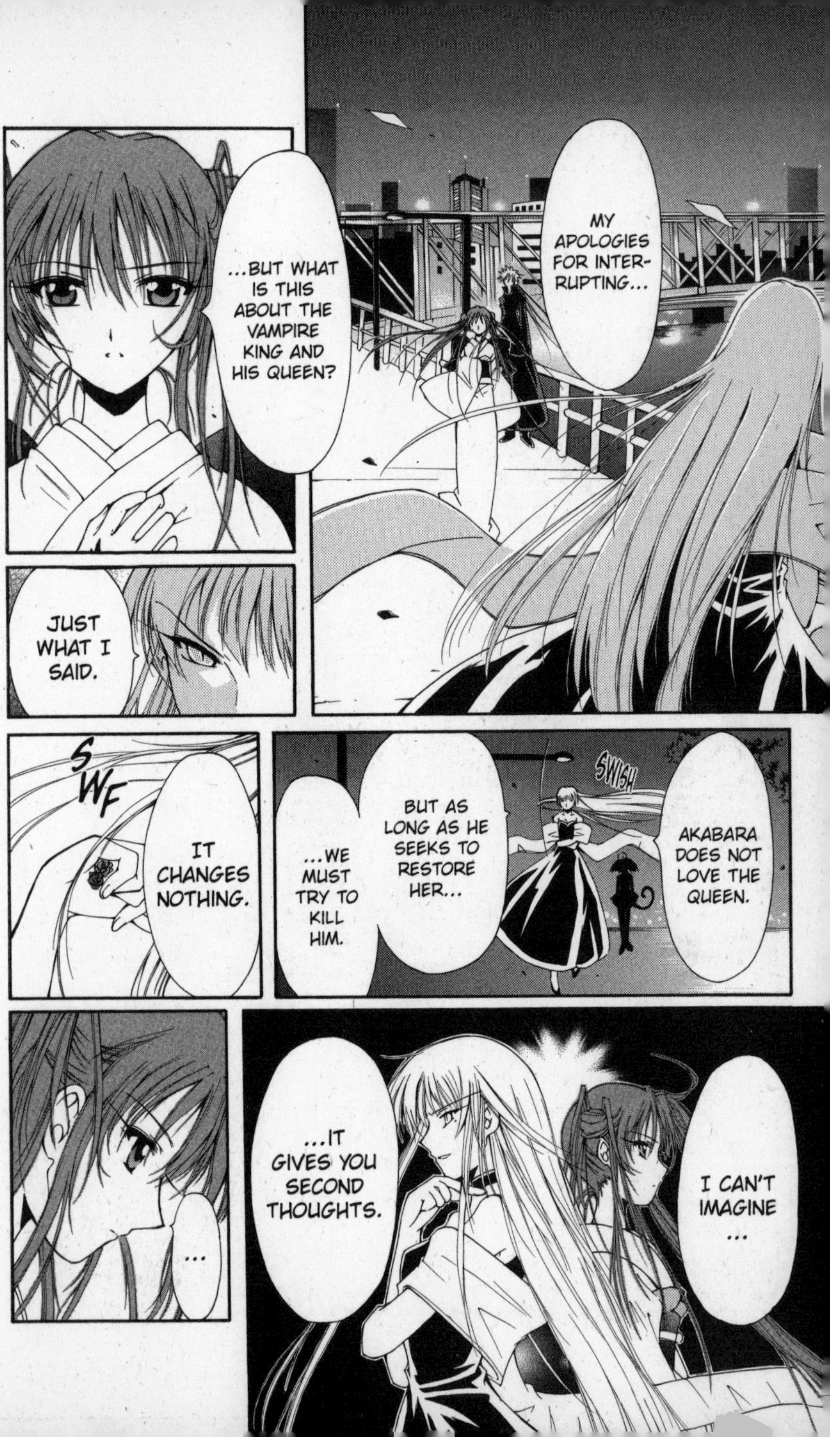
MY APOLOGIES FOR INTER-RUPTING...
...BUT WHAT IS THIS ABOUT THE VAMPIRE KING AND HIS QUEEN?
JUST WHAT I SAID.
AKABARA DOES NOT LOVE THE QUEEN.
SWISH
BUT AS LONG AS HE SEEKS TO RESTORE HER...
...WE MUST TRY TO KILL HIM.
SWF
IT CHANGES NOTHING.
I CAN'T IMAGINE ...
...IT GIVES YOU SECOND THOUGHTS.
...

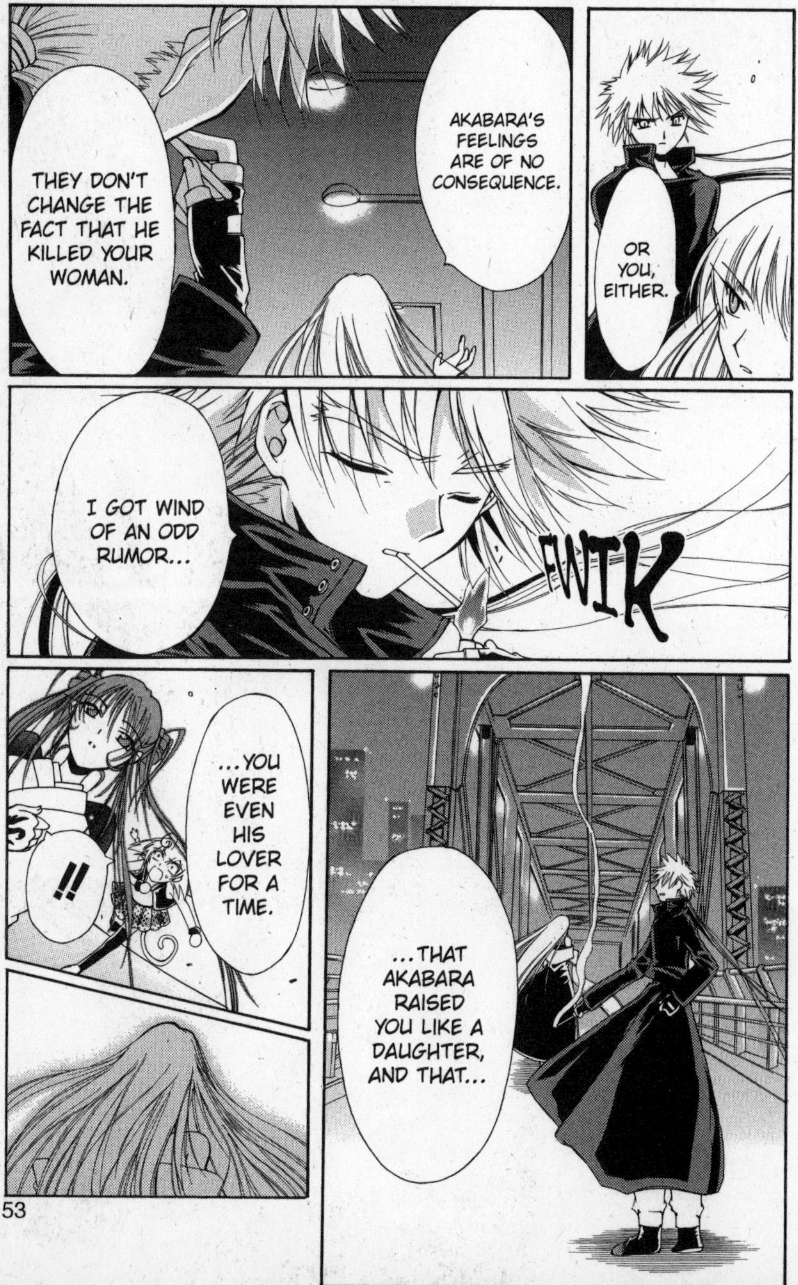
OR YOU, EITHER.
AKABARA'S FEELINGS ARE OF NO CONSEQUENCE.
THEY DON'T CHANGE THE FACT THAT HE KILLED YOUR WOMAN.
FWIK
I GOT WIND OF AN ODD RUMOR...
...THAT AKABARA RAISED YOU LIKE A DAUGHTER, AND THAT...
...YOU WERE EVEN HIS LOVER FOR A TIME.
!!

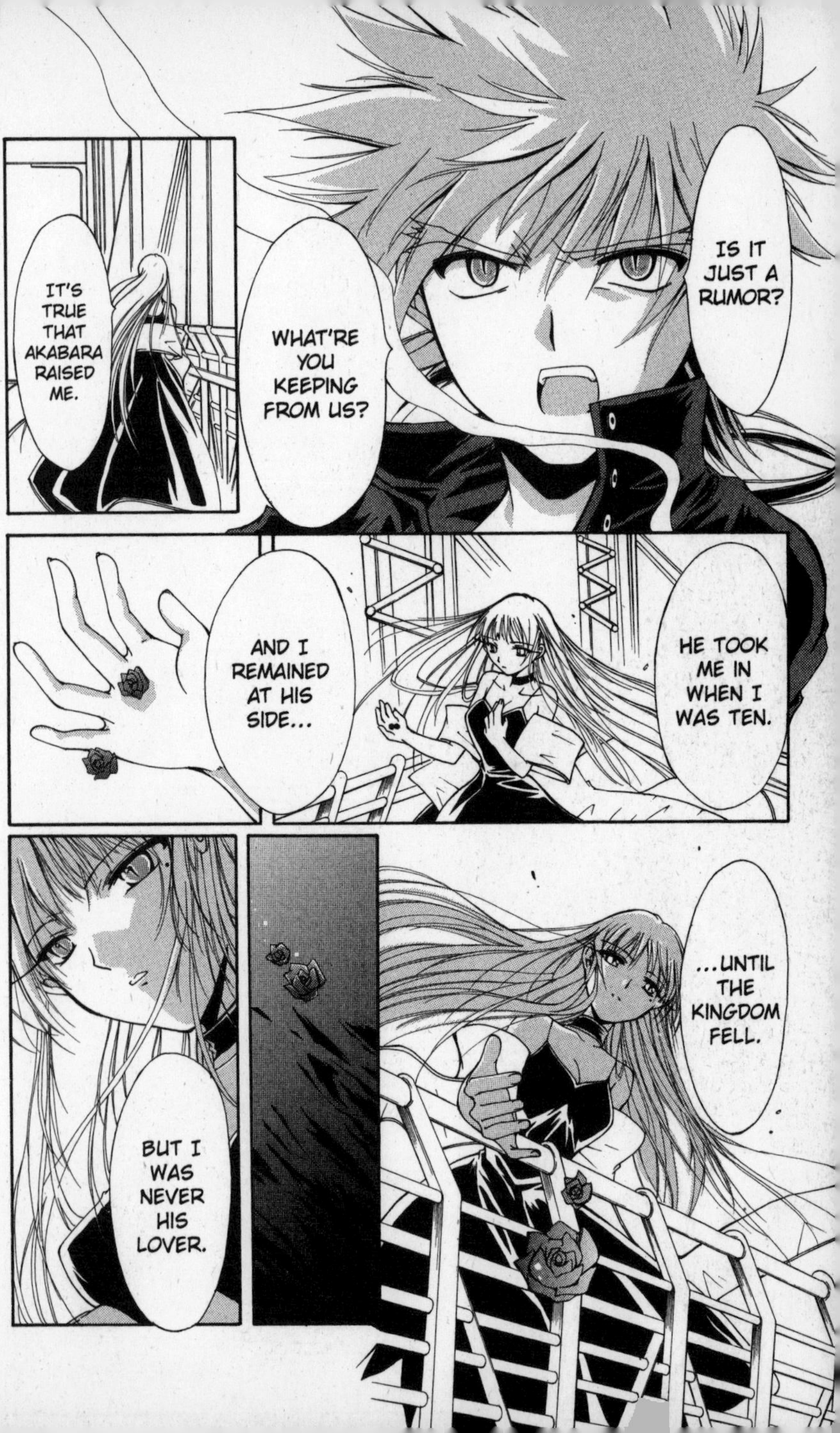
IS IT JUST A RUMOR?
WHAT'RE YOU KEEPING FROM US?
IT'S TRUE THAT AKABARA RAISED ME.
HE TOOK ME IN WHEN I WAS TEN.
AND I REMAINED AT HIS SIDE...
...UNTIL THE KINGDOM FELL.
BUT I WAS NEVER HIS LOVER.

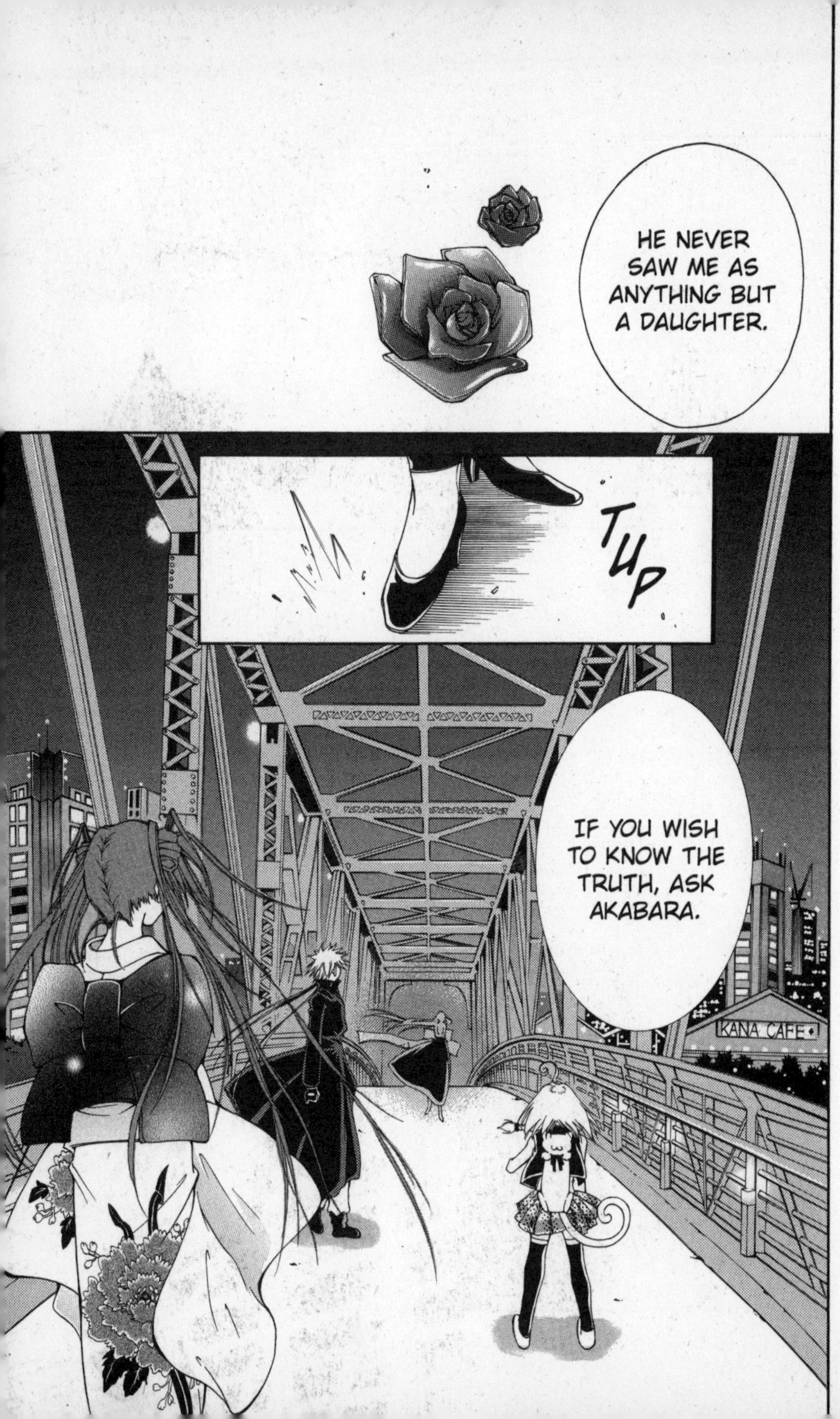
HE NEVER SAW ME AS ANYTHING BUT A DAUGHTER.
TUP
IF YOU WISH TO KNOW THE TRUTH, ASK AKABARA.
KANA CAFE

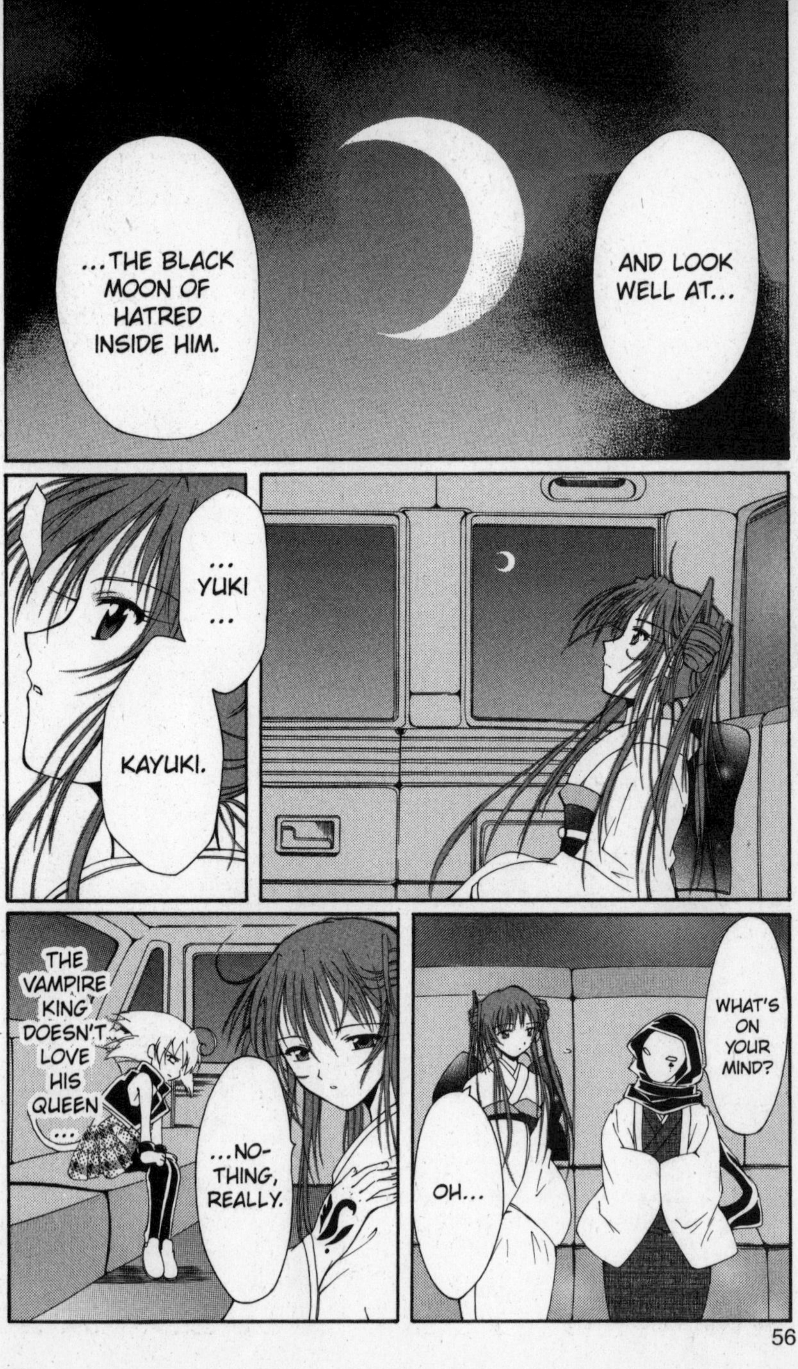
AND LOOK WELL AT...
...THE BLACK MOON OF HATRED INSIDE HIM.
...YUKI...
KAYUKI.
WHAT'S ON YOUR MIND?
OH...
THE VAMPIRE KING DOESN'T LOVE HIS QUEEN...
...NO-THING, REALLY.

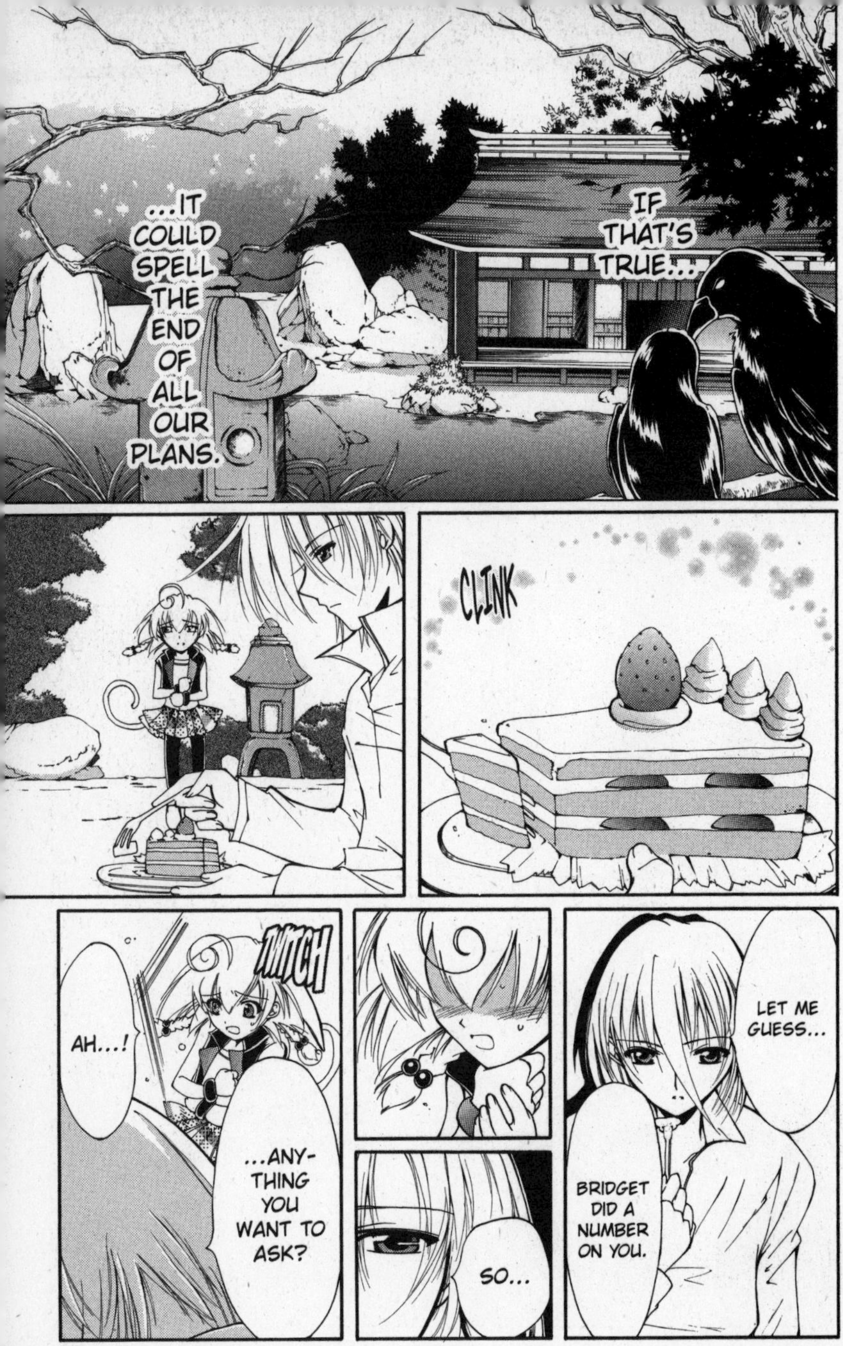
IF THAT'S TRUE...
...IT COULD SPELL THE END OF ALL OUR PLANS.
CLINK
LET ME GUESS...
BRIDGET DID A NUMBER ON YOU.
SO...
TWITCH
AH...!
...ANYTHING YOU WANT TO ASK?

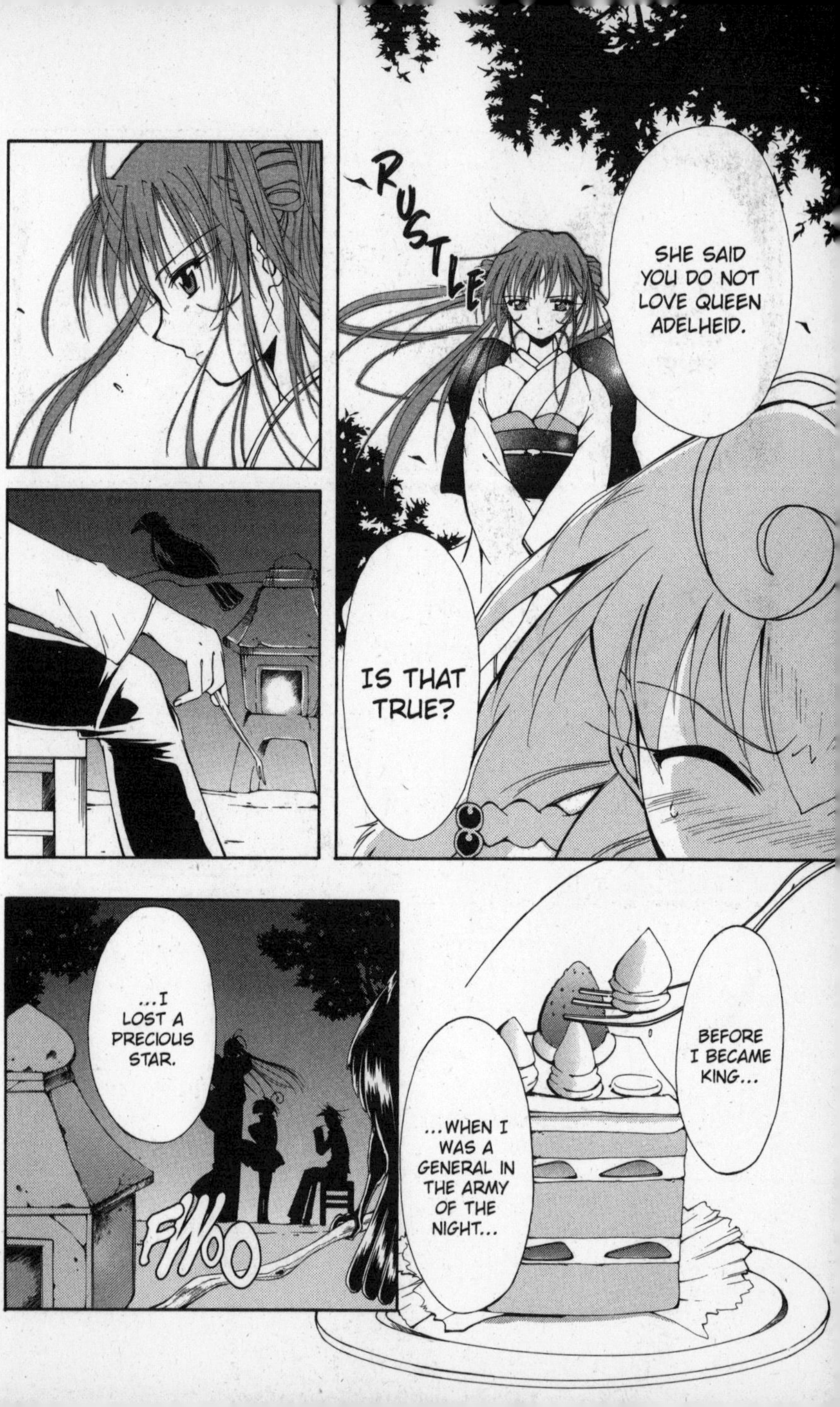
SHE SAID YOU DO NOT LOVE QUEEN ADELHEID.
RUSTLE
IS THAT TRUE?
BEFORE I BECAME KING...
...WHEN I WAS A GENERAL IN THE ARMY OF THE NIGHT...
...I LOST A PRECIOUS STAR.
FWOO

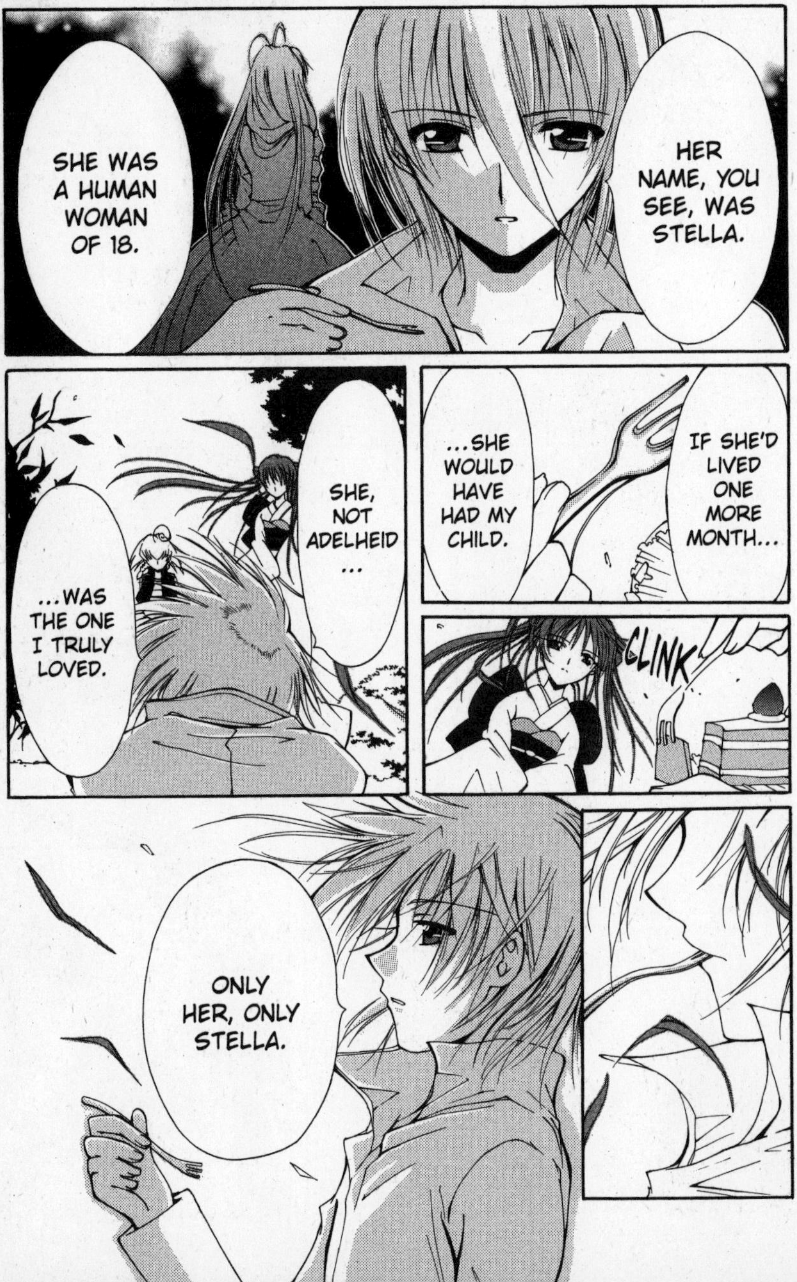
HER NAME, YOU SEE, WAS STELLA.
SHE WAS A HUMAN WOMAN OF 18.
IF SHE'D LIVED ONE MORE MONTH...
...SHE WOULD HAVE HAD MY CHILD.
CLINK
SHE, NOT ADELHEID...
...WAS THE ONE I TRULY LOVED.
ONLY HER, ONLY STELLA.

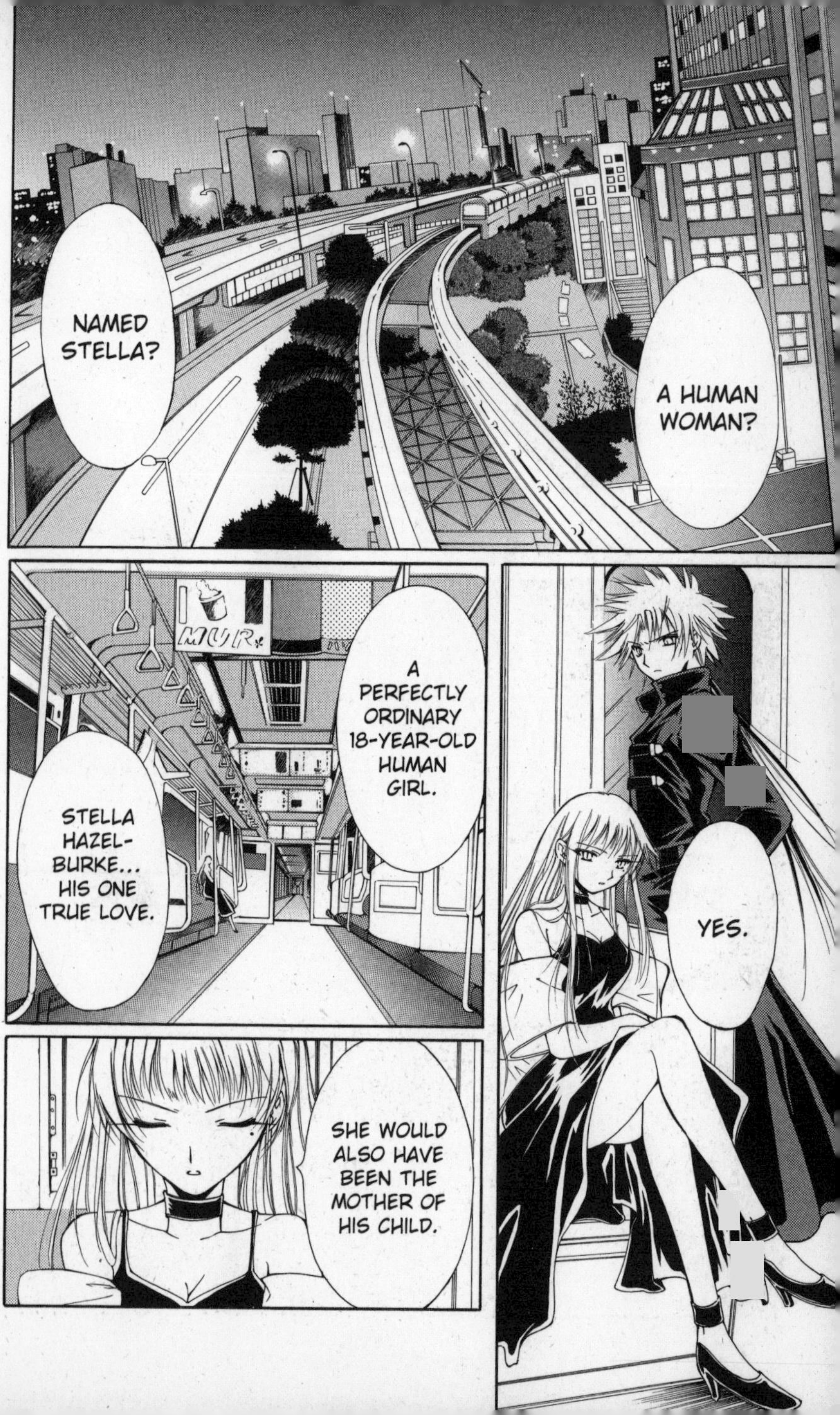
A HUMAN WOMAN?
NAMED STELLA?
YES.
A PERFECTLY ORDINARY 18-YEAR-OLD HUMAN GIRL.
STELLA HAZEL-BURKE... HIS ONE TRUE LOVE.
SHE WOULD ALSO HAVE BEEN THE MOTHER OF HIS CHILD.

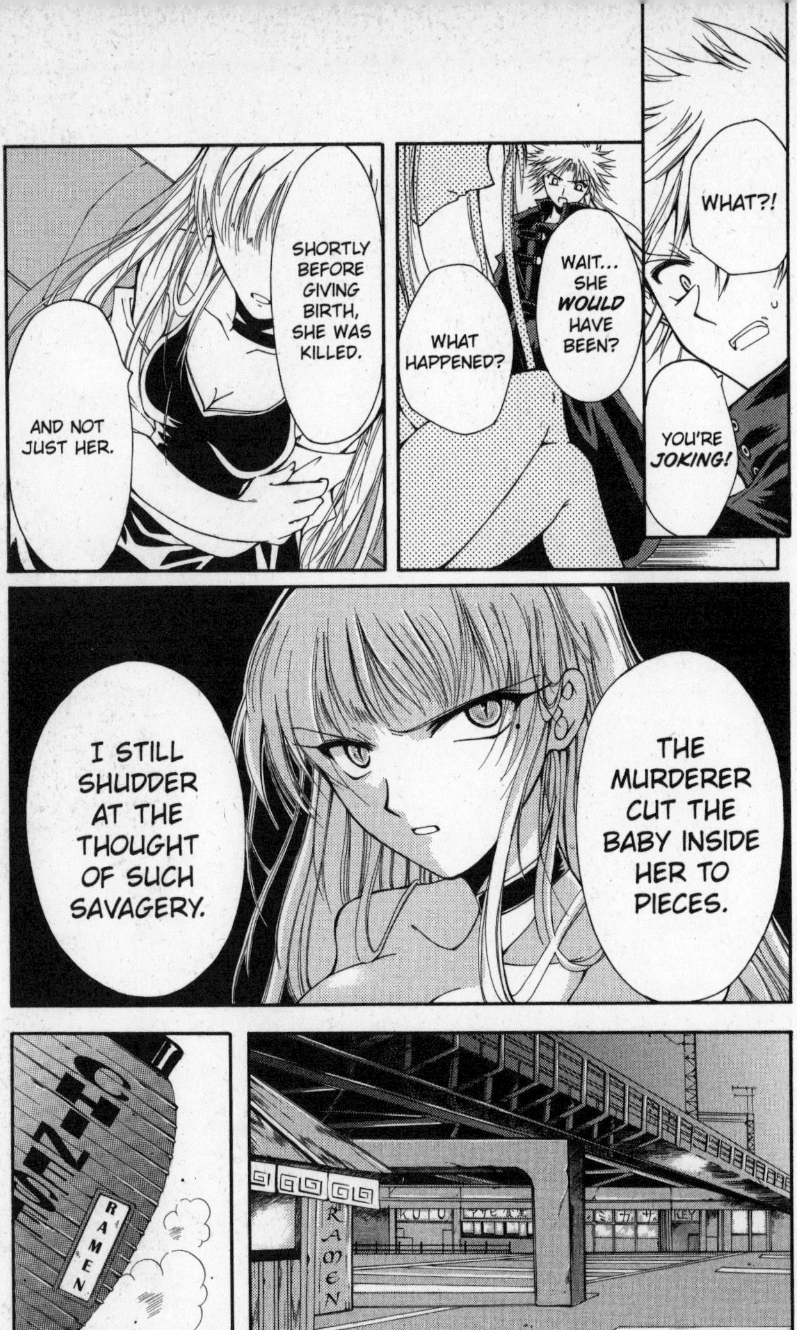
WHAT?!
YOU'RE JOKING!
WAIT... SHE WOULD HAVE BEEN?
WHAT HAPPENED?
SHORTLY BEFORE GIVING BIRTH, SHE WAS KILLED.
AND NOT JUST HER.
THE MURDERER CUT THE BABY INSIDE HER TO PIECES.
I STILL SHUDDER AT THE THOUGHT OF SUCH SAVAGERY.
RAMEN
RAMEN

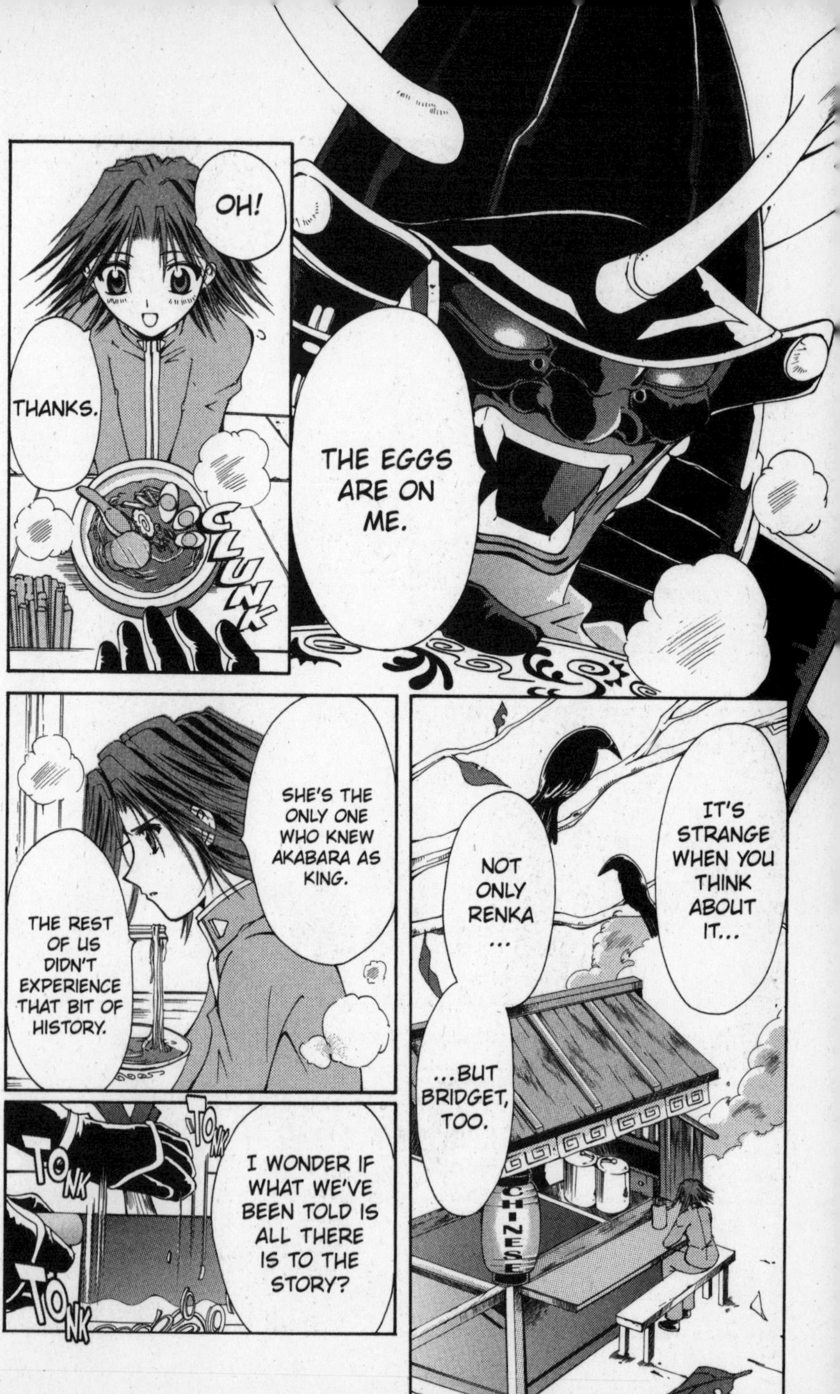
THE EGGS ARE ON ME.
OH!
THANKS.
CLUNK
IT'S STRANGE WHEN YOU THINK ABOUT IT...
NOT ONLY RENKA...
...BUT BRIDGET, TOO.
CHINESE
SHE'S THE ONLY ONE WHO KNEW AKABARA AS KING.
THE REST OF US DIDN'T EXPERIENCE THAT BIT OF HISTORY.
TONK
TONK
TONK
I WONDER IF WHAT WE'VE BEEN TOLD IS ALL THERE IS TO THE STORY?

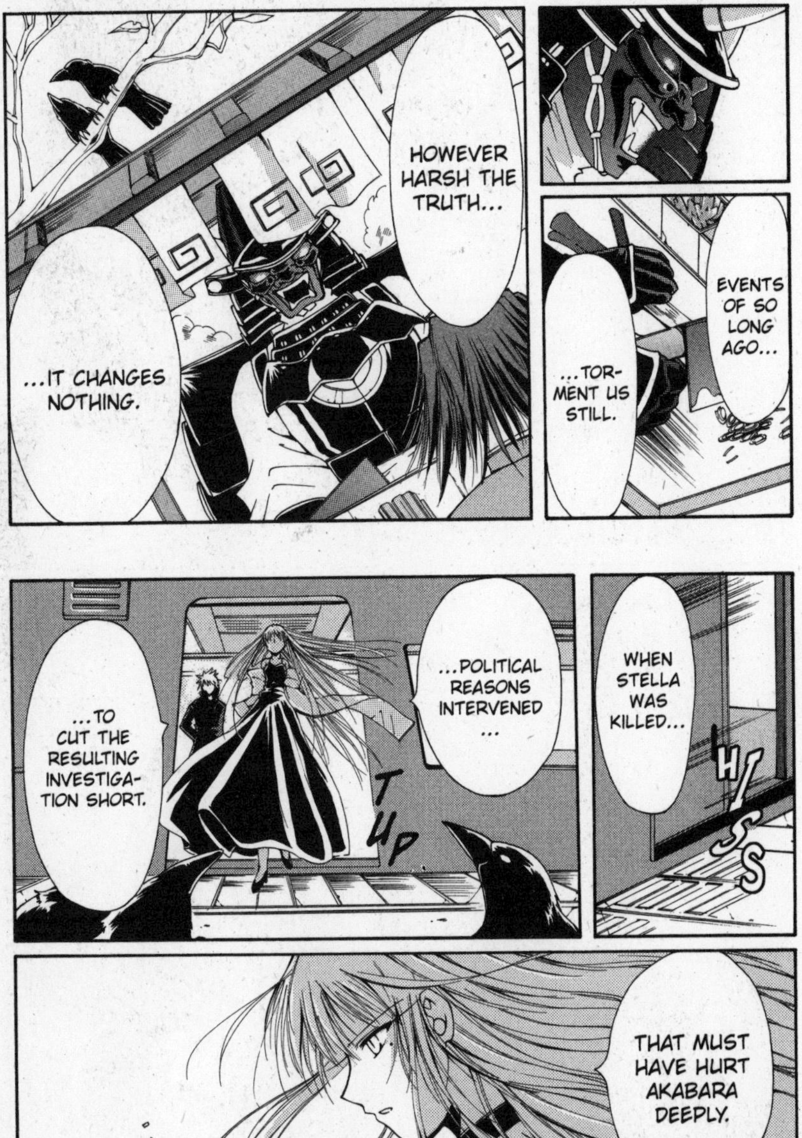
EVENTS OF SO LONG AGO...
...TORMENT US STILL.
HOWEVER HARSH THE TRUTH...
...IT CHANGES NOTHING.
WHEN STELLA WAS KILLED...
HISS
...POLITICAL REASONS INTERVENED...
TUP
...TO CUT THE RESULTING INVESTIGATION SHORT.
THAT MUST HAVE HURT AKABARA DEEPLY.

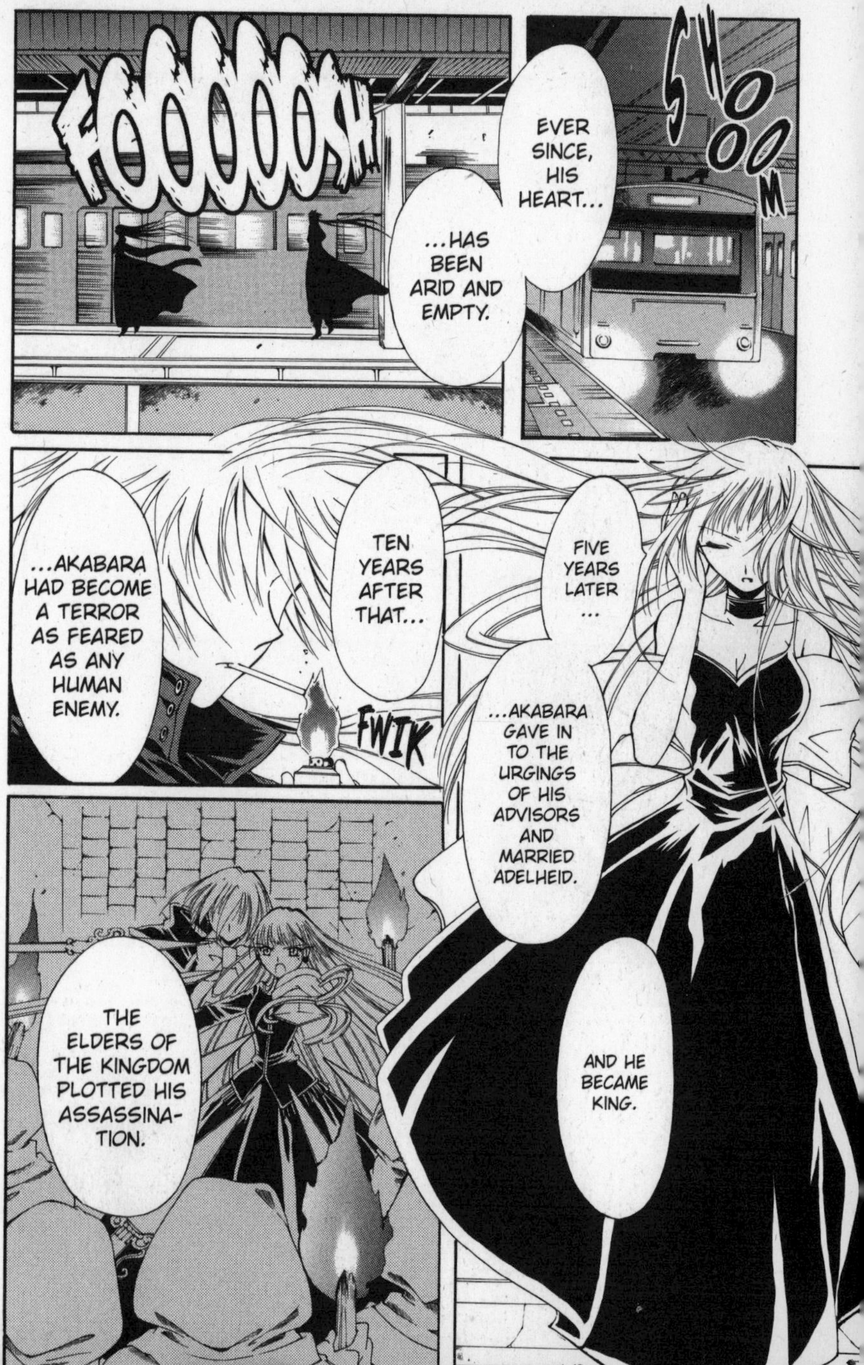
SHOOOM
EVER SINCE, HIS HEART...
...HAS BEEN ARID AND EMPTY.
FOOOOOSH
FIVE YEARS LATER...
...AKABARA GAVE IN TO THE URGINGS OF HIS ADVISORS AND MARRIED ADELHEID.
AND HE BECAME KING.
TEN YEARS AFTER THAT...
...AKABARA HAD BECOME A TERROR AS FEARED AS ANY HUMAN ENEMY.
FWIK
THE ELDERS OF THE KINGDOM PLOTTED HIS ASSASSINA-TION.

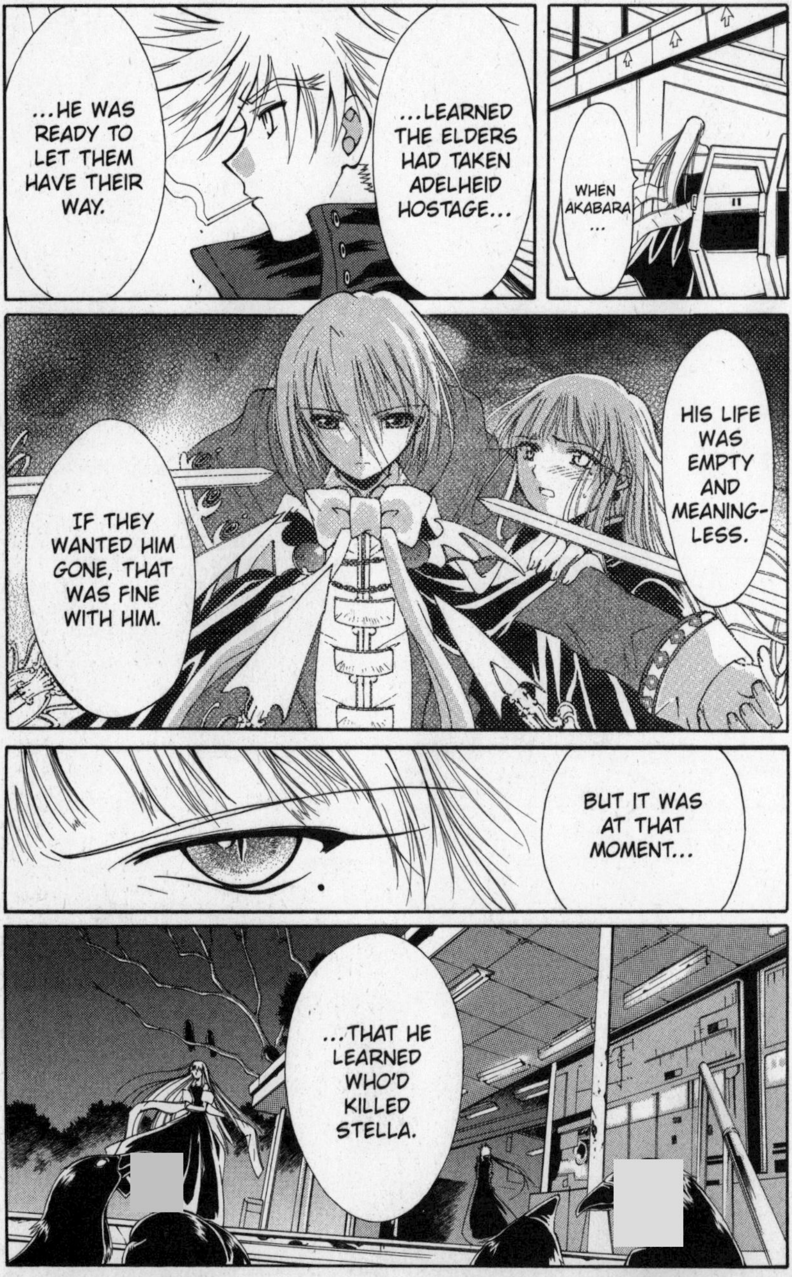
WHEN AKABARA ...
...LEARNED THE ELDERS HAD TAKEN ADELHEID HOSTAGE...
...HE WAS READY TO LET THEM HAVE THEIR WAY.
HIS LIFE WAS EMPTY AND MEANING-LESS.
IF THEY WANTED HIM GONE, THAT WAS FINE WITH HIM.
BUT IT WAS AT THAT MOMENT...
...THAT HE LEARNED WHO'D KILLED STELLA.

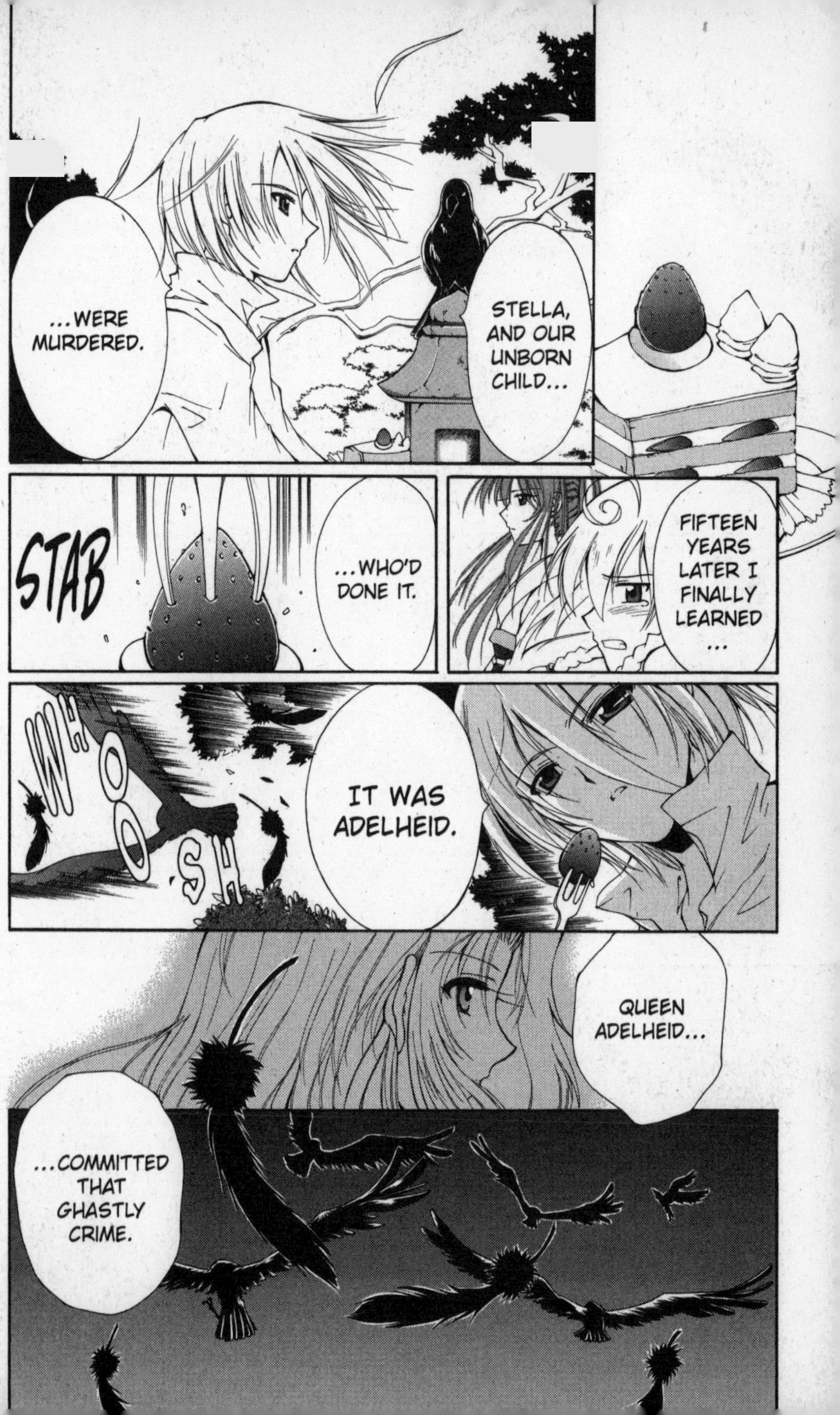
STELLA, AND OUR UNBORN CHILD...
...WERE MURDERED.
FIFTEEN YEARS LATER I FINALLY LEARNED...
...WHO'D DONE IT.
STAB
IT WAS ADELHEID.
WHOOSH
QUEEN ADELHEID...
...COMMITTED THAT GHASTLY CRIME.

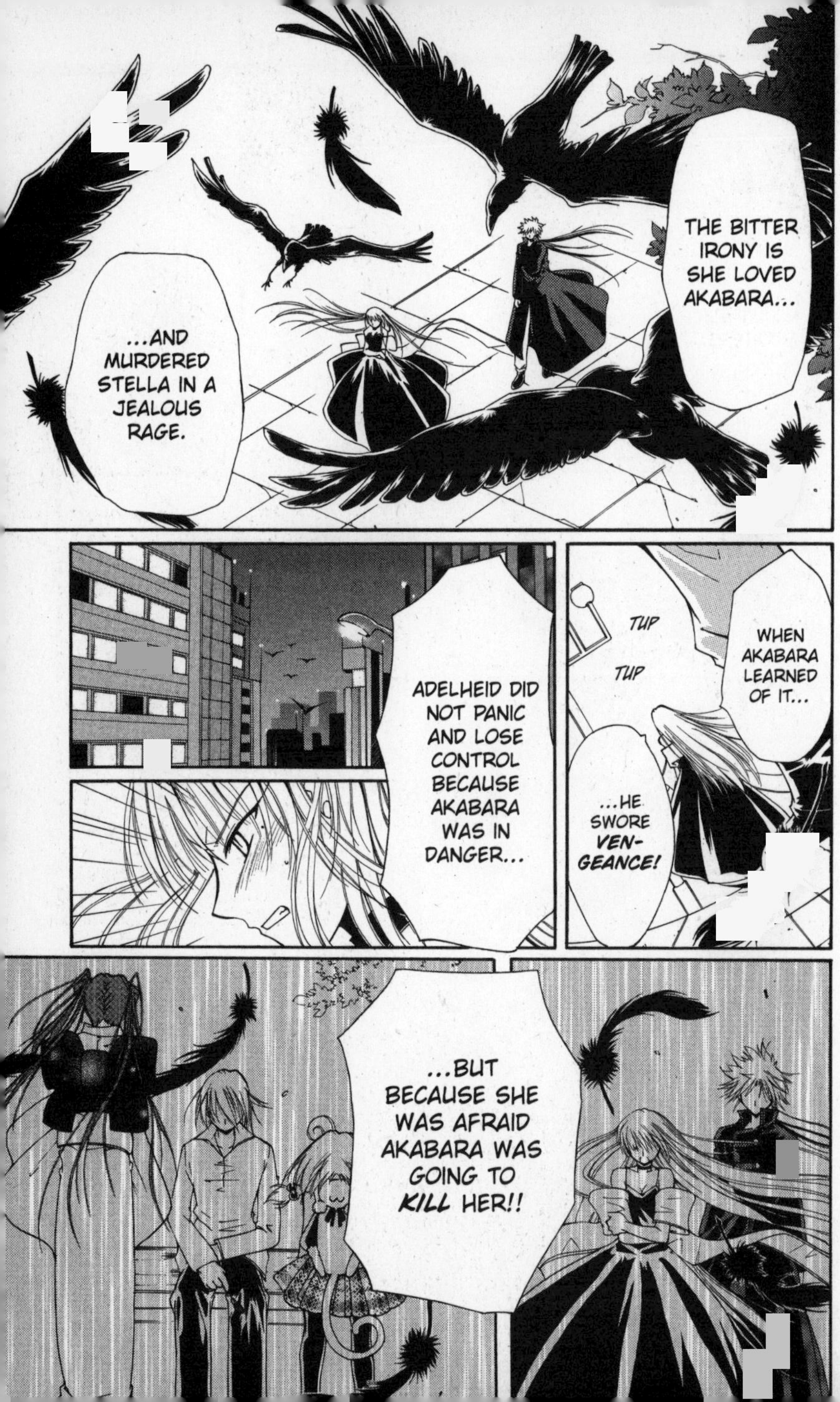
THE BITTER IRONY IS SHE LOVED AKABARA...
...AND MURDERED STELLA IN A JEALOUS RAGE.
WHEN AKABARA LEARNED OF IT...
TUP
TUP
...HE SWORE VEN-GEANCE!
ADELHEID DID NOT PANIC AND LOSE CONTROL BECAUSE AKABARA WAS IN DANGER...
...BUT BECAUSE SHE WAS AFRAID AKABARA WAS GOING TO KILL HER!!

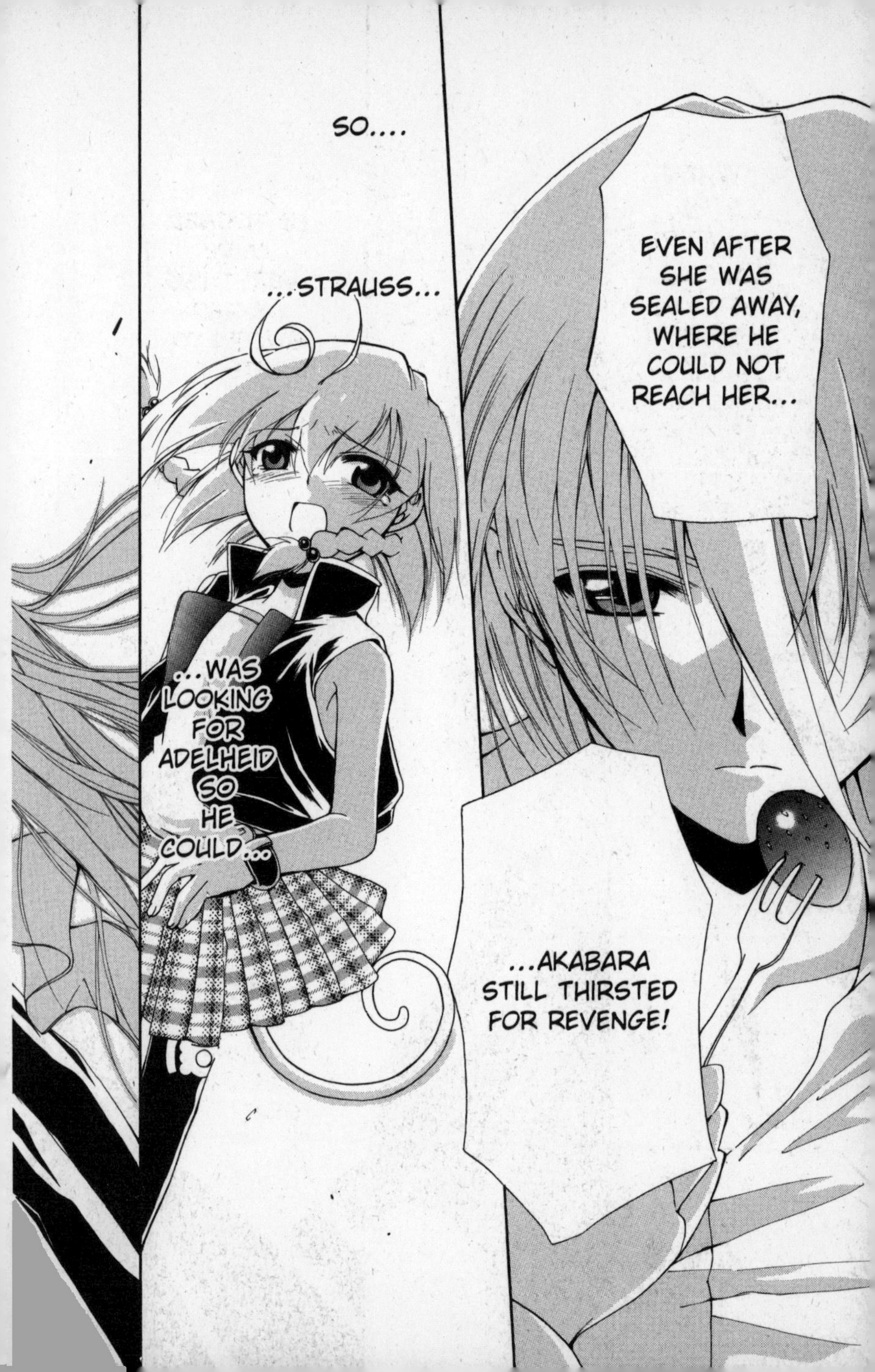

EVEN AFTER SHE WAS SEALED AWAY, WHERE HE COULD NOT REACH HER...
...AKABARA STILL THIRSTED FOR REVENGE!
SO....
...STRAUSS...
...WAS LOOKING FOR ADELHEID SO HE COULD...

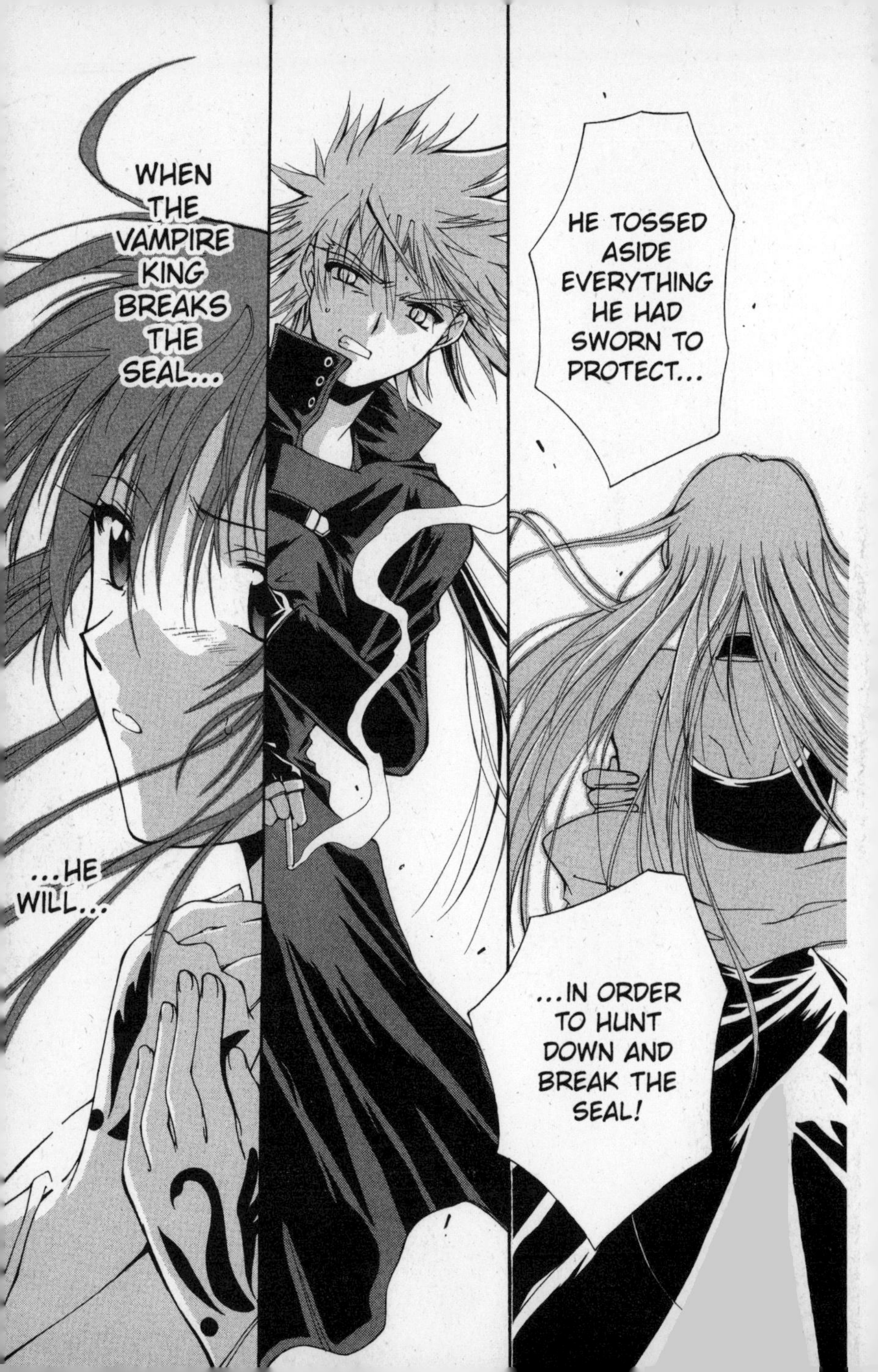
HE TOSSED ASIDE EVERYTHING HE HAD SWORN TO PROTECT...
...IN ORDER TO HUNT DOWN AND BREAK THE SEAL!
WHEN THE VAMPIRE KING BREAKS THE SEAL...
...HE WILL...

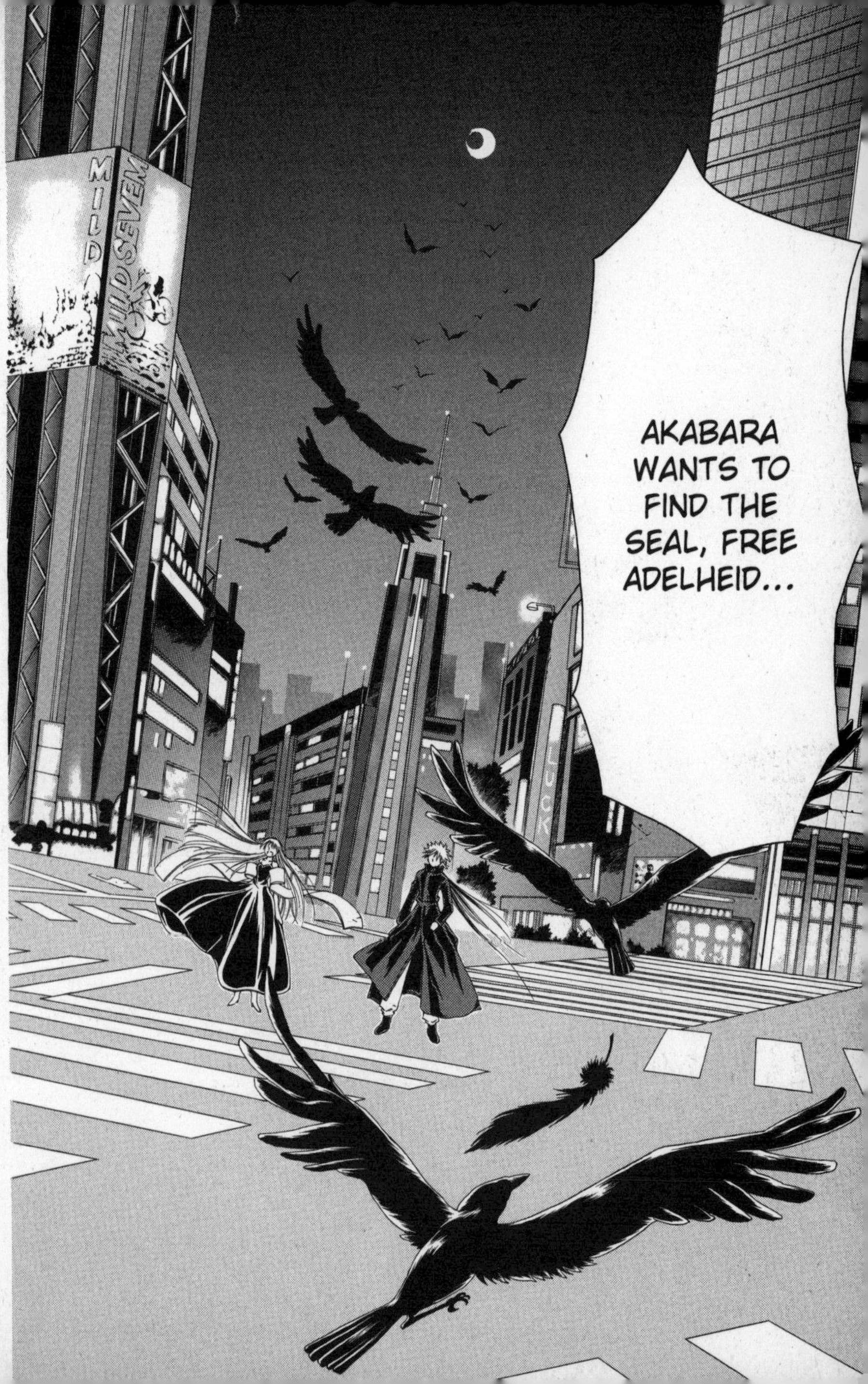
AKABARA WANTS TO FIND THE SEAL, FREE ADELHEID...
MILD SEVEN
LUCK

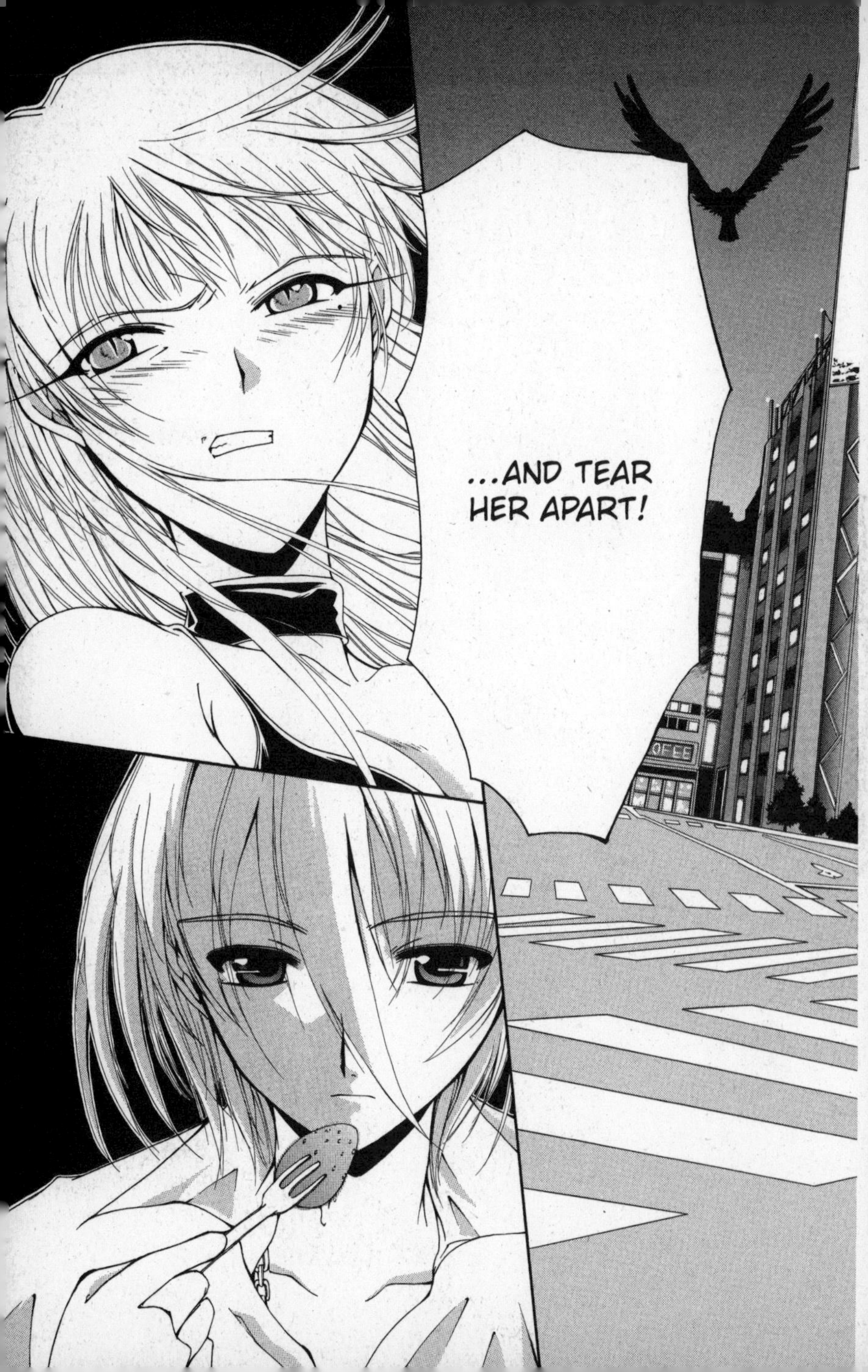
...AND TEAR HER APART!

THE RECORD OF A
FALLEN VAMPIRE

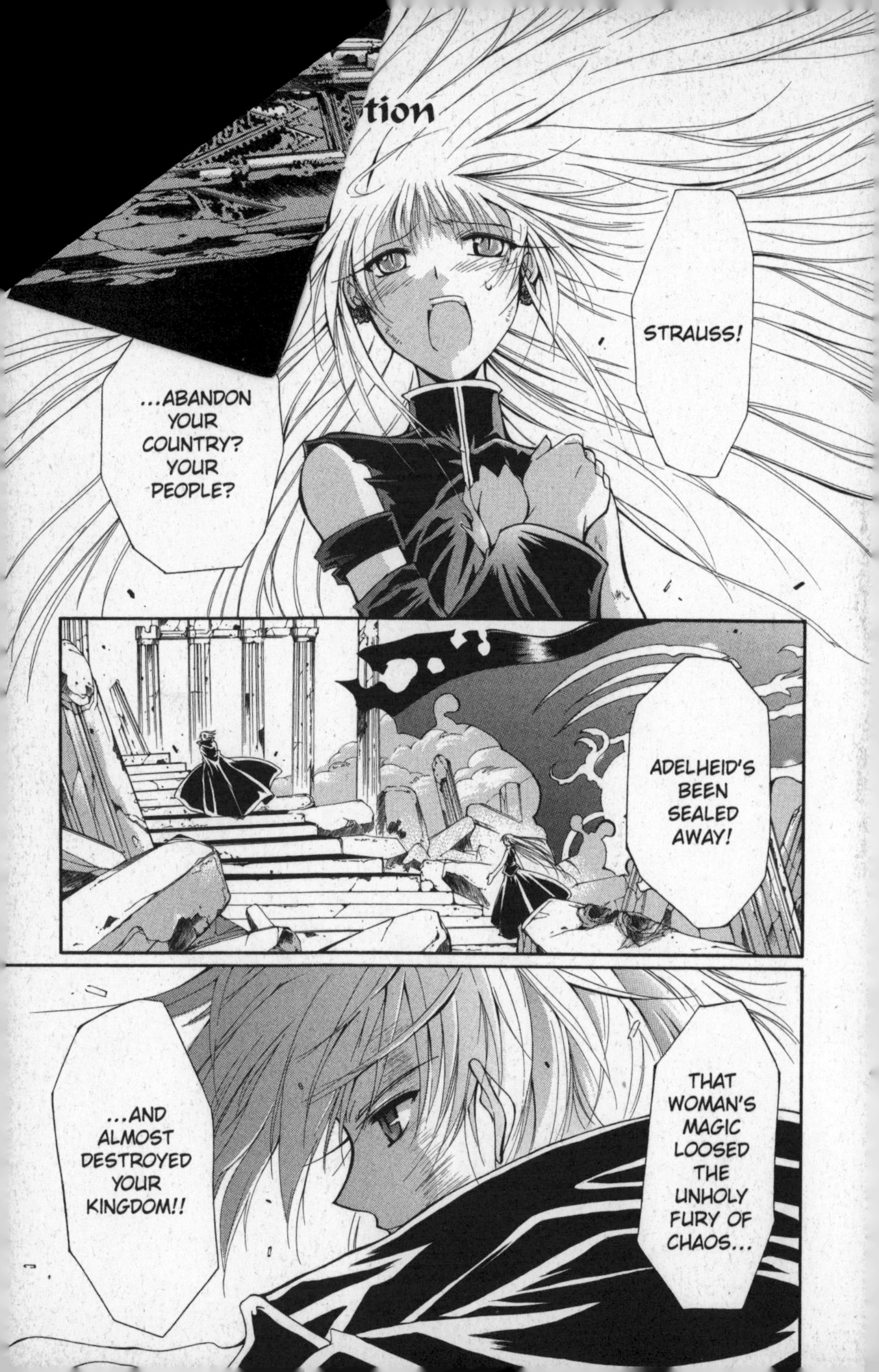
STRAUSS!
...ABANDON YOUR COUNTRY? YOUR PEOPLE?
ADELHEID'S BEEN SEALED AWAY!
THAT WOMAN'S MAGIC LOOSED THE UNHOLY FURY OF CHAOS...
...AND ALMOST DESTROYED YOUR KINGDOM!!

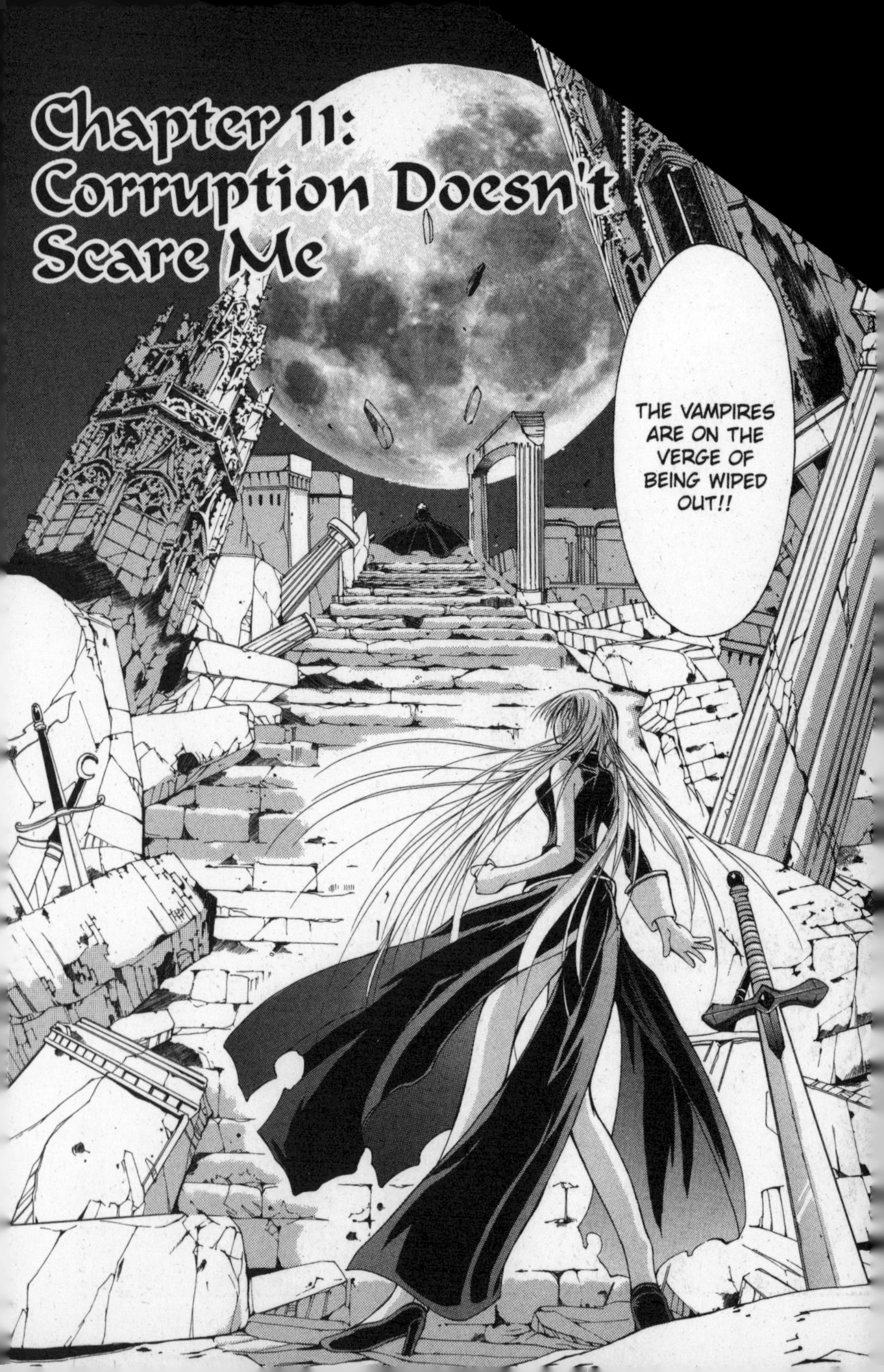
Chapter 11: Corruption Doesn't Scare Me
THE VAMPIRES ARE ON THE VERGE OF BEING WIPED OUT!!

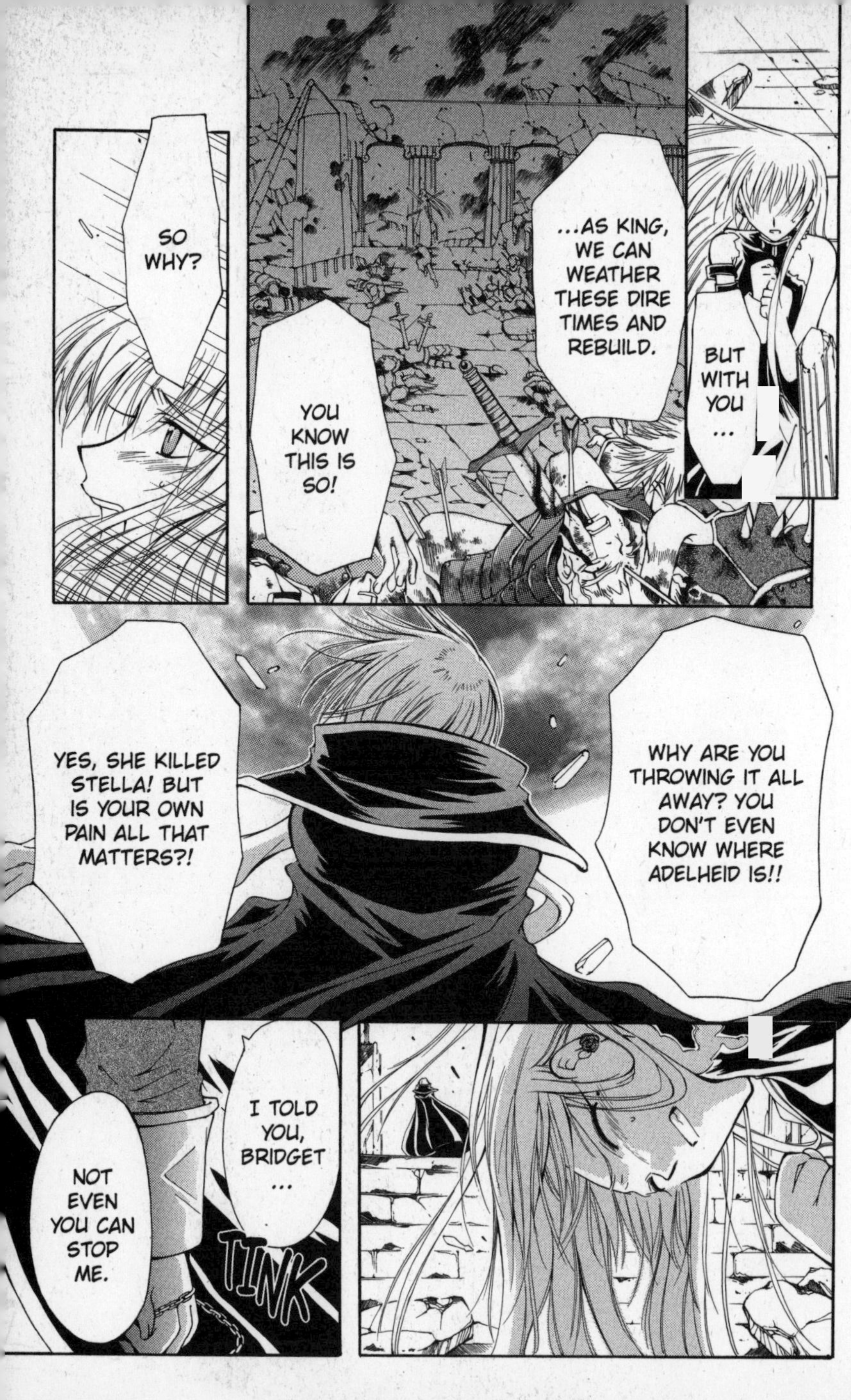
BUT WITH YOU ...
...AS KING, WE CAN WEATHER THESE DIRE TIMES AND REBUILD.
YOU KNOW THIS IS SO!
SO WHY?
WHY ARE YOU THROWING IT ALL AWAY? YOU DON'T EVEN KNOW WHERE ADELHEID IS!!
YES, SHE KILLED STELLA! BUT IS YOUR OWN PAIN ALL THAT MATTERS?!
I TOLD YOU, BRIDGET ...
NOT EVEN YOU CAN STOP ME.
TINK

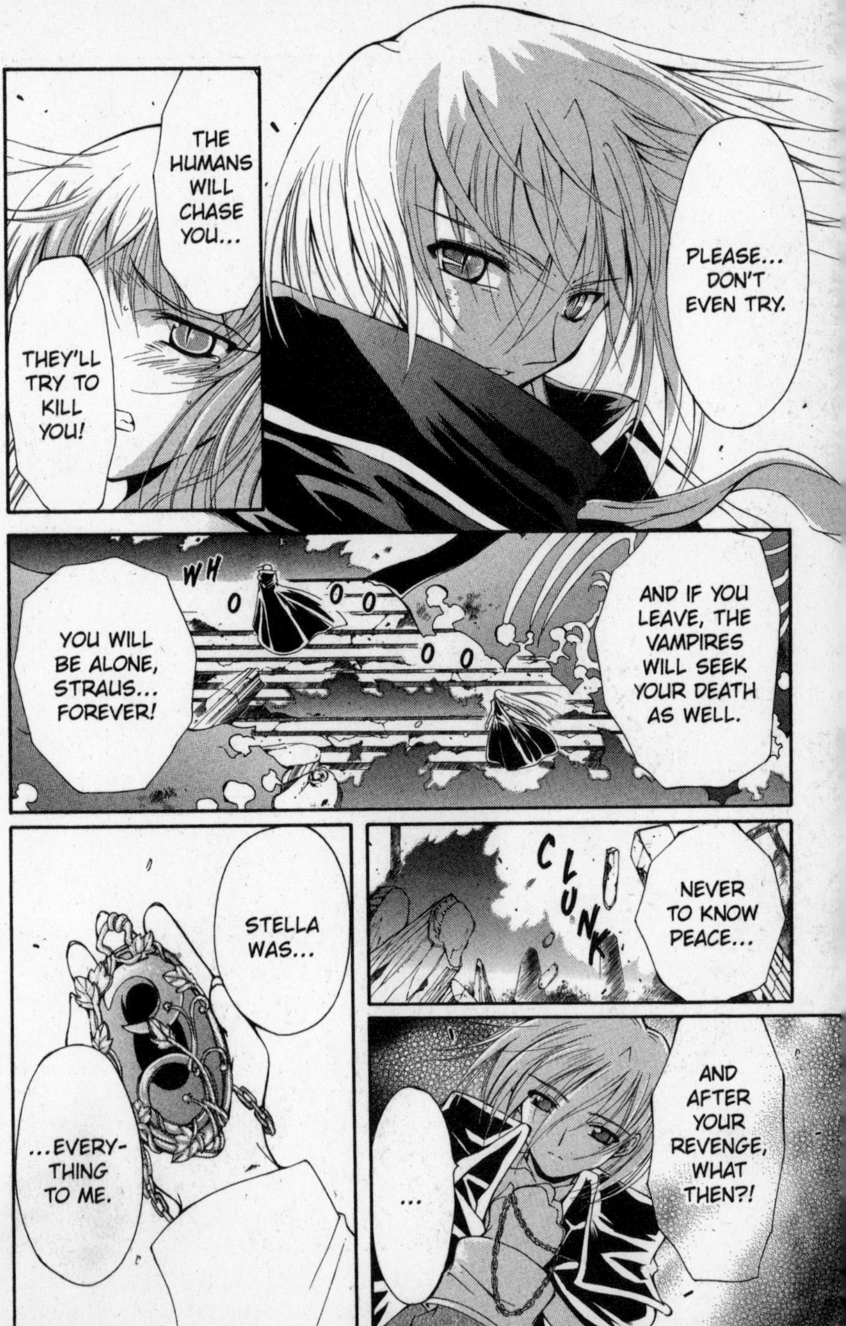

PLEASE... DON'T EVEN TRY.
THE HUMANS WILL CHASE YOU...
THEY'LL TRY TO KILL YOU!
AND IF YOU LEAVE, THE VAMPIRES WILL SEEK YOUR DEATH AS WELL.
WHOOOOOO
YOU WILL BE ALONE, STRAUS... FOREVER!
NEVER TO KNOW PEACE...
CLUNK
AND AFTER YOUR REVENGE, WHAT THEN?!
...
STELLA WAS...
...EVERY-THING TO ME.

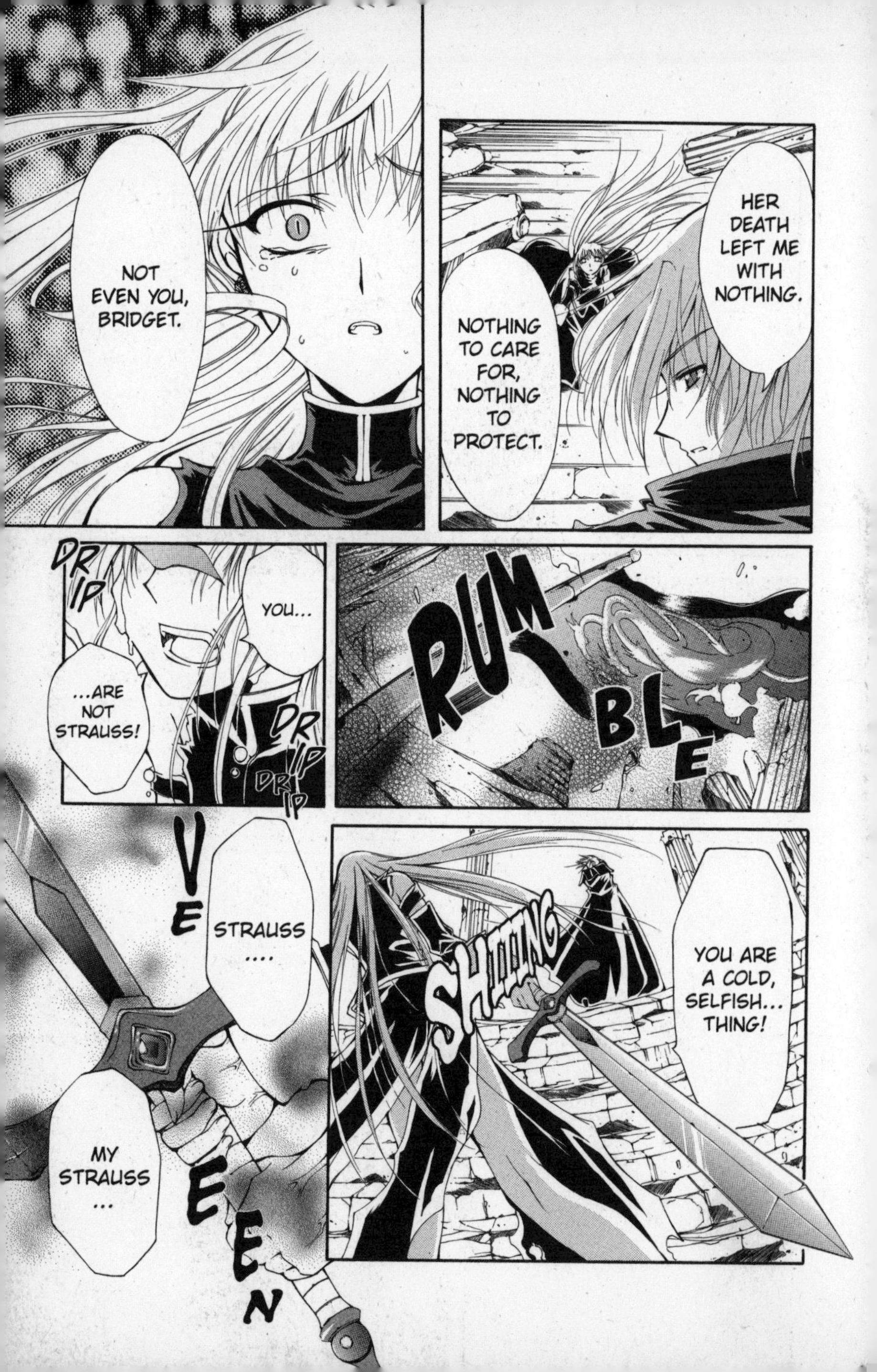
HER DEATH LEFT ME WITH NOTHING.
NOTHING TO CARE FOR, NOTHING TO PROTECT.
NOT EVEN YOU, BRIDGET.
RUMBLE
DRIP
YOU...
...ARE NOT STRAUSS!
DRIP
DRIP
SHIIING
YOU ARE A COLD, SELFISH... THING!
VEEEN
STRAUSS ....
MY STRAUSS ...

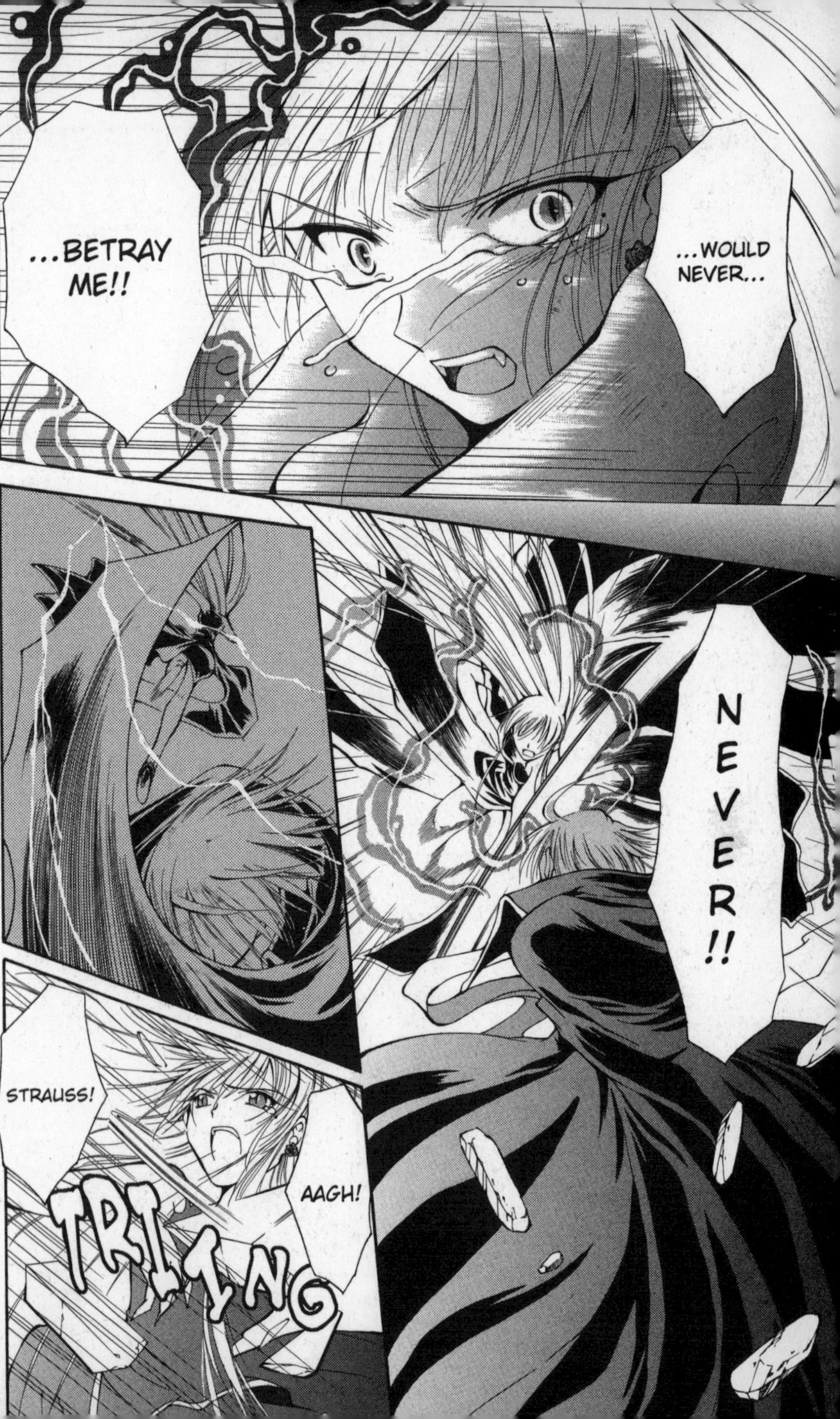

...WOULD NEVER...
...BETRAY ME!!
NEVER!!
STRAUSS!
AAGH!
TRIING

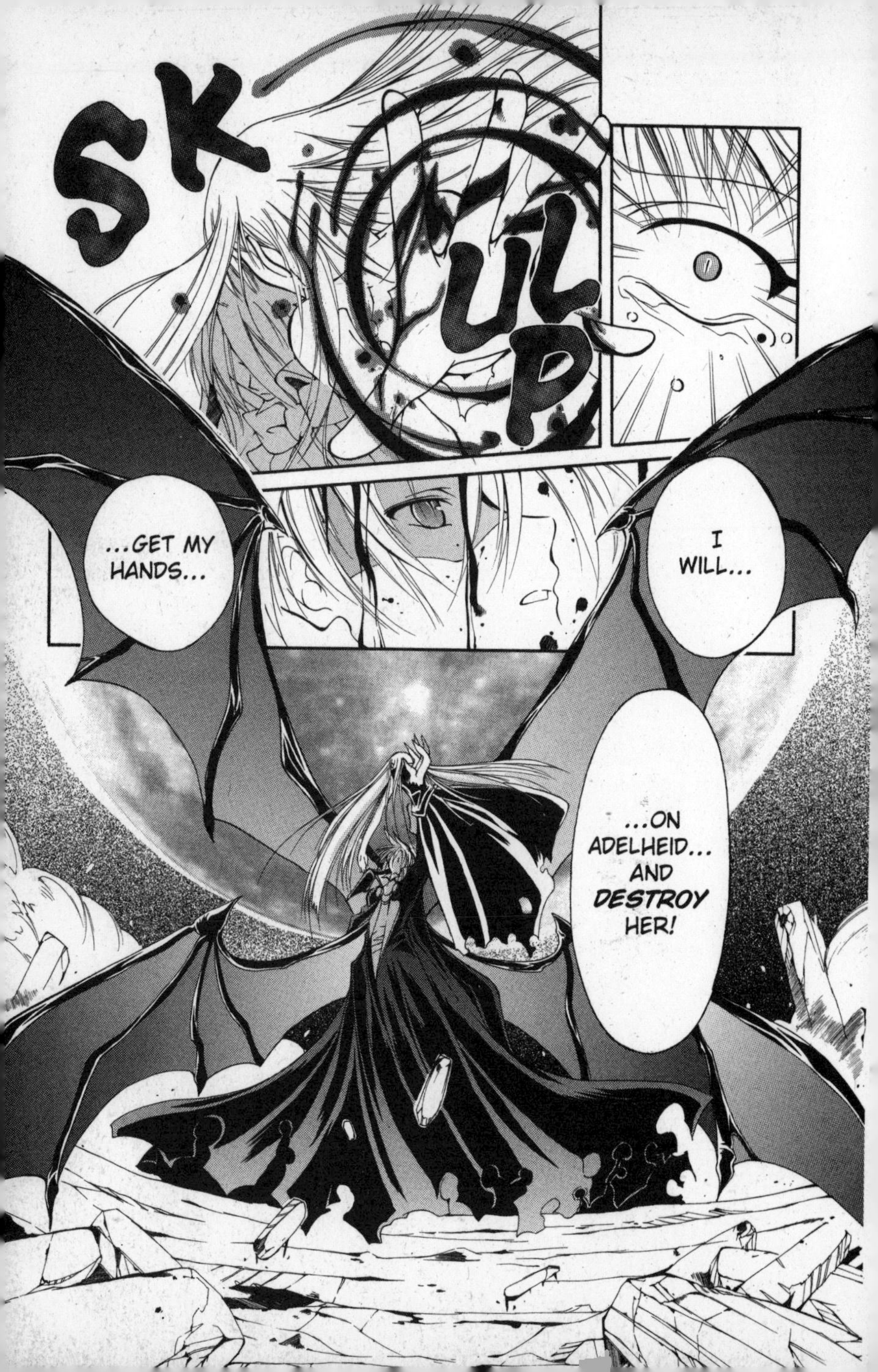
SKULP
I WILL...
...GET MY HANDS...
...ON ADELHEID... AND DESTROY HER!

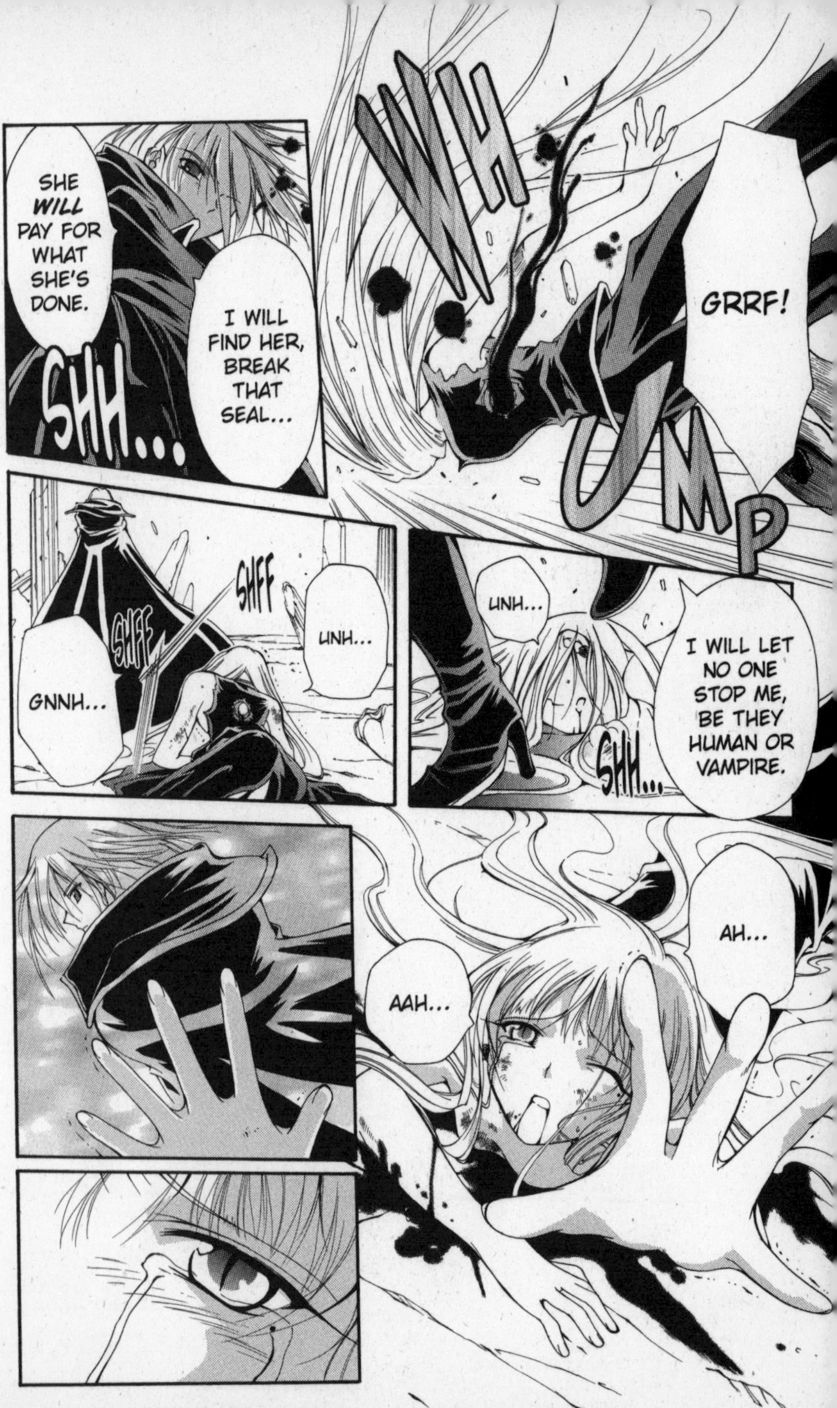
GRRF!
WHUMP
I WILL FIND HER, BREAK THAT SEAL...
SHE **WILL** PAY FOR WHAT SHE'S DONE.
SHH...
I WILL LET NO ONE STOP ME, BE THEY HUMAN OR VAMPIRE.
UNH...
SHH...
UNH...
SHFF
SHFF
GNNH...
AH...
AAH...

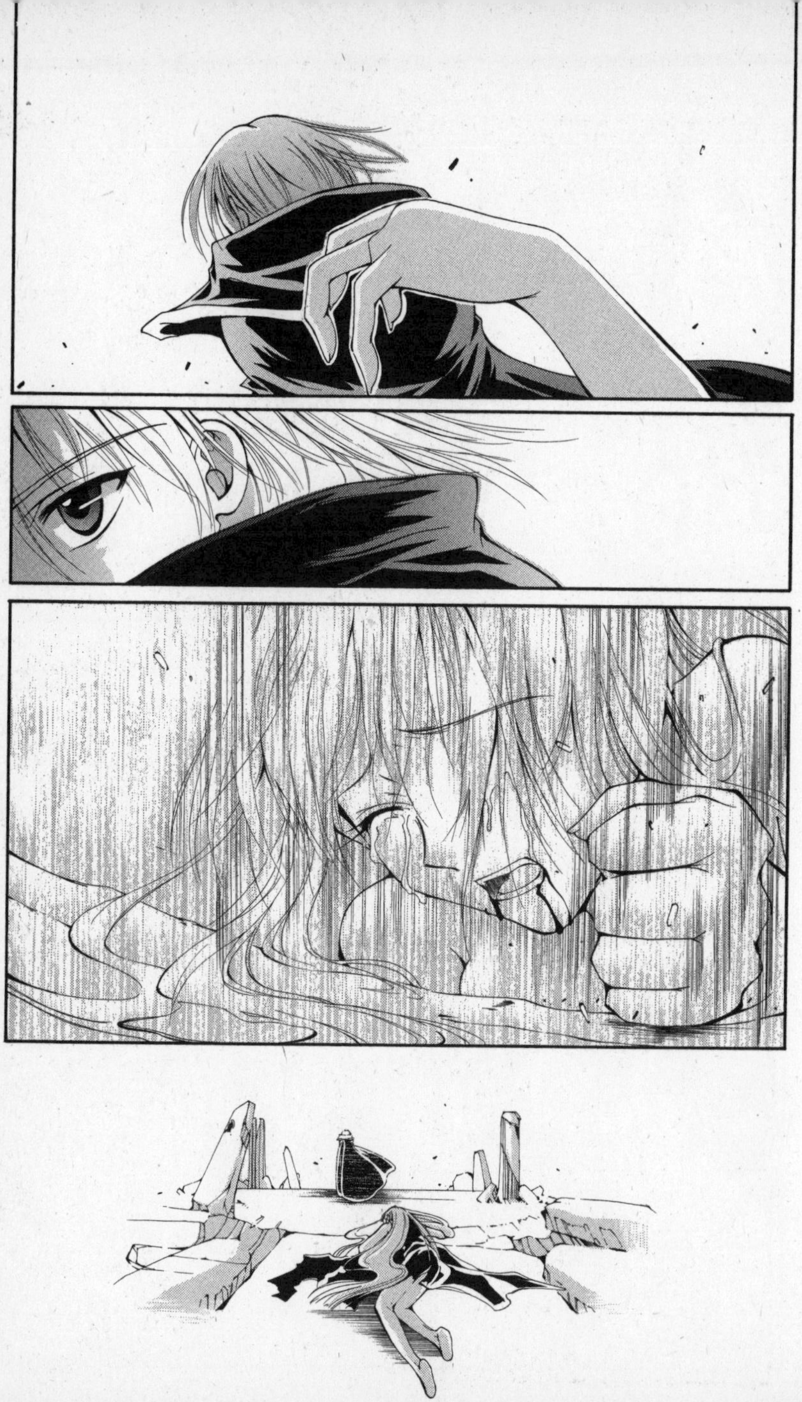

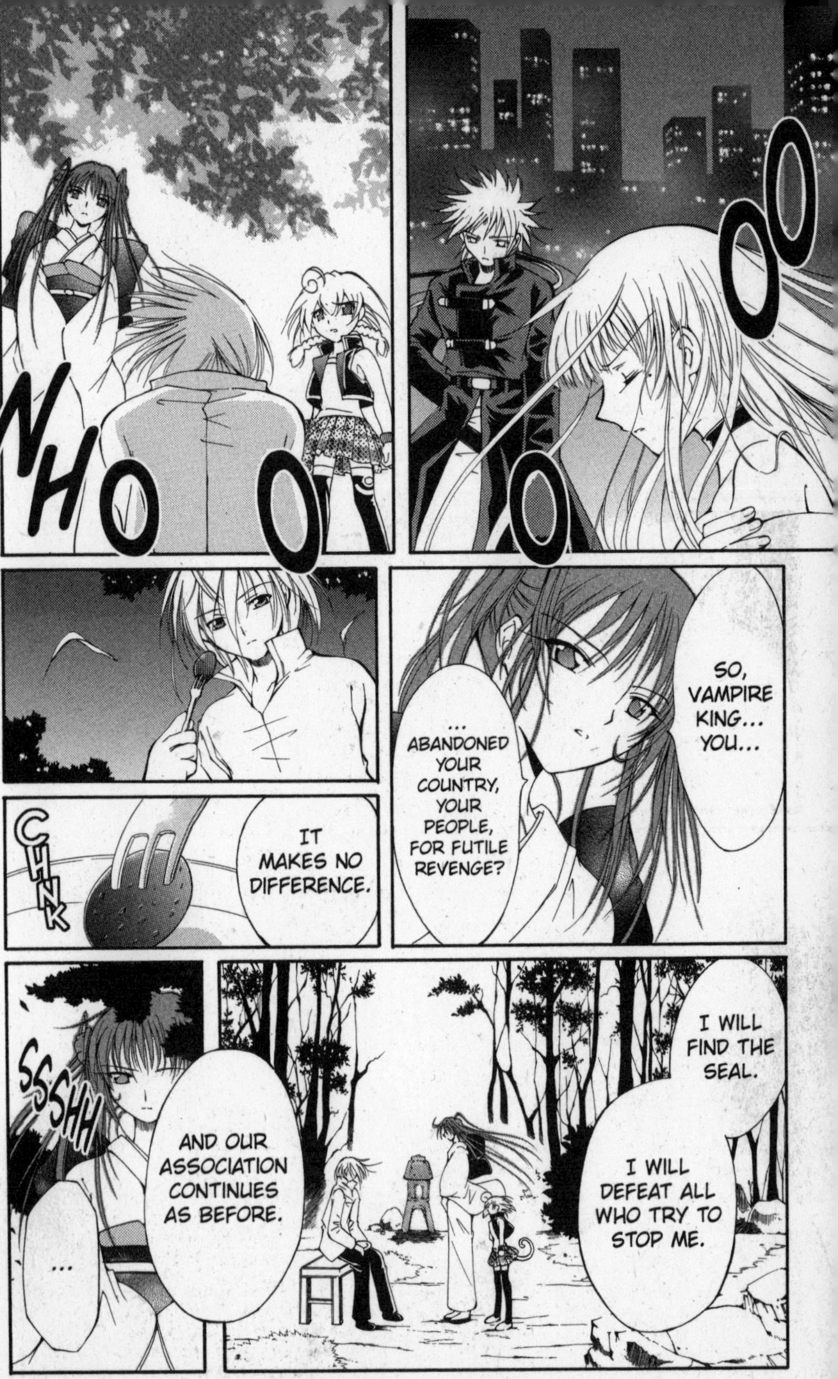
WHOOOOOO
SO, VAMPIRE KING... YOU...
...ABANDONED YOUR COUNTRY, YOUR PEOPLE, FOR FUTILE REVENGE?
IT MAKES NO DIFFERENCE.
CHNK
I WILL FIND THE SEAL.
I WILL DEFEAT ALL WHO TRY TO STOP ME.
SSSHH
AND OUR ASSOCIATION CONTINUES AS BEFORE.
...

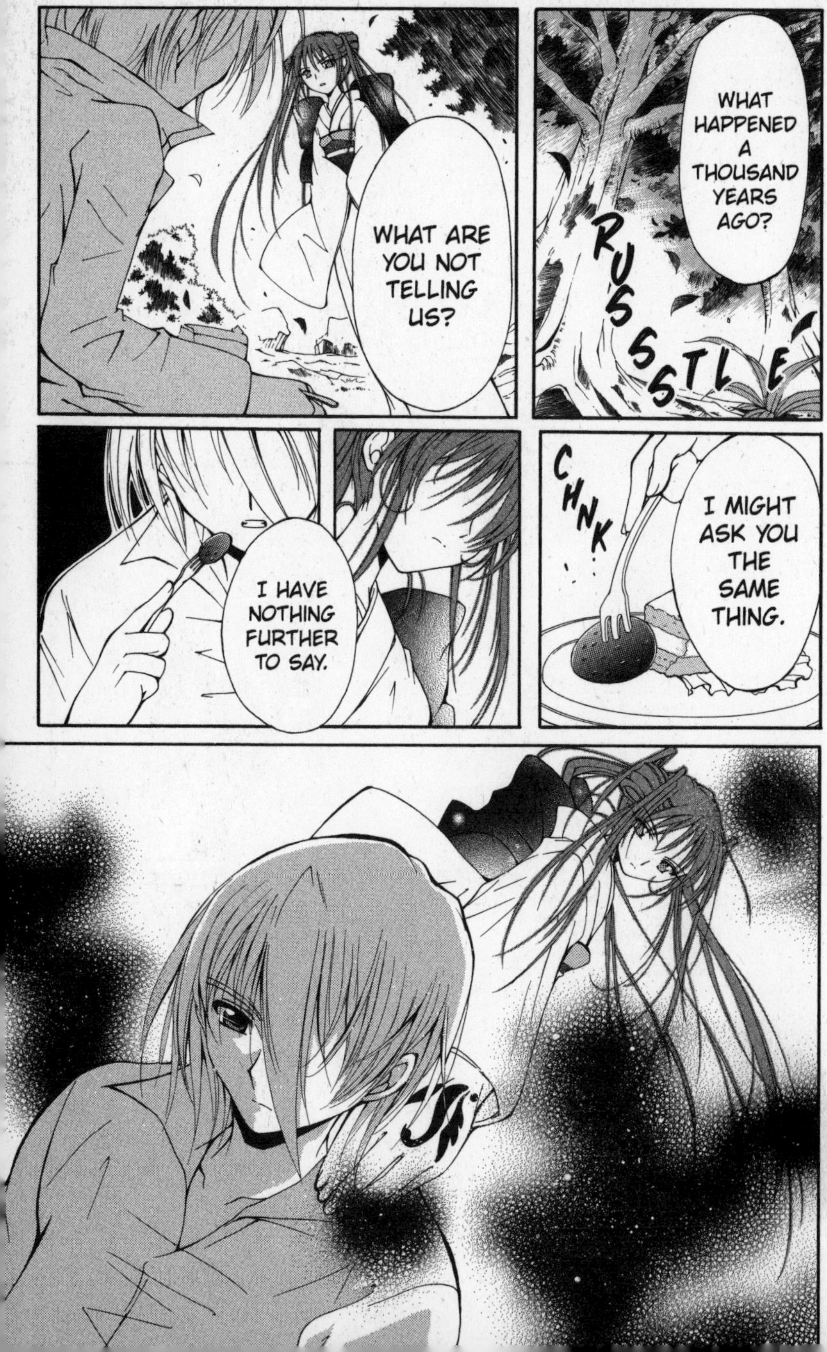
WHAT HAPPENED A THOUSAND YEARS AGO?
RUSSSTLE
WHAT ARE YOU NOT TELLING US?
CHNK
I MIGHT ASK YOU THE SAME THING.
I HAVE NOTHING FURTHER TO SAY.

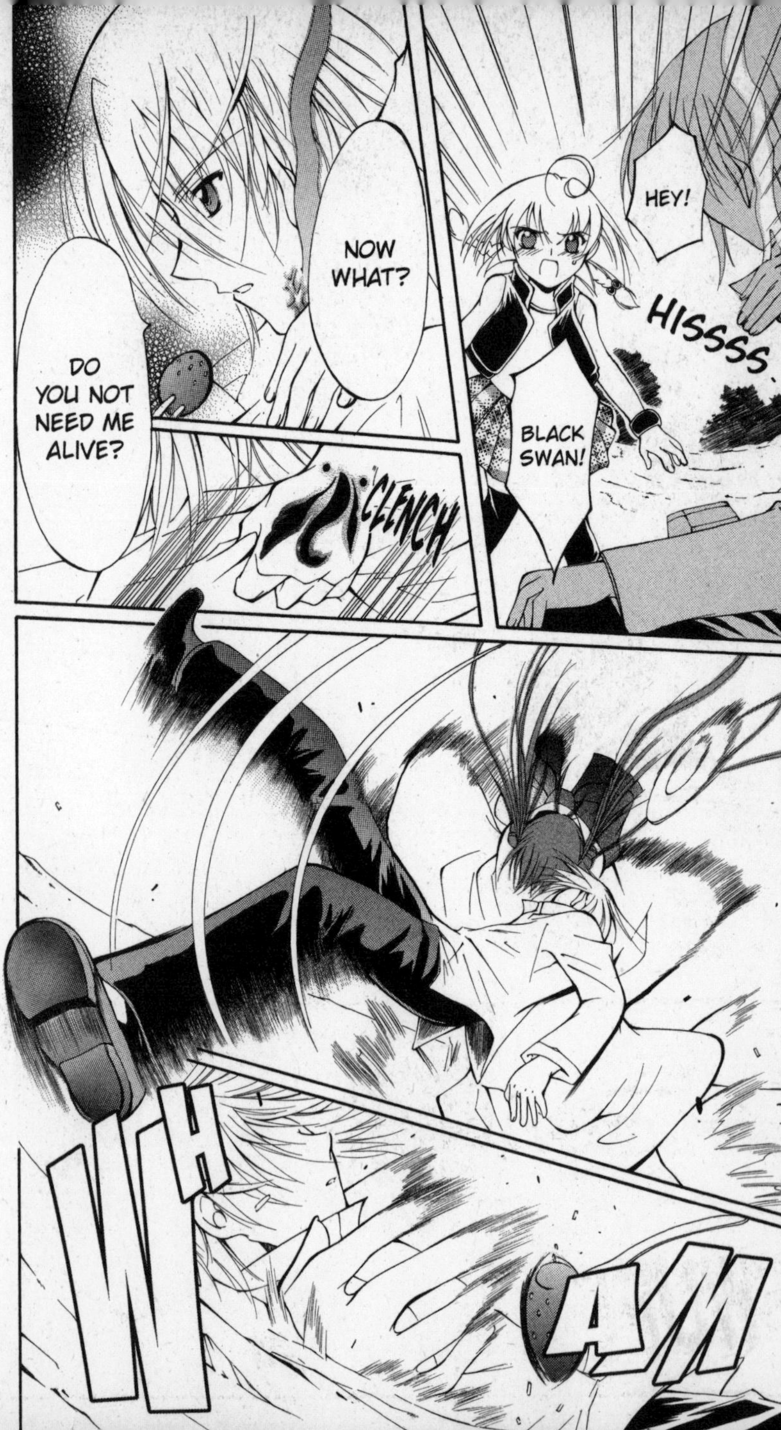
HEY!
HISSSS..
BLACK SWAN!
NOW WHAT?
DO YOU NOT NEED ME ALIVE?
CLENCH
WHAM

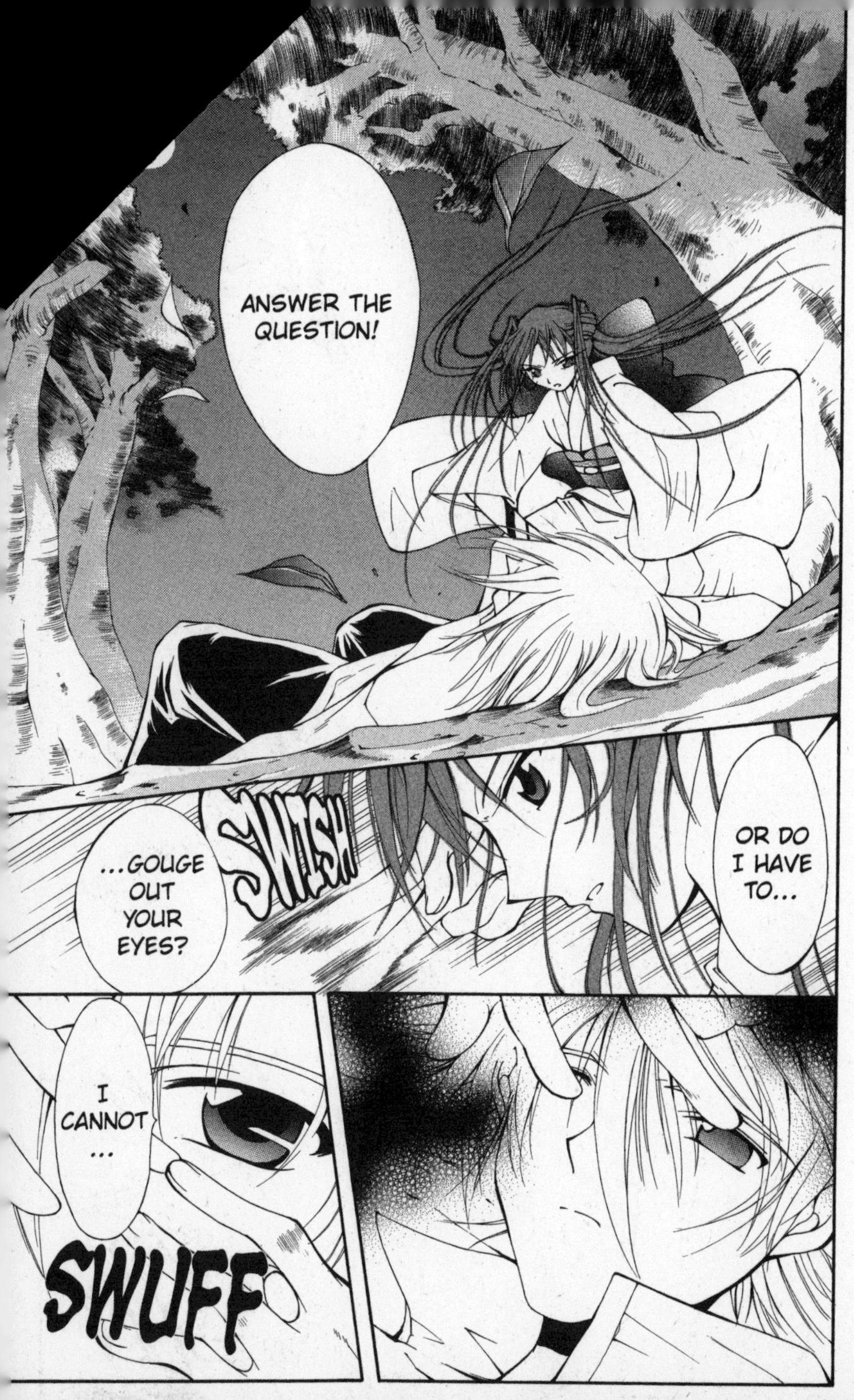
ANSWER THE QUESTION!
OR DO I HAVE TO...
SWISH
...GOUGE OUT YOUR EYES?
I CANNOT ...
SWUFF

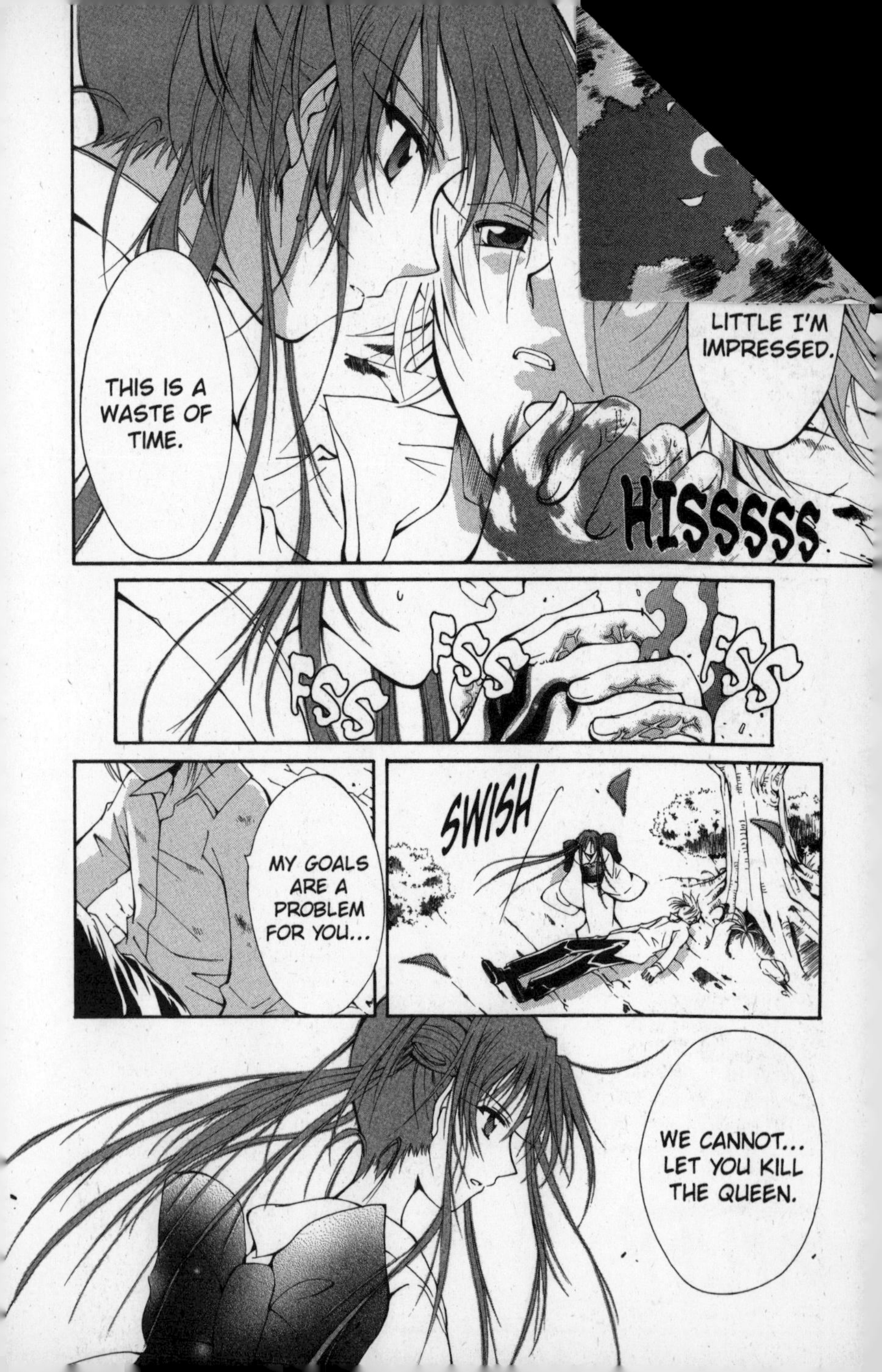
LITTLE I'M IMPRESSED.
HISSSSS
THIS IS A WASTE OF TIME.
FSS
FSS
FSS
SWISH
MY GOALS ARE A PROBLEM FOR YOU...
WE CANNOT... LET YOU KILL THE QUEEN.

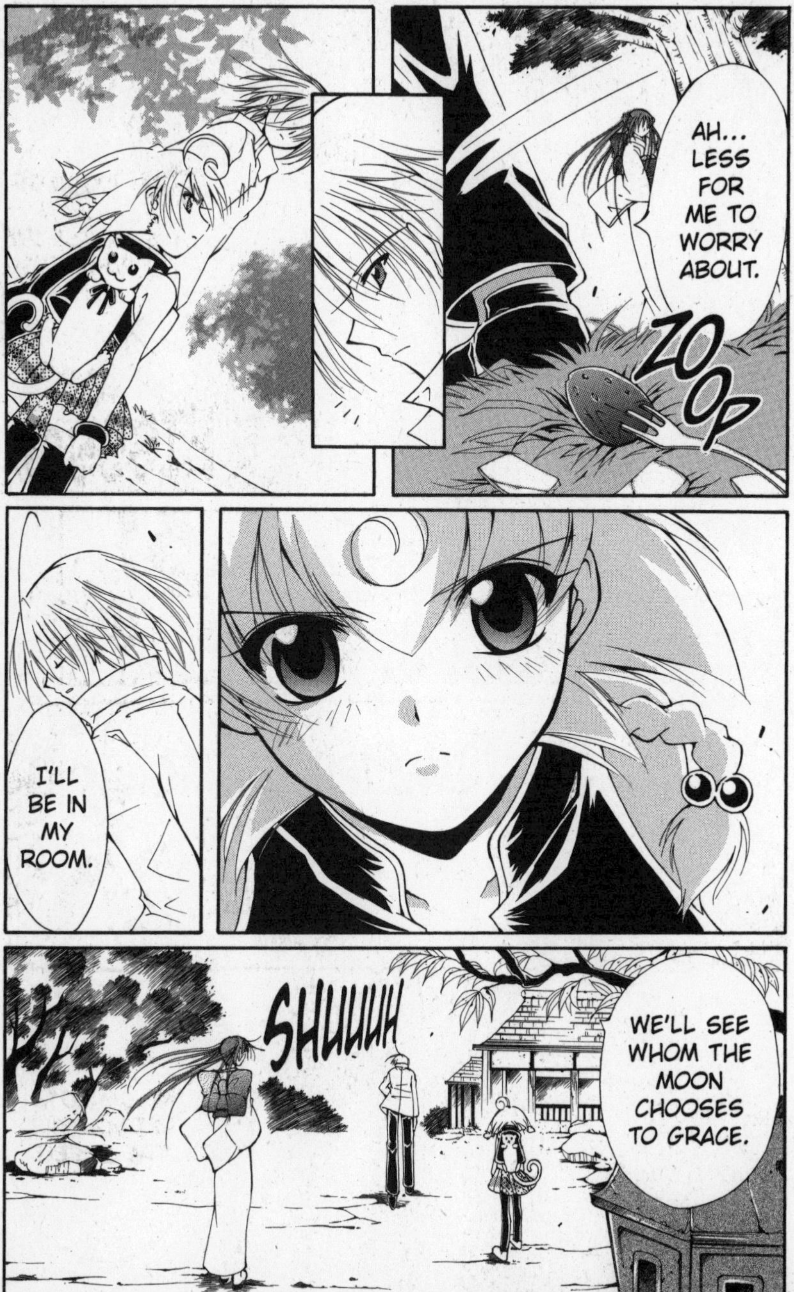
AH... LESS FOR ME TO WORRY ABOUT.
ZOOP
I'LL BE IN MY ROOM.
WE'LL SEE WHOM THE MOON CHOOSES TO GRACE.
SHUUUH

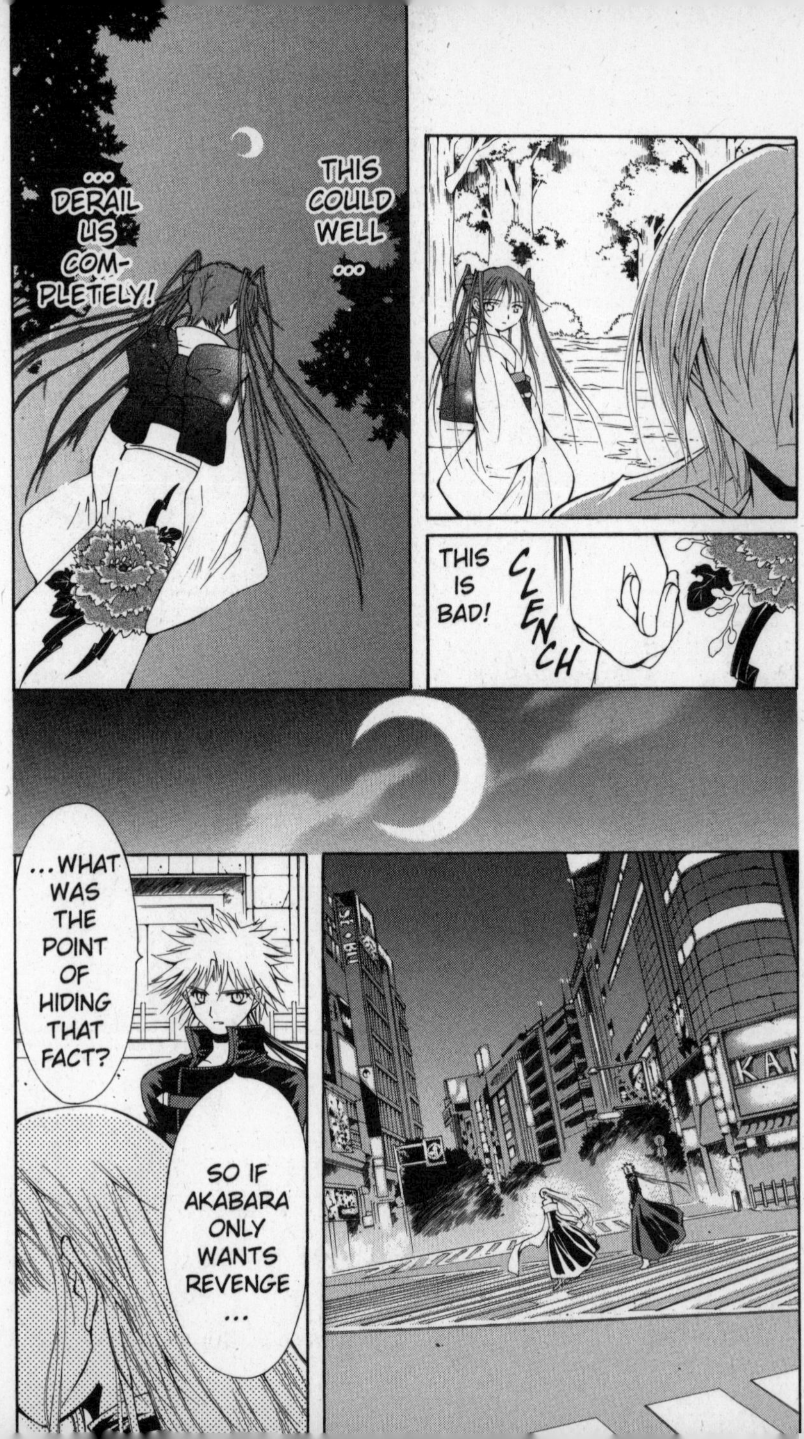
THIS IS BAD!
CLENCH
THIS COULD WELL...
...DERAIL US COM-PLETELY!
SO IF AKABARA ONLY WANTS REVENGE...
...WHAT WAS THE POINT OF HIDING THAT FACT?

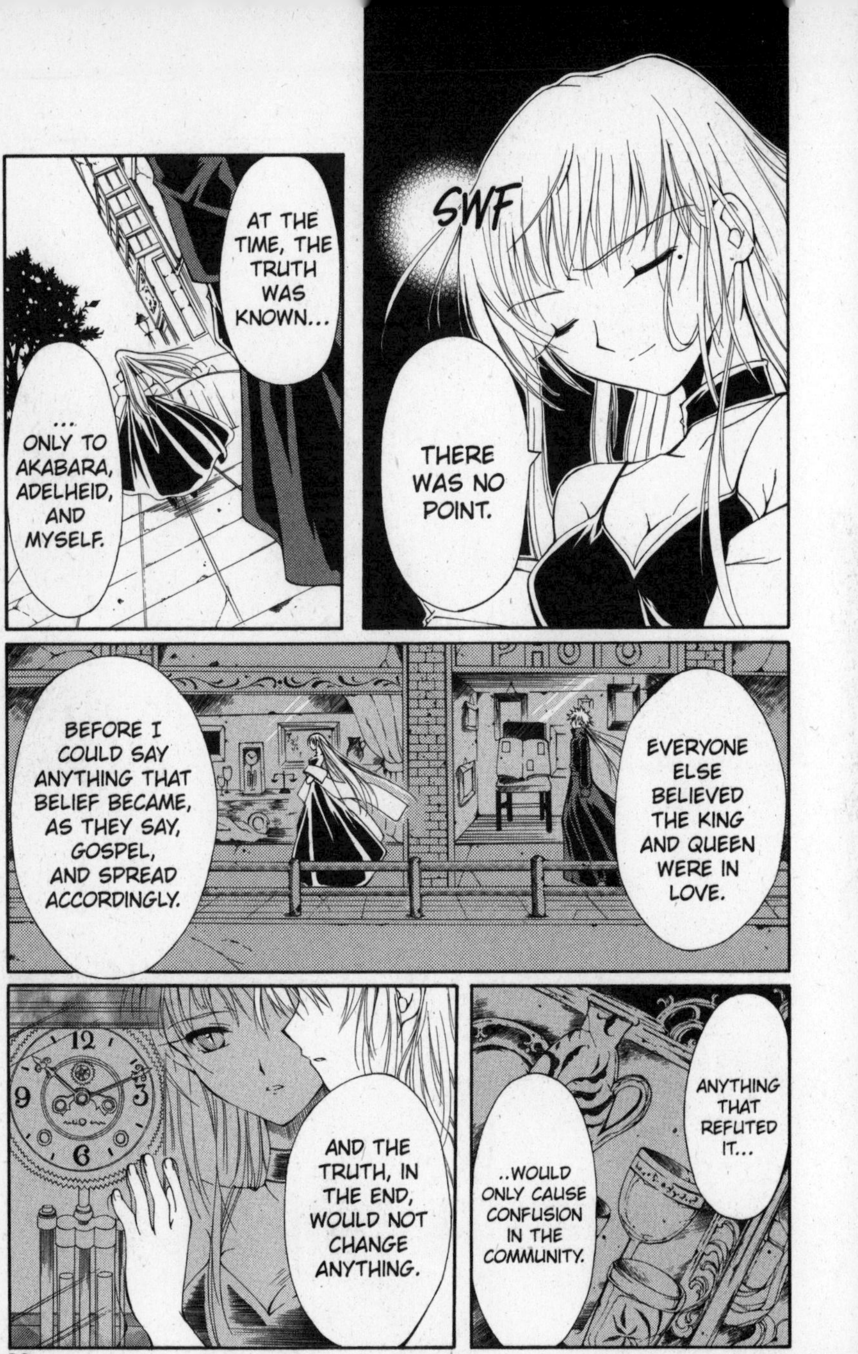
SWF
THERE WAS NO POINT.
AT THE TIME, THE TRUTH WAS KNOWN...
... ONLY TO AKABARA, ADELHEID, AND MYSELF.
EVERYONE ELSE BELIEVED THE KING AND QUEEN WERE IN LOVE.
BEFORE I COULD SAY ANYTHING THAT BELIEF BECAME, AS THEY SAY, GOSPEL, AND SPREAD ACCORDINGLY.
ANYTHING THAT REFUTED IT...
..WOULD ONLY CAUSE CONFUSION IN THE COMMUNITY.
AND THE TRUTH, IN THE END, WOULD NOT CHANGE ANYTHING.

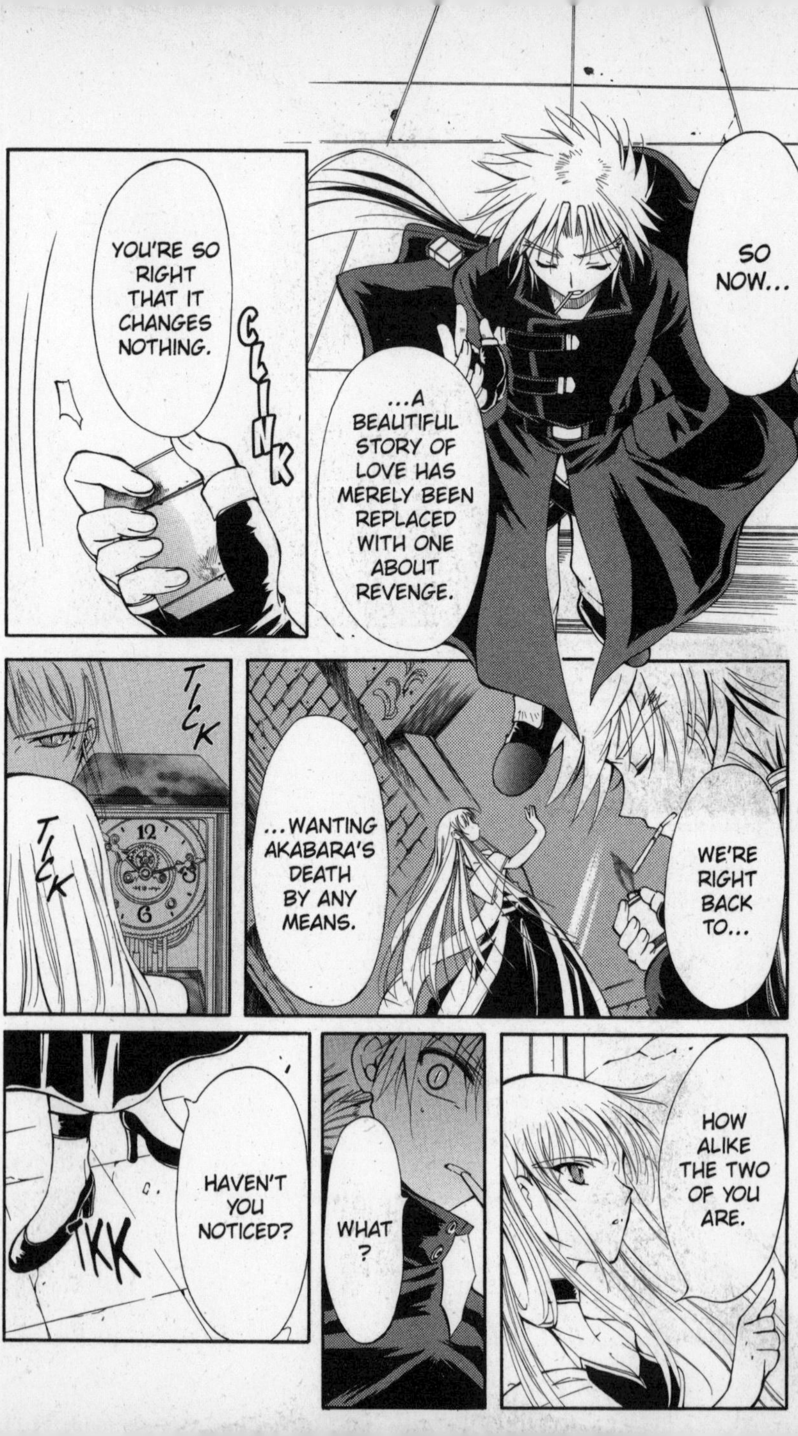
SO NOW...
...A BEAUTIFUL STORY OF LOVE HAS MERELY BEEN REPLACED WITH ONE ABOUT REVENGE.
YOU'RE SO RIGHT THAT IT CHANGES NOTHING.
CLINK
WE'RE RIGHT BACK TO...
...WANTING AKABARA'S DEATH BY ANY MEANS.
TICK
TICK
HOW ALIKE THE TWO OF YOU ARE.
WHAT?
HAVEN'T YOU NOTICED?
TKK

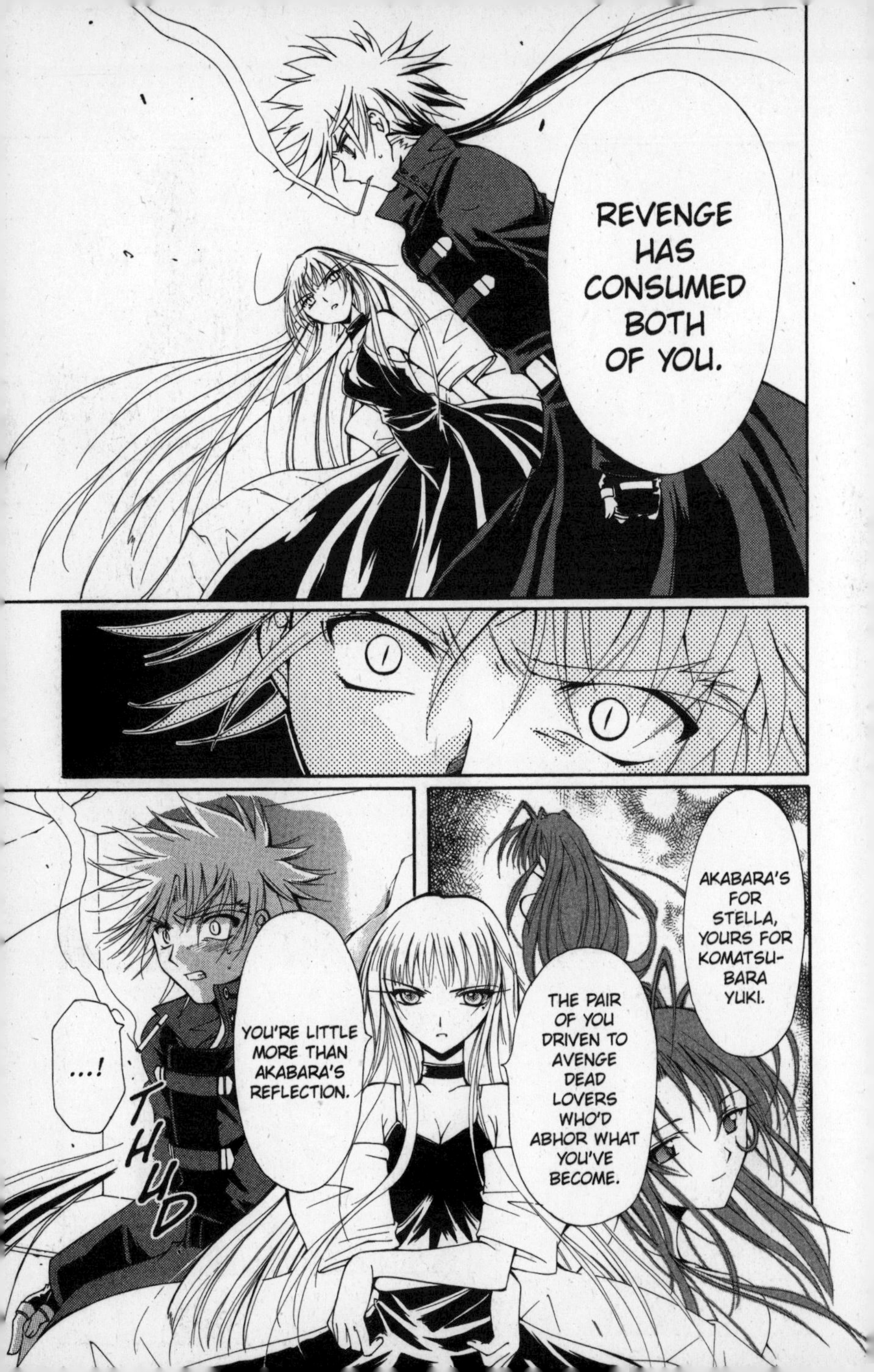
REVENGE HAS CONSUMED BOTH OF YOU.
AKABARA'S FOR STELLA, YOURS FOR KOMATSU-BARA YUKI.
THE PAIR OF YOU DRIVEN TO AVENGE DEAD LOVERS WHO'D ABHOR WHAT YOU'VE BECOME.
YOU'RE LITTLE MORE THAN AKABARA'S REFLECTION.
...!
THUD

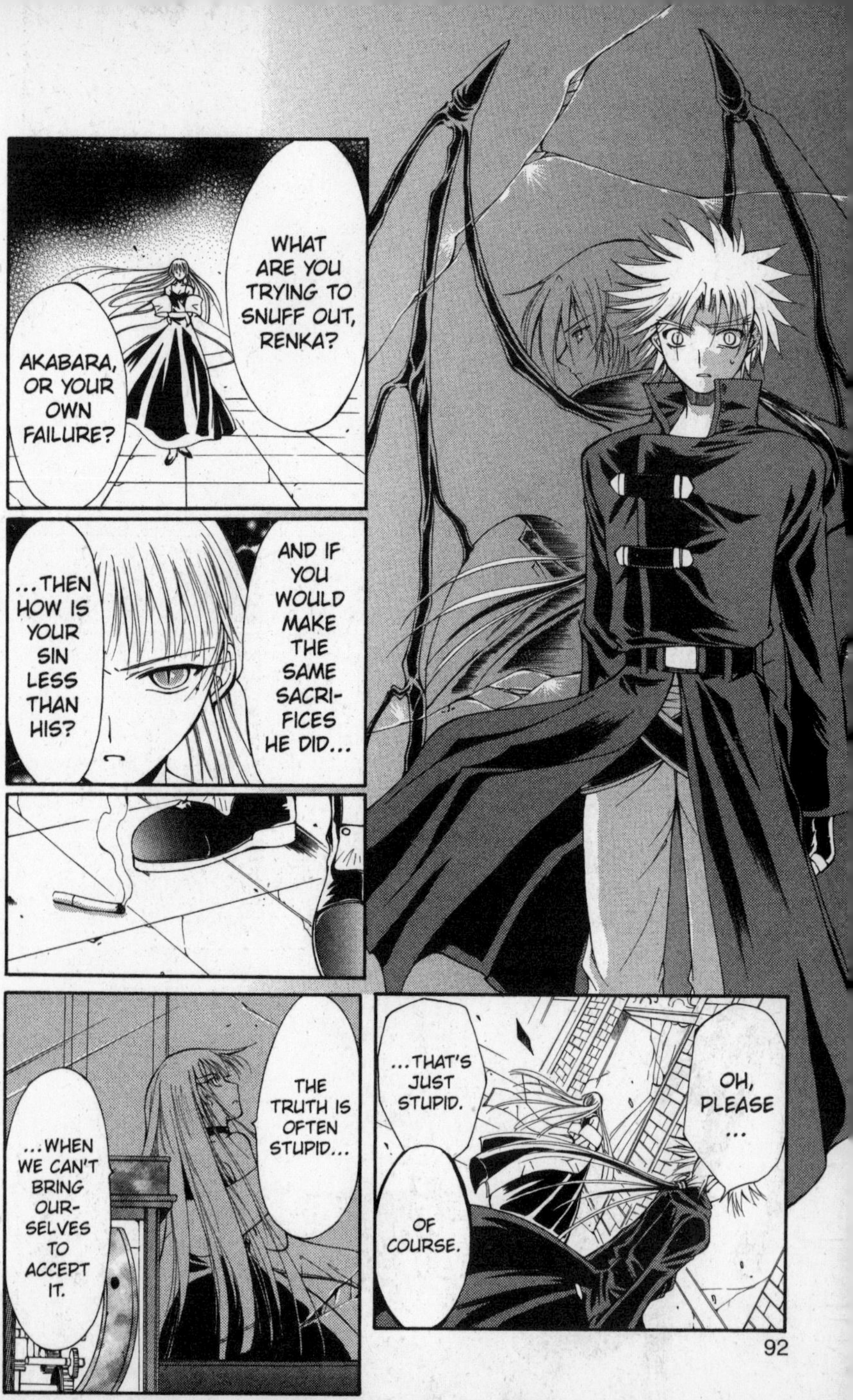
WHAT ARE YOU TRYING TO SNUFF OUT, RENKA?
AKABARA, OR YOUR OWN FAILURE?
AND IF YOU WOULD MAKE THE SAME SACRI-FICES HE DID...
...THEN HOW IS YOUR SIN LESS THAN HIS?
OH, PLEASE ...
...THAT'S JUST STUPID.
OF COURSE.
THE TRUTH IS OFTEN STUPID...
...WHEN WE CAN'T BRING OUR-SELVES TO ACCEPT IT.

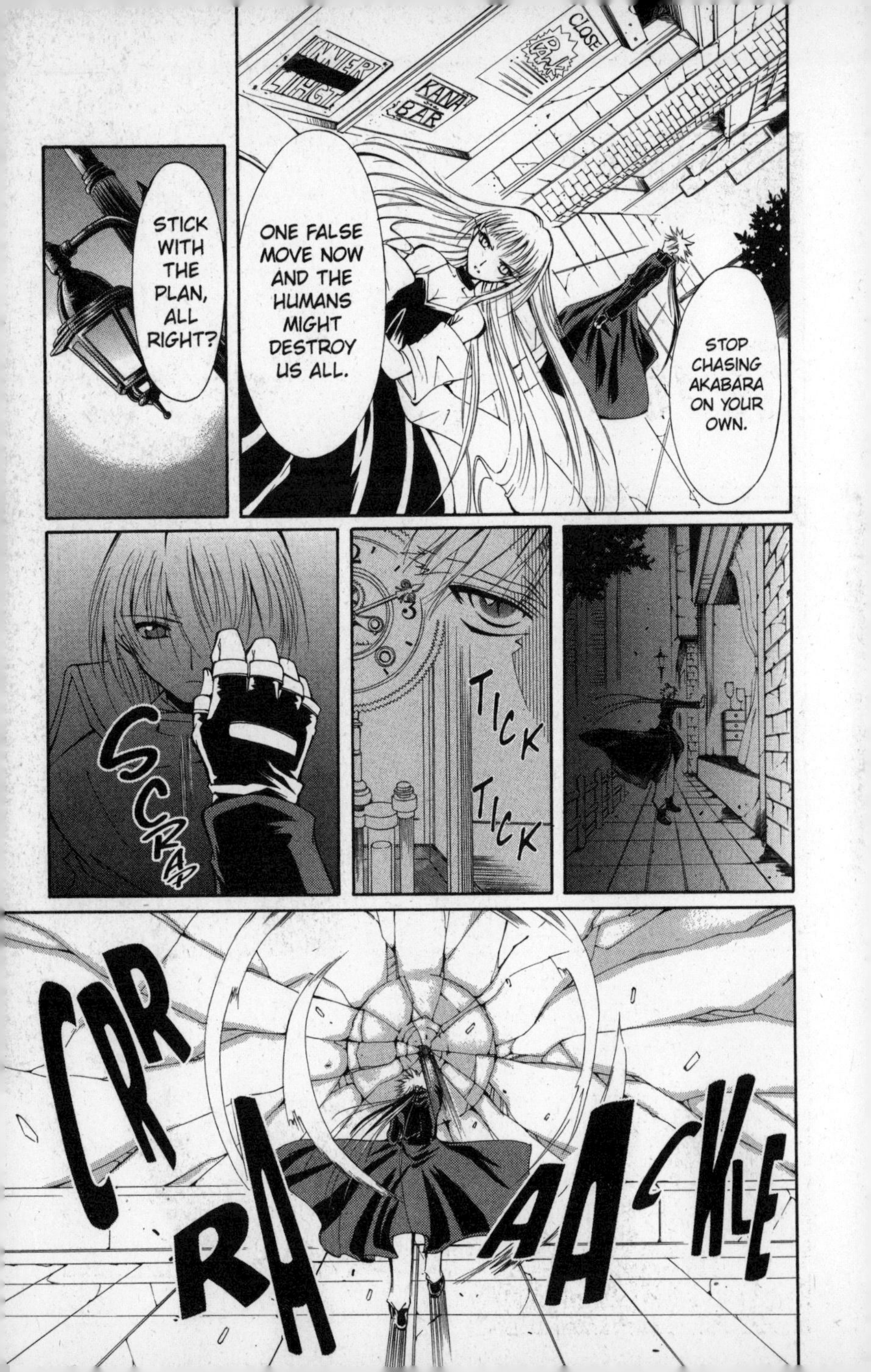
CLOSE
KANA BAR
STOP CHASING AKABARA ON YOUR OWN.
ONE FALSE MOVE NOW AND THE HUMANS MIGHT DESTROY US ALL.
STICK WITH THE PLAN, ALL RIGHT?
TICK TICK
SCRAP
CRRAAACKLE

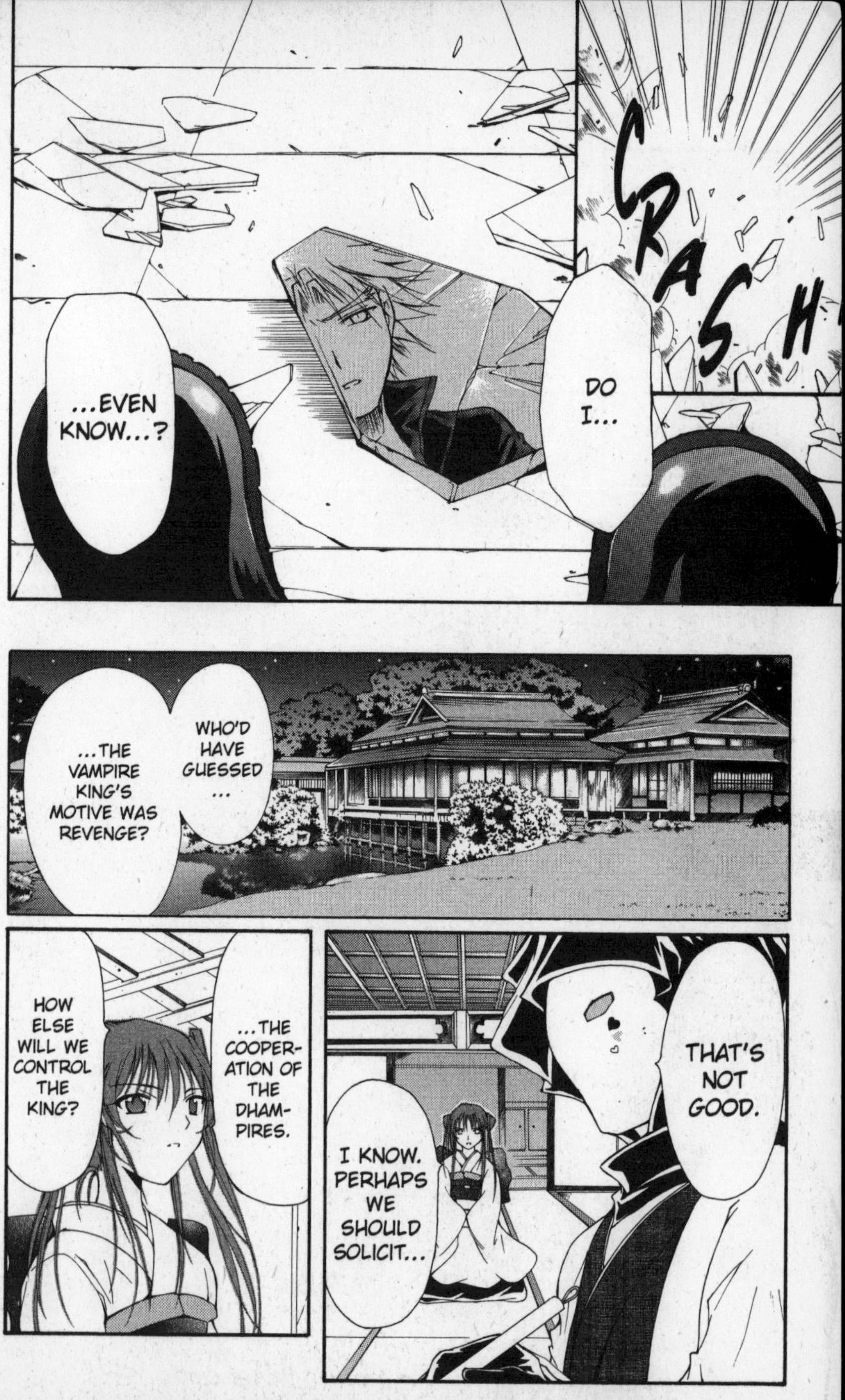
CRASH
DO I...
...EVEN KNOW...?
WHO'D HAVE GUESSED...
...THE VAMPIRE KING'S MOTIVE WAS REVENGE?
THAT'S NOT GOOD.
I KNOW. PERHAPS WE SHOULD SOLICIT...
...THE COOPERATION OF THE DHAMPIRES.
HOW ELSE WILL WE CONTROL THE KING?

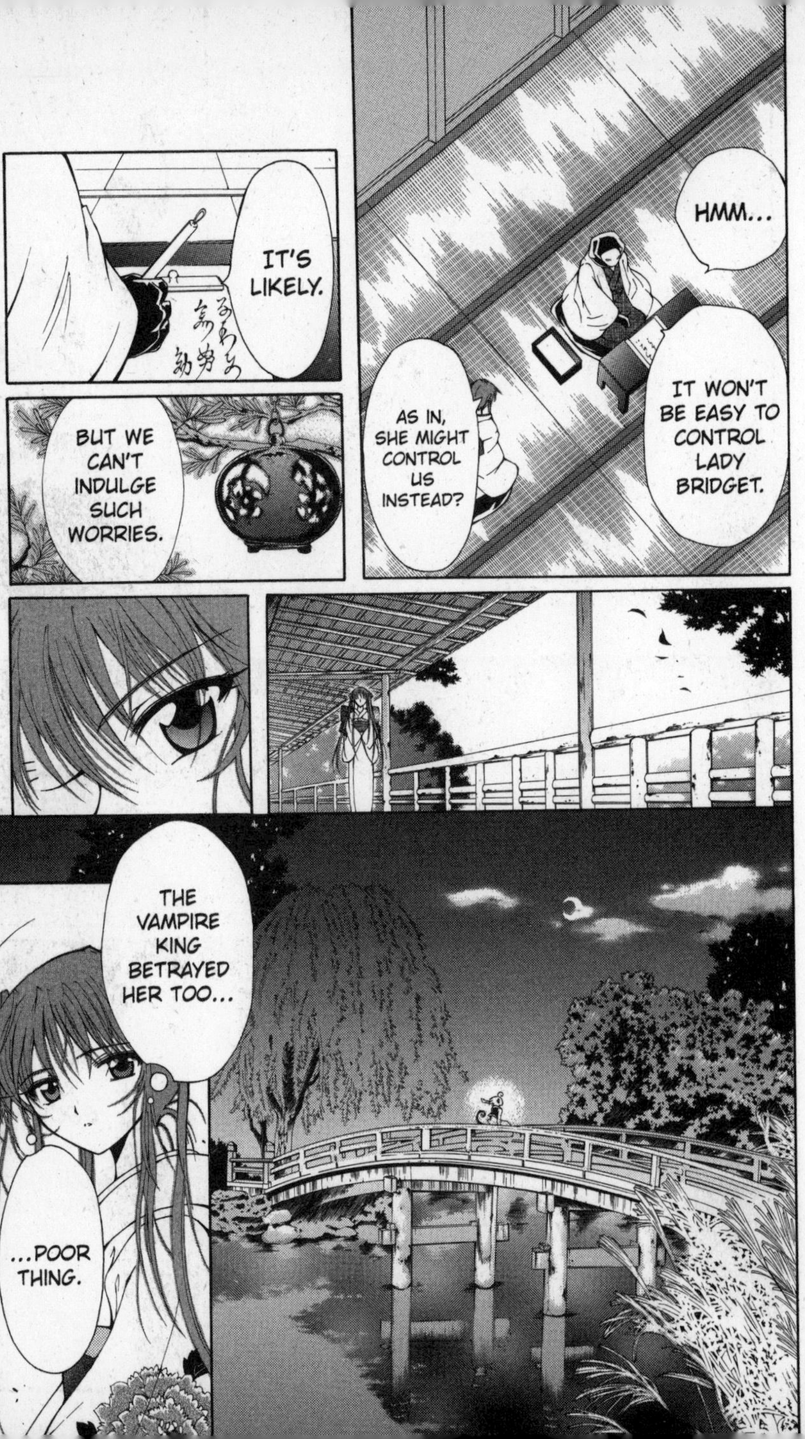
HMM...
IT WON'T BE EASY TO CONTROL LADY BRIDGET.
AS IN, SHE MIGHT CONTROL US INSTEAD?
IT'S LIKELY.
BUT WE CAN'T INDULGE SUCH WORRIES.
THE VAMPIRE KING BETRAYED HER TOO...
...POOR THING.

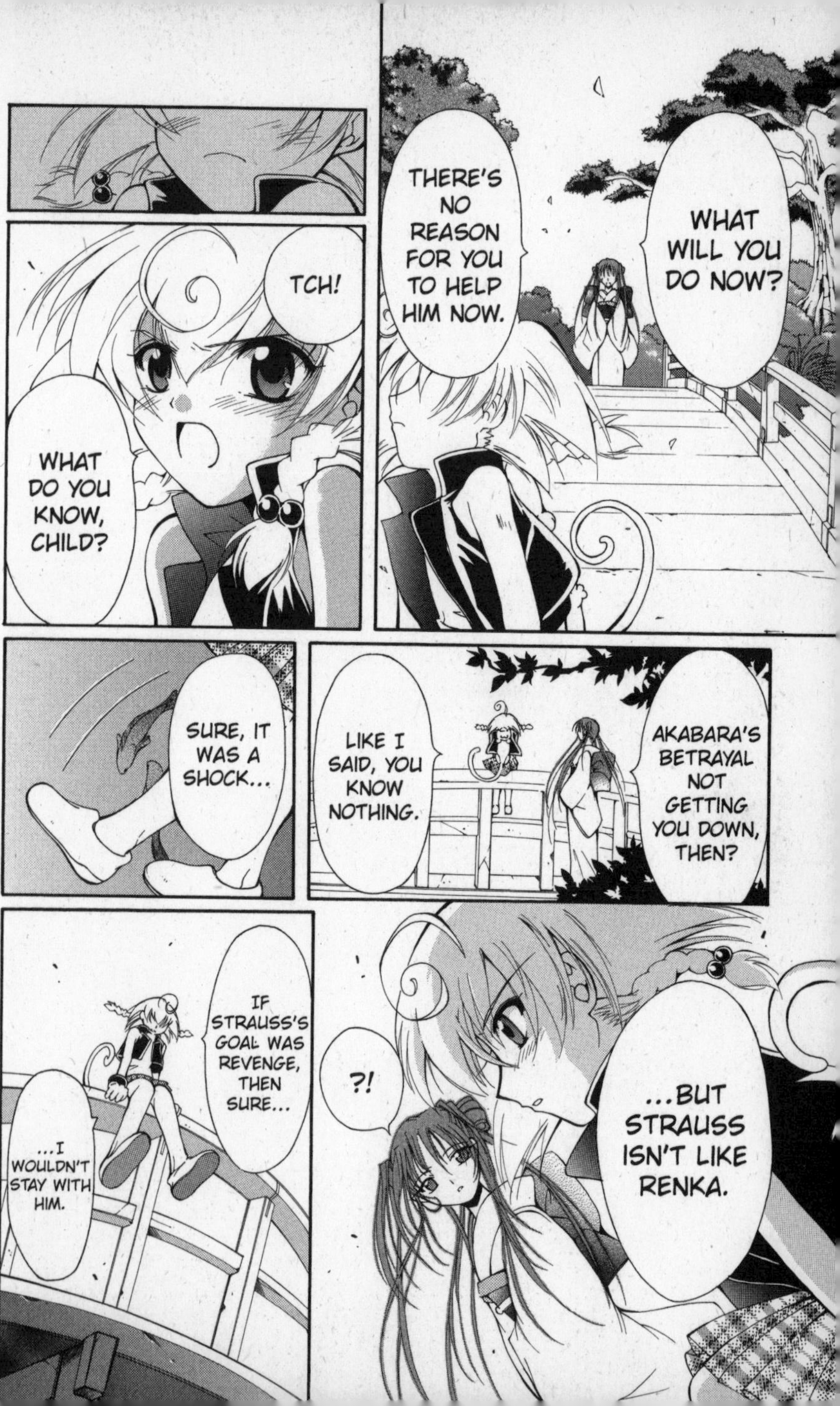
WHAT WILL YOU DO NOW?
THERE'S NO REASON FOR YOU TO HELP HIM NOW.
TCH!
WHAT DO YOU KNOW, CHILD?
AKABARA'S BETRAYAL NOT GETTING YOU DOWN, THEN?
LIKE I SAID, YOU KNOW NOTHING.
SURE, IT WAS A SHOCK...
...BUT STRAUSS ISN'T LIKE RENKA.
?!
IF STRAUSS'S GOAL WAS REVENGE, THEN SURE...
...I WOULDN'T STAY WITH HIM.

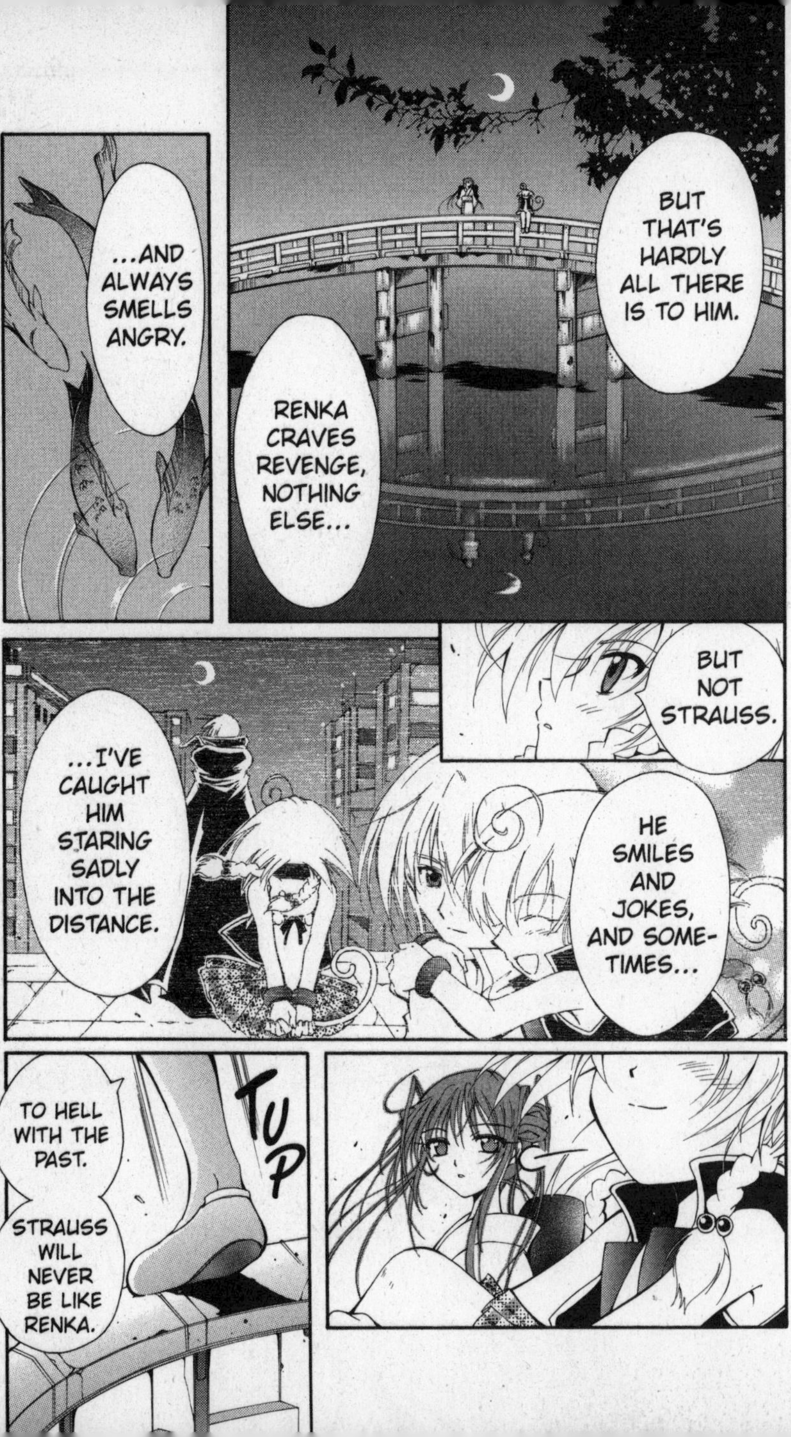
BUT THAT'S HARDLY ALL THERE IS TO HIM.
RENKA CRAVES REVENGE, NOTHING ELSE...
...AND ALWAYS SMELLS ANGRY.
BUT NOT STRAUSS.
HE SMILES AND JOKES, AND SOME-TIMES...
...I'VE CAUGHT HIM STARING SADLY INTO THE DISTANCE.
TUP
TO HELL WITH THE PAST.
STRAUSS WILL NEVER BE LIKE RENKA.

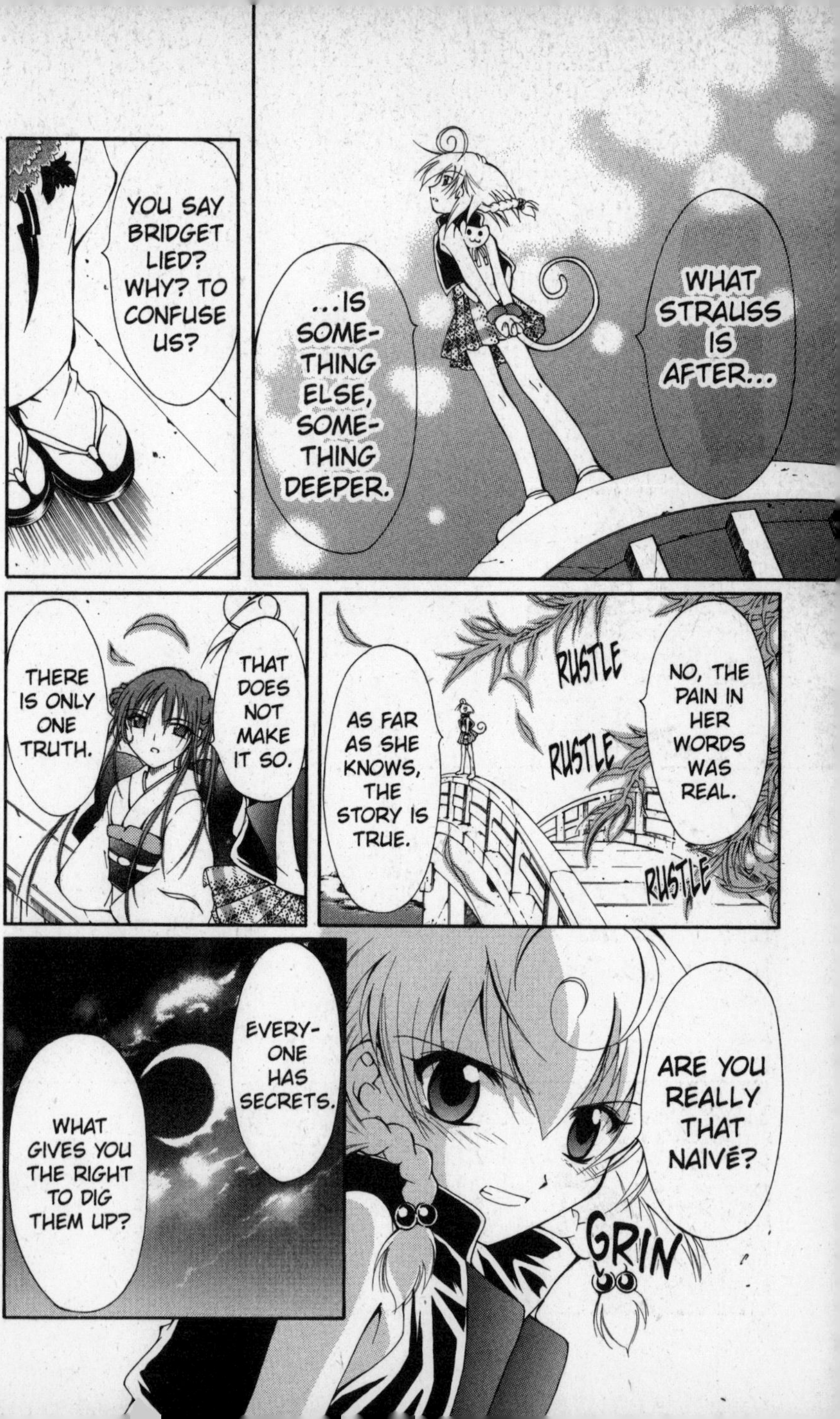
WHAT STRAUSS IS AFTER...
...IS SOMETHING ELSE, SOMETHING DEEPER.
YOU SAY BRIDGET LIED? WHY? TO CONFUSE US?
NO, THE PAIN IN HER WORDS WAS REAL.
RUSTLE
RUSTLE
RUSTLE
AS FAR AS SHE KNOWS, THE STORY IS TRUE.
THAT DOES NOT MAKE IT SO.
THERE IS ONLY ONE TRUTH.
ARE YOU REALLY THAT NAIVE?
GRIN
EVERYONE HAS SECRETS.
WHAT GIVES YOU THE RIGHT TO DIG THEM UP?

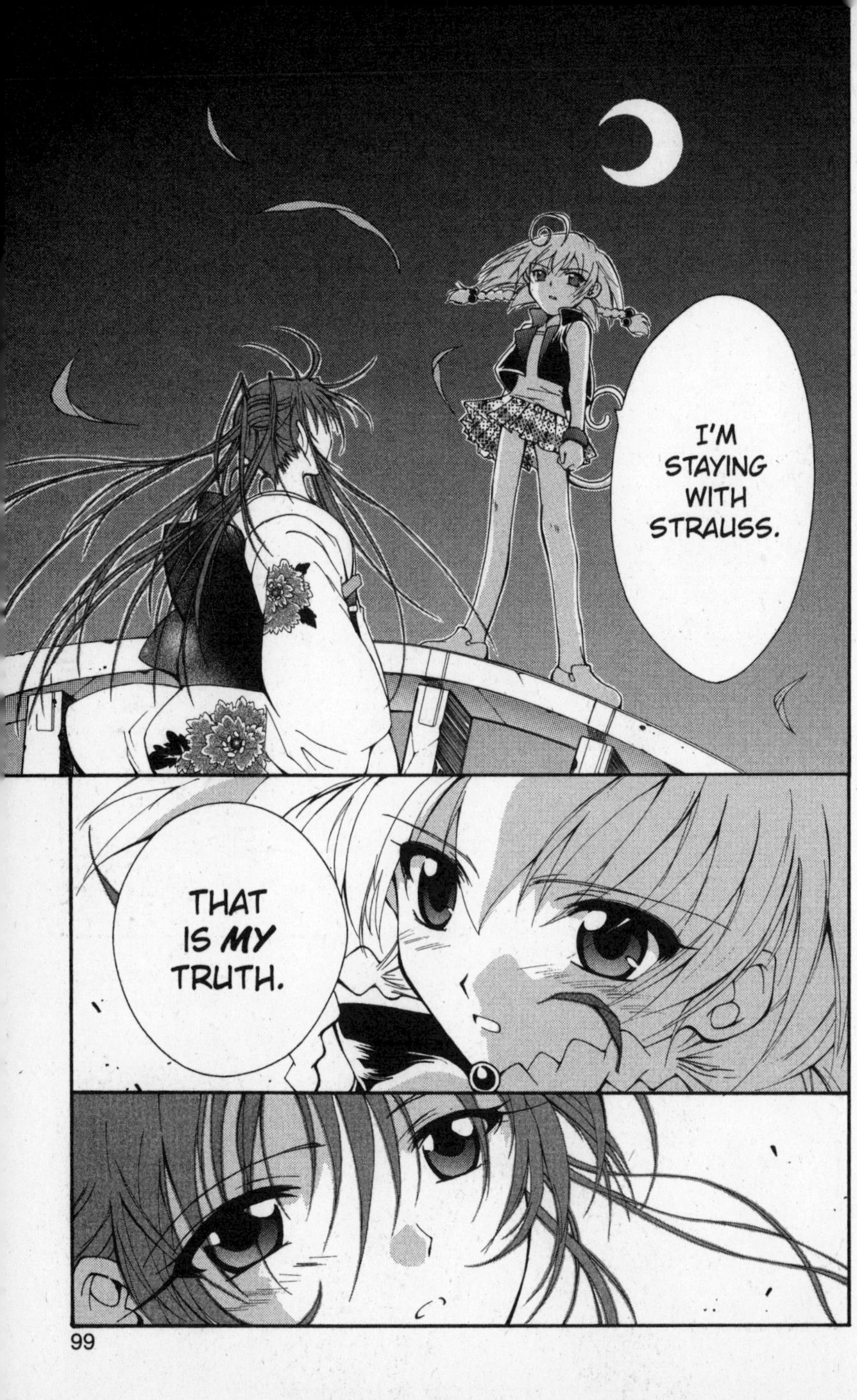
I'M STAYING WITH STRAUSS.
THAT IS *MY* TRUTH.

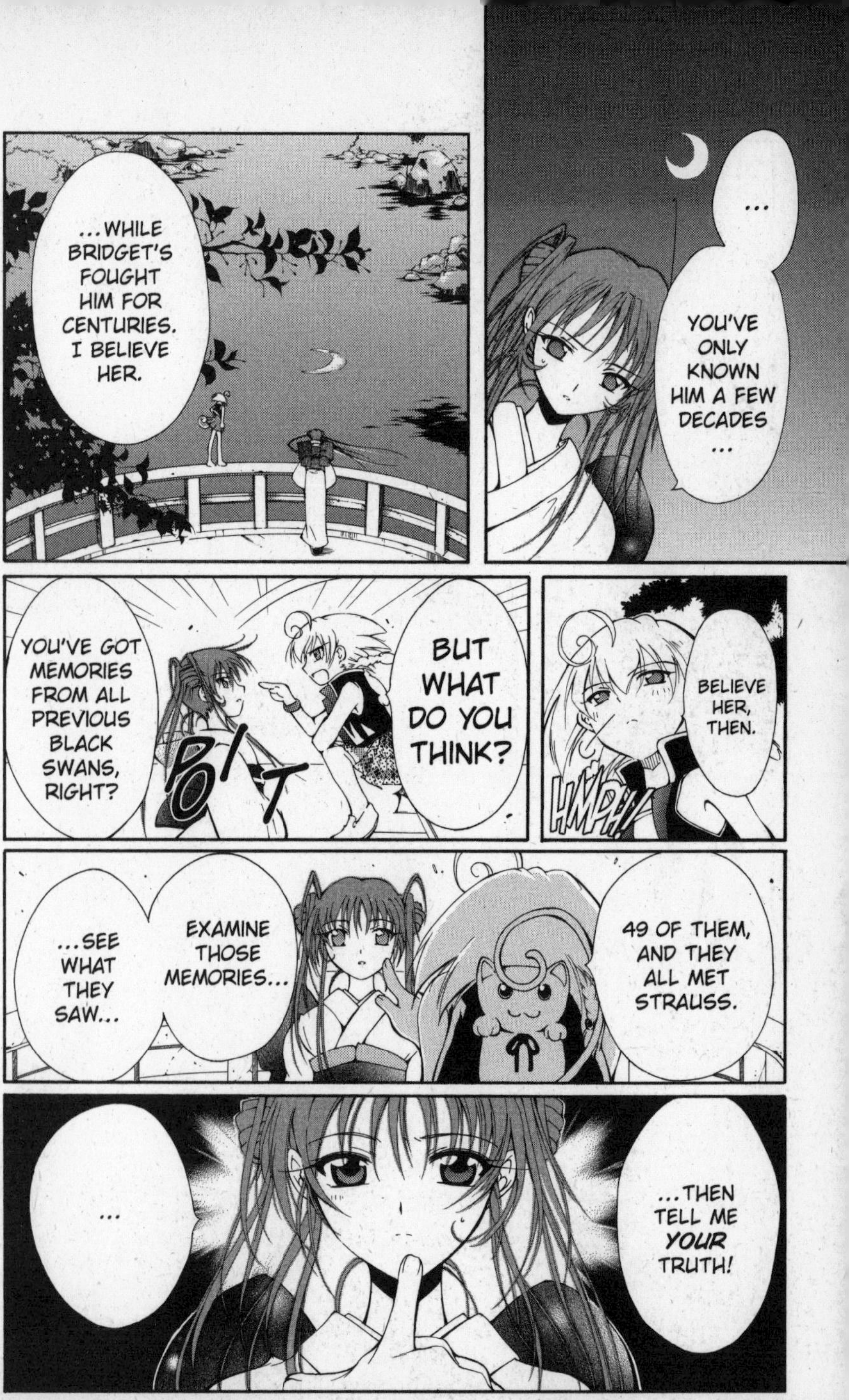
...
YOU'VE ONLY KNOWN HIM A FEW DECADES ...
...WHILE BRIDGET'S FOUGHT HIM FOR CENTURIES. I BELIEVE HER.
BELIEVE HER, THEN.
HMPH!
BUT WHAT DO YOU THINK?
YOU'VE GOT MEMORIES FROM ALL PREVIOUS BLACK SWANS, RIGHT?
49 OF THEM, AND THEY ALL MET STRAUSS.
EXAMINE THOSE MEMORIES...
...SEE WHAT THEY SAW...
...THEN TELL ME *YOUR* TRUTH!
...

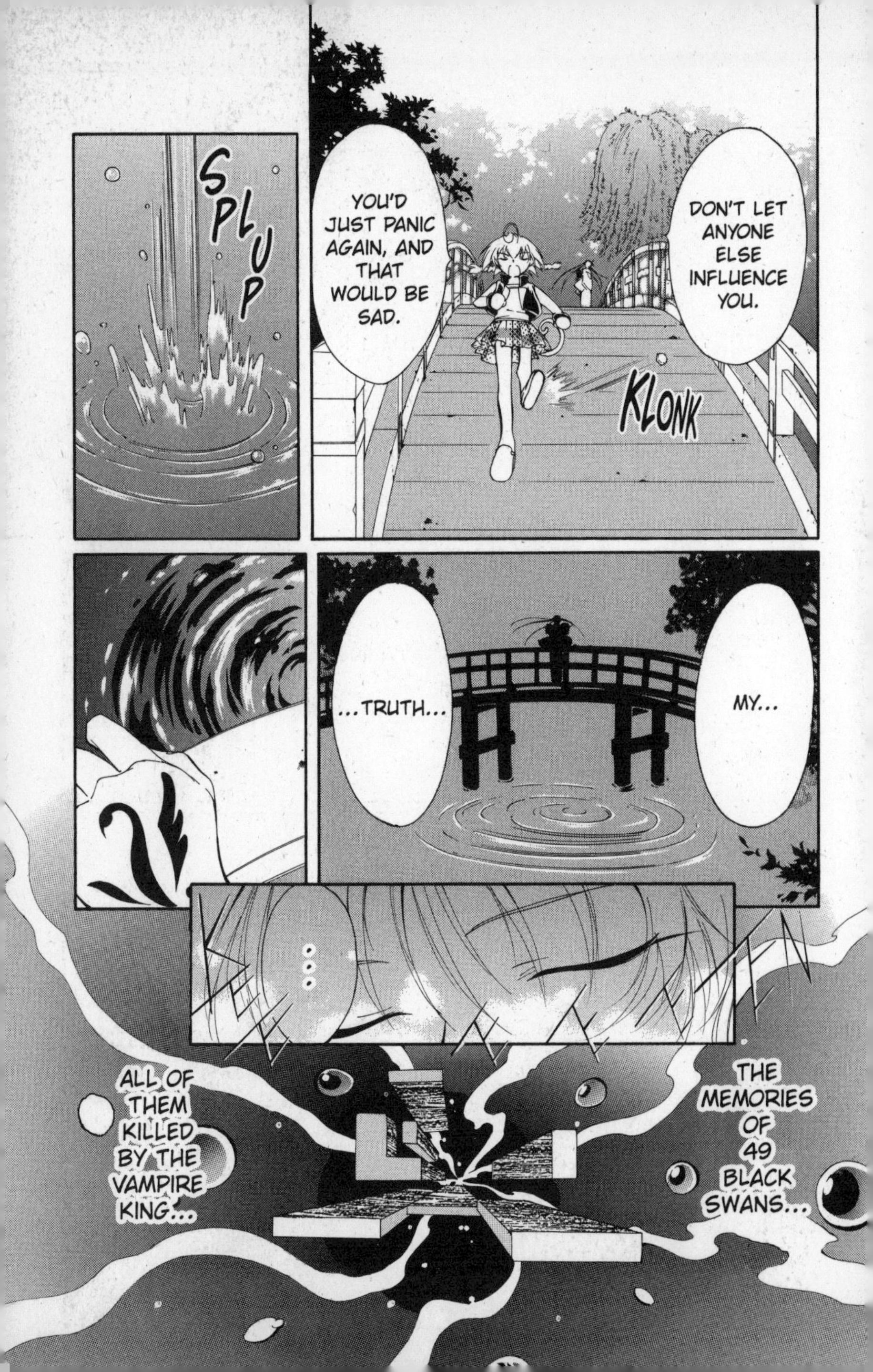
DON'T LET ANYONE ELSE INFLUENCE YOU.
YOU'D JUST PANIC AGAIN, AND THAT WOULD BE SAD.
KLONK
SPLUP
MY...
...TRUTH...
...
THE MEMORIES OF 49 BLACK SWANS...
ALL OF THEM KILLED BY THE VAMPIRE KING...

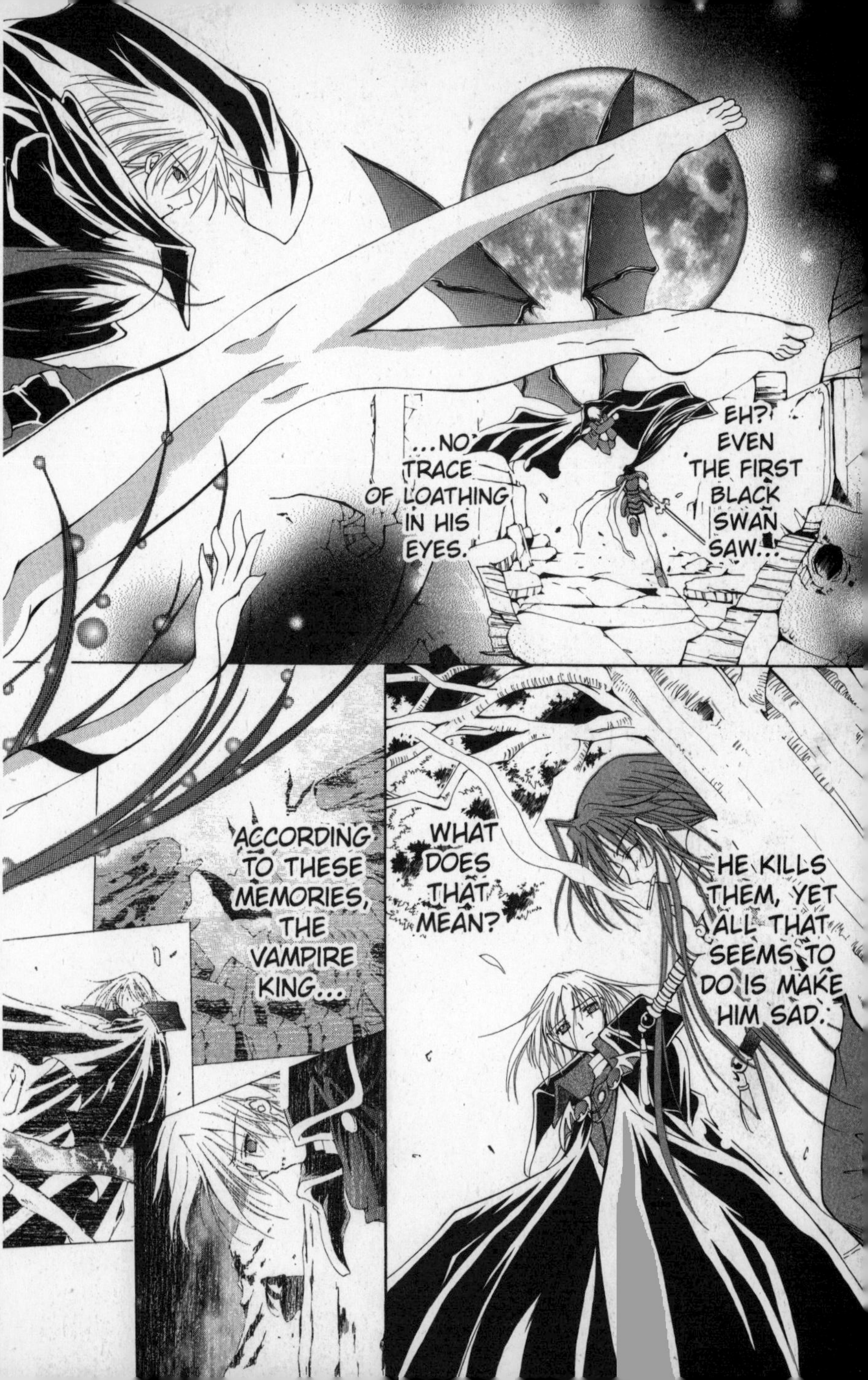
EH? EVEN THE FIRST BLACK SWAN SAW...
...NO TRACE OF LOATHING IN HIS EYES.
HE KILLS THEM, YET ALL THAT SEEMS TO DO IS MAKE HIM SAD.
WHAT DOES THAT MEAN?
ACCORDING TO THESE MEMORIES, THE VAMPIRE KING...

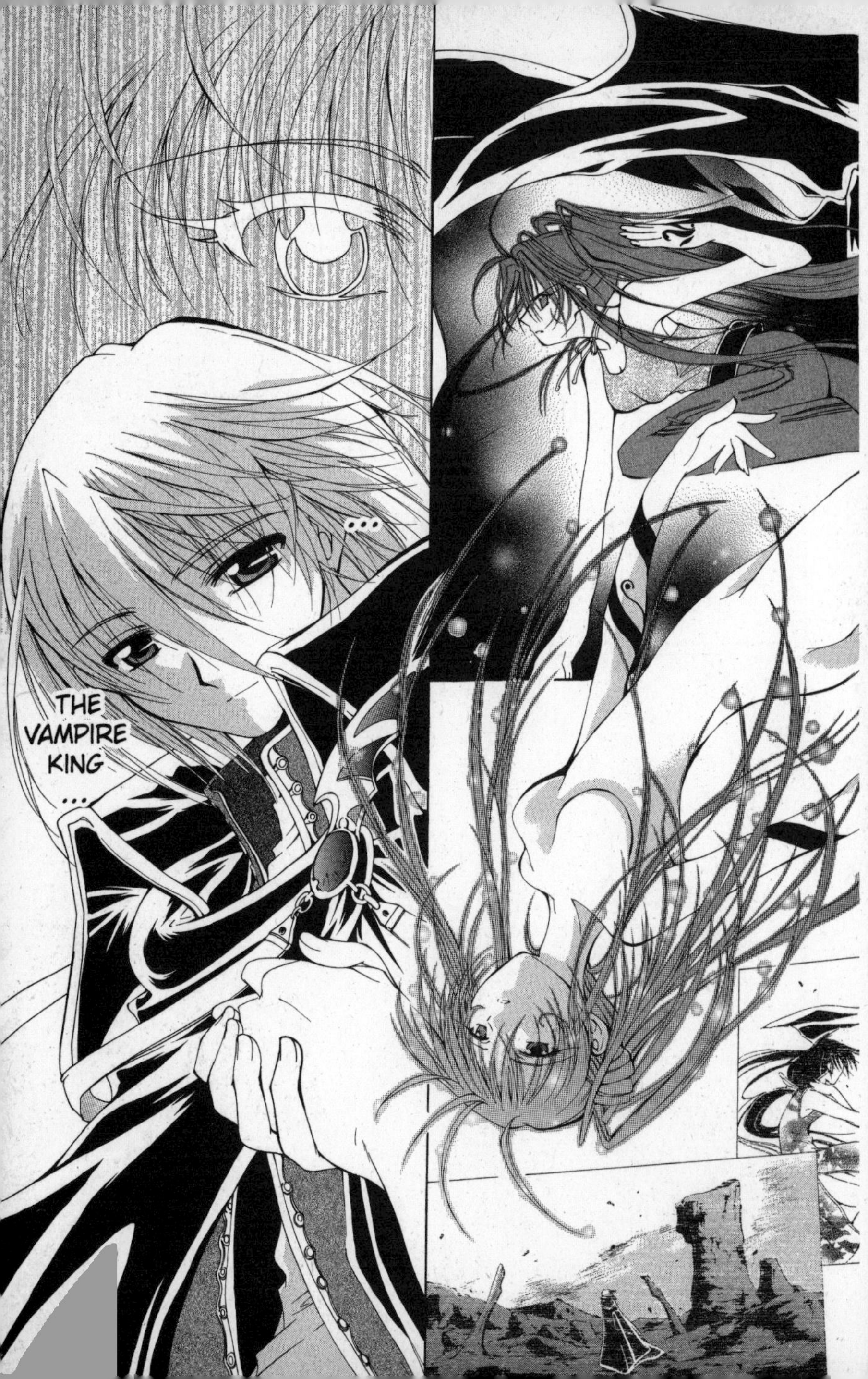
...
THE VAMPIRE KING ...

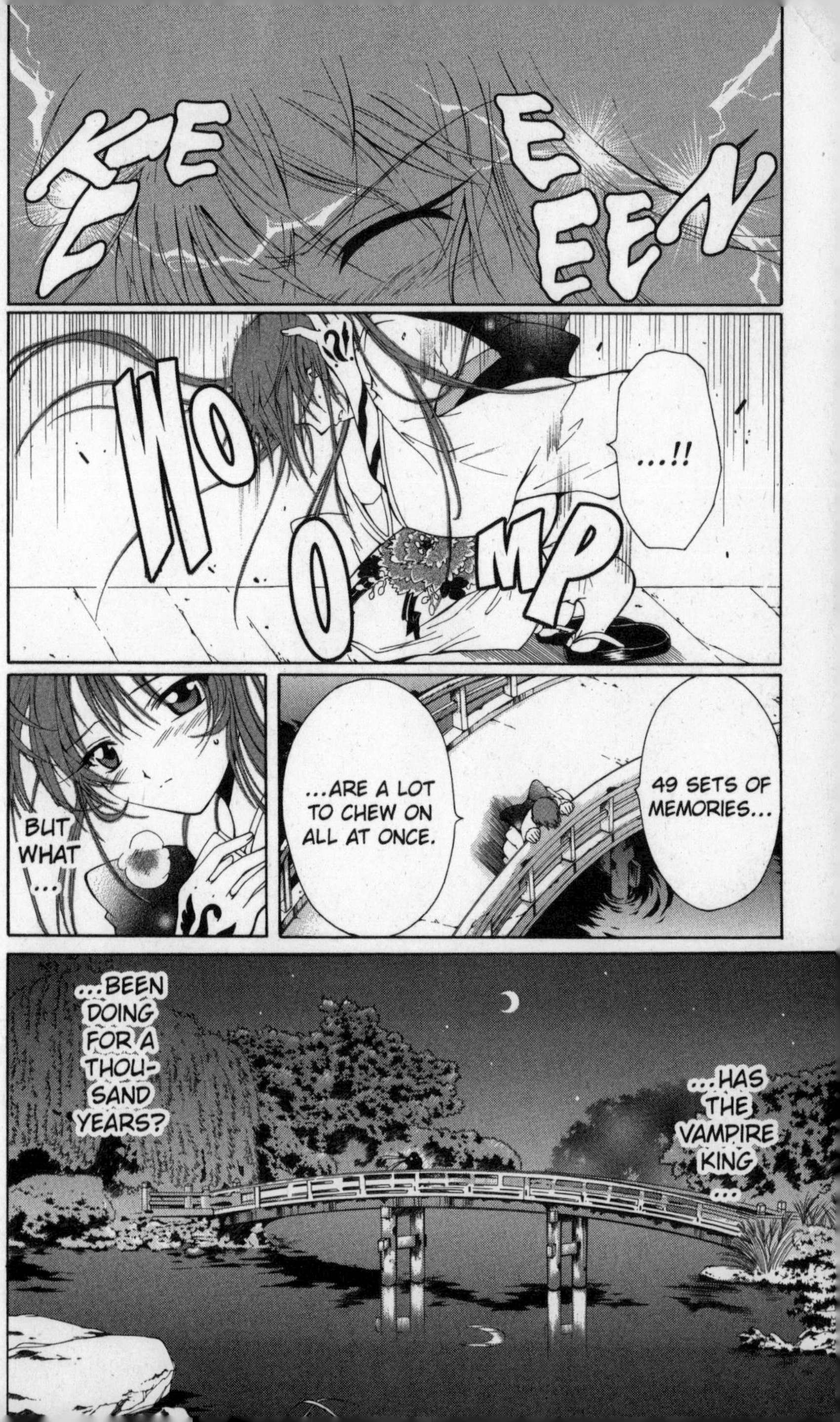

KEEEEN
WOOOMP
?!
...!!
49 SETS OF MEMORIES...
...ARE A LOT TO CHEW ON ALL AT ONCE.
BUT WHAT ...
...HAS THE VAMPIRE KING ...
...BEEN DOING FOR A THOU-SAND YEARS?

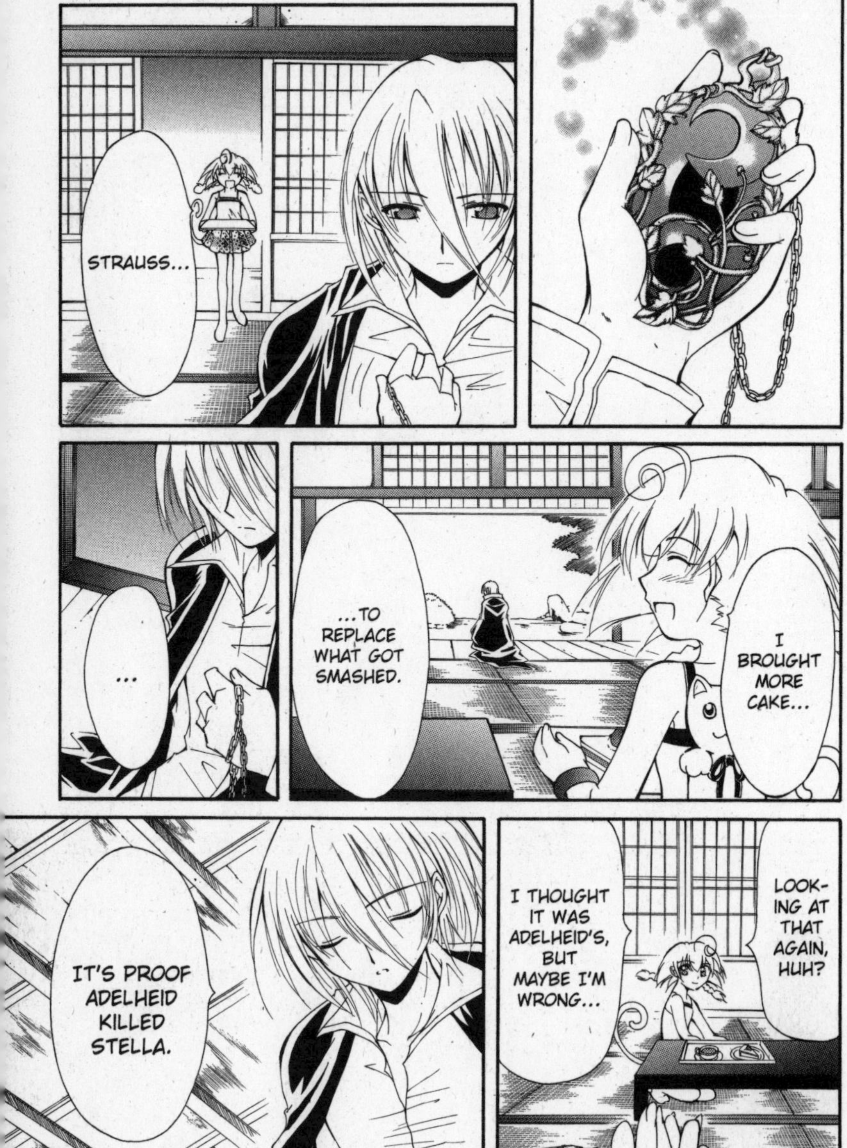
STRAUSS...
I BROUGHT MORE CAKE...
...TO REPLACE WHAT GOT SMASHED.
...
LOOKING AT THAT AGAIN, HUH?
I THOUGHT IT WAS ADELHEID'S, BUT MAYBE I'M WRONG...
IT'S PROOF ADELHEID KILLED STELLA.

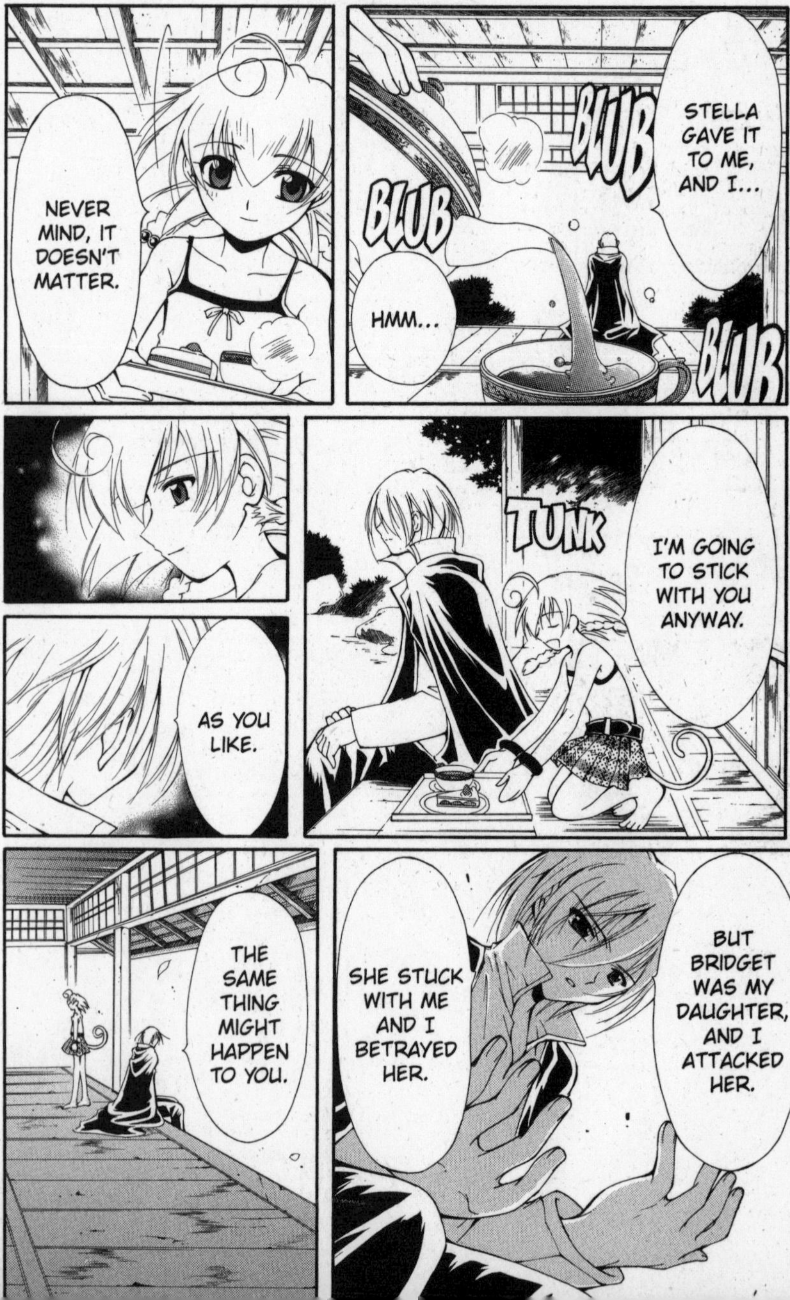
STELLA GAVE IT TO ME, AND I...
BLUB
BLUB
BLUB
HMM...
NEVER MIND, IT DOESN'T MATTER.
TUNK
I'M GOING TO STICK WITH YOU ANYWAY.
AS YOU LIKE.
BUT BRIDGET WAS MY DAUGHTER, AND I ATTACKED HER.
SHE STUCK WITH ME AND I BETRAYED HER.
THE SAME THING MIGHT HAPPEN TO YOU.

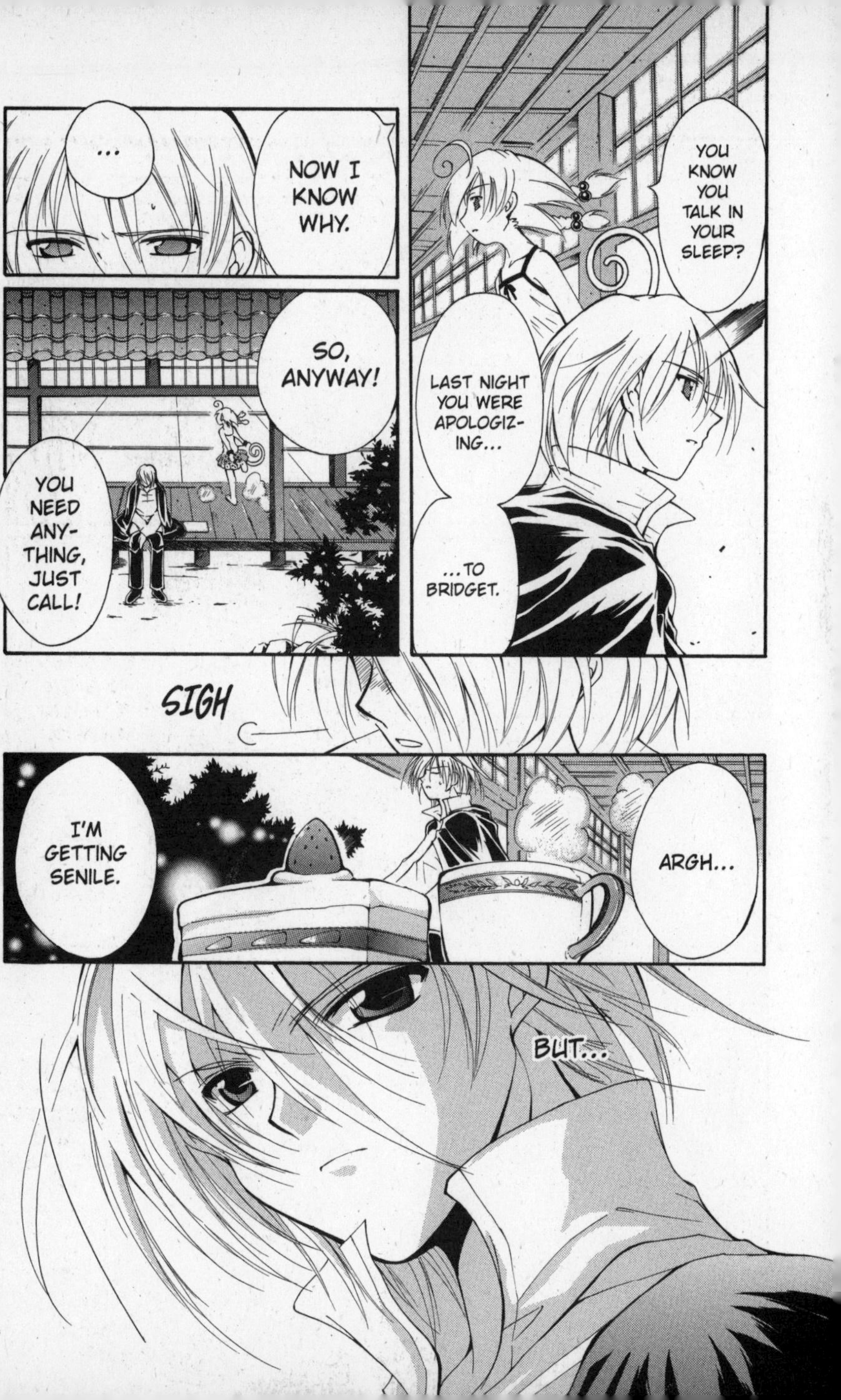
YOU KNOW YOU TALK IN YOUR SLEEP?
LAST NIGHT YOU WERE APOLOGIZING...
...TO BRIDGET.
NOW I KNOW WHY.
...
SO, ANYWAY!
YOU NEED ANYTHING, JUST CALL!
SIGH
ARGH...
I'M GETTING SENILE.
BUT...

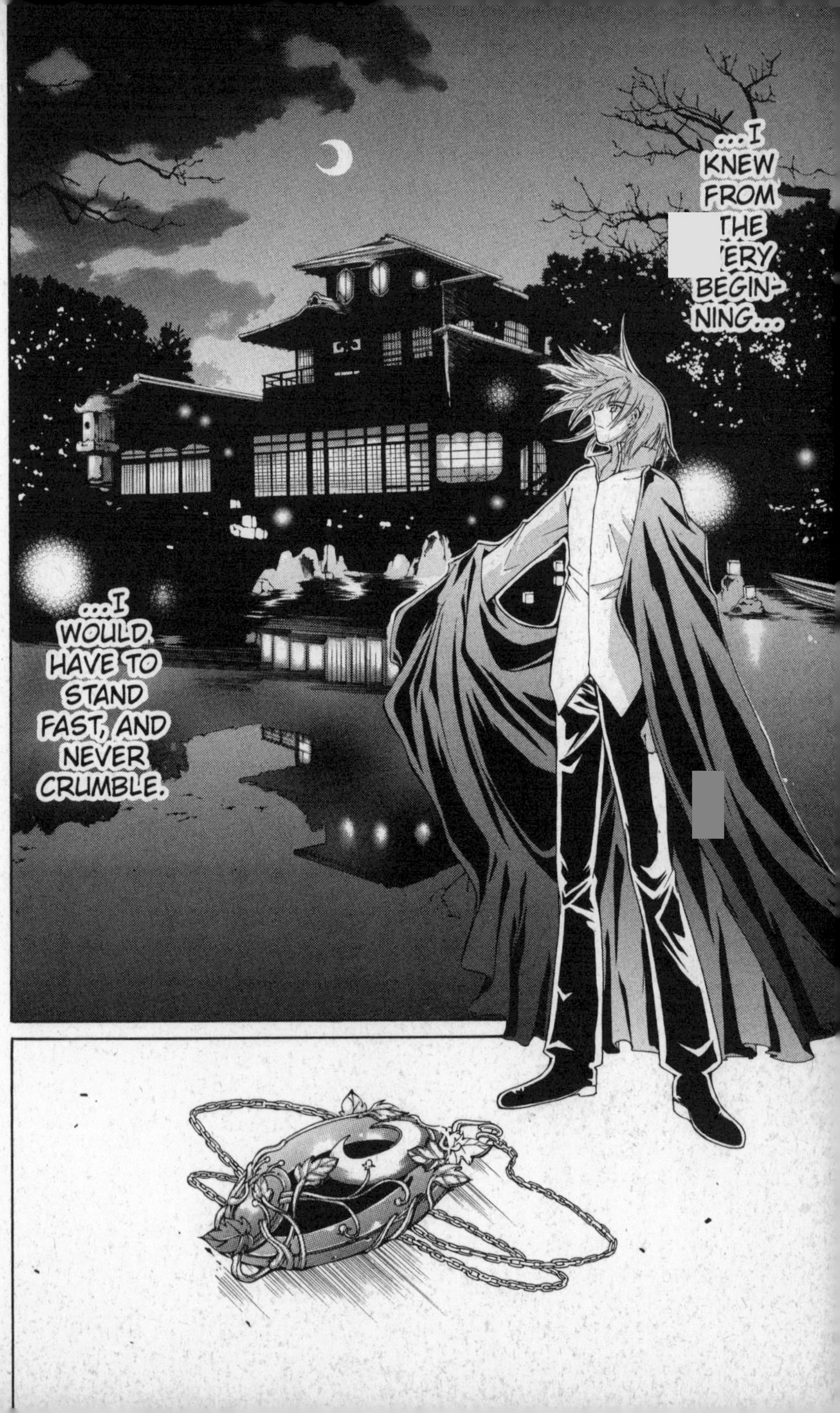
...I KNEW FROM THE VERY BEGIN-NING...
...I WOULD HAVE TO STAND FAST, AND NEVER CRUMBLE.

THE RECORD OF A

FALLEN VAMPIRE

THE RECORD OF A
FALLEN VAMPIRE

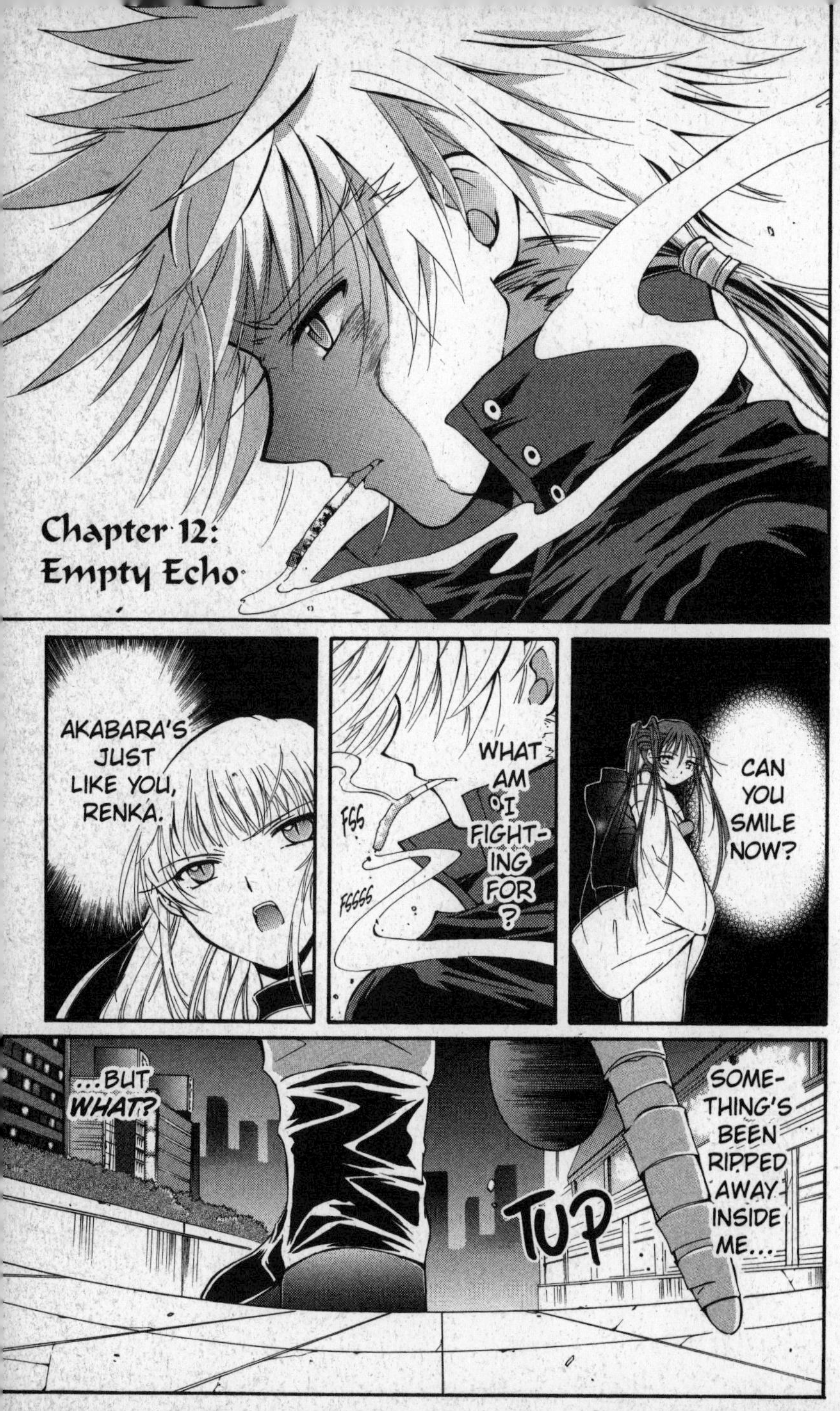
Chapter 12:
Empty Echo
CAN YOU SMILE NOW?
WHAT AM I FIGHTING FOR?
FSS
FSSSS
AKABARA'S JUST LIKE YOU, RENKA.
SOMETHING'S BEEN RIPPED AWAY INSIDE ME...
TUP
...BUT WHAT?

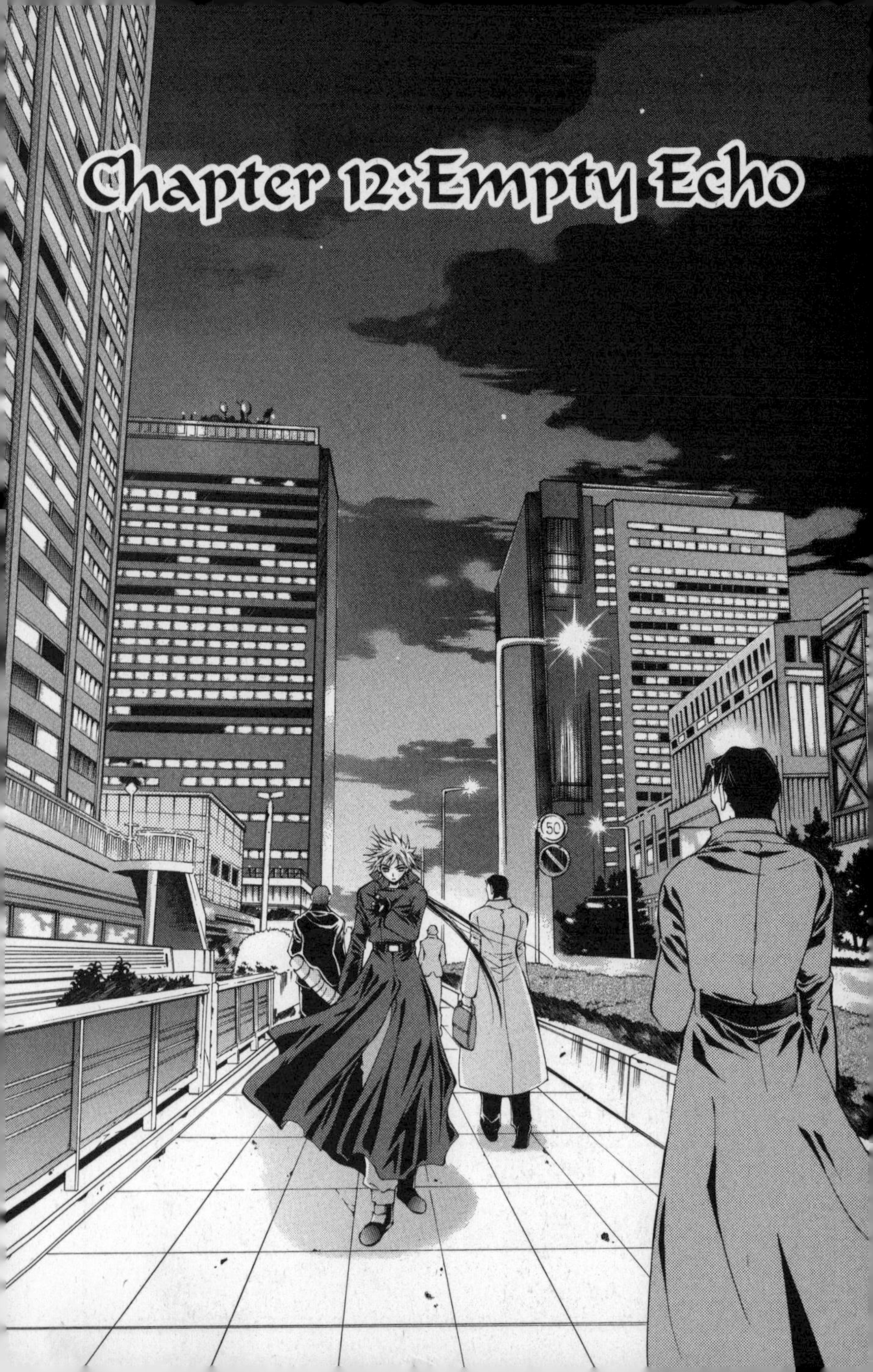
Chapter 12: Empty Echo
50

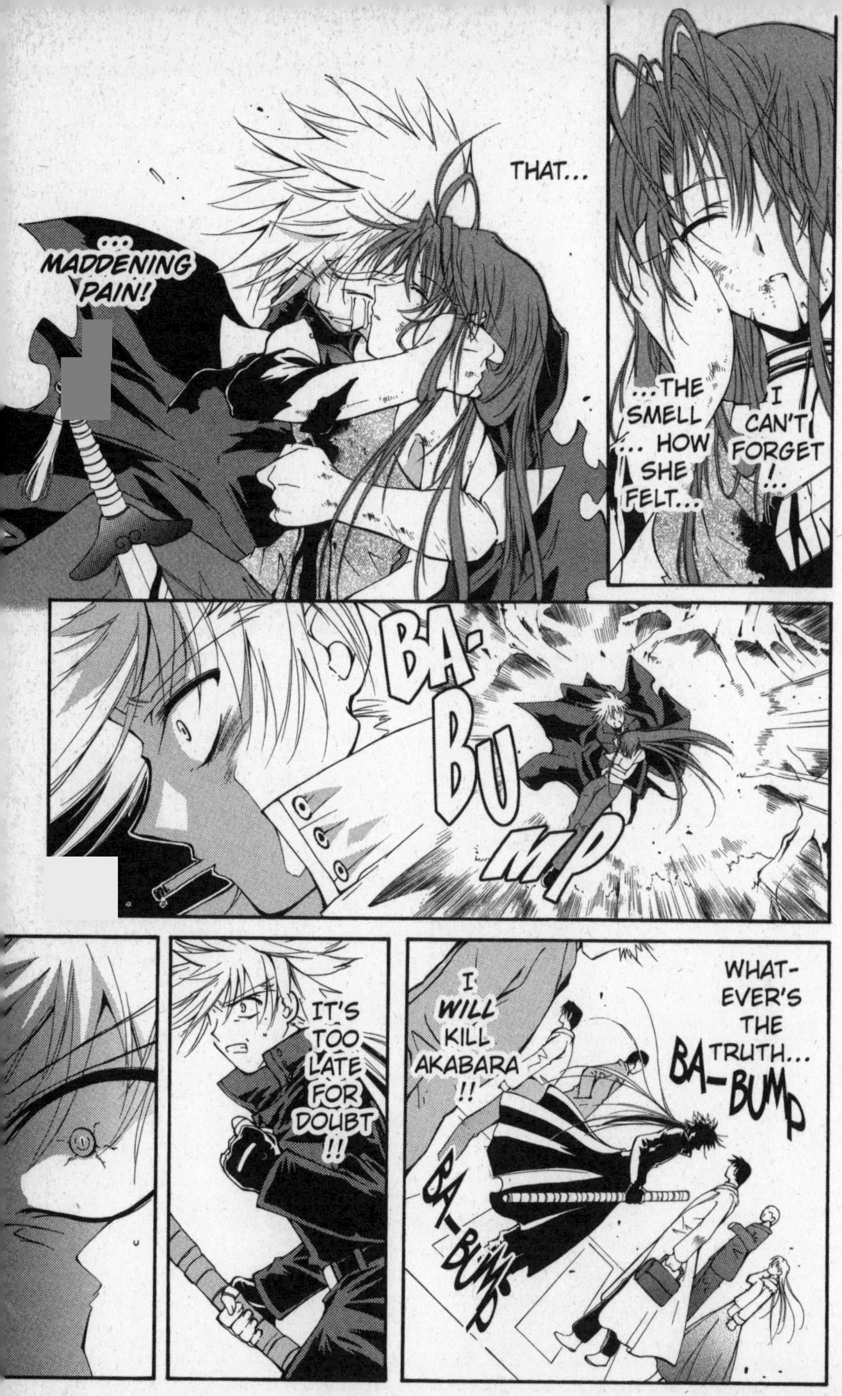
I CAN'T FORGET!...
...THE SMELL ... HOW SHE FELT...
THAT...
...MADDENING PAIN!
BA-BUMP
WHATEVER'S THE TRUTH...
BA-BUMP
I WILL KILL AKABARA!!
BA-BUMP
IT'S TOO LATE FOR DOUBT!!

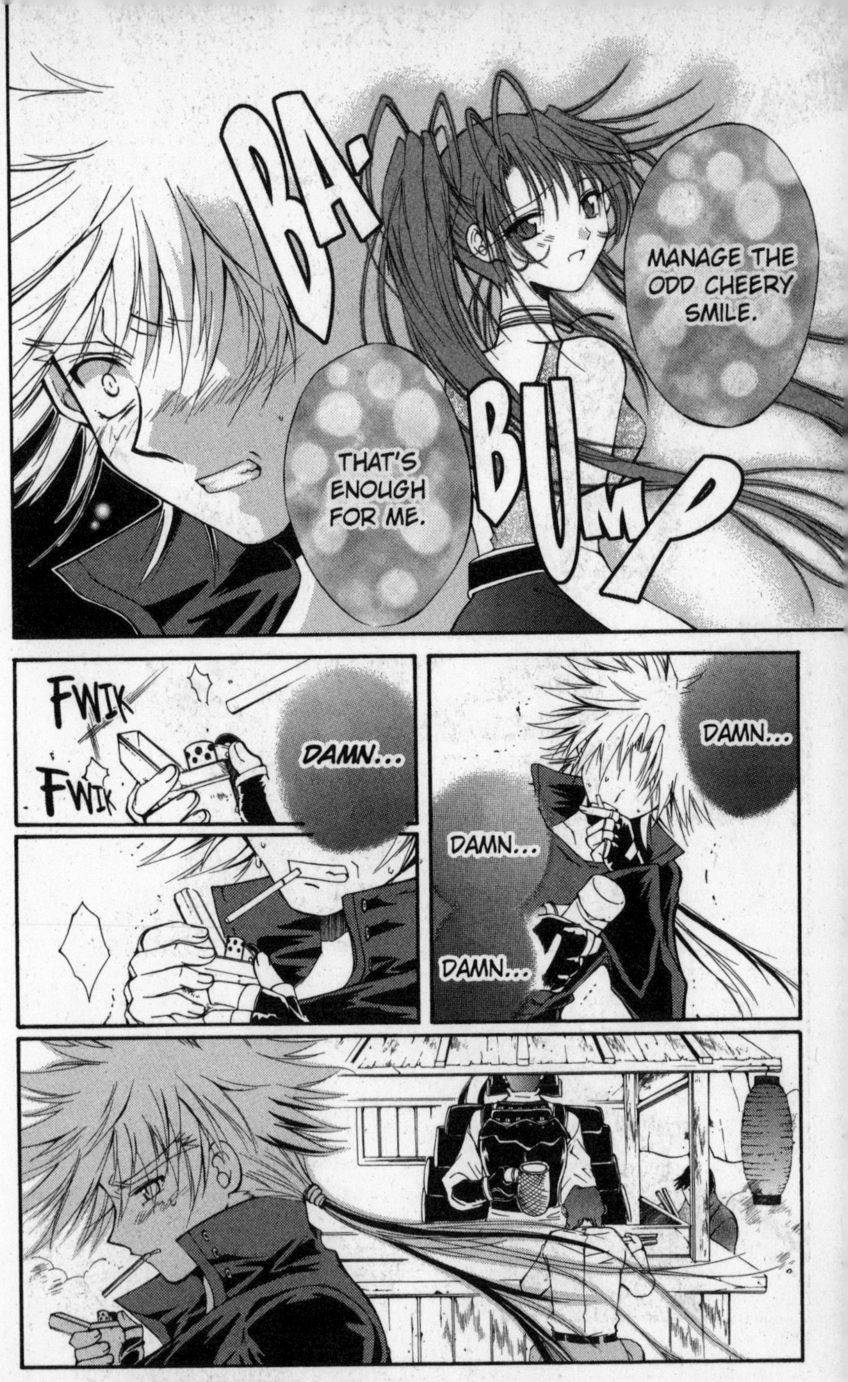
MANAGE THE ODD CHEERY SMILE.
BA-BUMP
THAT'S ENOUGH FOR ME.
DAMN...
DAMN...
DAMN...
FWIK
FWIK
DAMN...

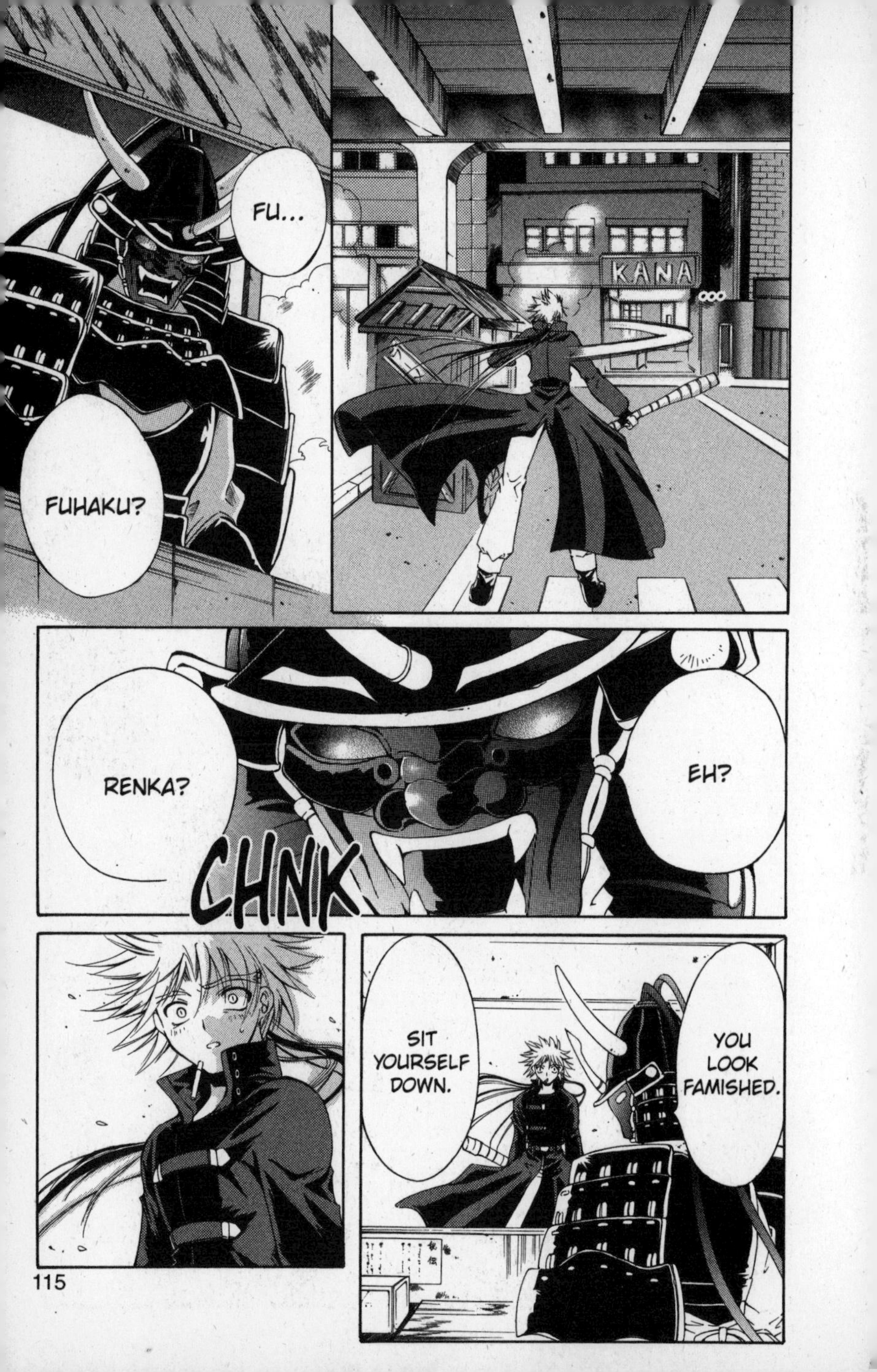
FU...
FUHAKU?
EH?
RENKA?
CHNK
YOU LOOK FAMISHED.
SIT YOURSELF DOWN.

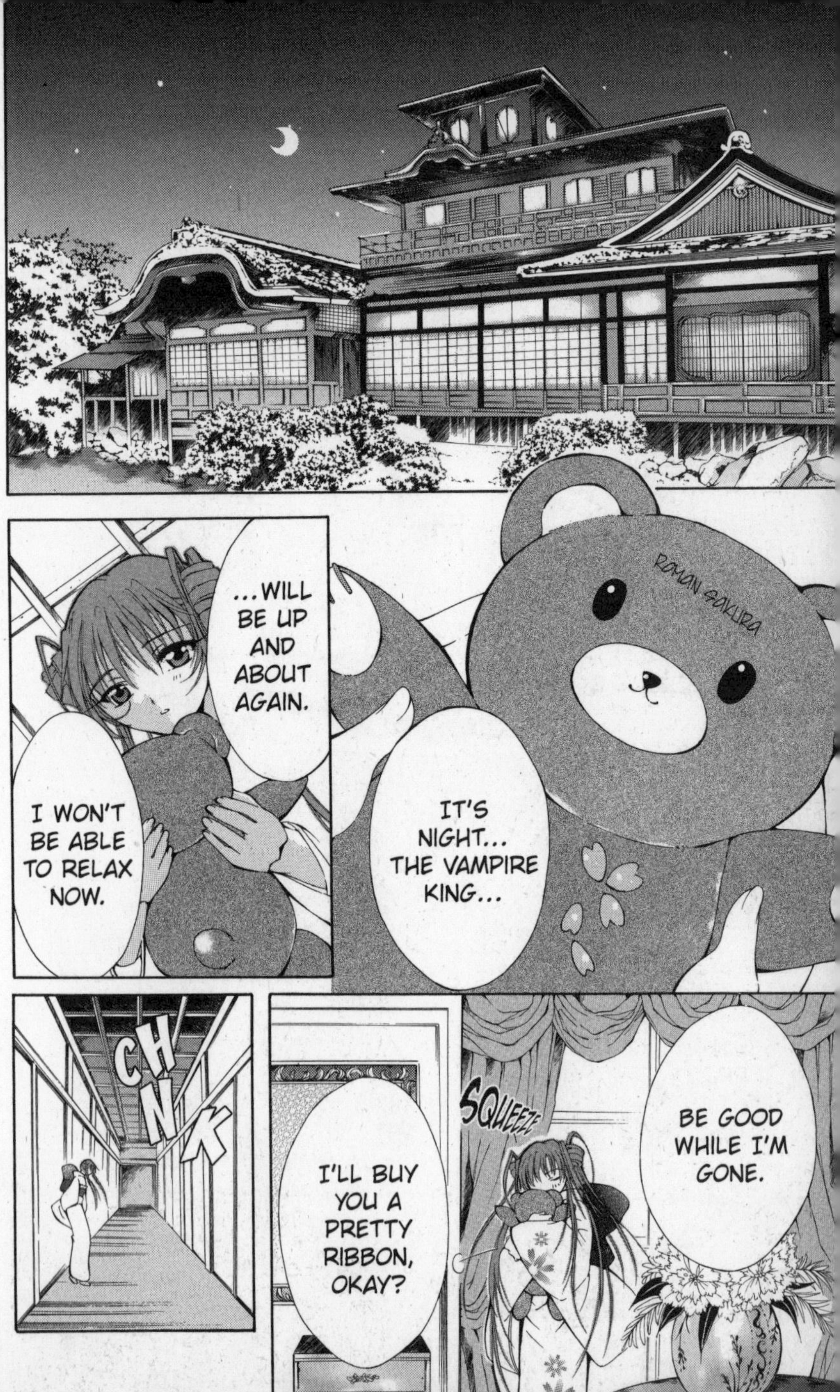
ROMAN SAKURA
IT'S NIGHT... THE VAMPIRE KING...
...WILL BE UP AND ABOUT AGAIN.
I WON'T BE ABLE TO RELAX NOW.
SQUEEZE
BE GOOD WHILE I'M GONE.
I'LL BUY YOU A PRETTY RIBBON, OKAY?
CHNK

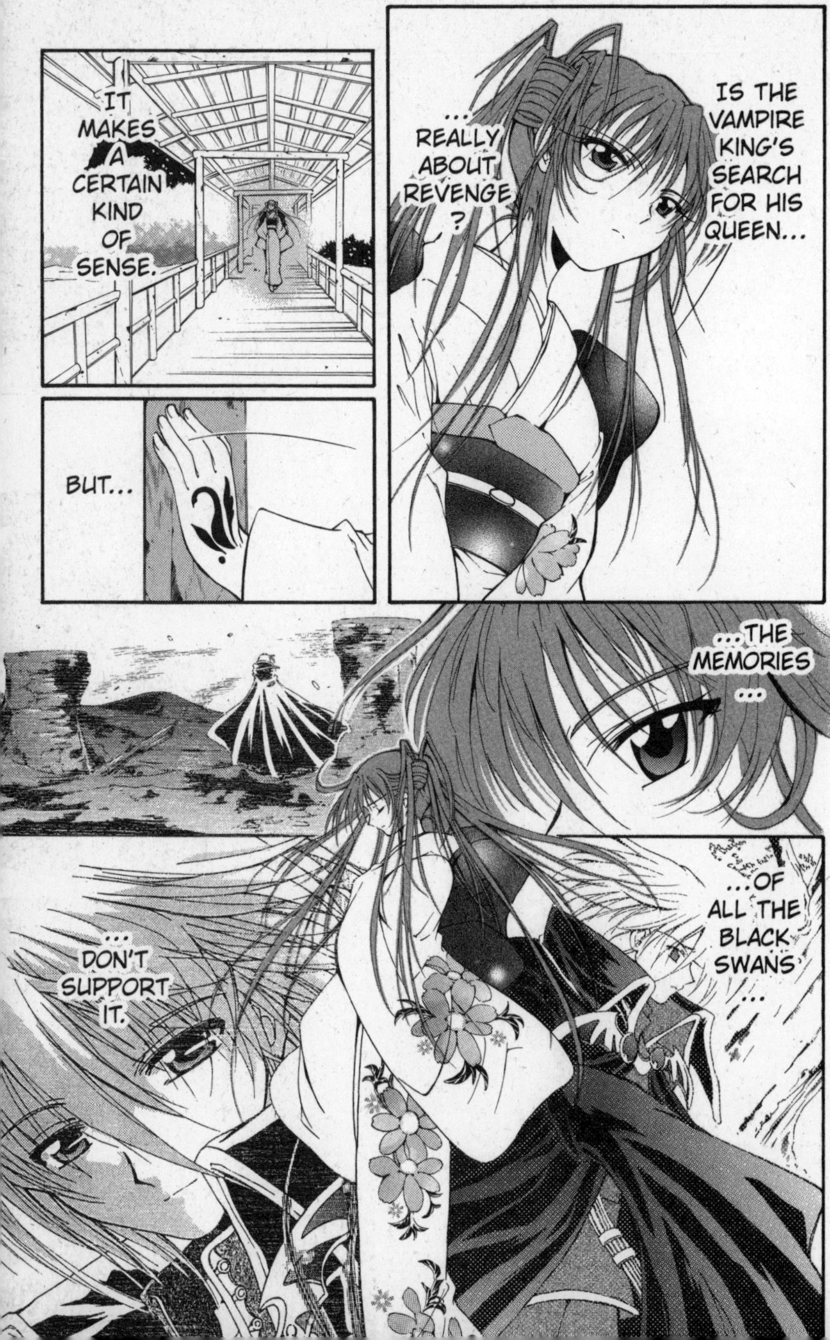
IS THE VAMPIRE KING'S SEARCH FOR HIS QUEEN...
...REALLY ABOUT REVENGE?
IT MAKES A CERTAIN KIND OF SENSE.
BUT...
...THE MEMORIES...
...OF ALL THE BLACK SWANS...
...DON'T SUPPORT IT.

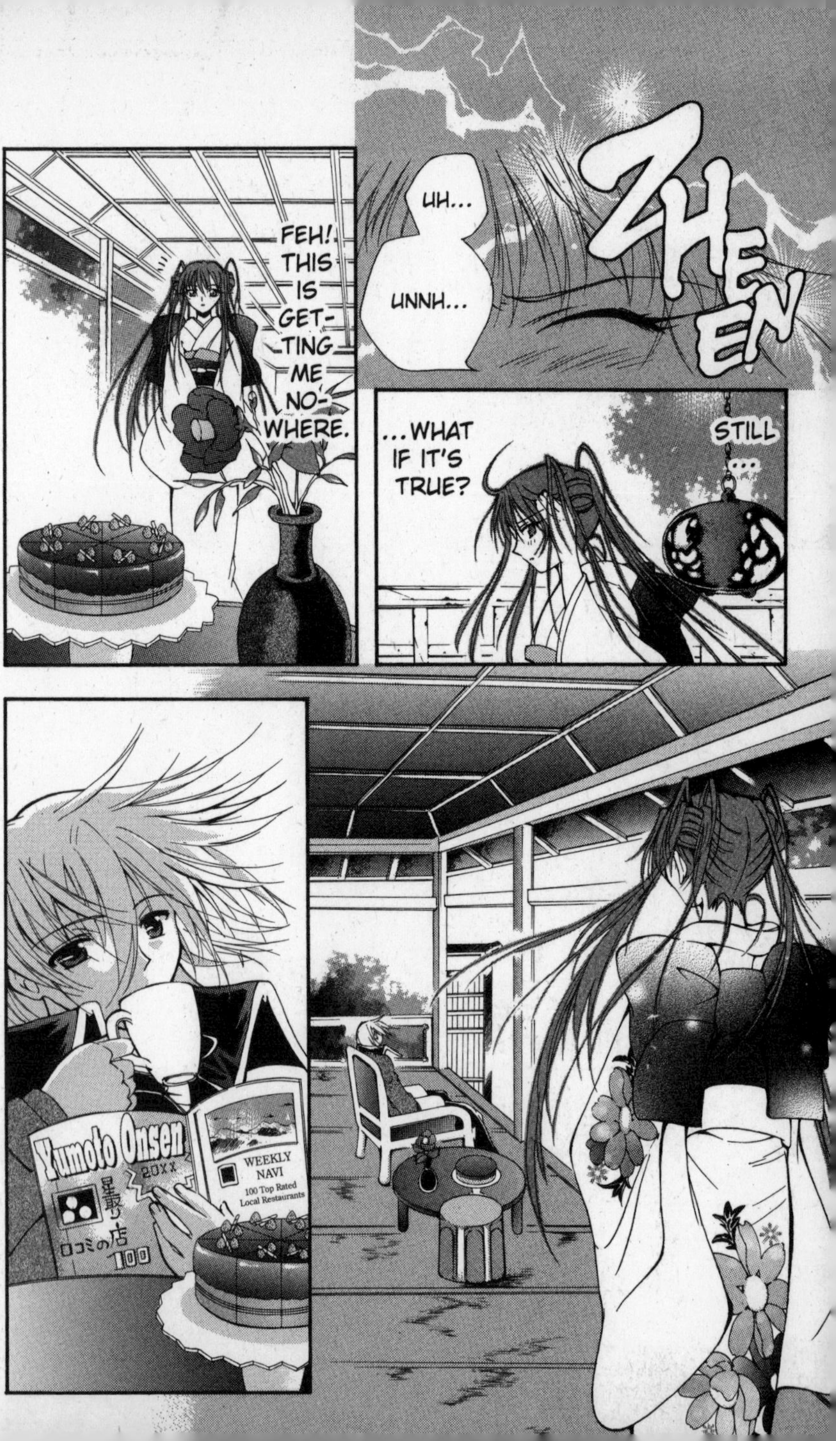
ZHEN
UH...
UNNH...
STILL...
...WHAT IF IT'S TRUE?
FEH! THIS IS GETTING ME NOWHERE.
Yumoto Onsen
20XX
WEEKLY NAVI
100 Top Rated Local Restaurants

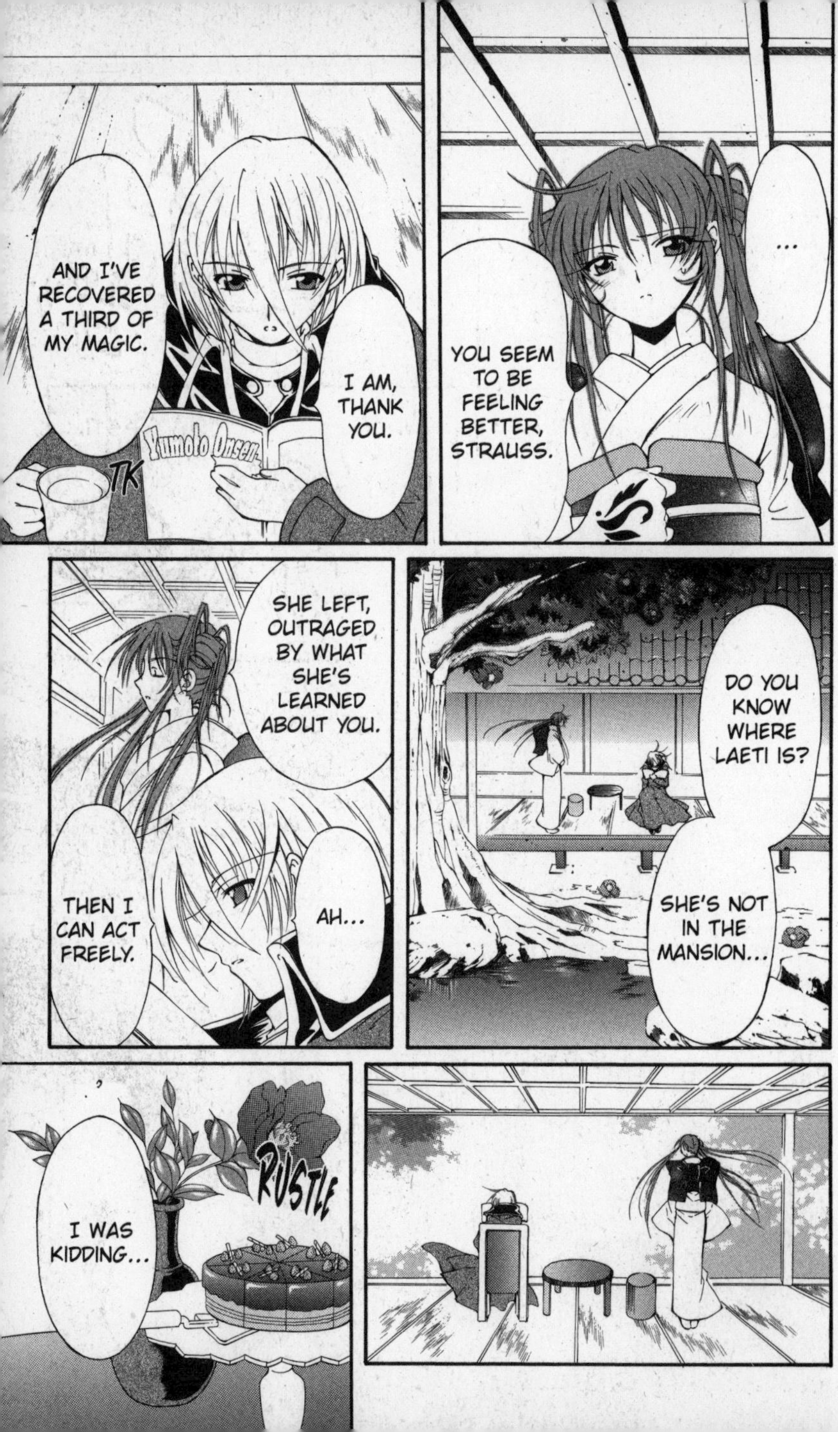
...
YOU SEEM TO BE FEELING BETTER, STRAUSS.
I AM, THANK YOU.
AND I'VE RECOVERED A THIRD OF MY MAGIC.
Yumoto Onsen
TK
DO YOU KNOW WHERE LAETI IS?
SHE'S NOT IN THE MANSION...
SHE LEFT, OUTRAGED BY WHAT SHE'S LEARNED ABOUT YOU.
AH...
THEN I CAN ACT FREELY.
RUSTLE
I WAS KIDDING...

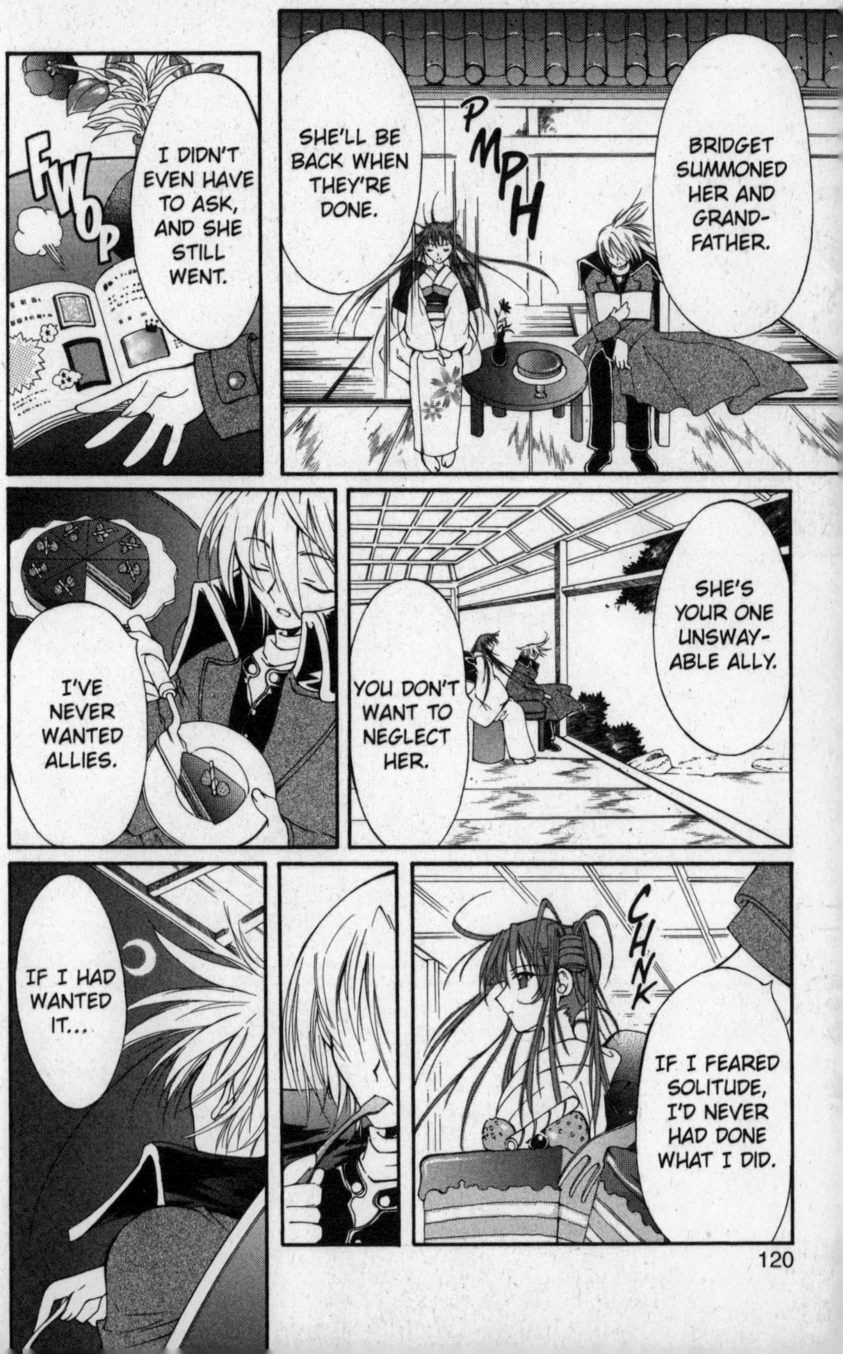
BRIDGET SUMMONED HER AND GRAND-FATHER.
PMPH
SHE'LL BE BACK WHEN THEY'RE DONE.
FWOP
I DIDN'T EVEN HAVE TO ASK, AND SHE STILL WENT.
SHE'S YOUR ONE UNSWAY-ABLE ALLY.
YOU DON'T WANT TO NEGLECT HER.
I'VE NEVER WANTED ALLIES.
CHNK
IF I FEARED SOLITUDE, I'D NEVER HAD DONE WHAT I DID.
IF I HAD WANTED IT...

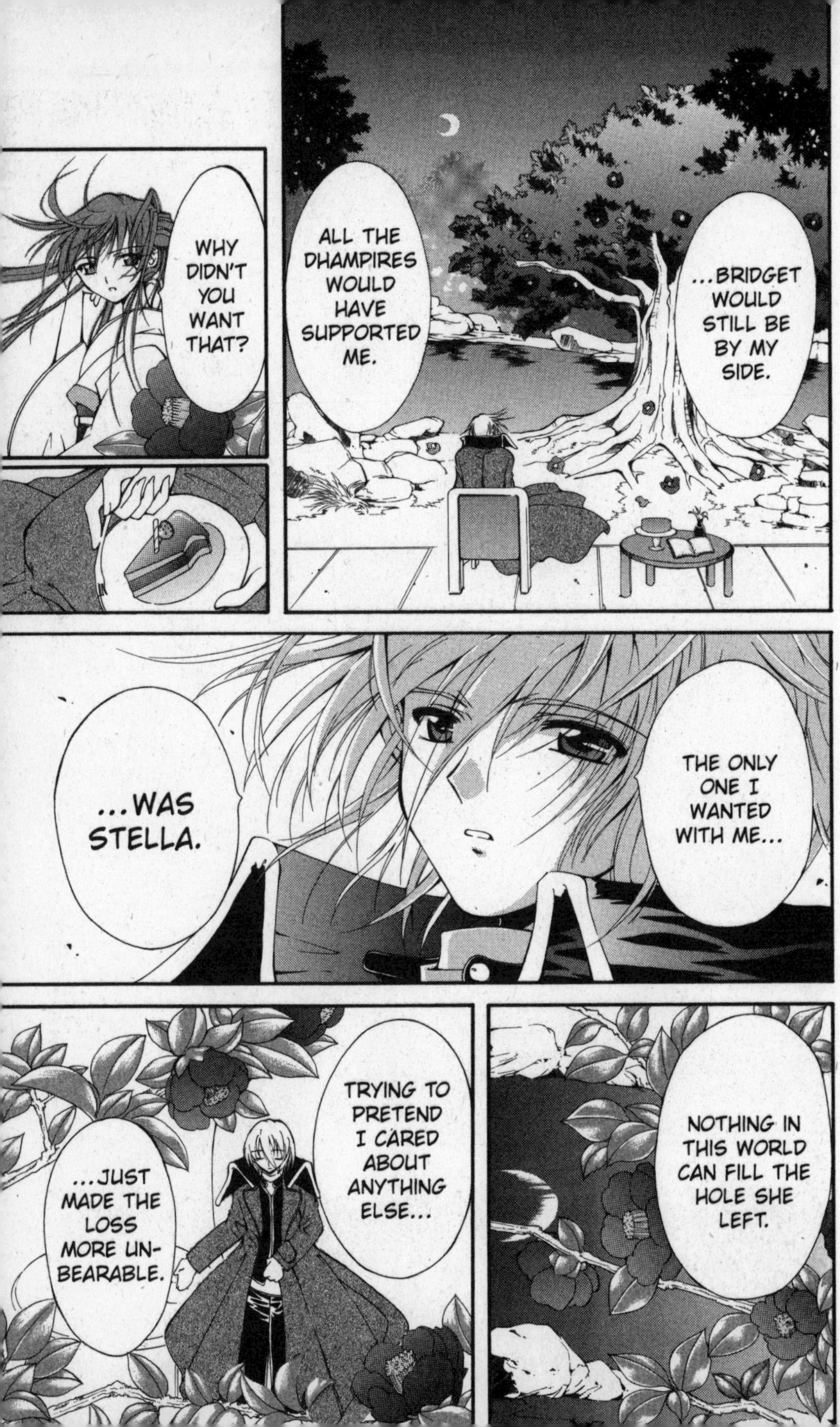
...BRIDGET WOULD STILL BE BY MY SIDE.
ALL THE DHAMPIRES WOULD HAVE SUPPORTED ME.
WHY DIDN'T YOU WANT THAT?
THE ONLY ONE I WANTED WITH ME...
...WAS STELLA.
NOTHING IN THIS WORLD CAN FILL THE HOLE SHE LEFT.
TRYING TO PRETEND I CARED ABOUT ANYTHING ELSE...
...JUST MADE THE LOSS MORE UN-BEARABLE.

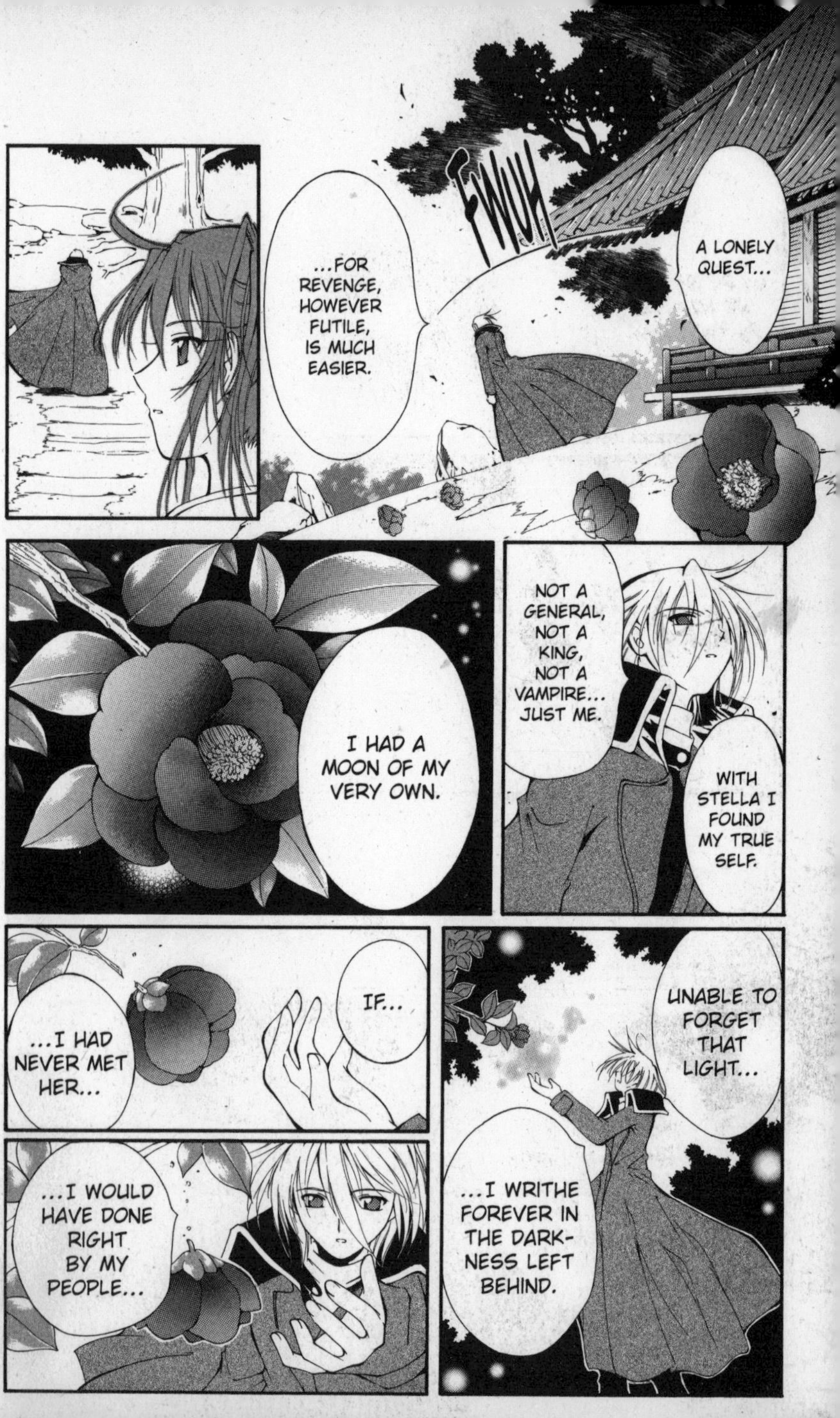
A LONELY QUEST...
FWUH
...FOR REVENGE, HOWEVER FUTILE, IS MUCH EASIER.
NOT A GENERAL, NOT A KING, NOT A VAMPIRE... JUST ME.
WITH STELLA I FOUND MY TRUE SELF.
I HAD A MOON OF MY VERY OWN.
UNABLE TO FORGET THAT LIGHT...
...I WRITHE FOREVER IN THE DARK-NESS LEFT BEHIND.
IF...
...I HAD NEVER MET HER...
...I WOULD HAVE DONE RIGHT BY MY PEOPLE...

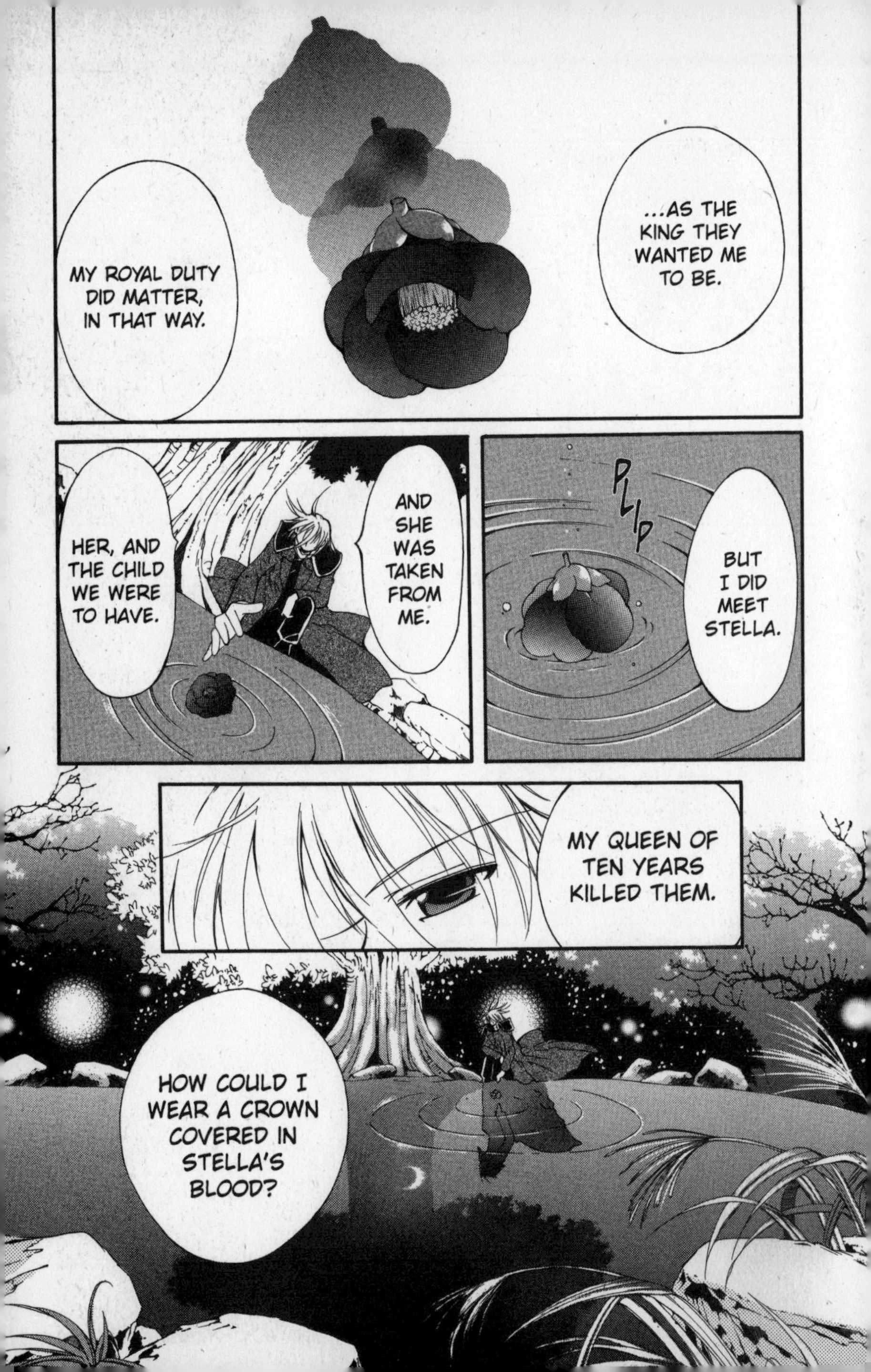
...AS THE KING THEY WANTED ME TO BE.
MY ROYAL DUTY DID MATTER, IN THAT WAY.
PLIP
BUT I DID MEET STELLA.
AND SHE WAS TAKEN FROM ME.
HER, AND THE CHILD WE WERE TO HAVE.
MY QUEEN OF TEN YEARS KILLED THEM.
HOW COULD I WEAR A CROWN COVERED IN STELLA'S BLOOD?

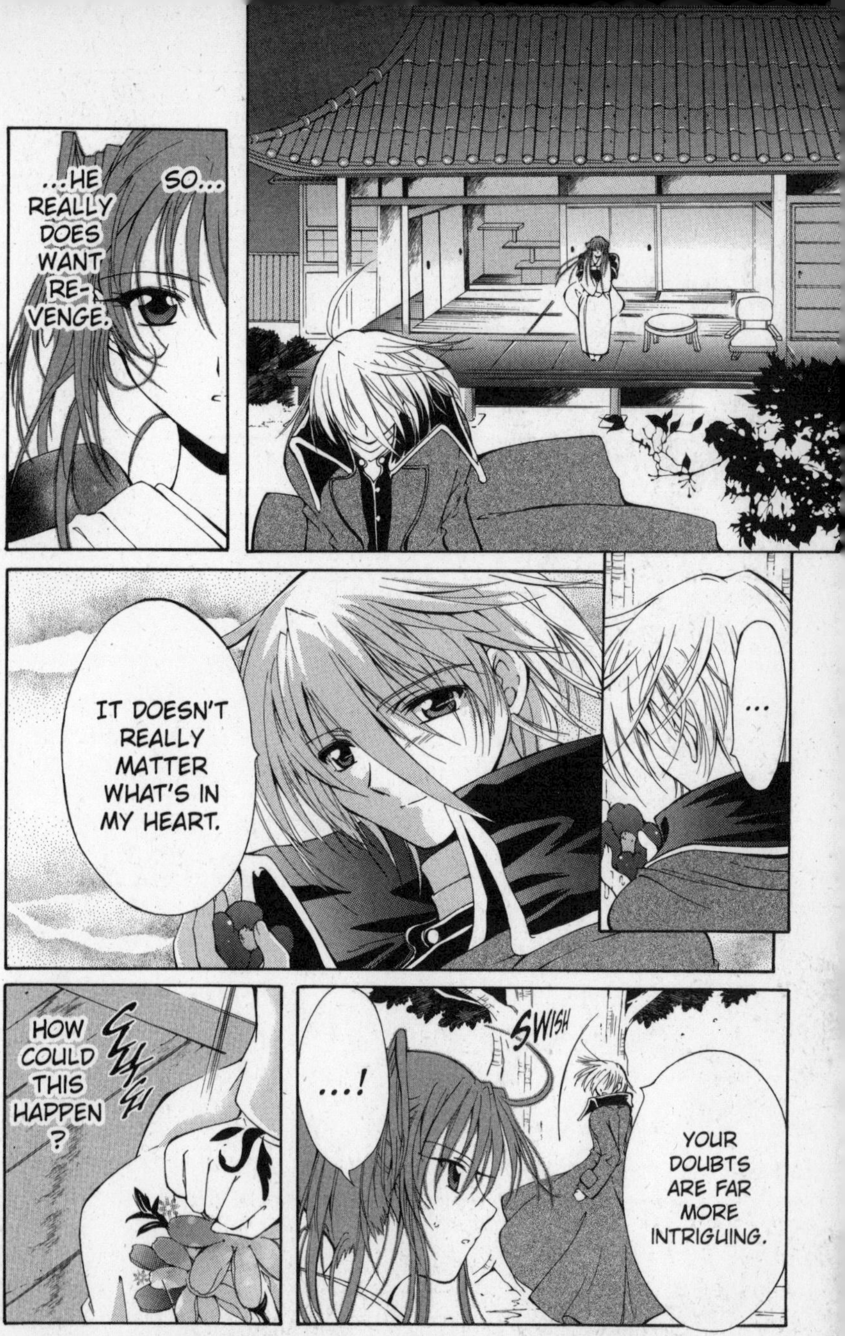
SO...
...HE REALLY DOES WANT RE-VENGE.
...
IT DOESN'T REALLY MATTER WHAT'S IN MY HEART.
SWISH
YOUR DOUBTS ARE FAR MORE INTRIGUING.
...!
HOW COULD THIS HAPPEN?

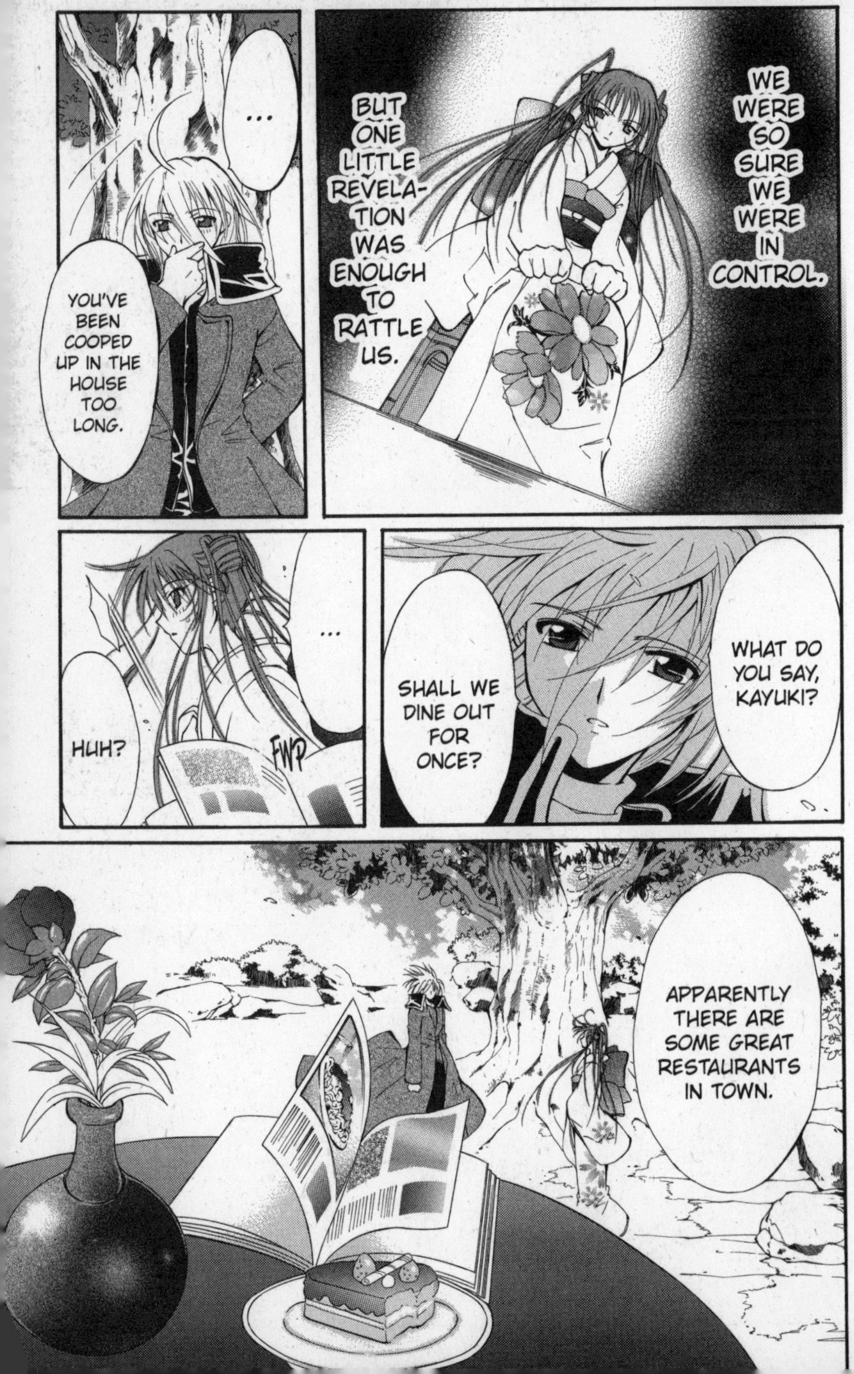
WE WERE SO SURE WE WERE IN CONTROL.
BUT ONE LITTLE REVELATION WAS ENOUGH TO RATTLE US.
...
YOU'VE BEEN COOPED UP IN THE HOUSE TOO LONG.
WHAT DO YOU SAY, KAYUKI?
SHALL WE DINE OUT FOR ONCE?
...
HUH?
FWP
APPARENTLY THERE ARE SOME GREAT RESTAURANTS IN TOWN.

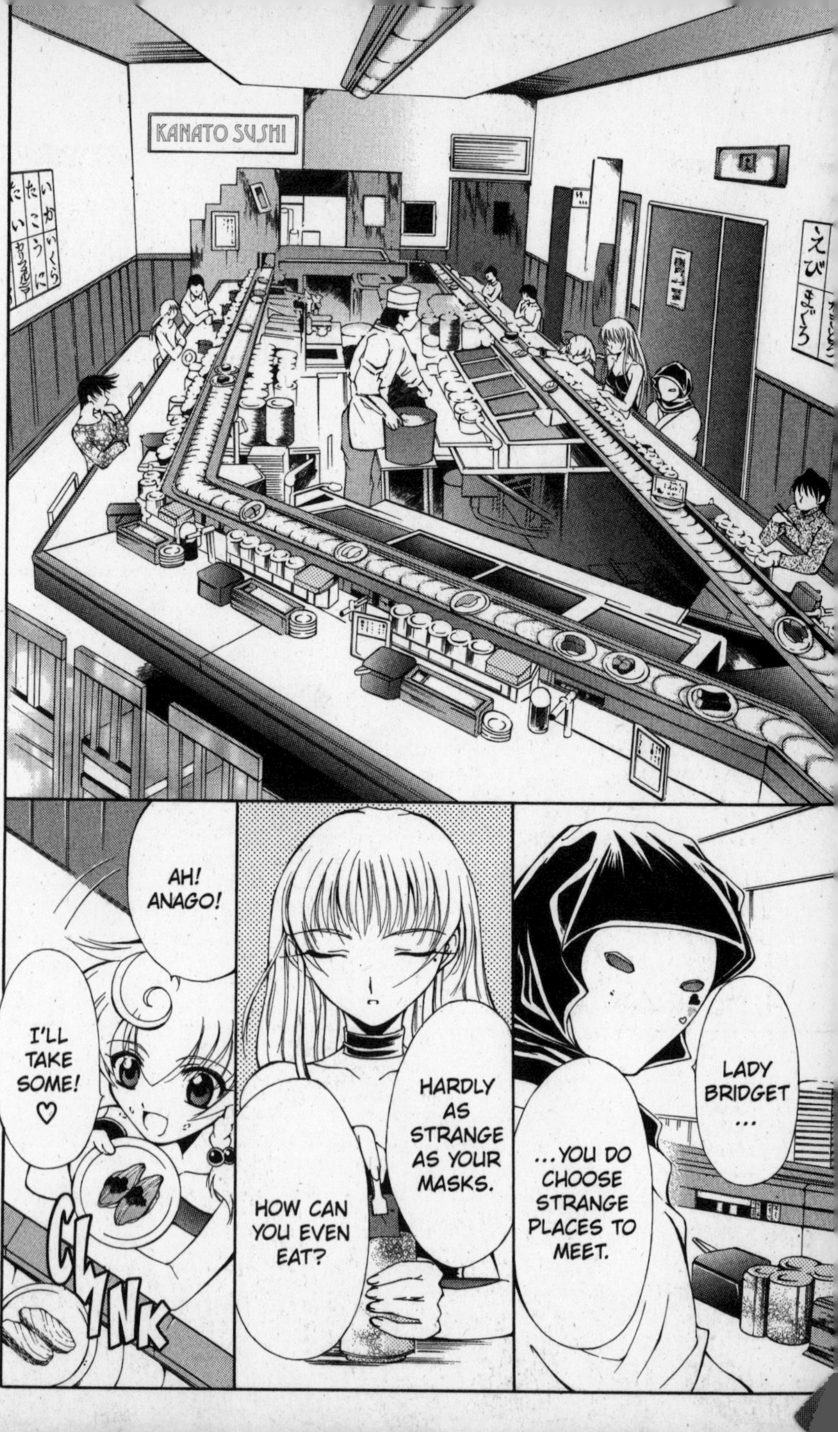
KANATO SUSHI
えび
まぐろ
LADY BRIDGET ...
...YOU DO CHOOSE STRANGE PLACES TO MEET.
HARDLY AS STRANGE AS YOUR MASKS.
HOW CAN YOU EVEN EAT?
AH! ANAGO!
I'LL TAKE SOME! ♡
CLINK

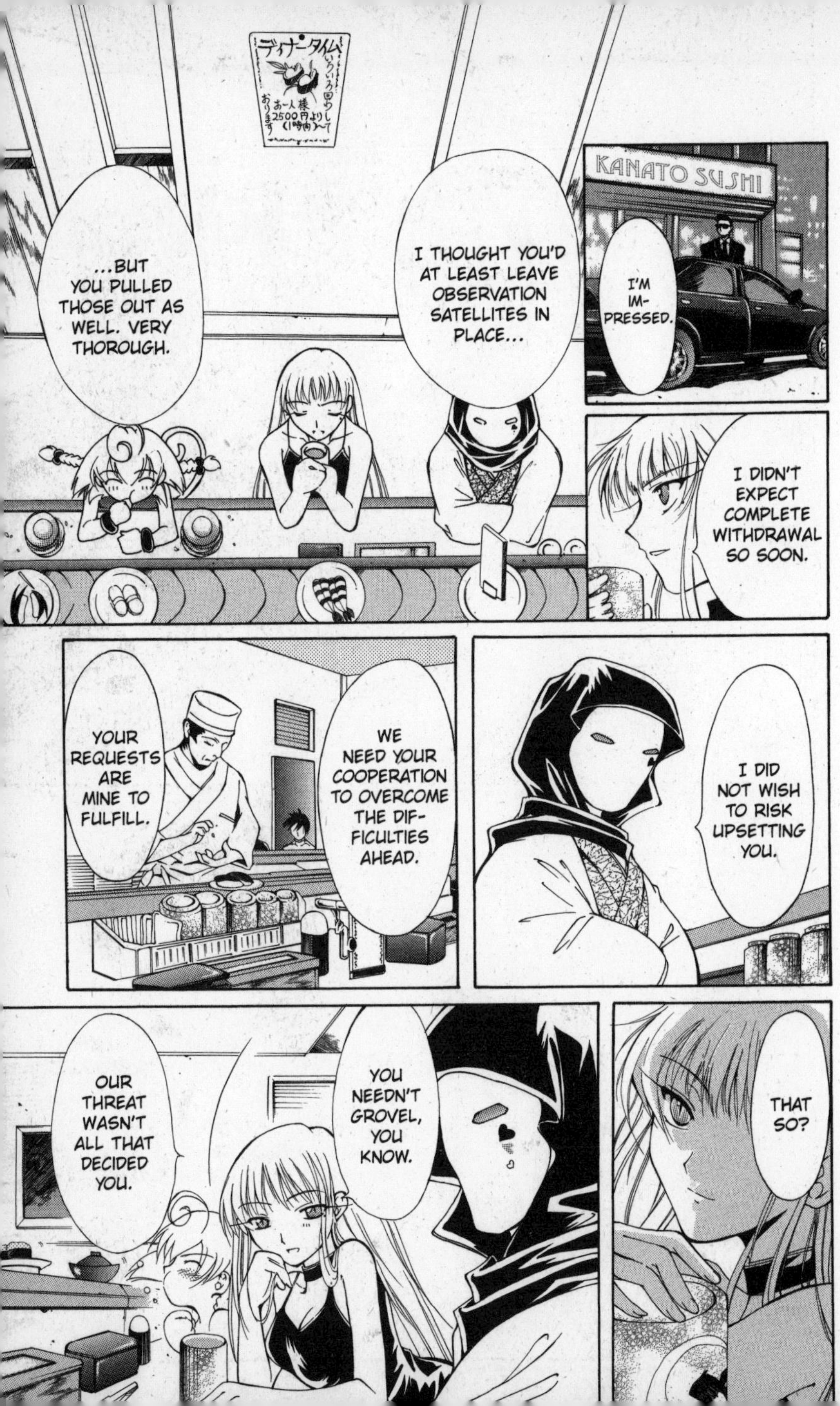
KANATO SUSHI
I'M IM-PRESSED.
I DIDN'T EXPECT COMPLETE WITHDRAWAL SO SOON.
ディナータイム
I THOUGHT YOU'D AT LEAST LEAVE OBSERVATION SATELLITES IN PLACE...
...BUT YOU PULLED THOSE OUT AS WELL. VERY THOROUGH.
I DID NOT WISH TO RISK UPSETTING YOU.
WE NEED YOUR COOPERATION TO OVERCOME THE DIF-FICULTIES AHEAD.
YOUR REQUESTS ARE MINE TO FULFILL.
THAT SO?
YOU NEEDN'T GROVEL, YOU KNOW.
OUR THREAT WASN'T ALL THAT DECIDED YOU.

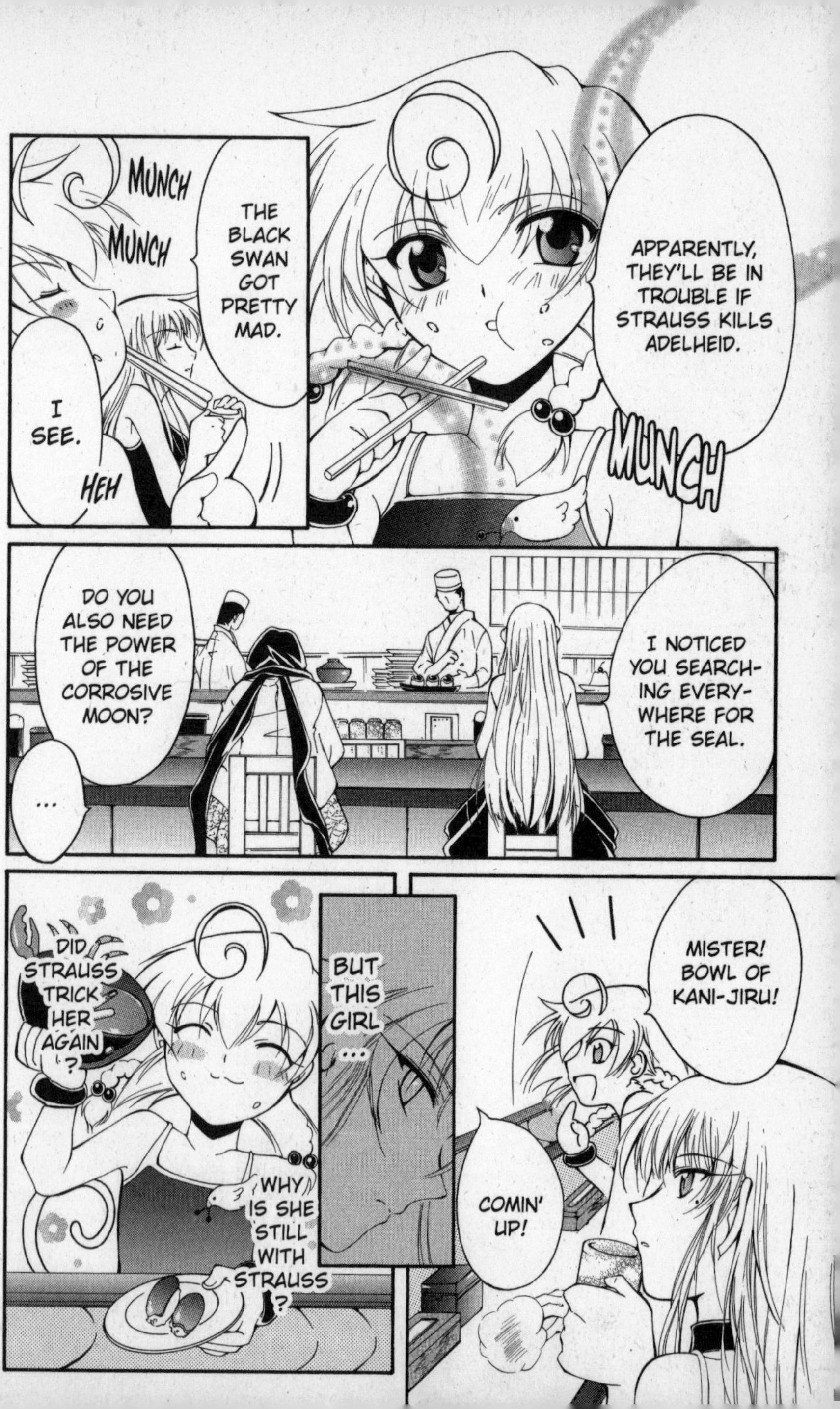
APPARENTLY, THEY'LL BE IN TROUBLE IF STRAUSS KILLS ADELHEID.
MUNCH
THE BLACK SWAN GOT PRETTY MAD.
MUNCH
MUNCH
I SEE.
HEH
I NOTICED YOU SEARCHING EVERYWHERE FOR THE SEAL.
DO YOU ALSO NEED THE POWER OF THE CORROSIVE MOON?
...
MISTER! BOWL OF KANI-JIRU!
COMIN' UP!
DID STRAUSS TRICK HER AGAIN?
BUT THIS GIRL...
WHY IS SHE STILL WITH STRAUSS?

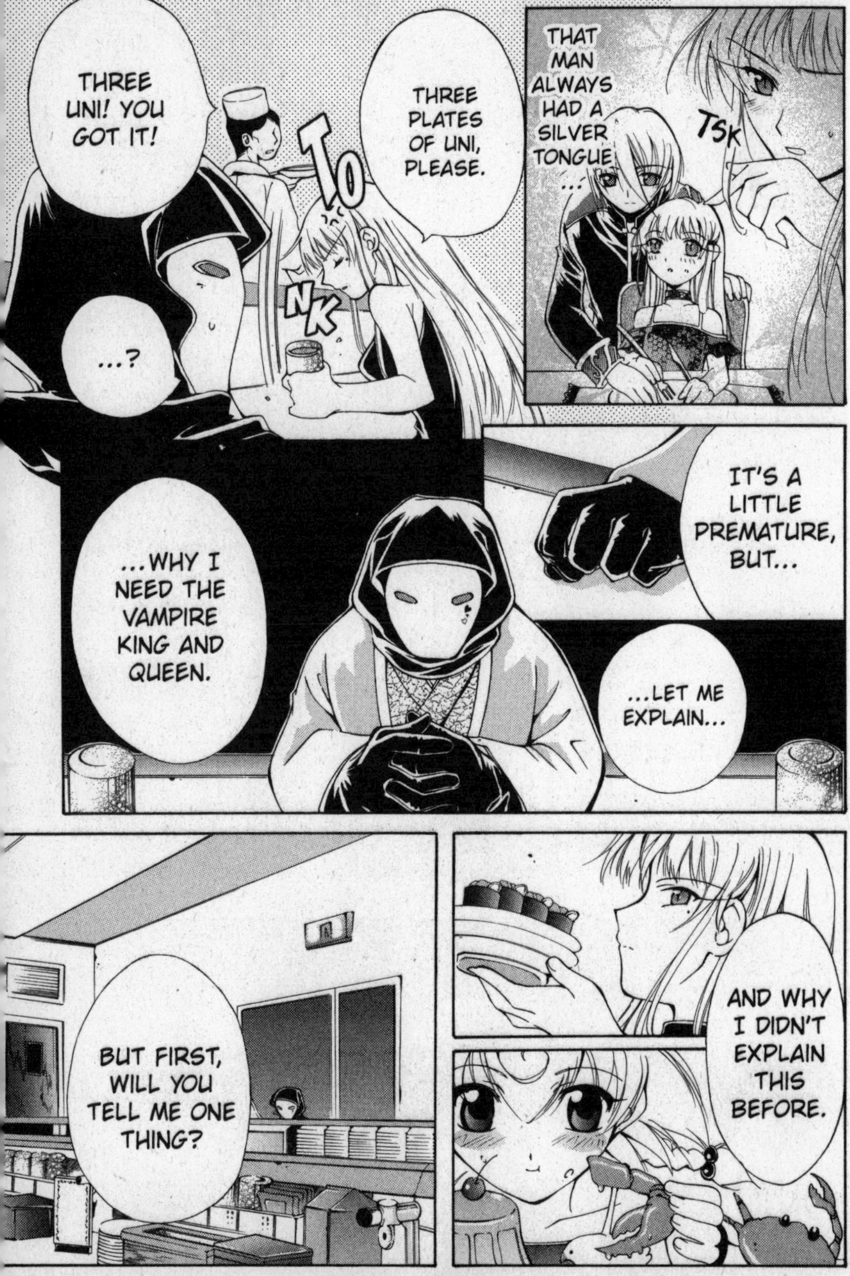
THAT MAN ALWAYS HAD A SILVER TONGUE
TSK
...
THREE PLATES OF UNI, PLEASE.
TO
NK
THREE UNI! YOU GOT IT!
...?
IT'S A LITTLE PREMATURE, BUT...
...LET ME EXPLAIN...
...WHY I NEED THE VAMPIRE KING AND QUEEN.
AND WHY I DIDN'T EXPLAIN THIS BEFORE.
BUT FIRST, WILL YOU TELL ME ONE THING?

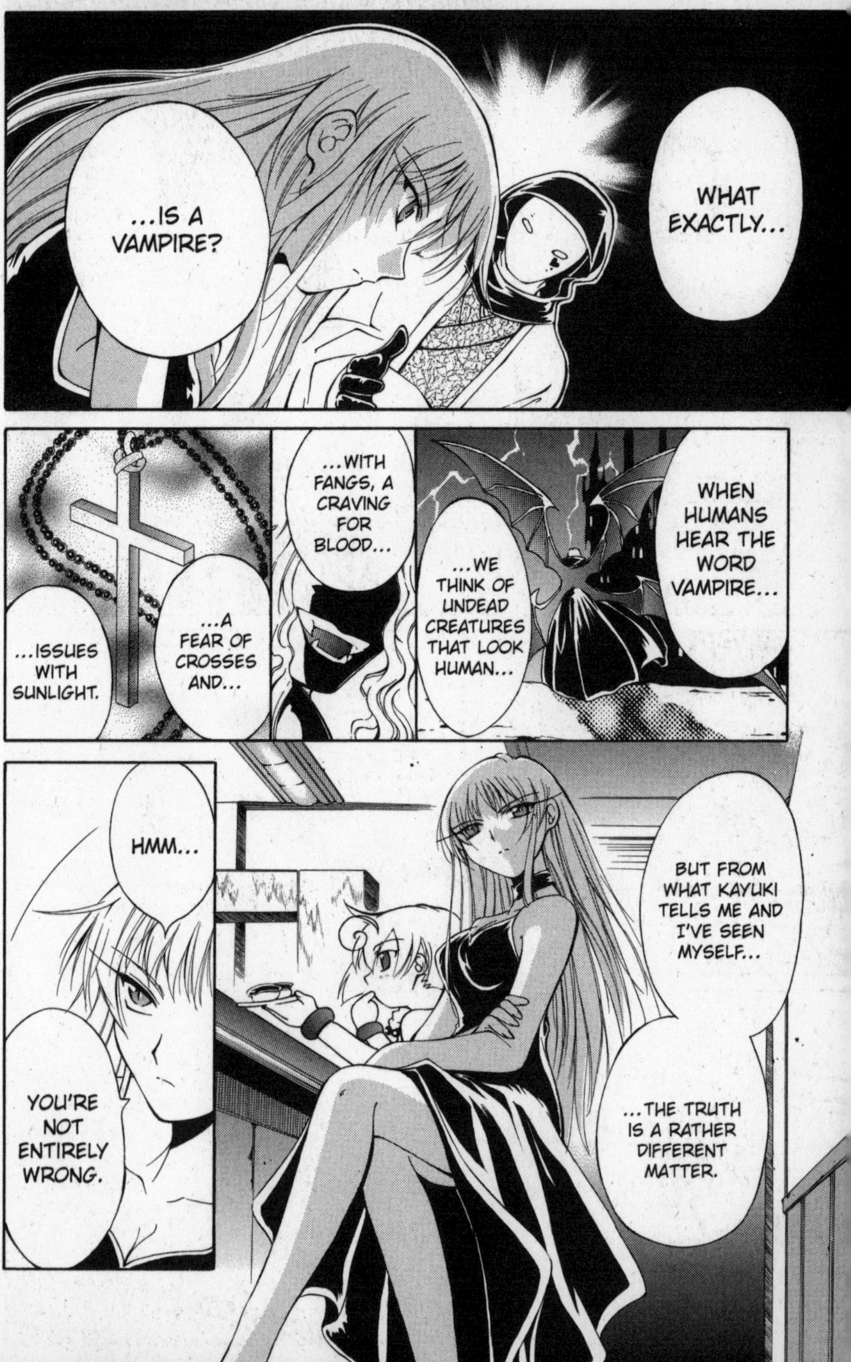
WHAT EXACTLY...
...IS A VAMPIRE?
WHEN HUMANS HEAR THE WORD VAMPIRE...
...WE THINK OF UNDEAD CREATURES THAT LOOK HUMAN...
...WITH FANGS, A CRAVING FOR BLOOD...
...A FEAR OF CROSSES AND...
...ISSUES WITH SUNLIGHT.
BUT FROM WHAT KAYUKI TELLS ME AND I'VE SEEN MYSELF...
...THE TRUTH IS A RATHER DIFFERENT MATTER.
HMM...
YOU'RE NOT ENTIRELY WRONG.

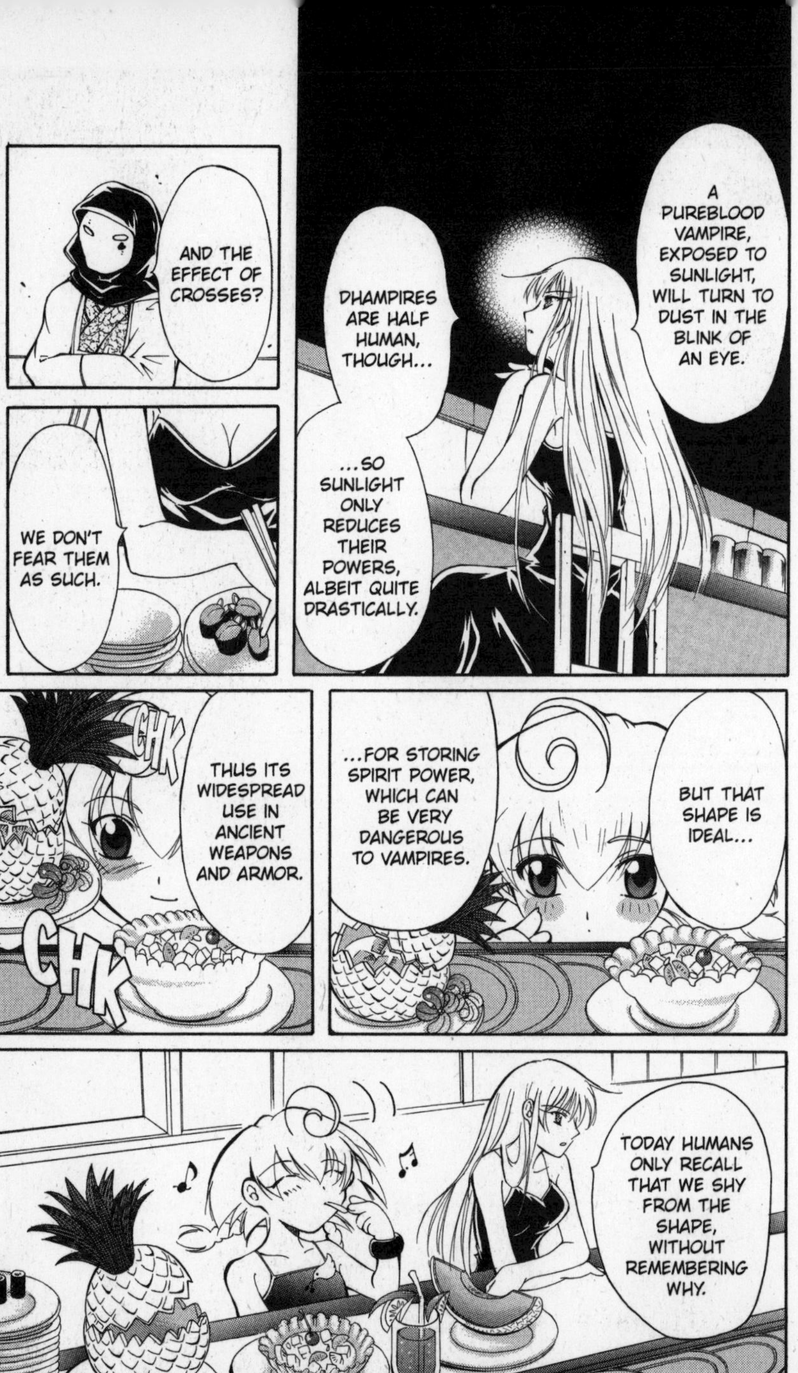
A PUREBLOOD VAMPIRE, EXPOSED TO SUNLIGHT, WILL TURN TO DUST IN THE BLINK OF AN EYE.
DHAMPIRES ARE HALF HUMAN, THOUGH...
...SO SUNLIGHT ONLY REDUCES THEIR POWERS, ALBEIT QUITE DRASTICALLY.
AND THE EFFECT OF CROSSES?
WE DON'T FEAR THEM AS SUCH.
BUT THAT SHAPE IS IDEAL...
...FOR STORING SPIRIT POWER, WHICH CAN BE VERY DANGEROUS TO VAMPIRES.
CHK
THUS ITS WIDESPREAD USE IN ANCIENT WEAPONS AND ARMOR.
CHK
TODAY HUMANS ONLY RECALL THAT WE SHY FROM THE SHAPE, WITHOUT REMEMBERING WHY.

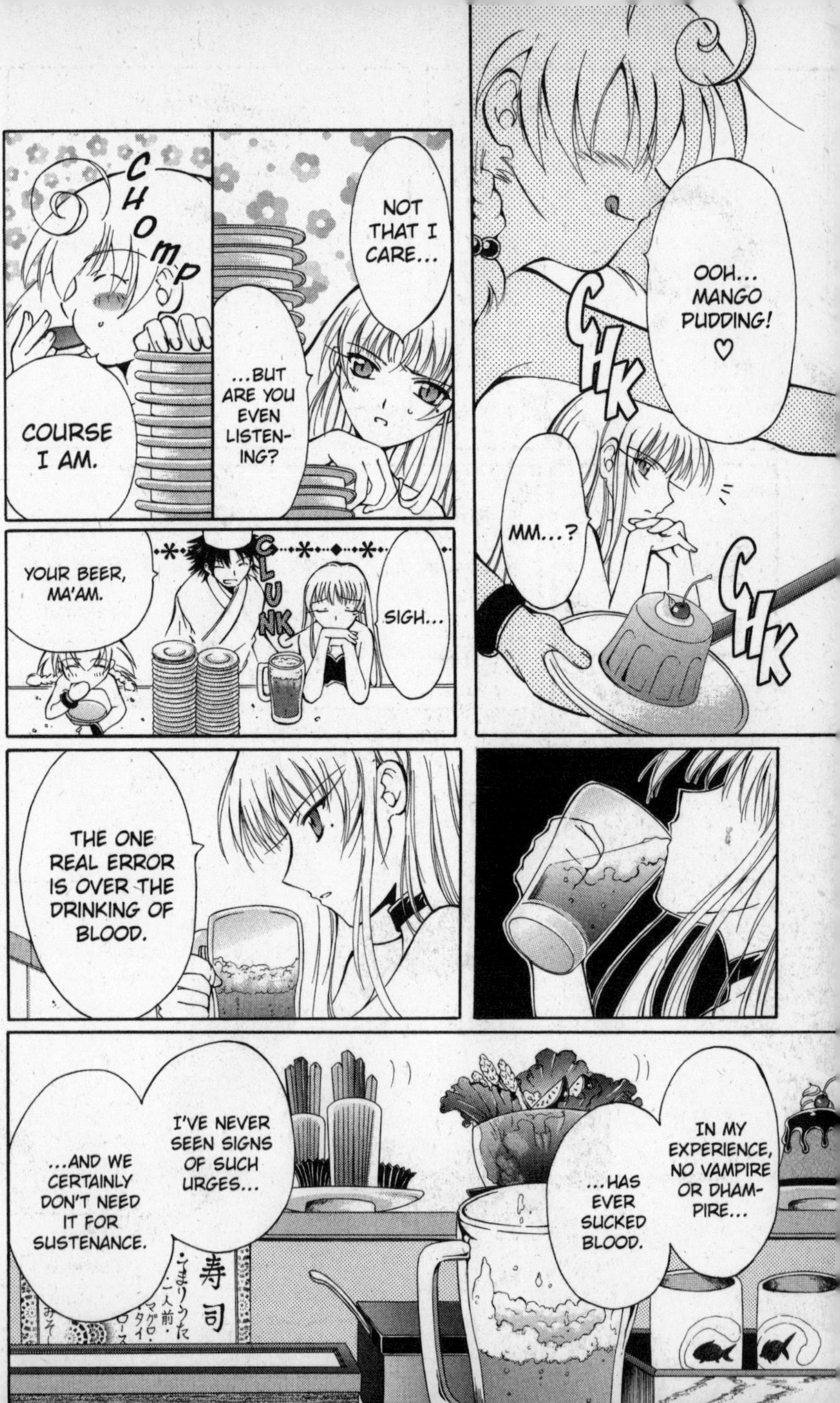
OOH... MANGO PUDDING! ♡
CHK
MM...?
CHK
NOT THAT I CARE...
...BUT ARE YOU EVEN LISTENING?
CHOMP
COURSE I AM.
SIGH...
CLUNK
YOUR BEER, MA'AM.
THE ONE REAL ERROR IS OVER THE DRINKING OF BLOOD.
IN MY EXPERIENCE, NO VAMPIRE OR DHAMPIRE...
...HAS EVER SUCKED BLOOD.
I'VE NEVER SEEN SIGNS OF SUCH URGES...
...AND WE CERTAINLY DON'T NEED IT FOR SUSTENANCE.
寿司

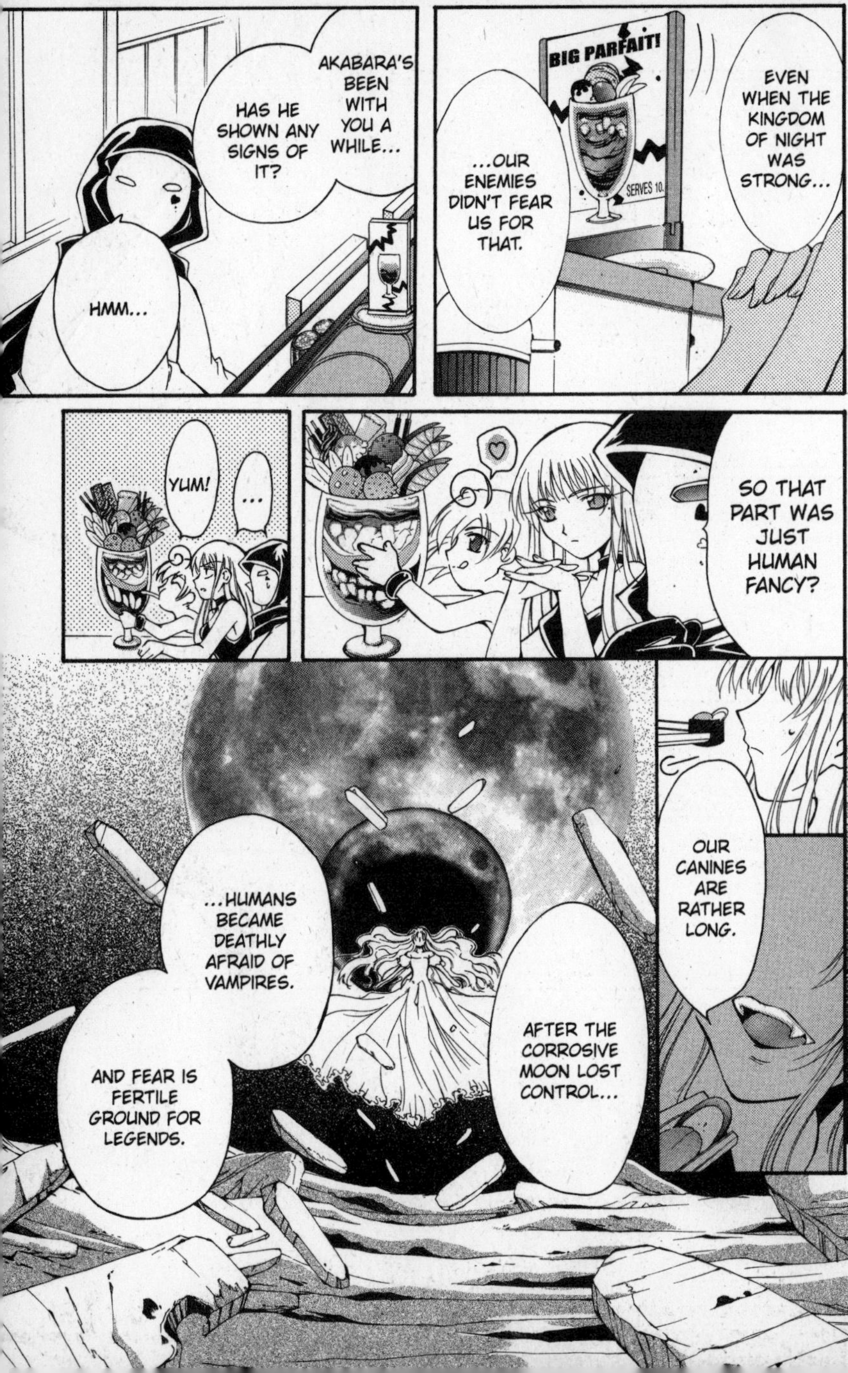
EVEN WHEN THE KINGDOM OF NIGHT WAS STRONG...
BIG PARFAIT!
SERVES 10.
...OUR ENEMIES DIDN'T FEAR US FOR THAT.
AKABARA'S BEEN WITH YOU A WHILE...
HAS HE SHOWN ANY SIGNS OF IT?
HMM...
SO THAT PART WAS JUST HUMAN FANCY?
...
YUM!
OUR CANINES ARE RATHER LONG.
AFTER THE CORROSIVE MOON LOST CONTROL...
...HUMANS BECAME DEATHLY AFRAID OF VAMPIRES.
AND FEAR IS FERTILE GROUND FOR LEGENDS.

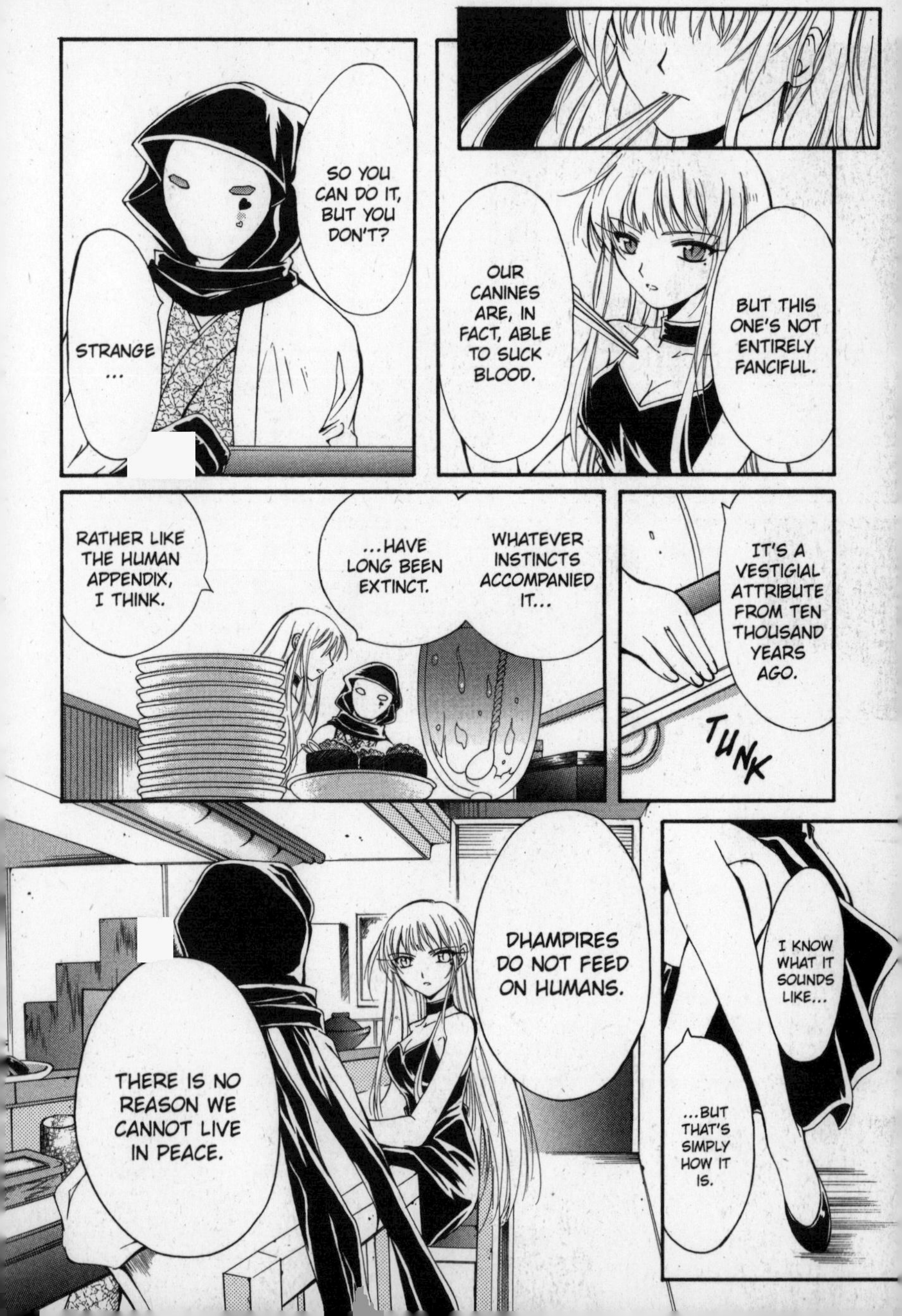
BUT THIS ONE'S NOT ENTIRELY FANCIFUL.
OUR CANINES ARE, IN FACT, ABLE TO SUCK BLOOD.
SO YOU CAN DO IT, BUT YOU DON'T?
STRANGE ...
IT'S A VESTIGIAL ATTRIBUTE FROM TEN THOUSAND YEARS AGO.
TUNK
WHATEVER INSTINCTS ACCOMPANIED IT...
...HAVE LONG BEEN EXTINCT.
RATHER LIKE THE HUMAN APPENDIX, I THINK.
I KNOW WHAT IT SOUNDS LIKE...
...BUT THAT'S SIMPLY HOW IT IS.
DHAMPIRES DO NOT FEED ON HUMANS.
THERE IS NO REASON WE CANNOT LIVE IN PEACE.

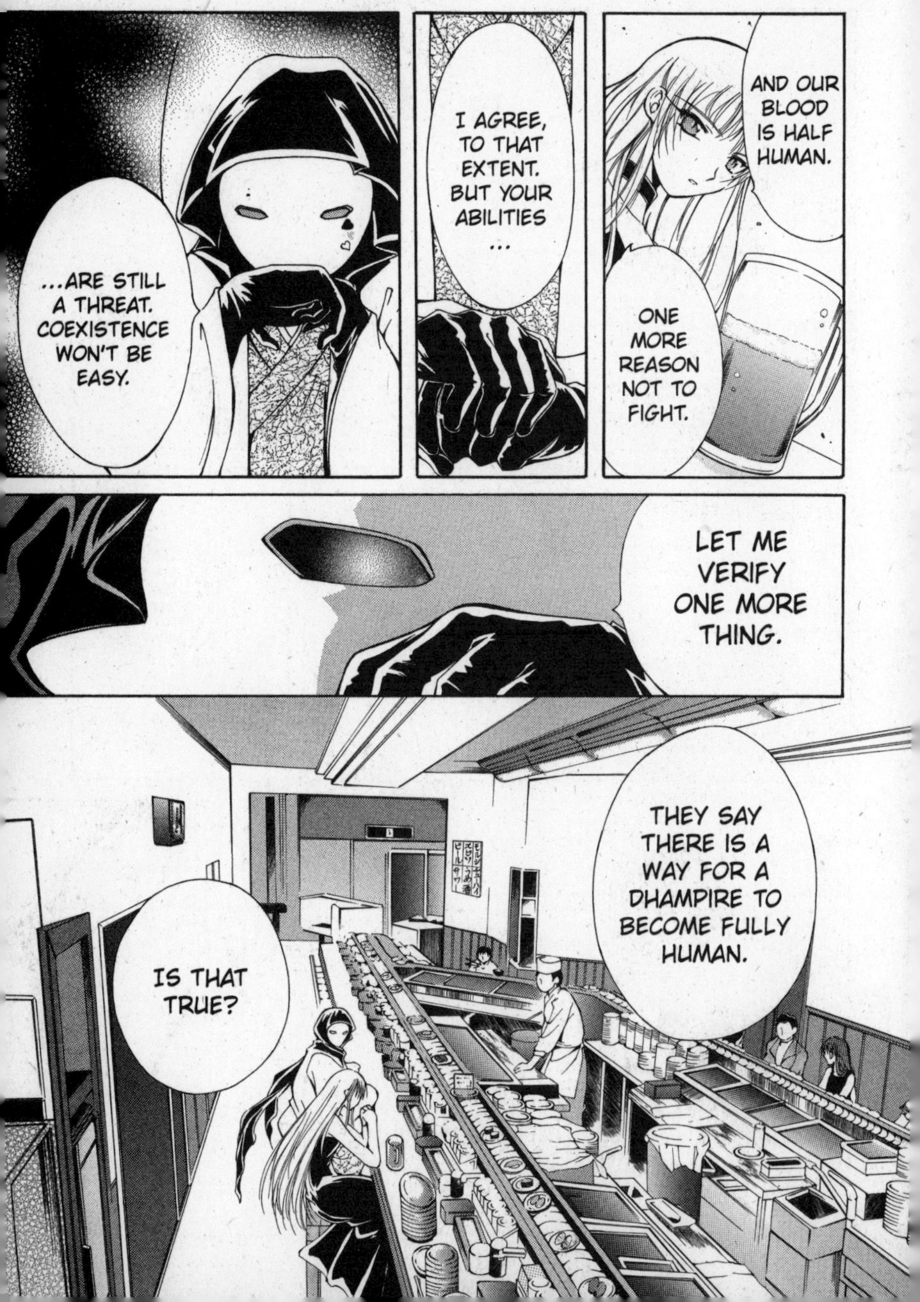
AND OUR BLOOD IS HALF HUMAN.
ONE MORE REASON NOT TO FIGHT.
I AGREE, TO THAT EXTENT. BUT YOUR ABILITIES ...
...ARE STILL A THREAT. COEXISTENCE WON'T BE EASY.
LET ME VERIFY ONE MORE THING.
THEY SAY THERE IS A WAY FOR A DHAMPIRE TO BECOME FULLY HUMAN.
IS THAT TRUE?

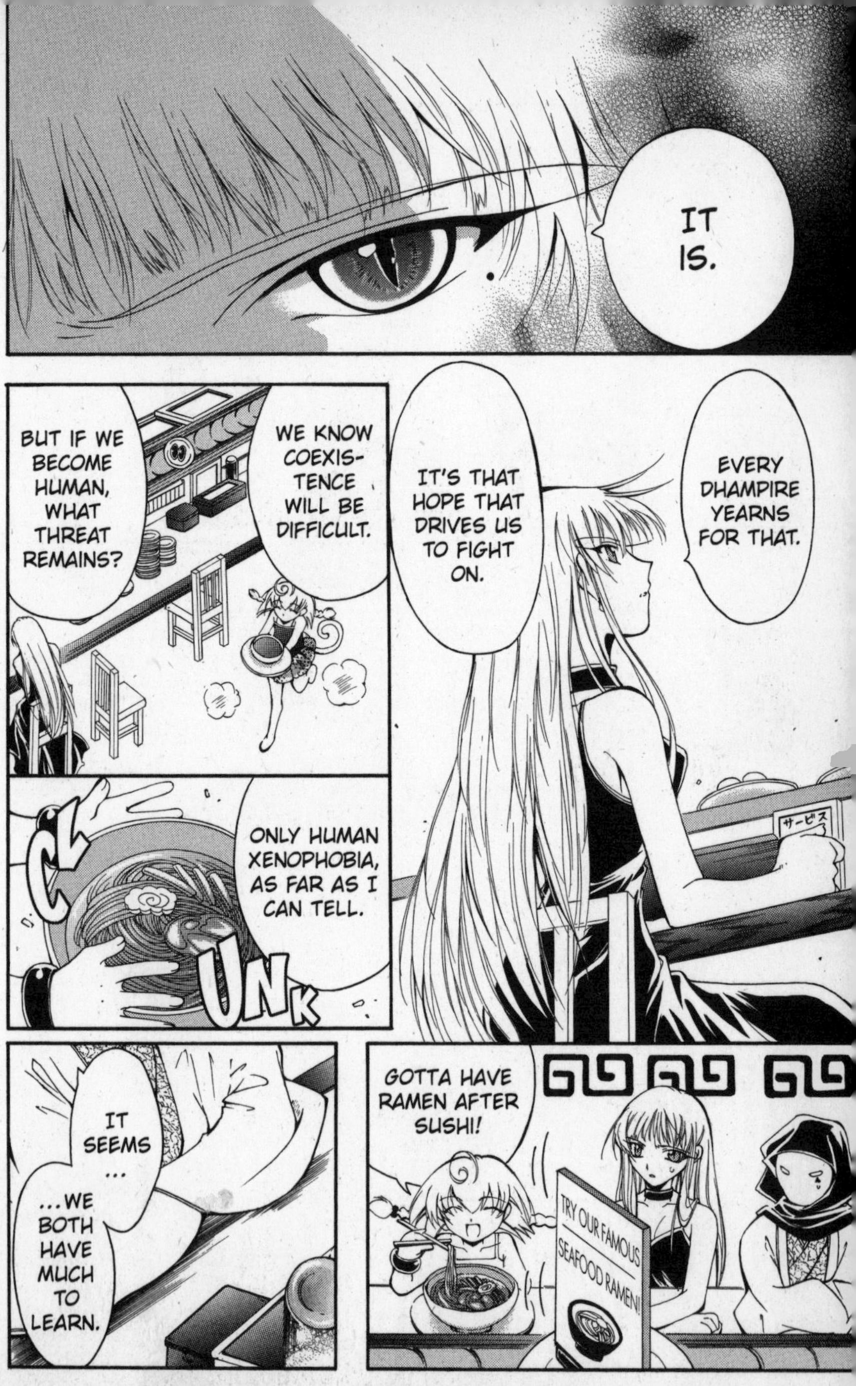
IT IS.
EVERY DHAMPIRE YEARNS FOR THAT.
IT'S THAT HOPE THAT DRIVES US TO FIGHT ON.
サービス
WE KNOW COEXIS-TENCE WILL BE DIFFICULT.
BUT IF WE BECOME HUMAN, WHAT THREAT REMAINS?
ONLY HUMAN XENOPHOBIA, AS FAR AS I CAN TELL.
CLUNK
GOTTA HAVE RAMEN AFTER SUSHI!
TRY OUR FAMOUS SEAFOOD RAMEN!
IT SEEMS...
...WE BOTH HAVE MUCH TO LEARN.

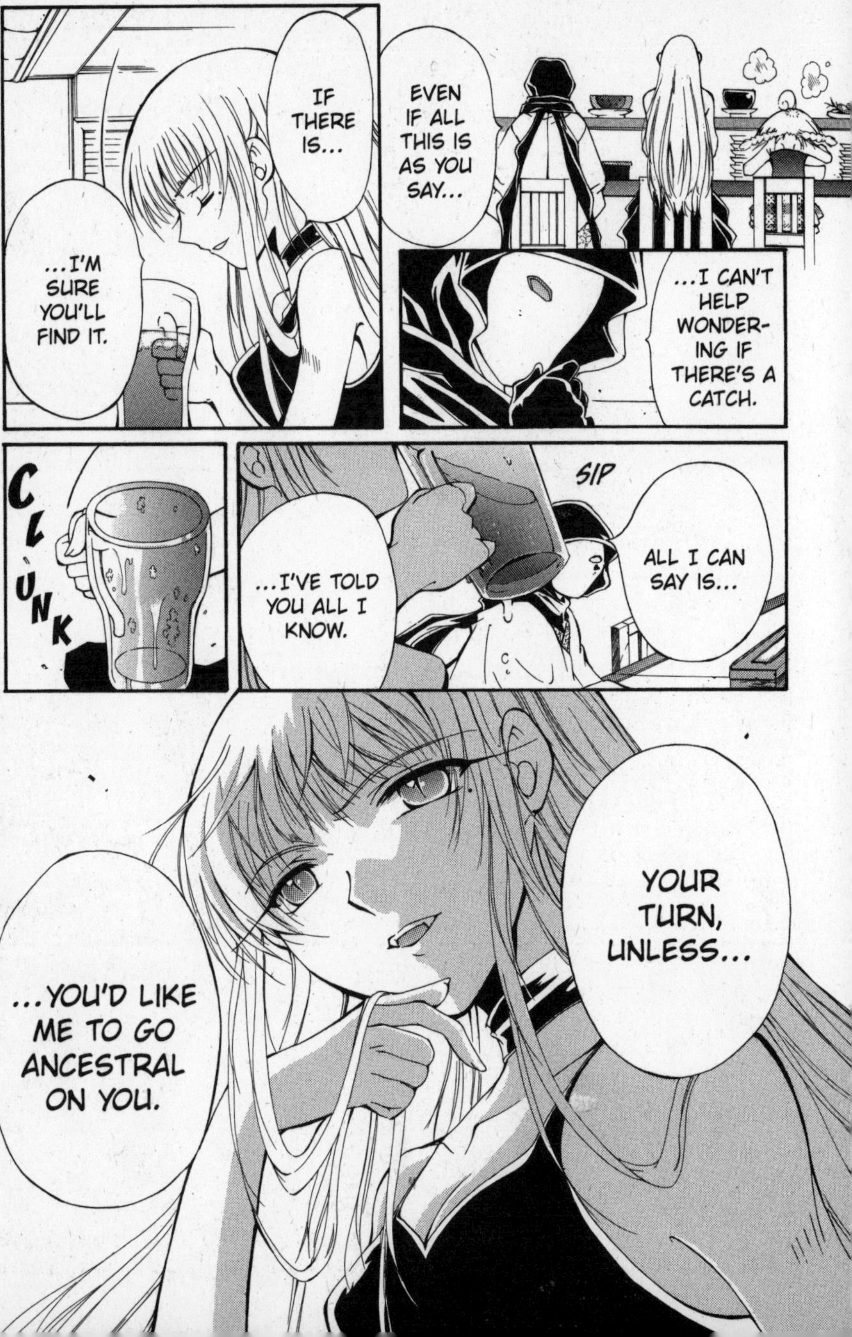
EVEN IF ALL THIS IS AS YOU SAY...
...I CAN'T HELP WONDERING IF THERE'S A CATCH.
IF THERE IS...
...I'M SURE YOU'LL FIND IT.
SIP
ALL I CAN SAY IS...
...I'VE TOLD YOU ALL I KNOW.
CLUNK
YOUR TURN, UNLESS...
...YOU'D LIKE ME TO GO ANCESTRAL ON YOU.

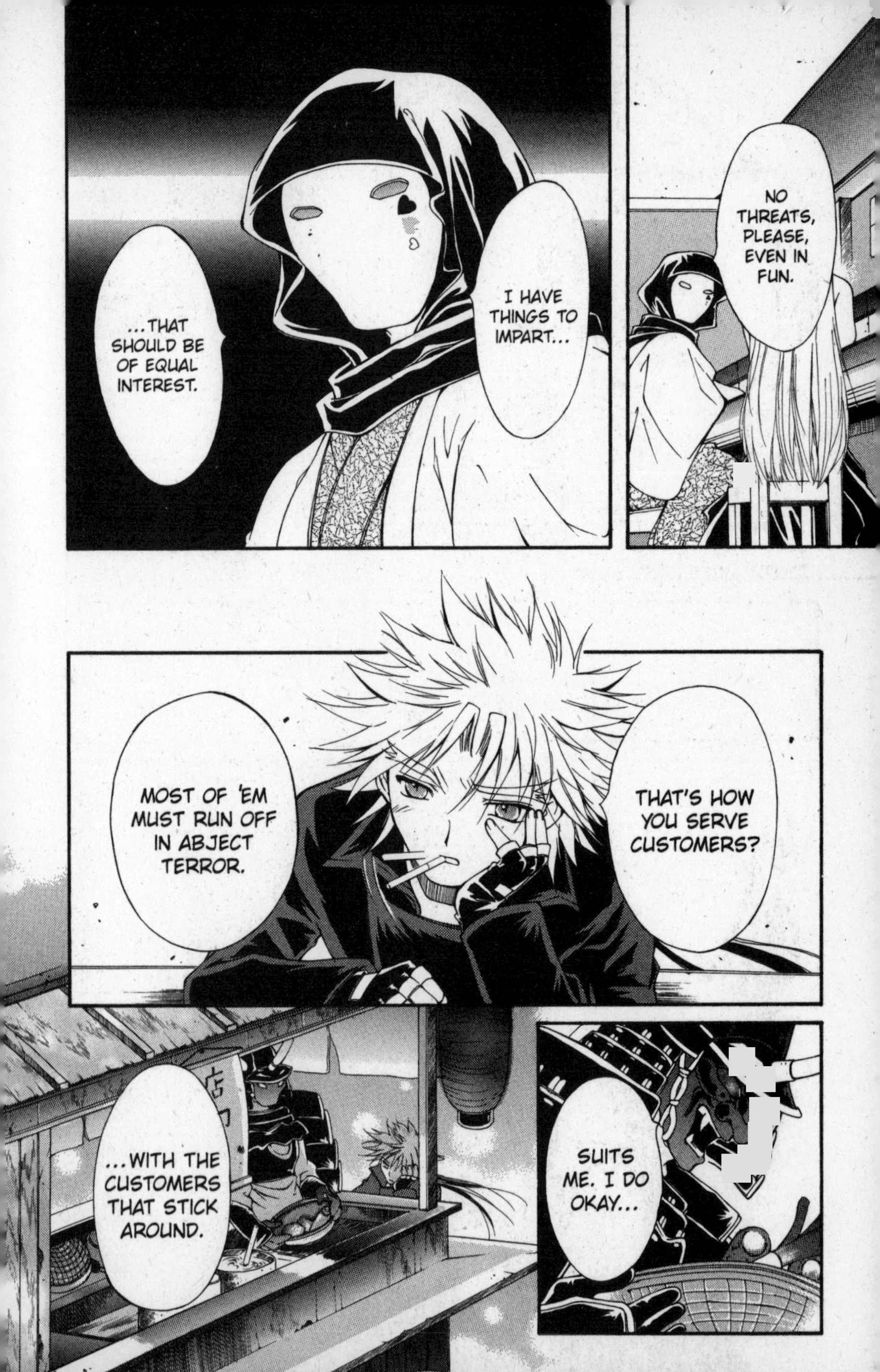
NO THREATS, PLEASE, EVEN IN FUN.
I HAVE THINGS TO IMPART...
...THAT SHOULD BE OF EQUAL INTEREST.
THAT'S HOW YOU SERVE CUSTOMERS?
MOST OF 'EM MUST RUN OFF IN ABJECT TERROR.
SUITS ME. I DO OKAY...
...WITH THE CUSTOMERS THAT STICK AROUND.

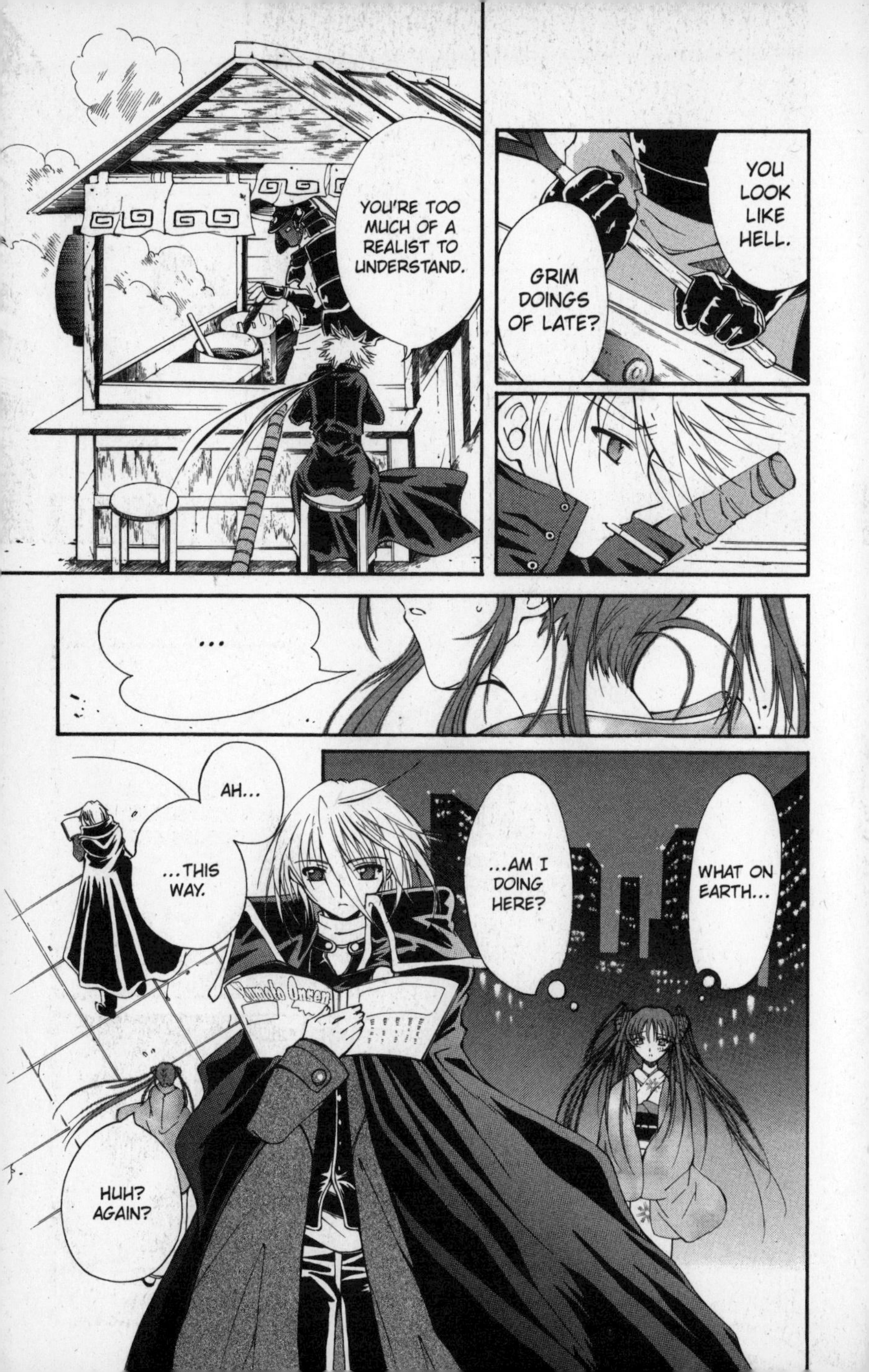
YOU LOOK LIKE HELL.
GRIM DOINGS OF LATE?
YOU'RE TOO MUCH OF A REALIST TO UNDERSTAND.
...
WHAT ON EARTH...
...AM I DOING HERE?
AH...
...THIS WAY.
HUH? AGAIN?

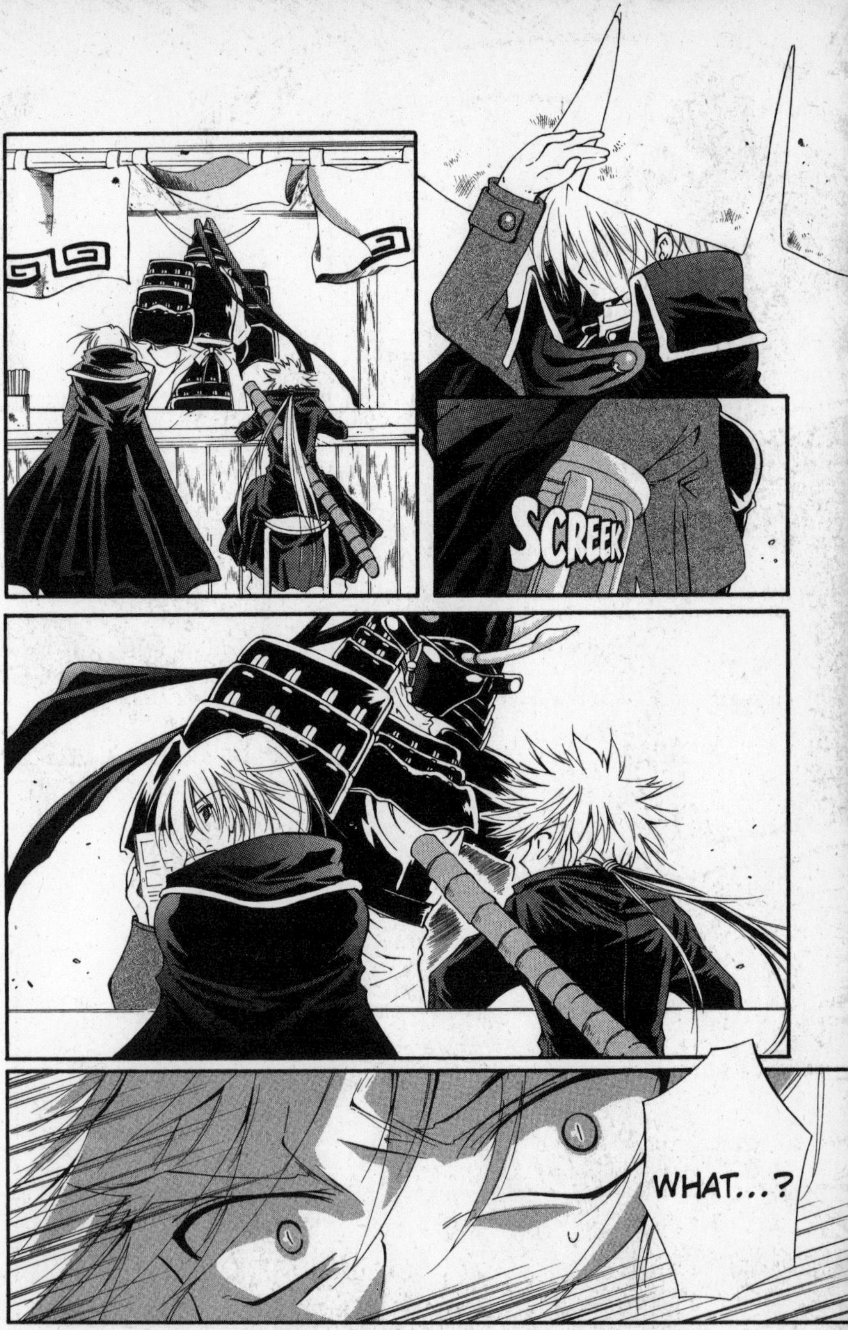
SCREEK
WHAT...?

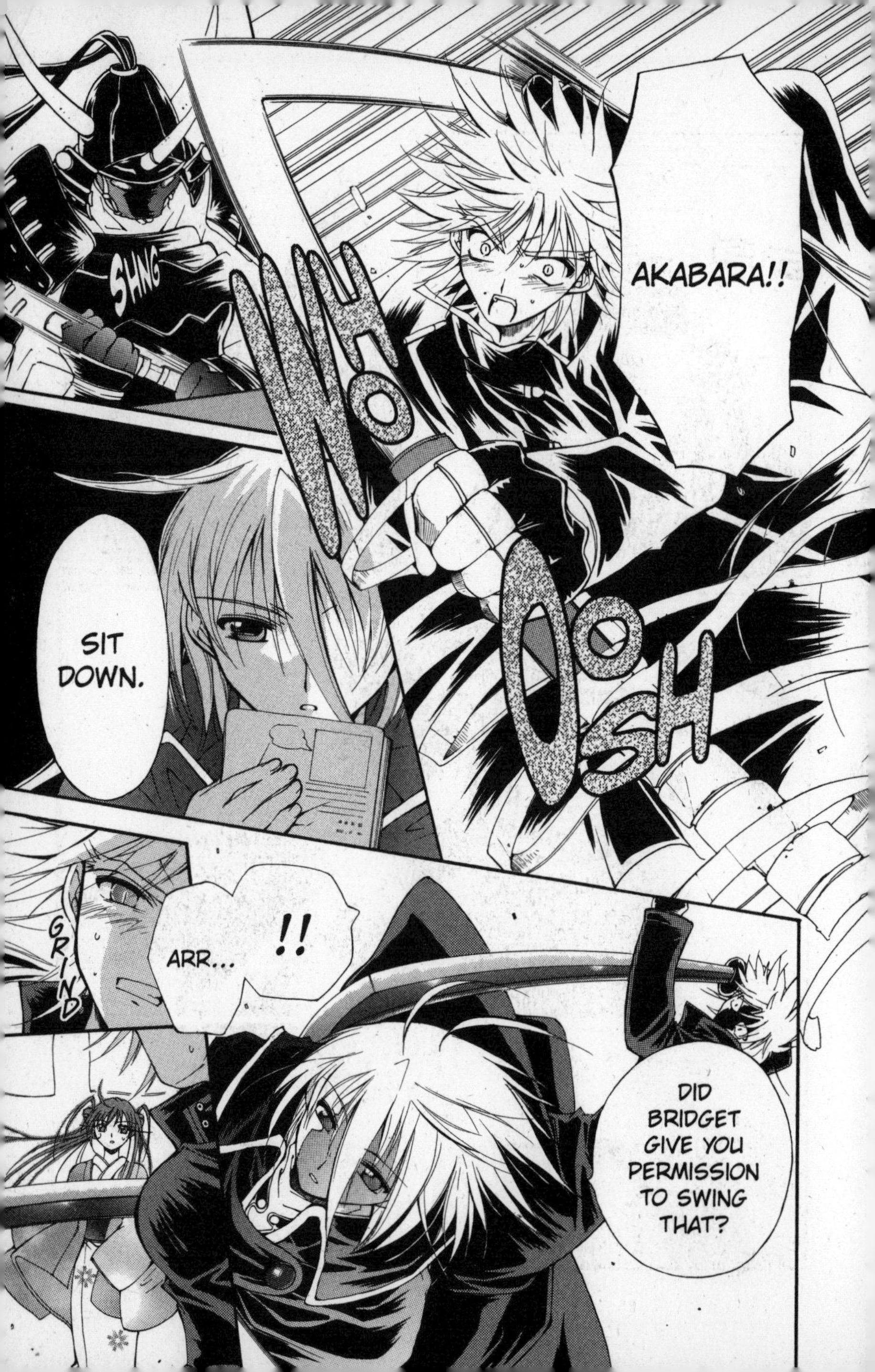
AKABARA!!
SHNG
WHOOOSH
SIT DOWN.
!!
ARR...
GRIND
DID BRIDGET GIVE YOU PERMISSION TO SWING THAT?

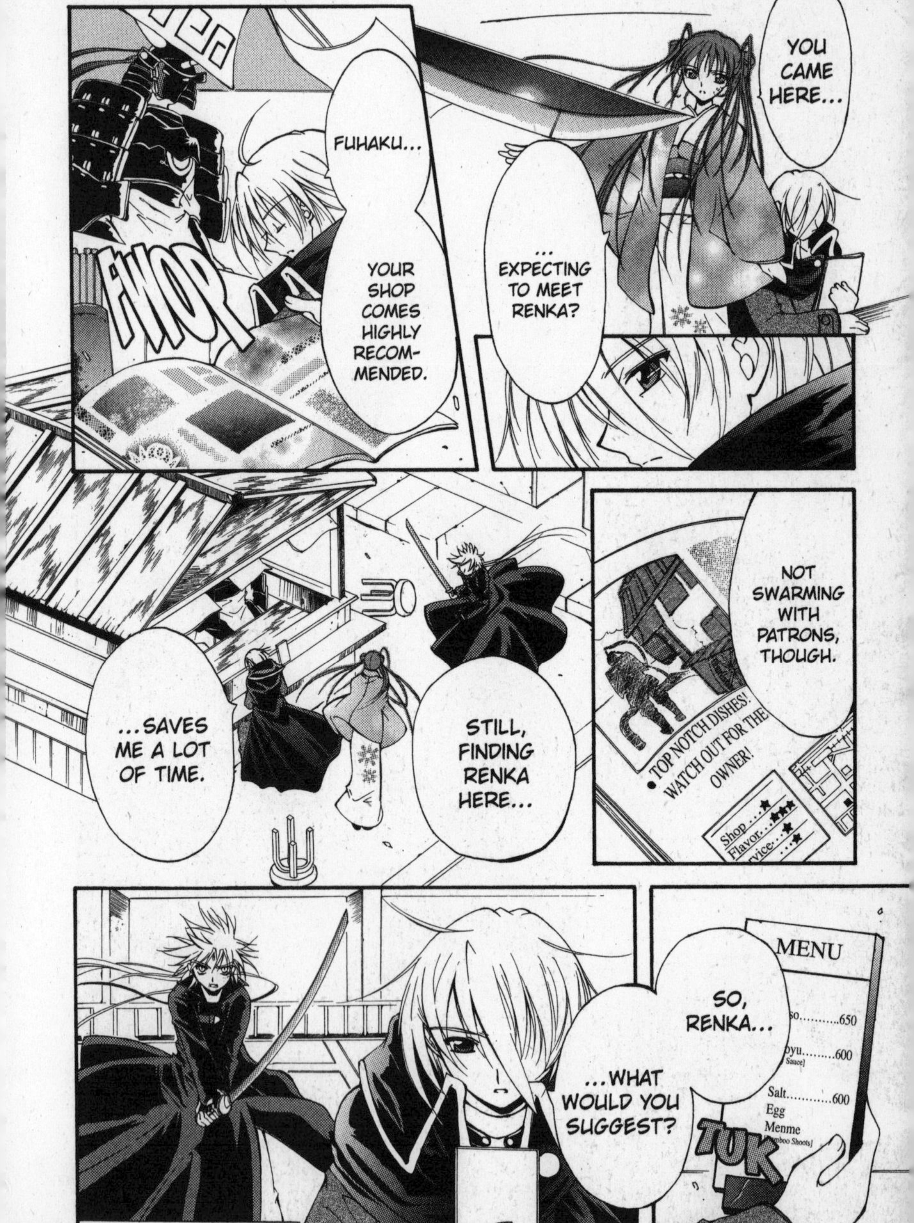
YOU CAME HERE...
...EXPECTING TO MEET RENKA?
FUHAKU...
YOUR SHOP COMES HIGHLY RECOM-MENDED.
FWOP
NOT SWARMING WITH PATRONS, THOUGH.
TOP NOTCH DISHES! WATCH OUT FOR THE OWNER!
STILL, FINDING RENKA HERE...
...SAVES ME A LOT OF TIME.
SO, RENKA...
...WHAT WOULD YOU SUGGEST?
MENU
Salt............600
Egg
Menme
TUK

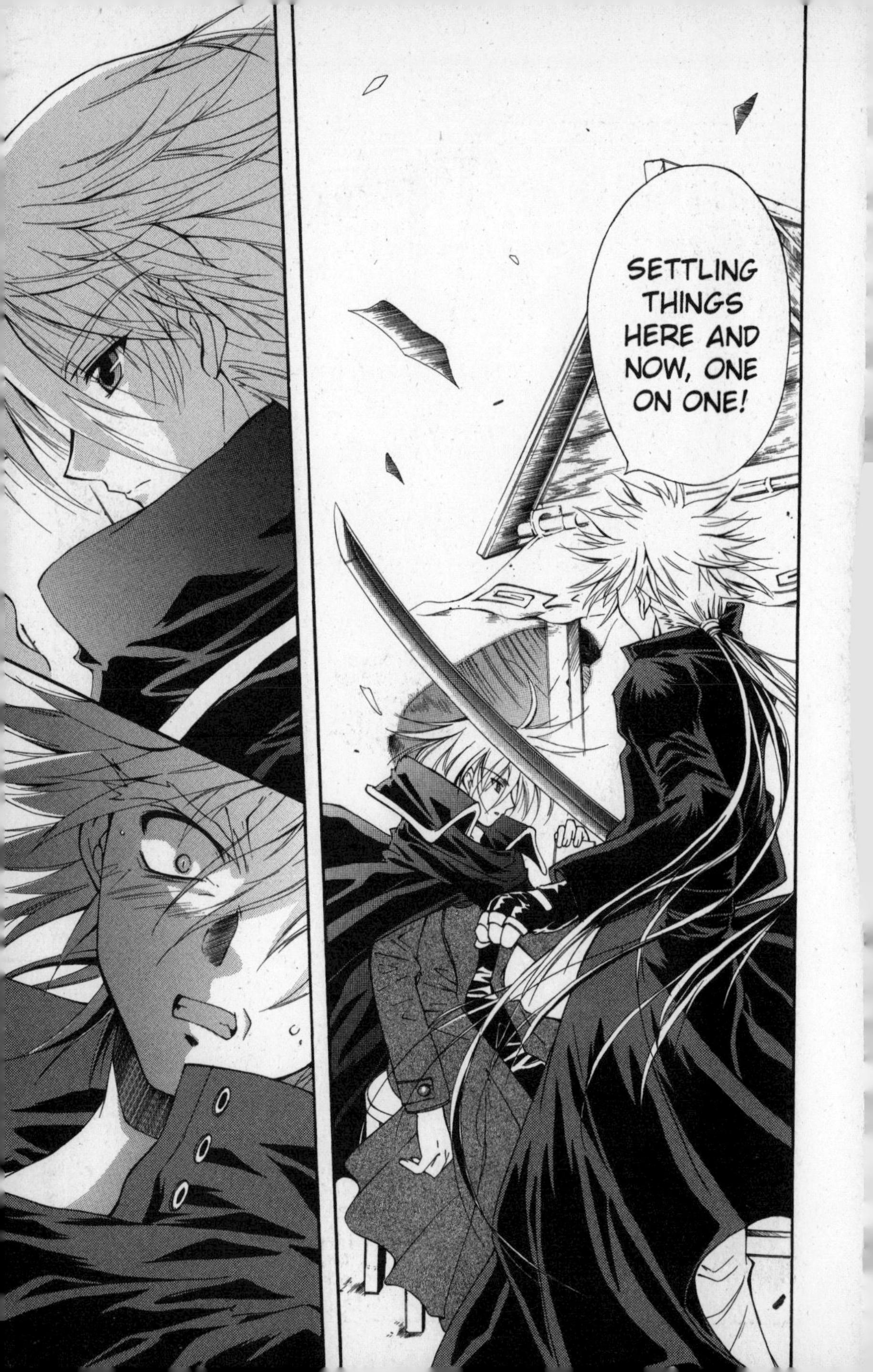
SETTLING THINGS HERE AND NOW, ONE ON ONE!

THE RECORD OF A

FALLEN VAMPIRE

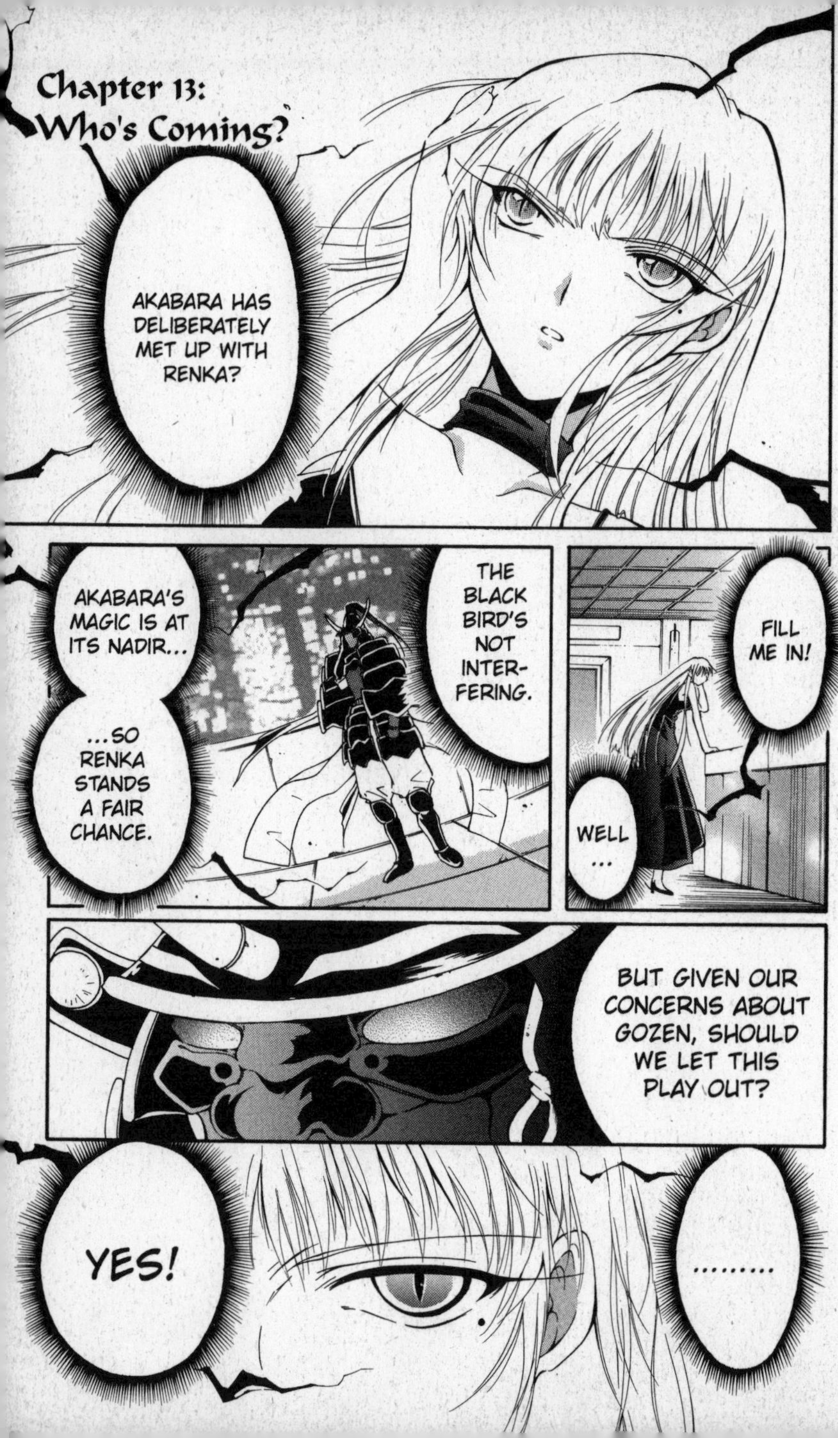
Chapter 13:
Who's Coming?
AKABARA HAS DELIBERATELY MET UP WITH RENKA?
FILL ME IN!
WELL ...
THE BLACK BIRD'S NOT INTER-FERING.
AKABARA'S MAGIC IS AT ITS NADIR...
...SO RENKA STANDS A FAIR CHANCE.
BUT GIVEN OUR CONCERNS ABOUT GOZEN, SHOULD WE LET THIS PLAY OUT?
....
YES!

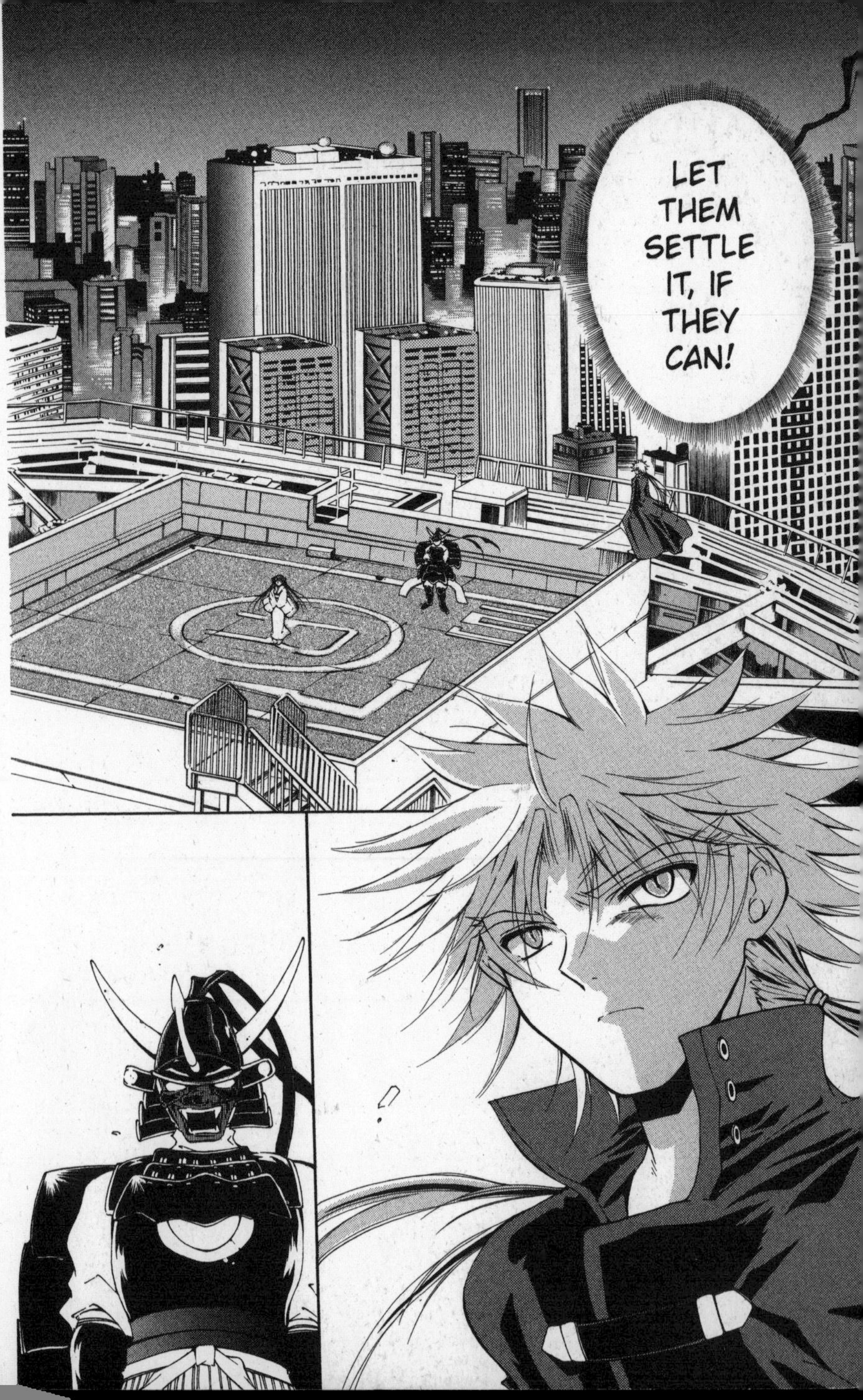
LET THEM SETTLE IT, IF THEY CAN!

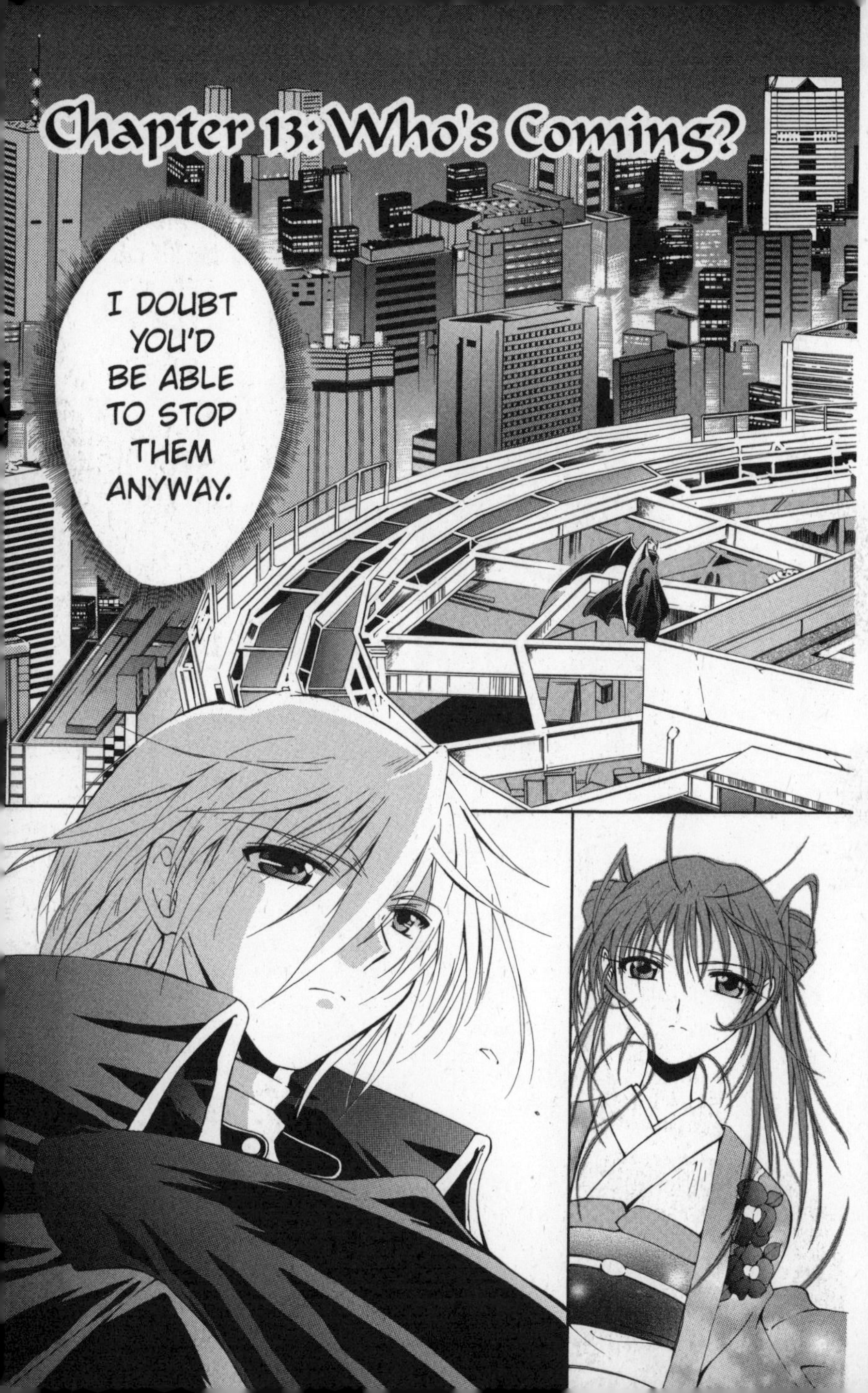
Chapter 13: Who's Coming?
I DOUBT YOU'D BE ABLE TO STOP THEM ANYWAY.

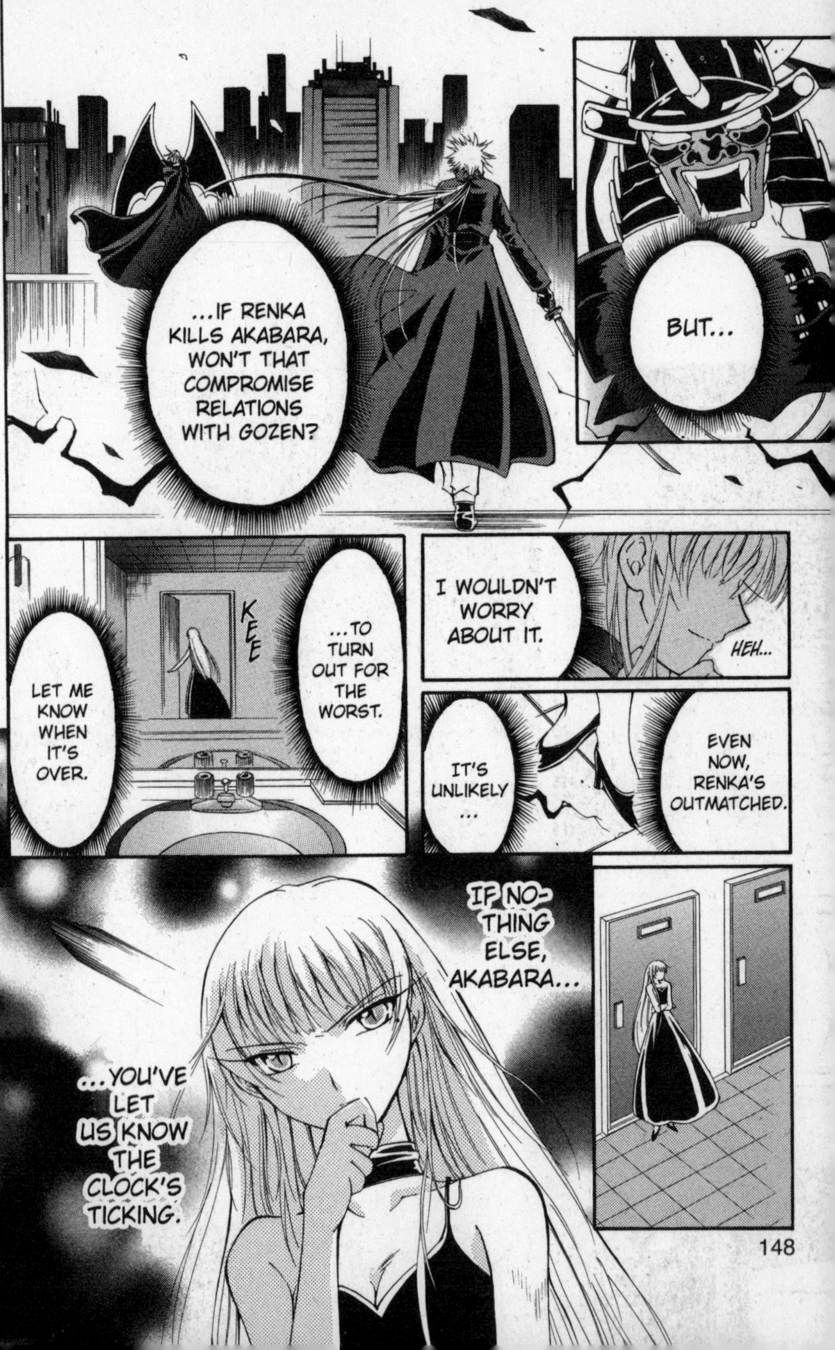
BUT...
...IF RENKA KILLS AKABARA, WON'T THAT COMPROMISE RELATIONS WITH GOZEN?
I WOULDN'T WORRY ABOUT IT.
HEH...
EVEN NOW, RENKA'S OUTMATCHED.
IT'S UNLIKELY ...
...TO TURN OUT FOR THE WORST.
KEE
LET ME KNOW WHEN IT'S OVER.
IF NO-THING ELSE, AKABARA...
...YOU'VE LET US KNOW THE CLOCK'S TICKING.

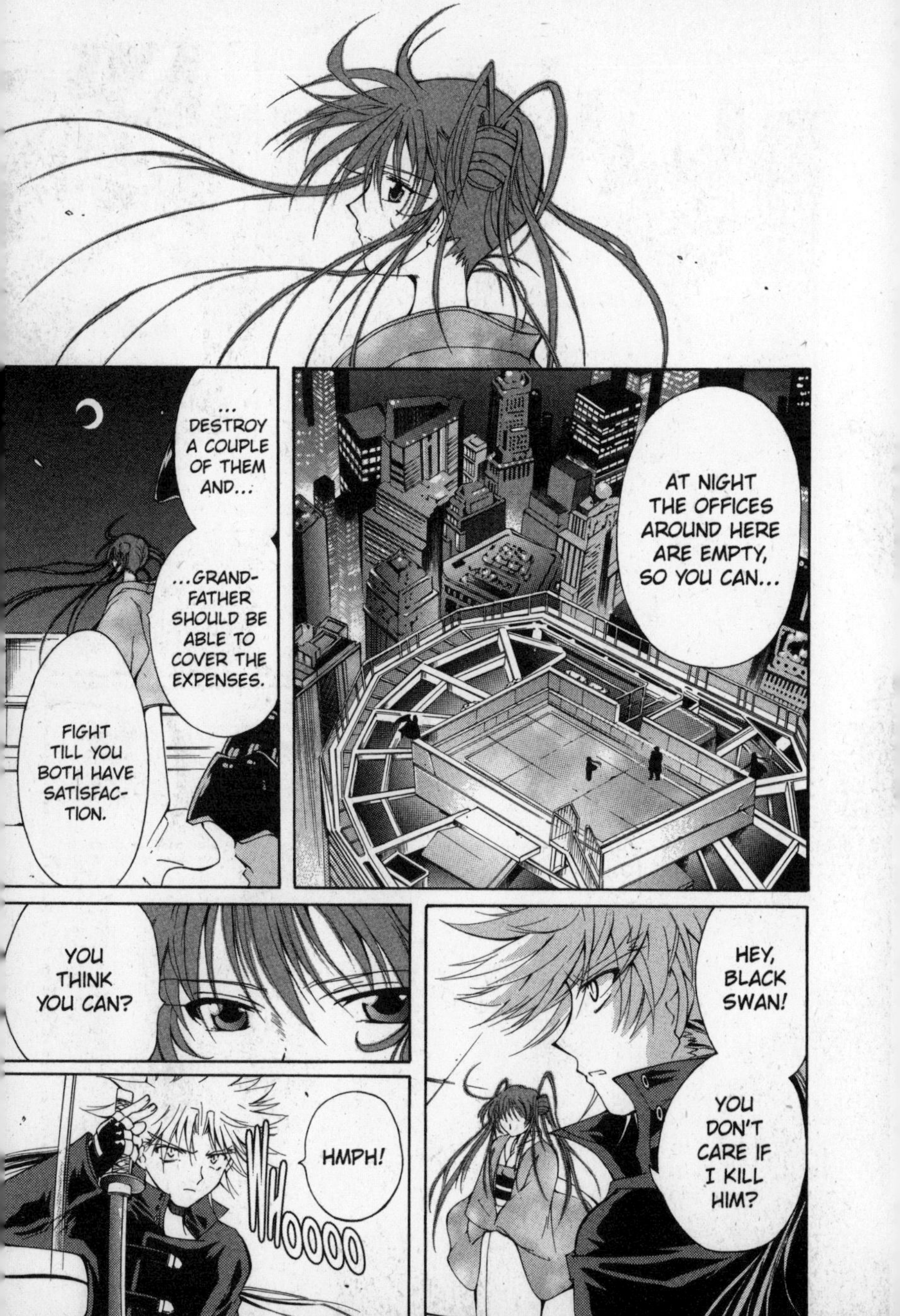
AT NIGHT THE OFFICES AROUND HERE ARE EMPTY, SO YOU CAN...
...DESTROY A COUPLE OF THEM AND...
...GRAND-FATHER SHOULD BE ABLE TO COVER THE EXPENSES.
FIGHT TILL YOU BOTH HAVE SATISFACTION.
HEY, BLACK SWAN!
YOU DON'T CARE IF I KILL HIM?
YOU THINK YOU CAN?
HMPH!
WHOOOO

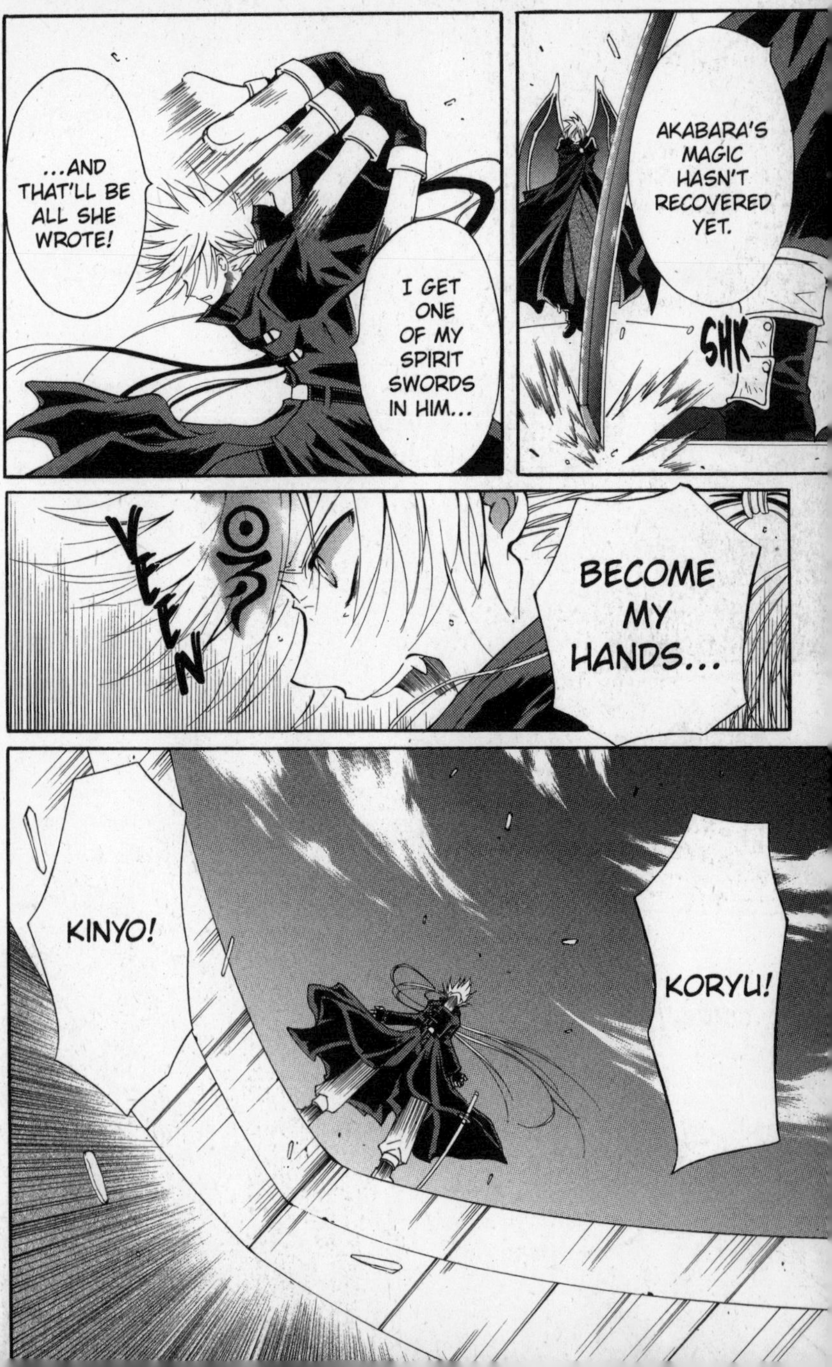
AKABARA'S MAGIC HASN'T RECOVERED YET.
SHK
I GET ONE OF MY SPIRIT SWORDS IN HIM...
...AND THAT'LL BE ALL SHE WROTE!
BECOME MY HANDS...
YEEEN
KORYU!
KINYO!

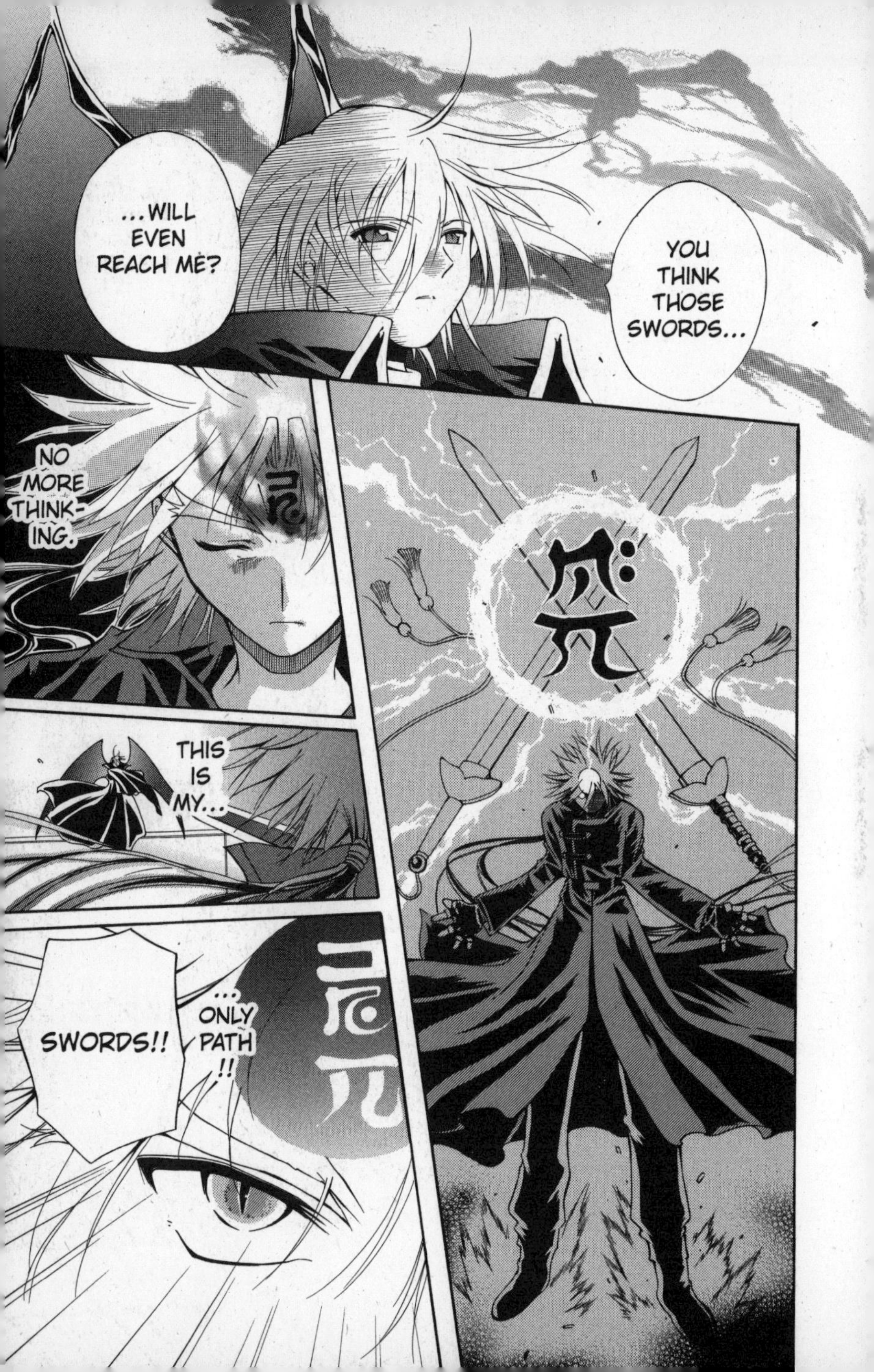
YOU THINK THOSE SWORDS...
...WILL EVEN REACH ME?
NO MORE THINK-ING.
THIS IS MY...
...ONLY PATH!!
SWORDS!!

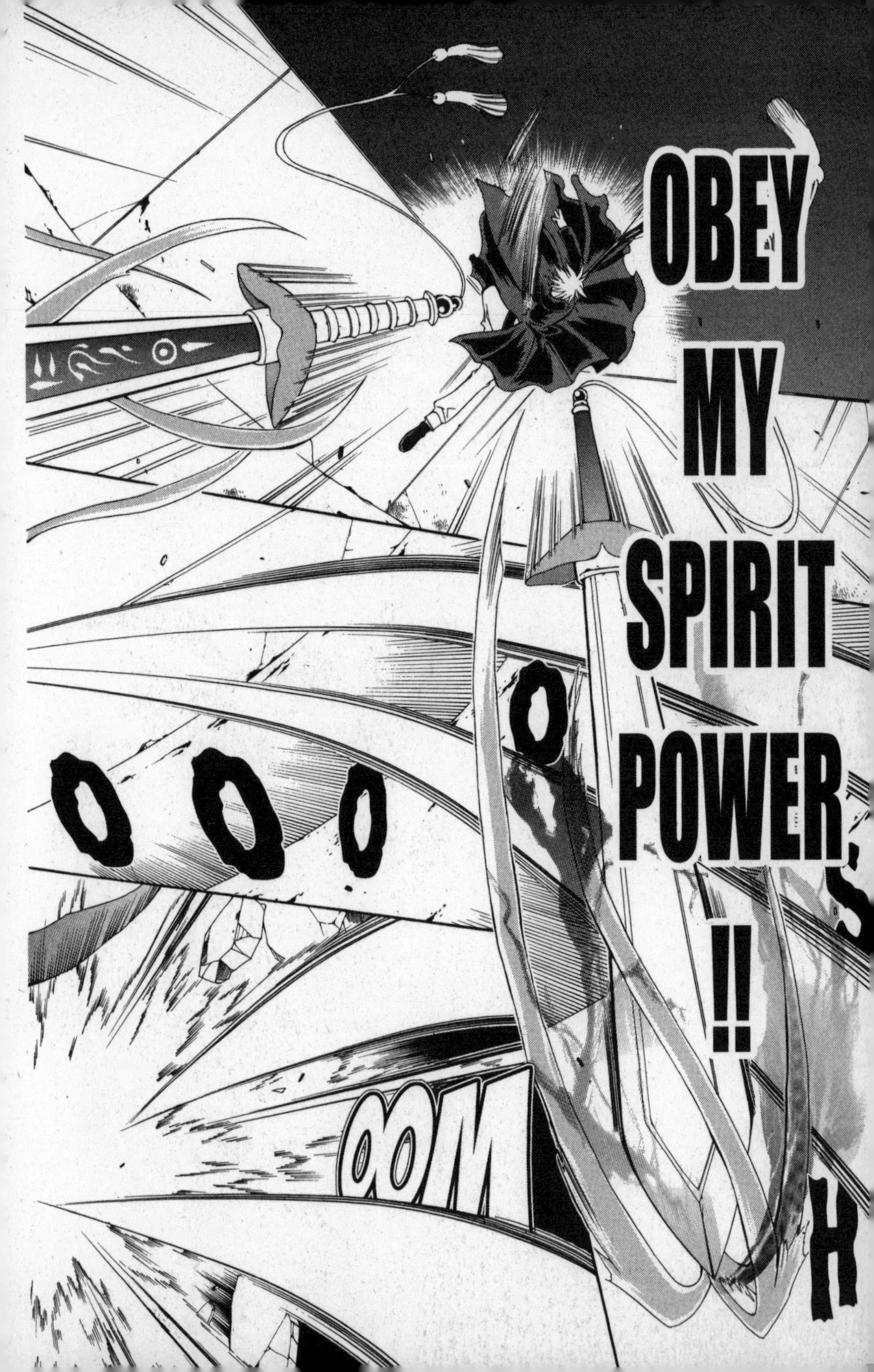
OBEY MY SPIRIT POWER!!

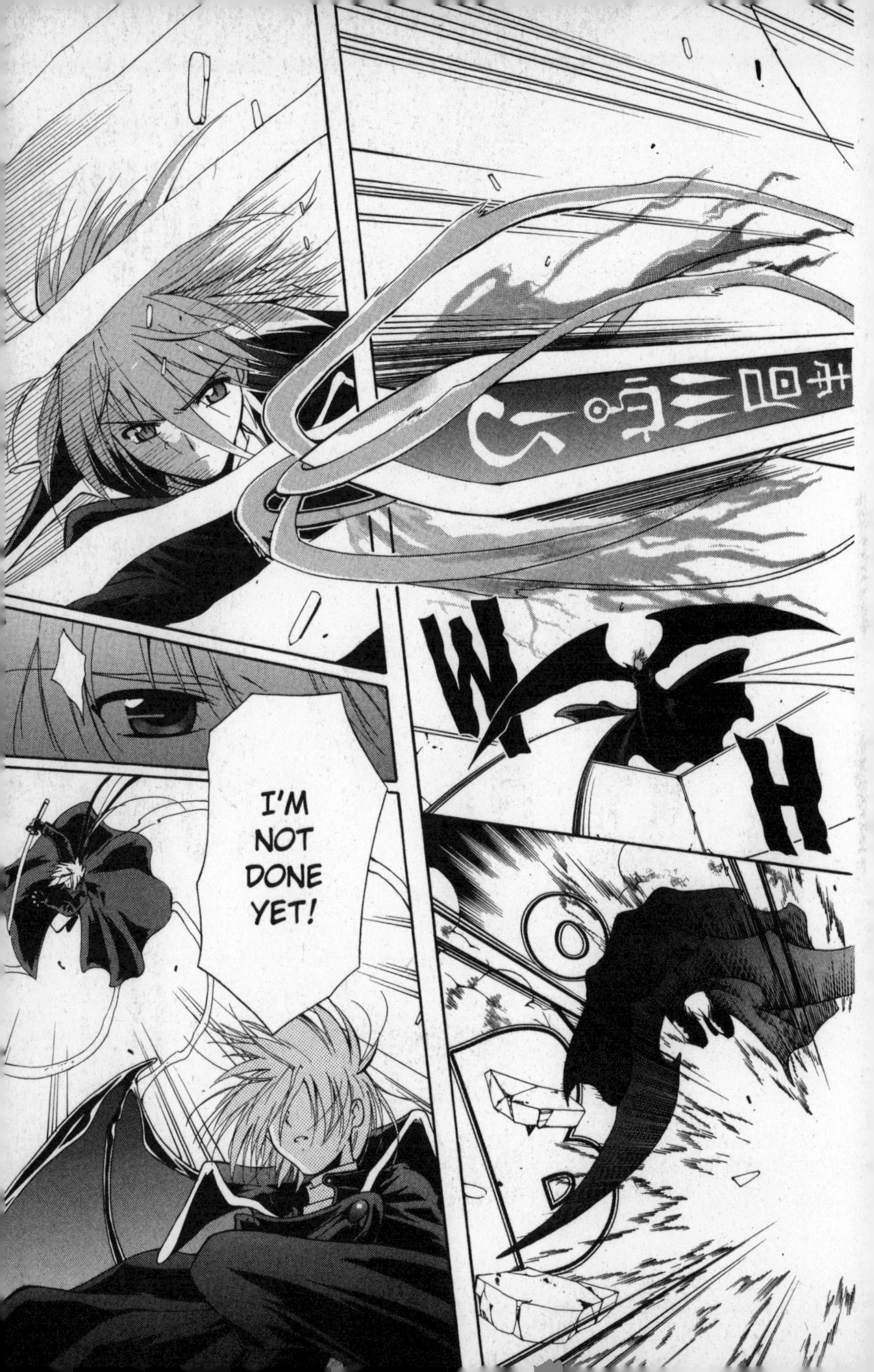
I'M NOT DONE YET!

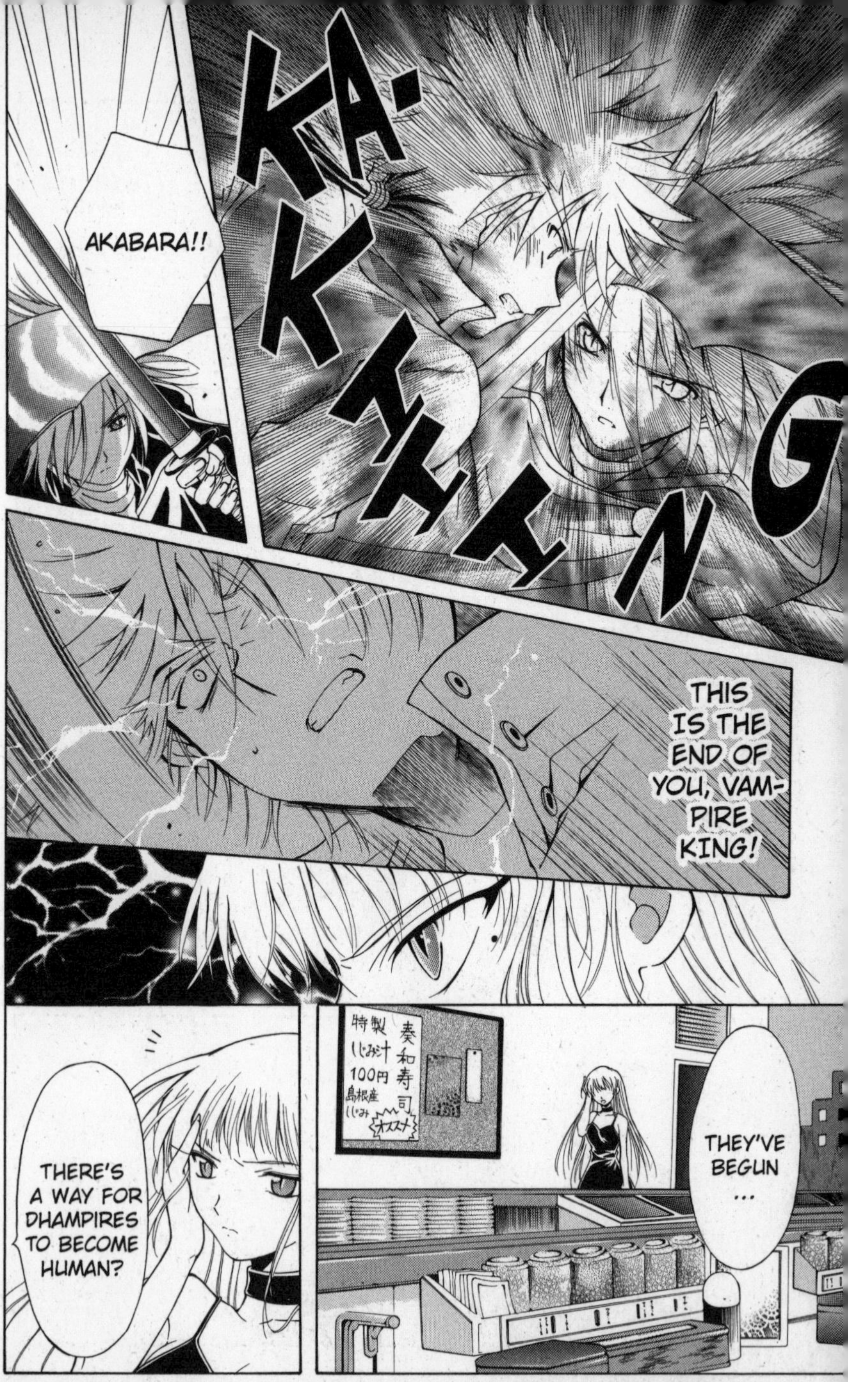
KA-KKHHHNG
AKABARA!!
THIS IS THE END OF YOU, VAMPIRE KING!
奏和寿司
特製
しじみ汁
100円
島根産
しじみ
オススメ
THEY'VE BEGUN ...
THERE'S A WAY FOR DHAMPIRES TO BECOME HUMAN?

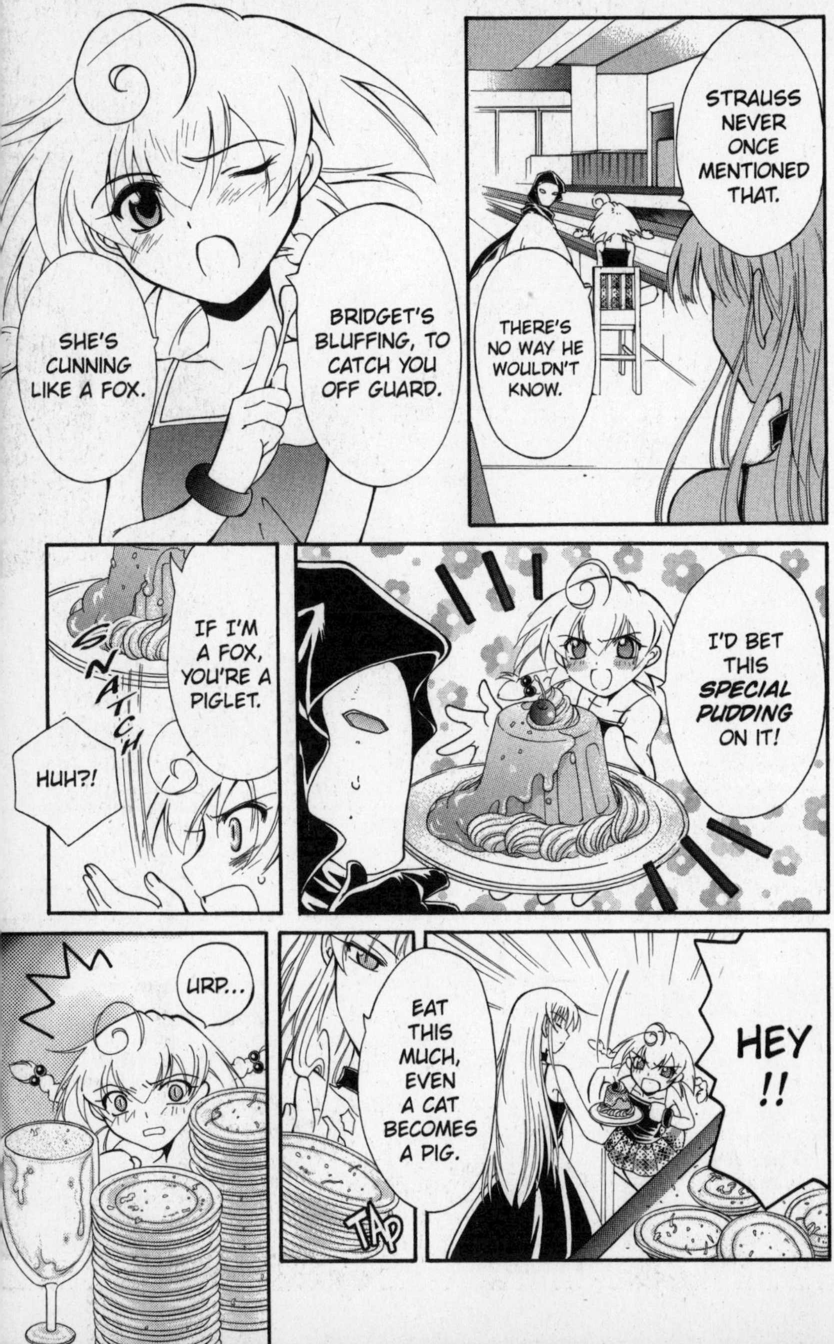
STRAUSS NEVER ONCE MENTIONED THAT.
THERE'S NO WAY HE WOULDN'T KNOW.
BRIDGET'S BLUFFING, TO CATCH YOU OFF GUARD.
SHE'S CUNNING LIKE A FOX.
I'D BET THIS SPECIAL PUDDING ON IT!
IF I'M A FOX, YOU'RE A PIGLET.
SNATCH
HUH?!
HEY!!
EAT THIS MUCH, EVEN A CAT BECOMES A PIG.
TAP
URP...

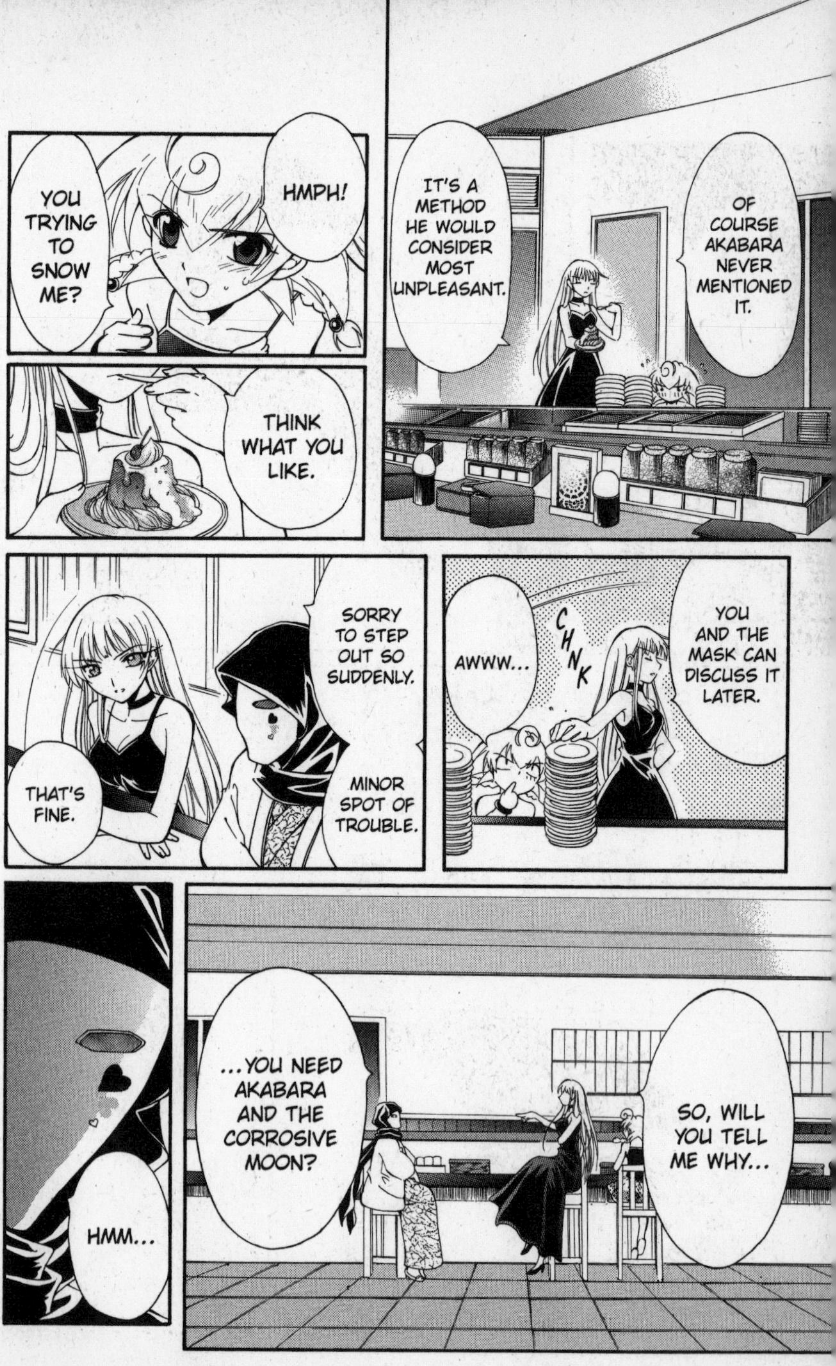
OF COURSE AKABARA NEVER MENTIONED IT.
IT'S A METHOD HE WOULD CONSIDER MOST UNPLEASANT.
HMPH!
YOU TRYING TO SNOW ME?
THINK WHAT YOU LIKE.
YOU AND THE MASK CAN DISCUSS IT LATER.
CHNK
AWWW...
SORRY TO STEP OUT SO SUDDENLY.
MINOR SPOT OF TROUBLE.
THAT'S FINE.
SO, WILL YOU TELL ME WHY...
...YOU NEED AKABARA AND THE CORROSIVE MOON?
HMM...

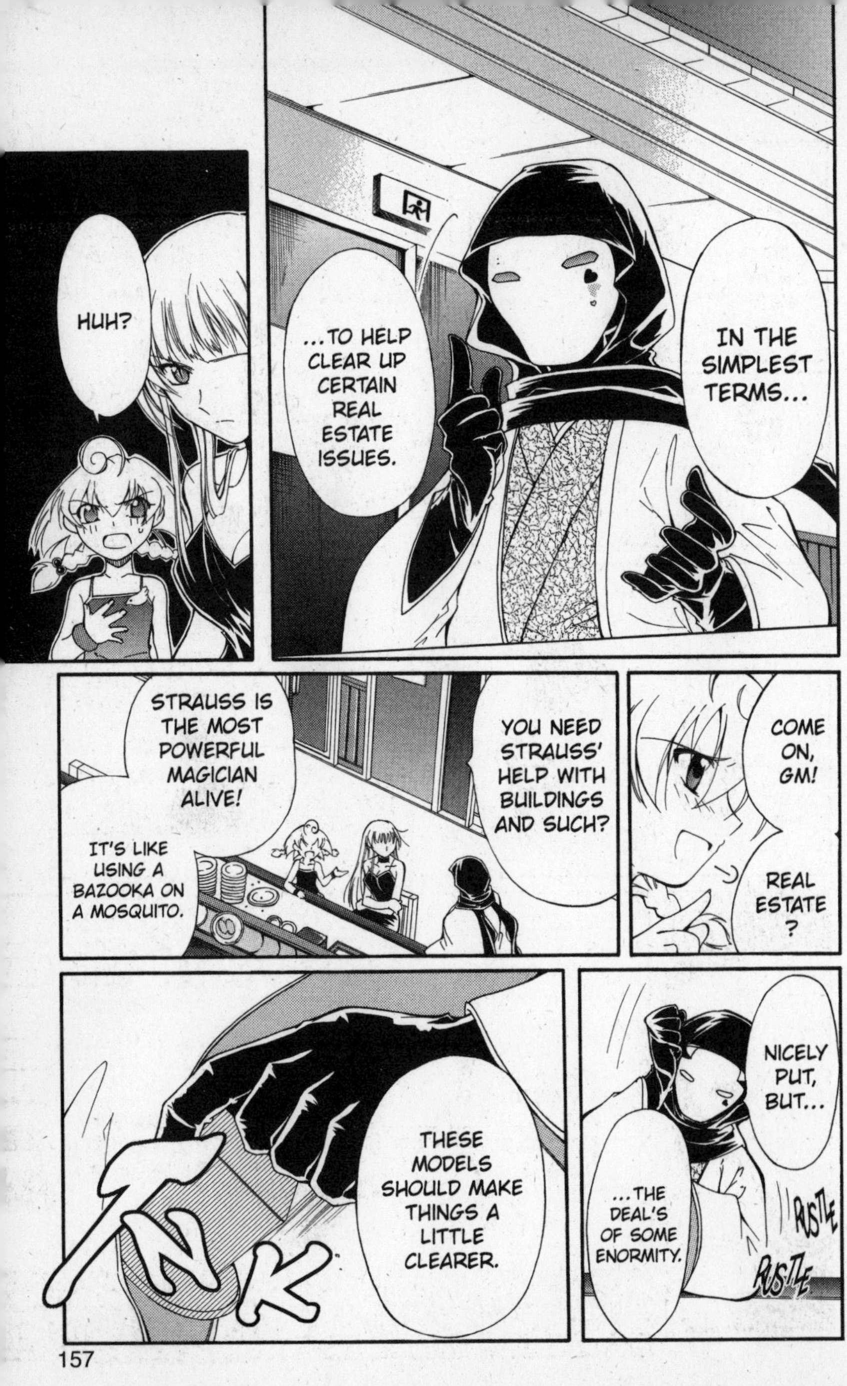
IN THE SIMPLEST TERMS...
...TO HELP CLEAR UP CERTAIN REAL ESTATE ISSUES.
HUH?
COME ON, GM!
REAL ESTATE ?
YOU NEED STRAUSS' HELP WITH BUILDINGS AND SUCH?
STRAUSS IS THE MOST POWERFUL MAGICIAN ALIVE!
IT'S LIKE USING A BAZOOKA ON A MOSQUITO.
NICELY PUT, BUT...
...THE DEAL'S OF SOME ENORMITY.
RUSTLE
RUSTLE
THESE MODELS SHOULD MAKE THINGS A LITTLE CLEARER.
NK

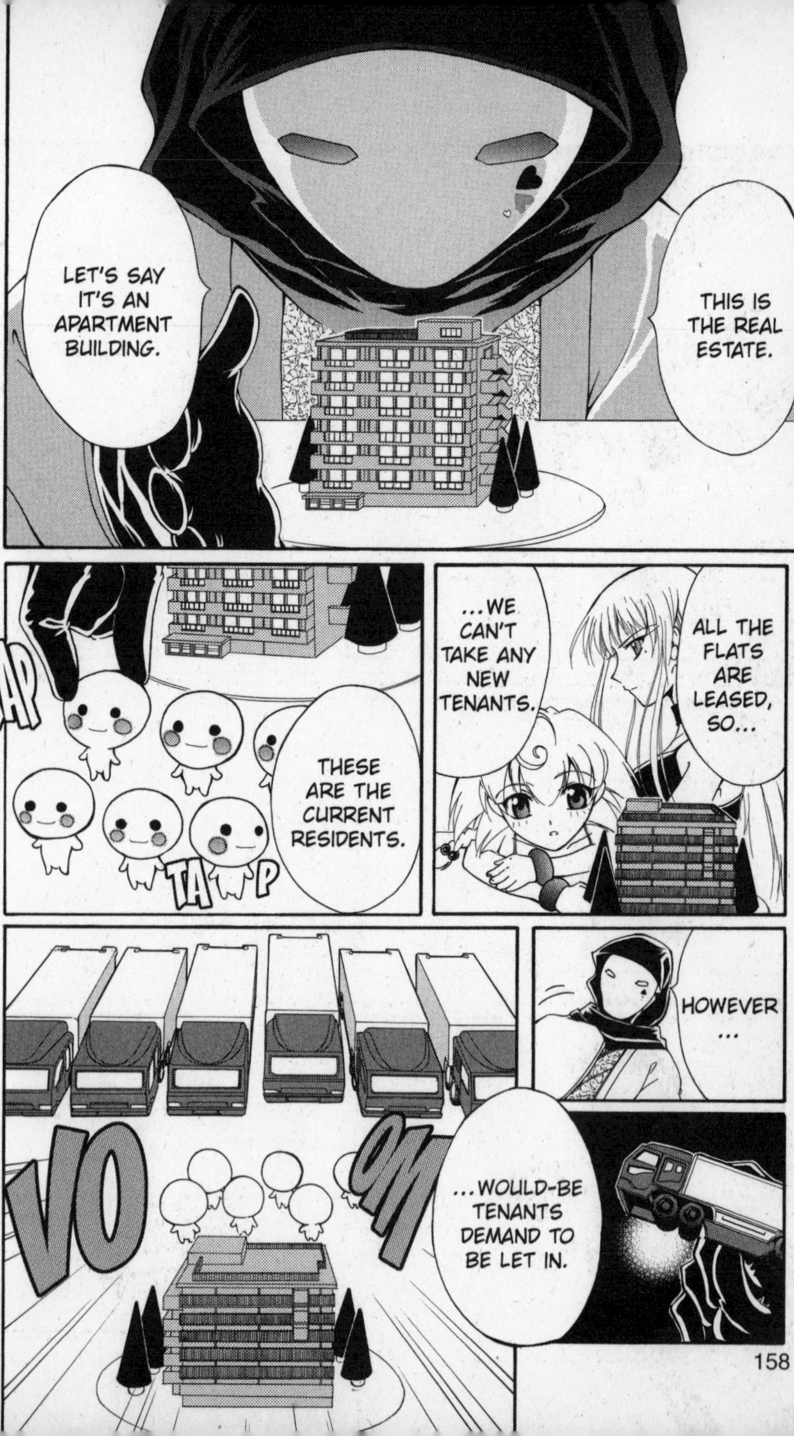
THIS IS THE REAL ESTATE.
LET'S SAY IT'S AN APARTMENT BUILDING.
ALL THE FLATS ARE LEASED, SO...
...WE CAN'T TAKE ANY NEW TENANTS.
THESE ARE THE CURRENT RESIDENTS.
TAP
TAP
HOWEVER ...
...WOULD-BE TENANTS DEMAND TO BE LET IN.
VOOM

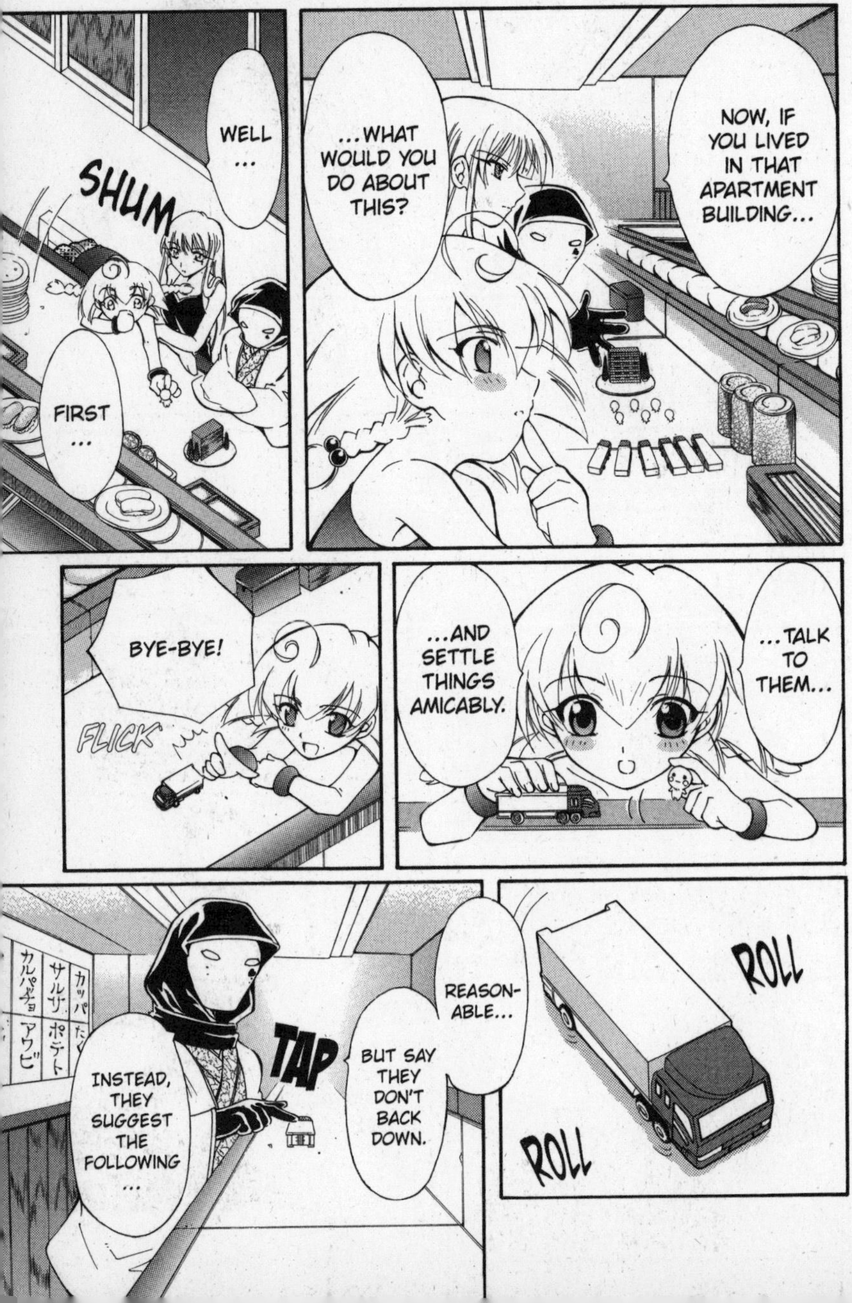
NOW, IF YOU LIVED IN THAT APARTMENT BUILDING...
...WHAT WOULD YOU DO ABOUT THIS?
WELL...
SHUM
FIRST...
...TALK TO THEM...
...AND SETTLE THINGS AMICABLY.
BYE-BYE!
FLICK
ROLL
ROLL
REASON-ABLE...
BUT SAY THEY DON'T BACK DOWN.
TAP
INSTEAD, THEY SUGGEST THE FOLLOWING...

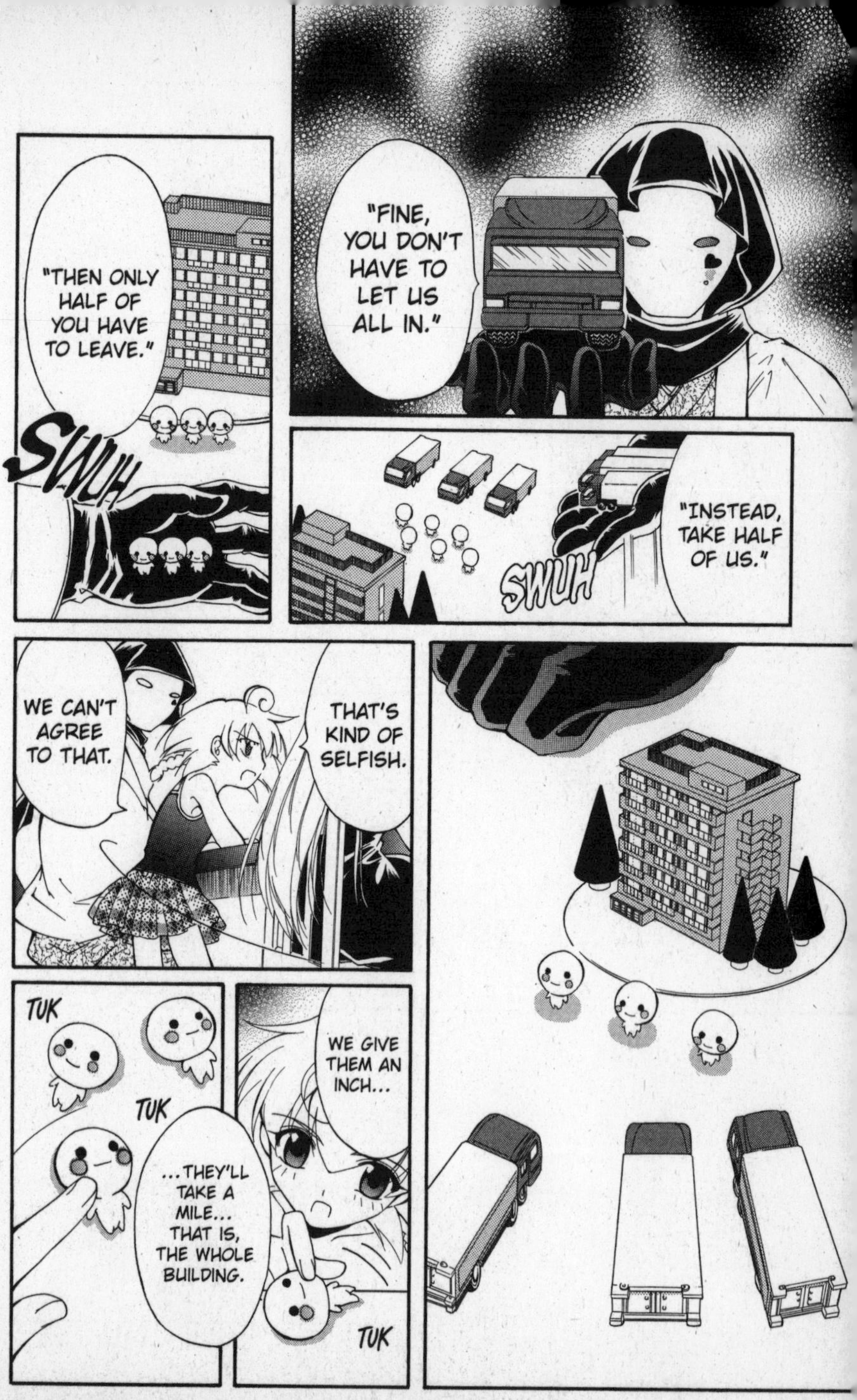
"FINE, YOU DON'T HAVE TO LET US ALL IN."
"INSTEAD, TAKE HALF OF US."
SWUH
"THEN ONLY HALF OF YOU HAVE TO LEAVE."
SWUH
THAT'S KIND OF SELFISH.
WE CAN'T AGREE TO THAT.
WE GIVE THEM AN INCH...
...THEY'LL TAKE A MILE... THAT IS, THE WHOLE BUILDING.
TUK
TUK
TUK

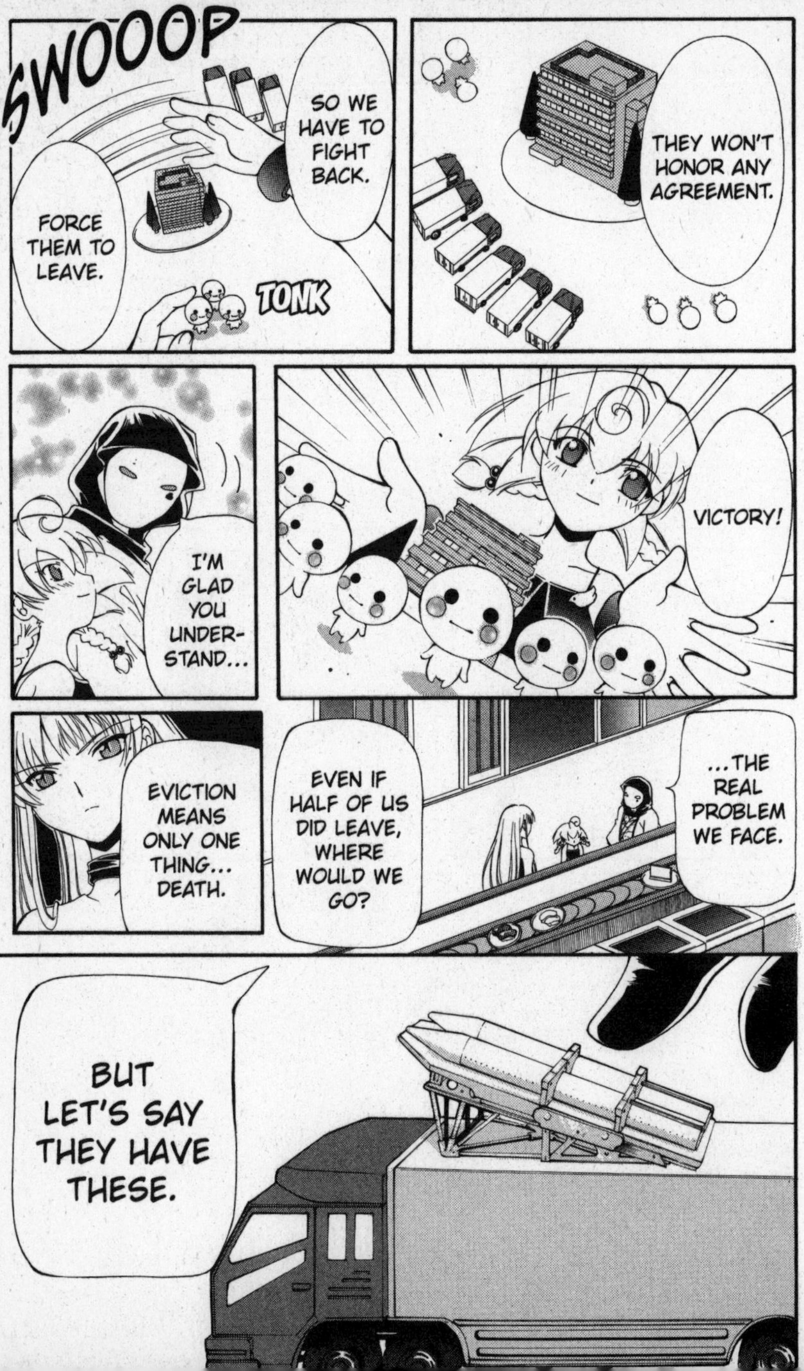
THEY WON'T HONOR ANY AGREEMENT.
SO WE HAVE TO FIGHT BACK.
SWOOOP
FORCE THEM TO LEAVE.
TONK
VICTORY!
I'M GLAD YOU UNDERSTAND...
...THE REAL PROBLEM WE FACE.
EVEN IF HALF OF US DID LEAVE, WHERE WOULD WE GO?
EVICTION MEANS ONLY ONE THING... DEATH.
BUT LET'S SAY THEY HAVE THESE.

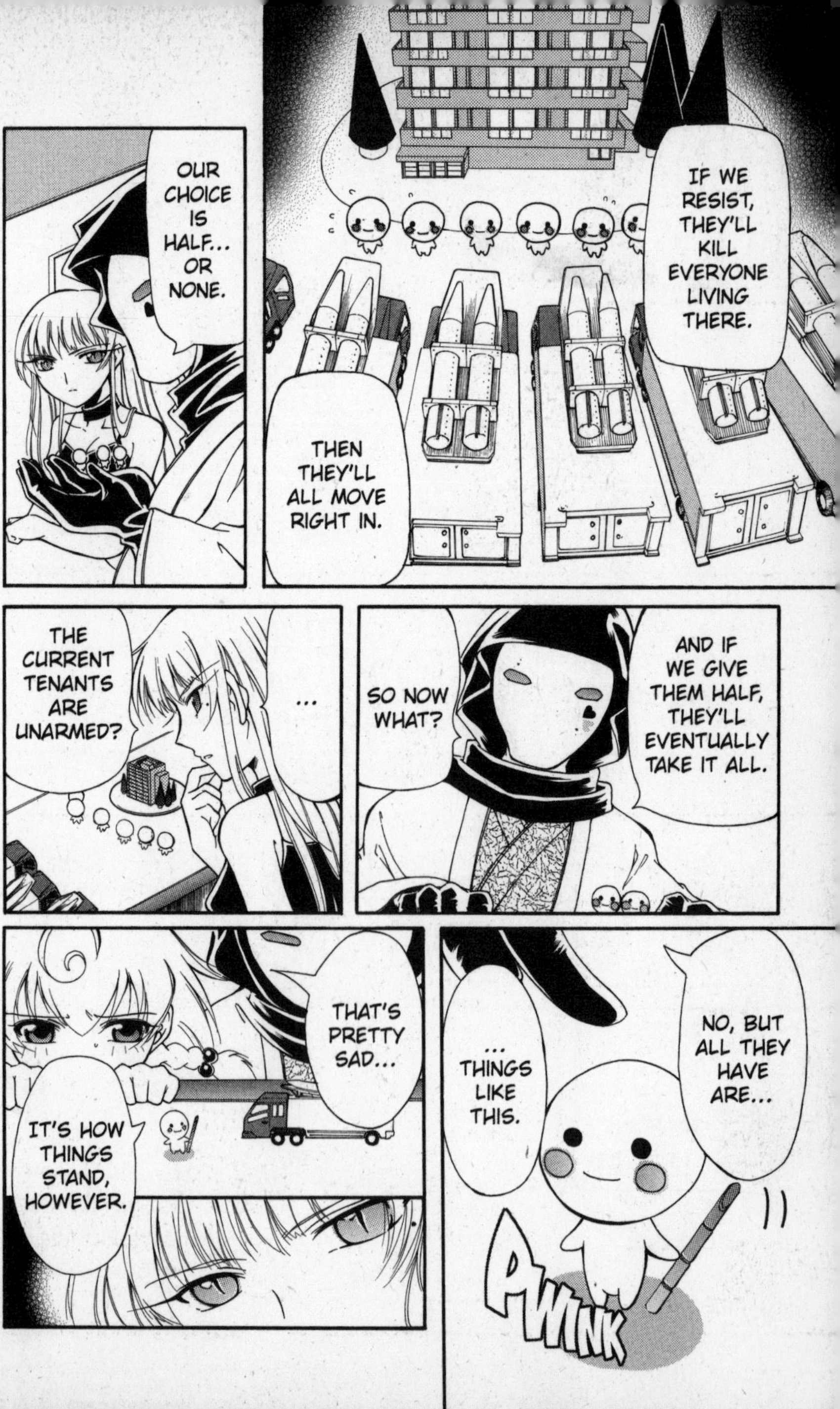
IF WE RESIST, THEY'LL KILL EVERYONE LIVING THERE.
THEN THEY'LL ALL MOVE RIGHT IN.
OUR CHOICE IS HALF... OR NONE.
AND IF WE GIVE THEM HALF, THEY'LL EVENTUALLY TAKE IT ALL.
SO NOW WHAT?
...
THE CURRENT TENANTS ARE UNARMED?
NO, BUT ALL THEY HAVE ARE...
...THINGS LIKE THIS.
PWINK
THAT'S PRETTY SAD...
IT'S HOW THINGS STAND, HOWEVER.

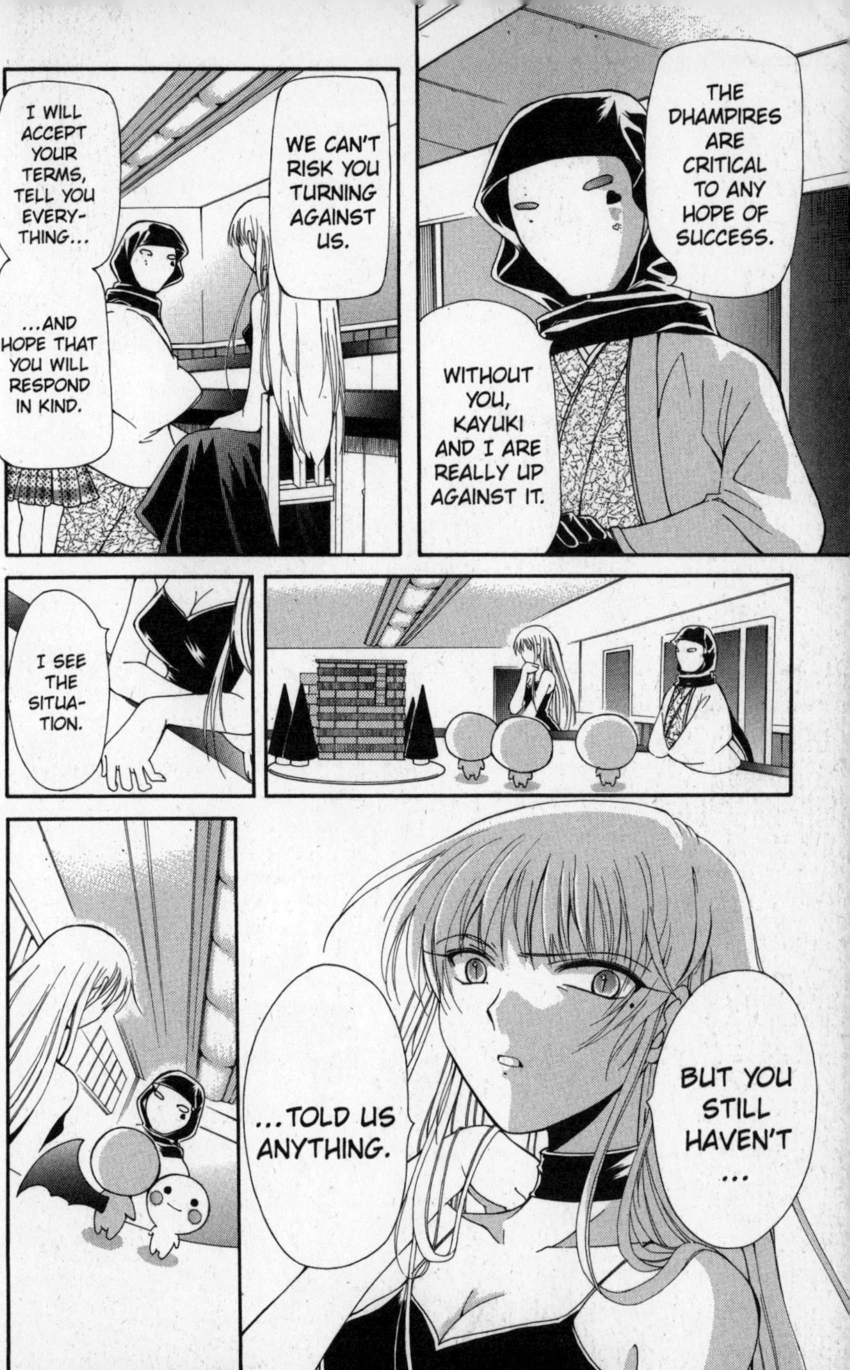
THE DHAMPIRES ARE CRITICAL TO ANY HOPE OF SUCCESS.
WITHOUT YOU, KAYUKI AND I ARE REALLY UP AGAINST IT.
WE CAN'T RISK YOU TURNING AGAINST US.
I WILL ACCEPT YOUR TERMS, TELL YOU EVERY-THING...
...AND HOPE THAT YOU WILL RESPOND IN KIND.
I SEE THE SITUA-TION.
BUT YOU STILL HAVEN'T ...
...TOLD US ANYTHING.

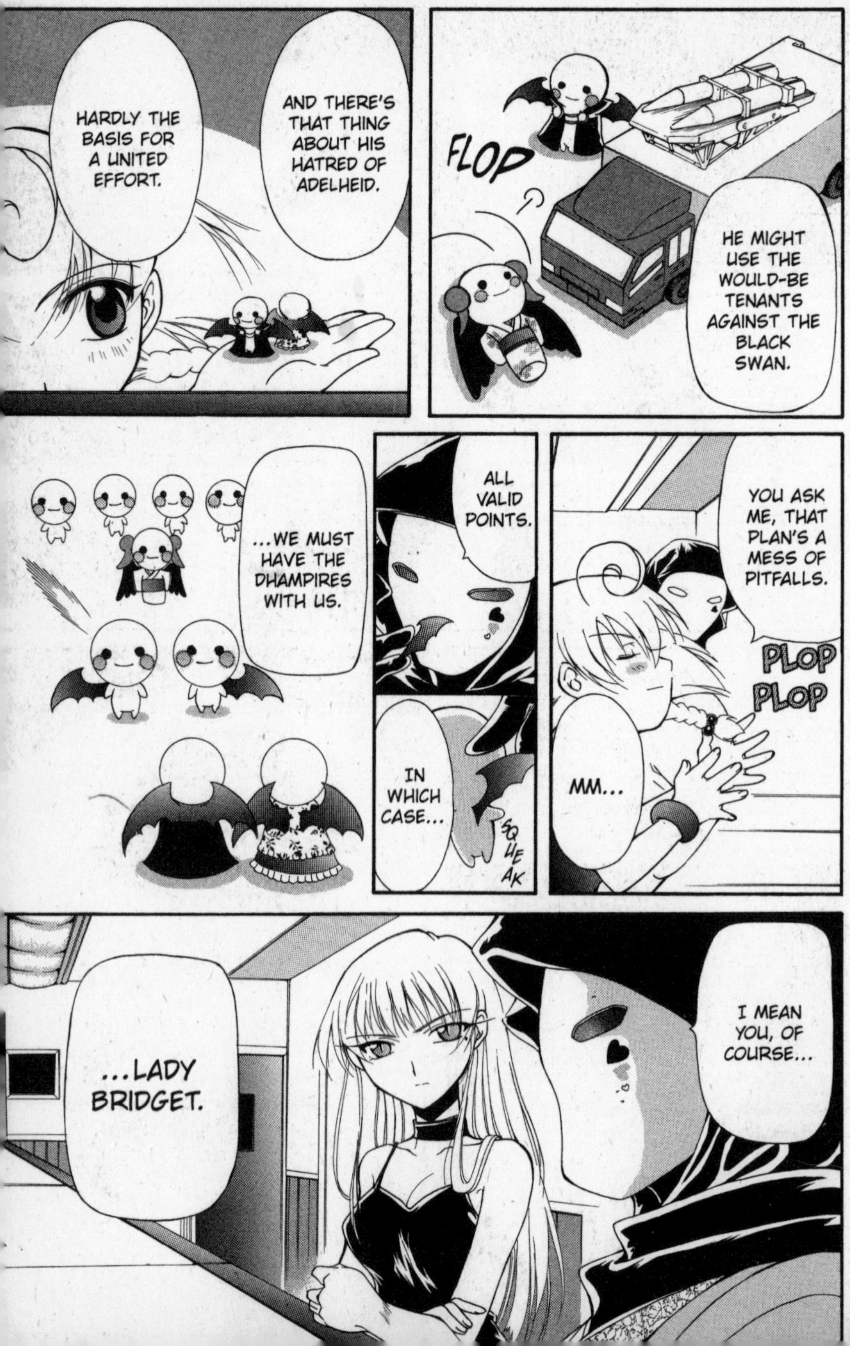
FLOP
HE MIGHT USE THE WOULD-BE TENANTS AGAINST THE BLACK SWAN.
AND THERE'S THAT THING ABOUT HIS HATRED OF ADELHEID.
HARDLY THE BASIS FOR A UNITED EFFORT.
YOU ASK ME, THAT PLAN'S A MESS OF PITFALLS.
PLOP PLOP
MM...
ALL VALID POINTS.
IN WHICH CASE...
SQUEAK
...WE MUST HAVE THE DHAMPIRES WITH US.
I MEAN YOU, OF COURSE...
...LADY BRIDGET.

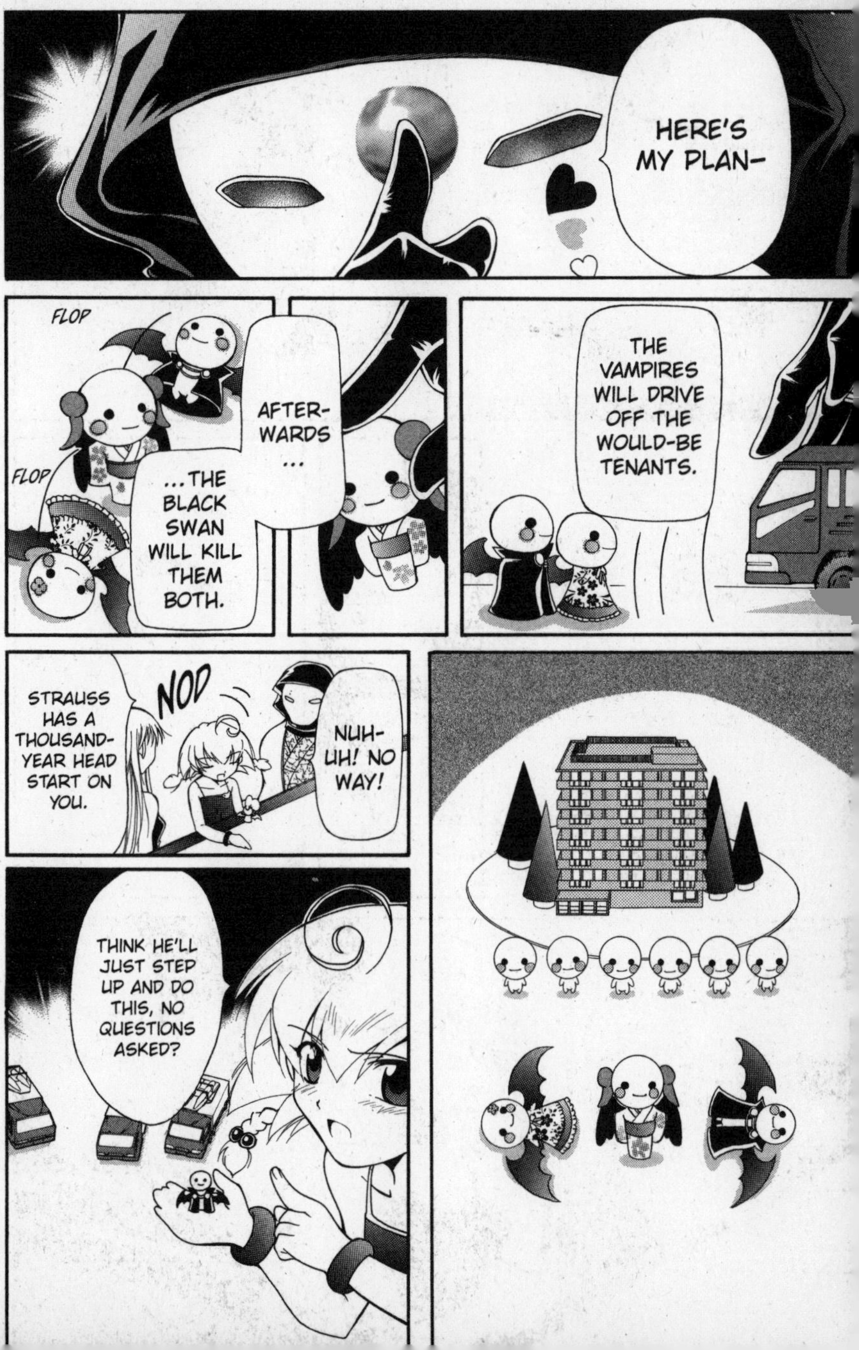
HERE'S MY PLAN-
THE VAMPIRES WILL DRIVE OFF THE WOULD-BE TENANTS.
AFTER-WARDS ...
FLOP
...THE BLACK SWAN WILL KILL THEM BOTH.
FLOP
NUH-UH! NO WAY!
NOD
STRAUSS HAS A THOUSAND-YEAR HEAD START ON YOU.
THINK HE'LL JUST STEP UP AND DO THIS, NO QUESTIONS ASKED?

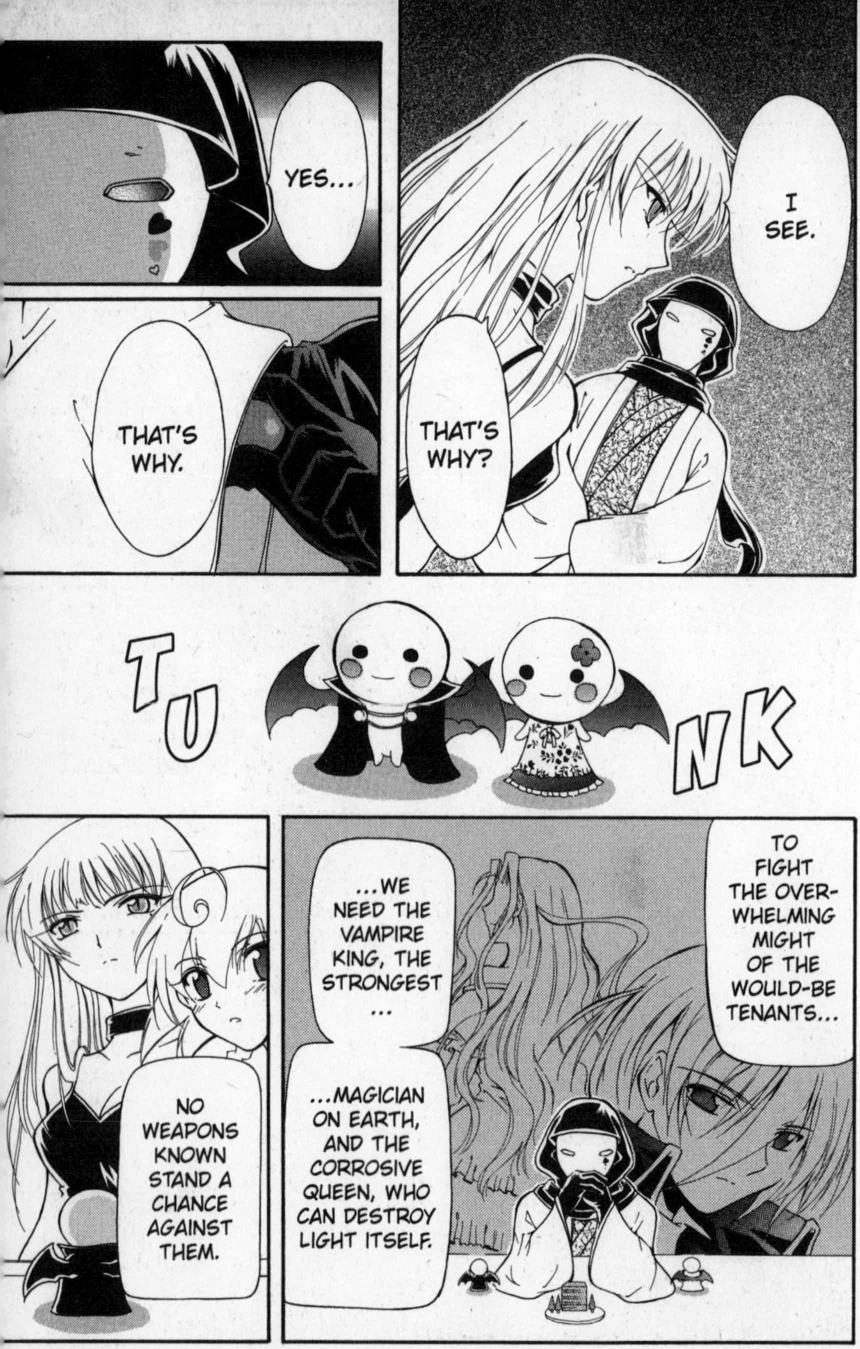
I SEE.
THAT'S WHY?
YES...
THAT'S WHY.
TUNK
TO FIGHT THE OVER-WHELMING MIGHT OF THE WOULD-BE TENANTS...
...WE NEED THE VAMPIRE KING, THE STRONGEST ...
...MAGICIAN ON EARTH, AND THE CORROSIVE QUEEN, WHO CAN DESTROY LIGHT ITSELF.
NO WEAPONS KNOWN STAND A CHANCE AGAINST THEM.

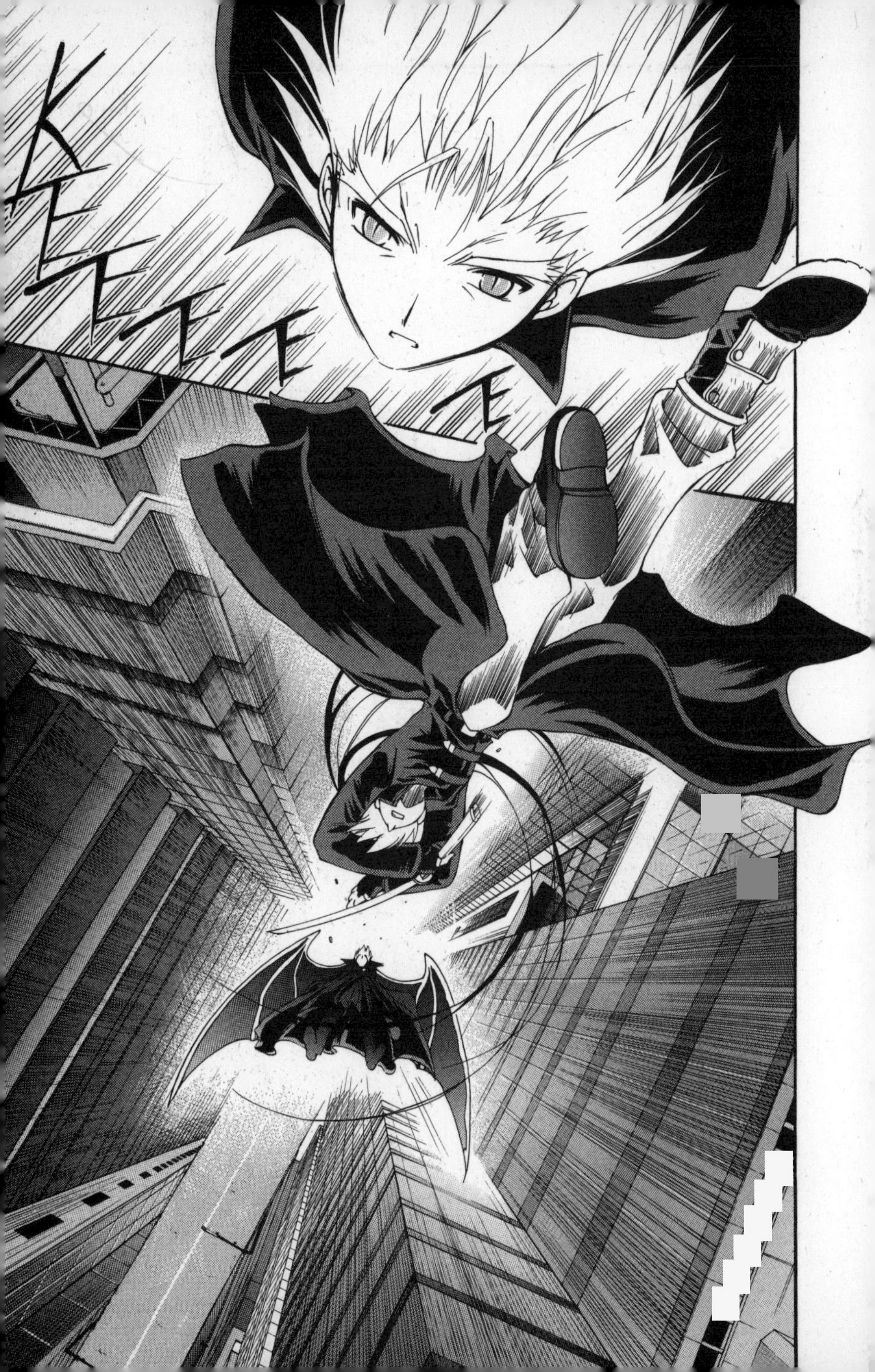
KEEEEEE

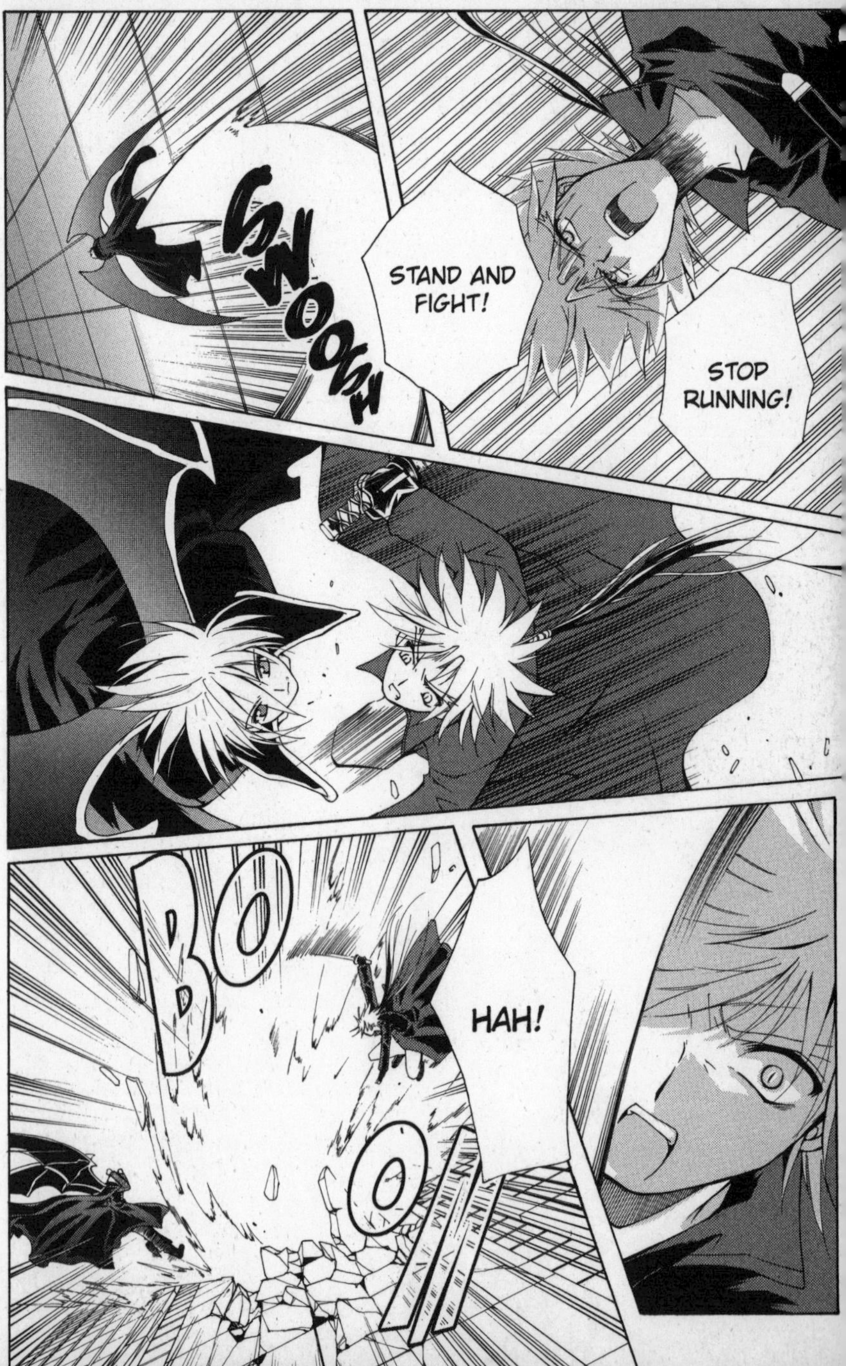
STOP RUNNING!
STAND AND FIGHT!
SWOOSH
HAH!
BOOM

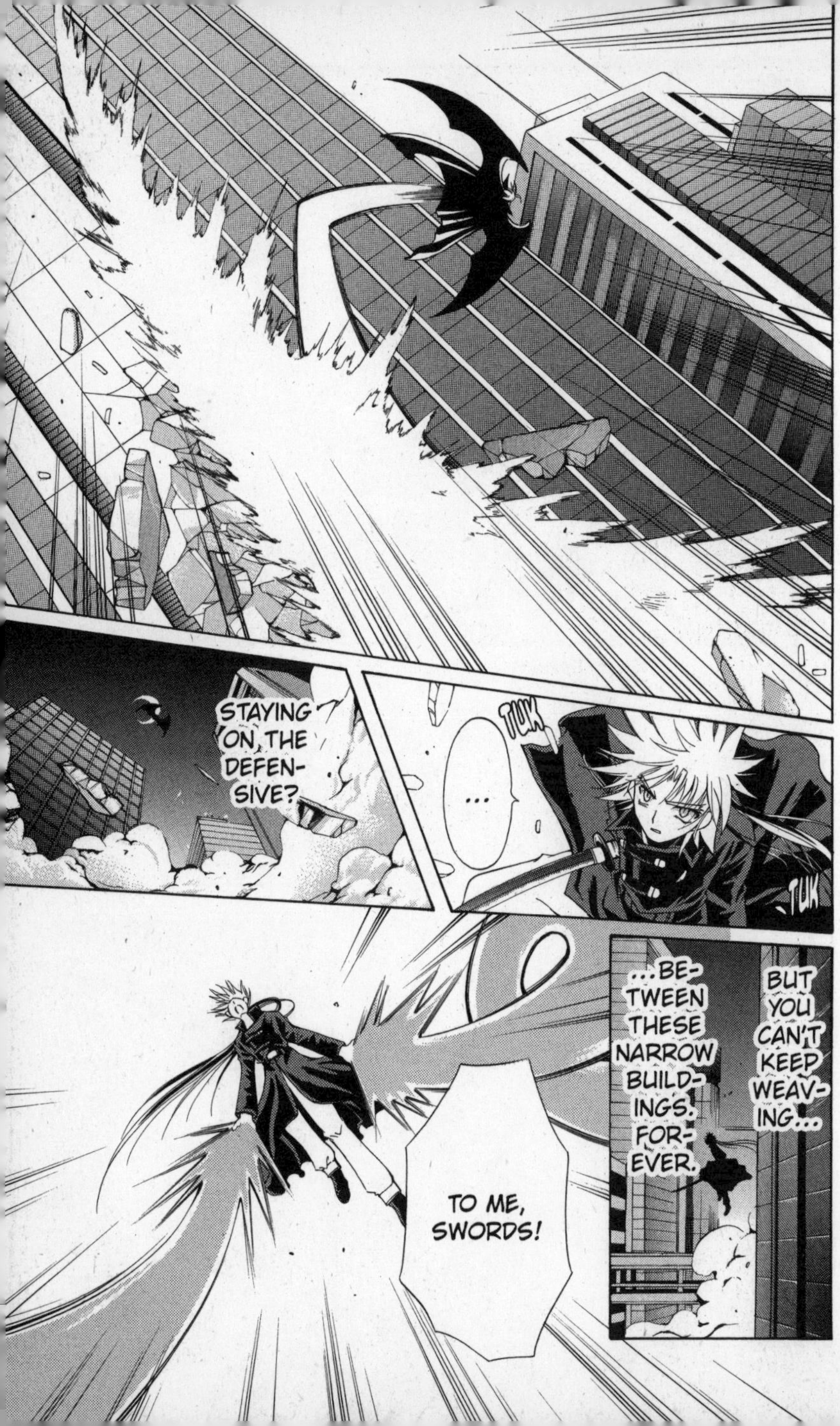
TUK
...
TUK
STAYING ON THE DEFEN-SIVE?
BUT YOU CAN'T KEEP WEAV-ING...
...BE-TWEEN THESE NARROW BUILD-INGS. FOR-EVER.
TO ME, SWORDS!

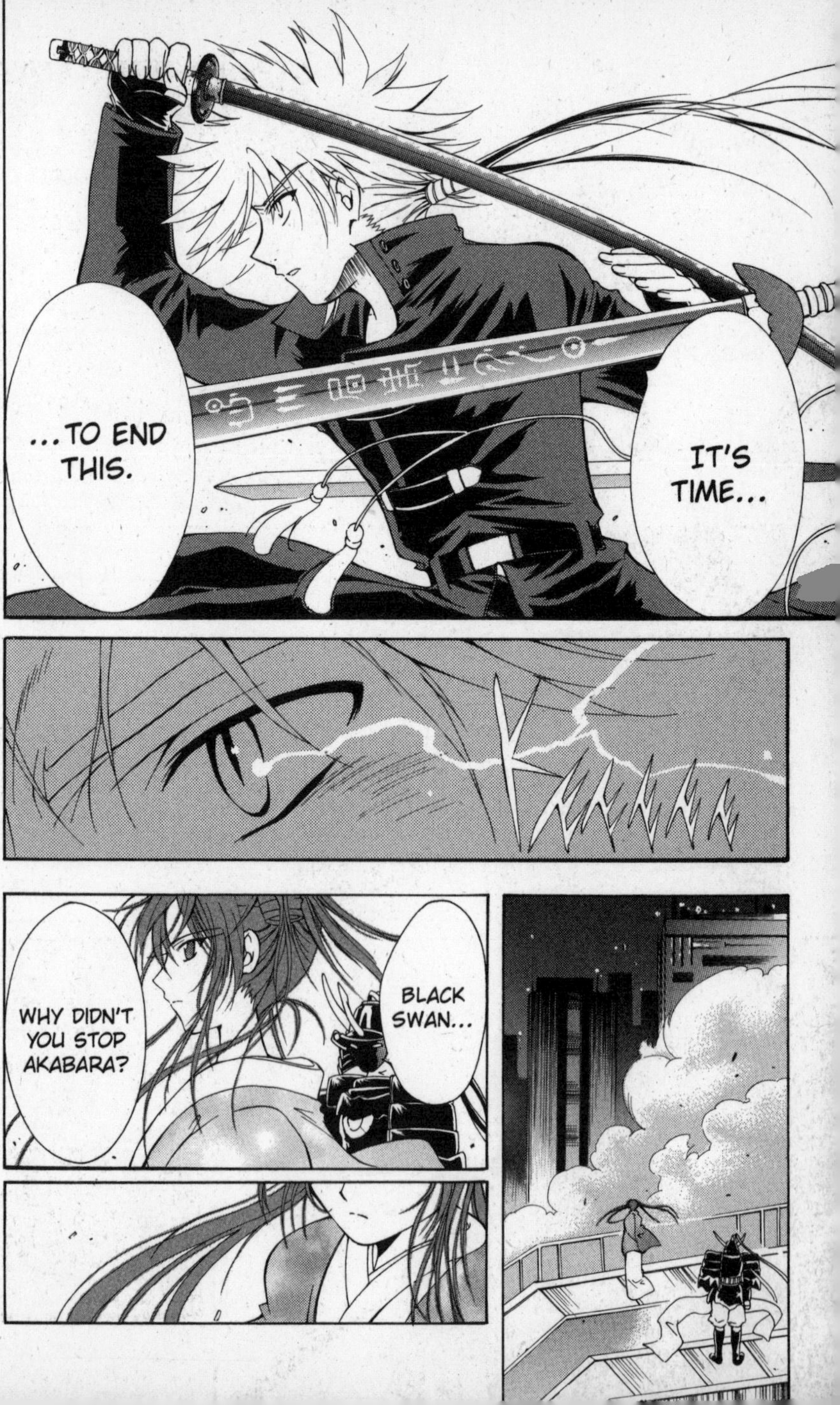
IT'S TIME...
...TO END THIS.
BLACK SWAN...
WHY DIDN'T YOU STOP AKABARA?

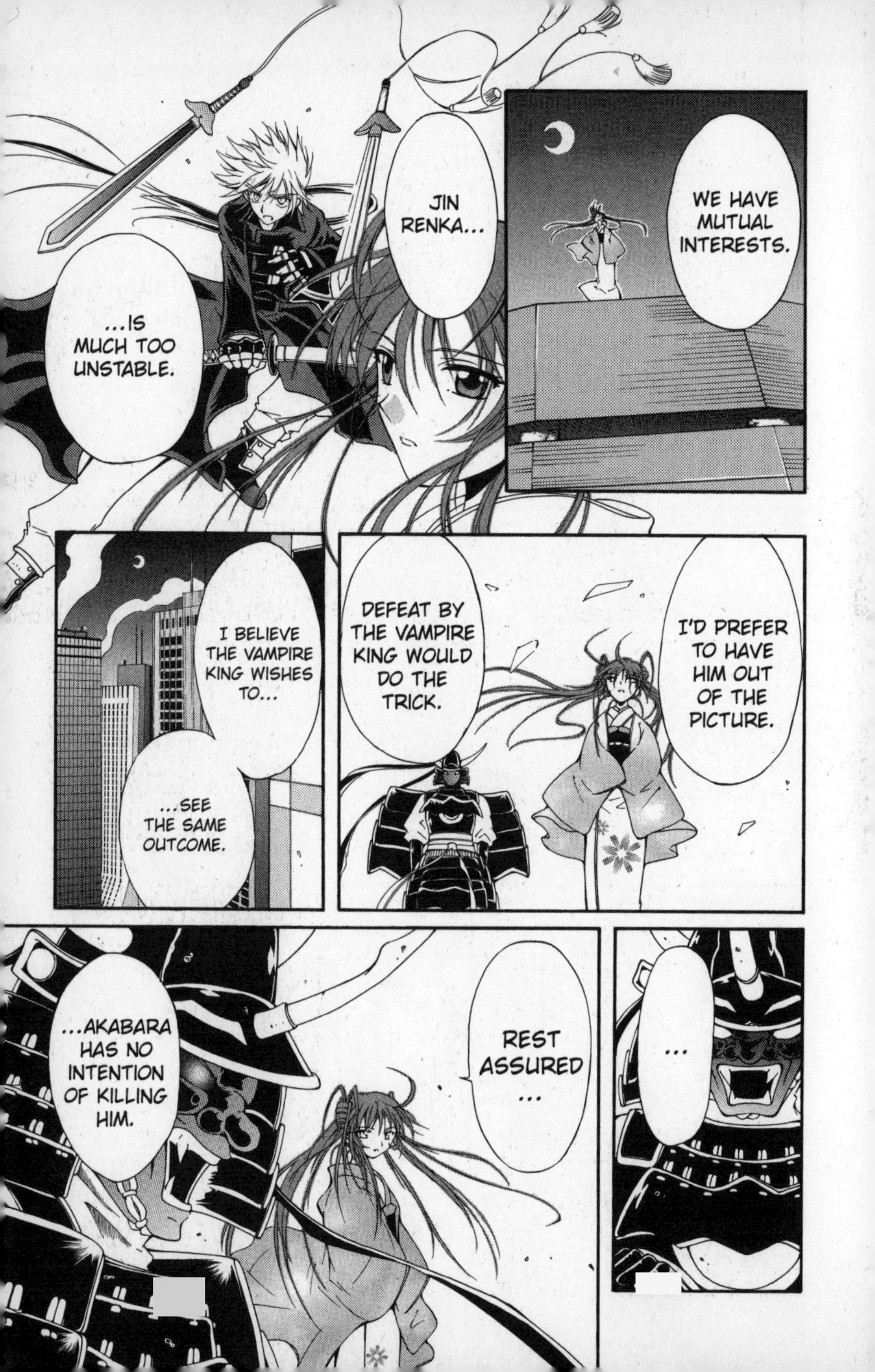
WE HAVE MUTUAL INTERESTS.
JIN RENKA...
...IS MUCH TOO UNSTABLE.
I'D PREFER TO HAVE HIM OUT OF THE PICTURE.
DEFEAT BY THE VAMPIRE KING WOULD DO THE TRICK.
I BELIEVE THE VAMPIRE KING WISHES TO...
...SEE THE SAME OUTCOME.
...
REST ASSURED...
...AKABARA HAS NO INTENTION OF KILLING HIM.

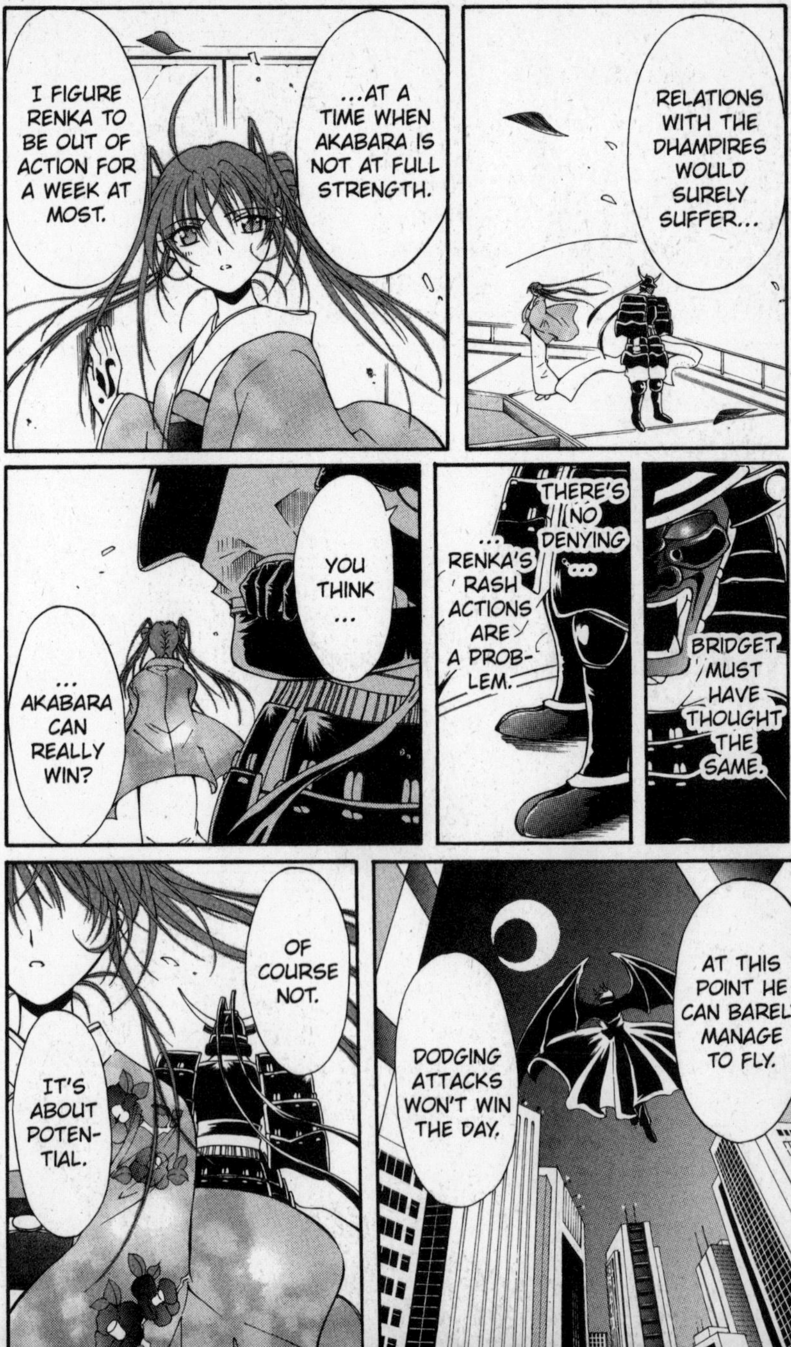
RELATIONS WITH THE DHAMPIRES WOULD SURELY SUFFER...
...AT A TIME WHEN AKABARA IS NOT AT FULL STRENGTH.
I FIGURE RENKA TO BE OUT OF ACTION FOR A WEEK AT MOST.
BRIDGET MUST HAVE THOUGHT THE SAME.
THERE'S NO DENYING...
...RENKA'S RASH ACTIONS ARE A PROB-LEM.
YOU THINK...
...AKABARA CAN REALLY WIN?
AT THIS POINT HE CAN BARELY MANAGE TO FLY.
DODGING ATTACKS WON'T WIN THE DAY.
OF COURSE NOT.
IT'S ABOUT POTEN-TIAL.

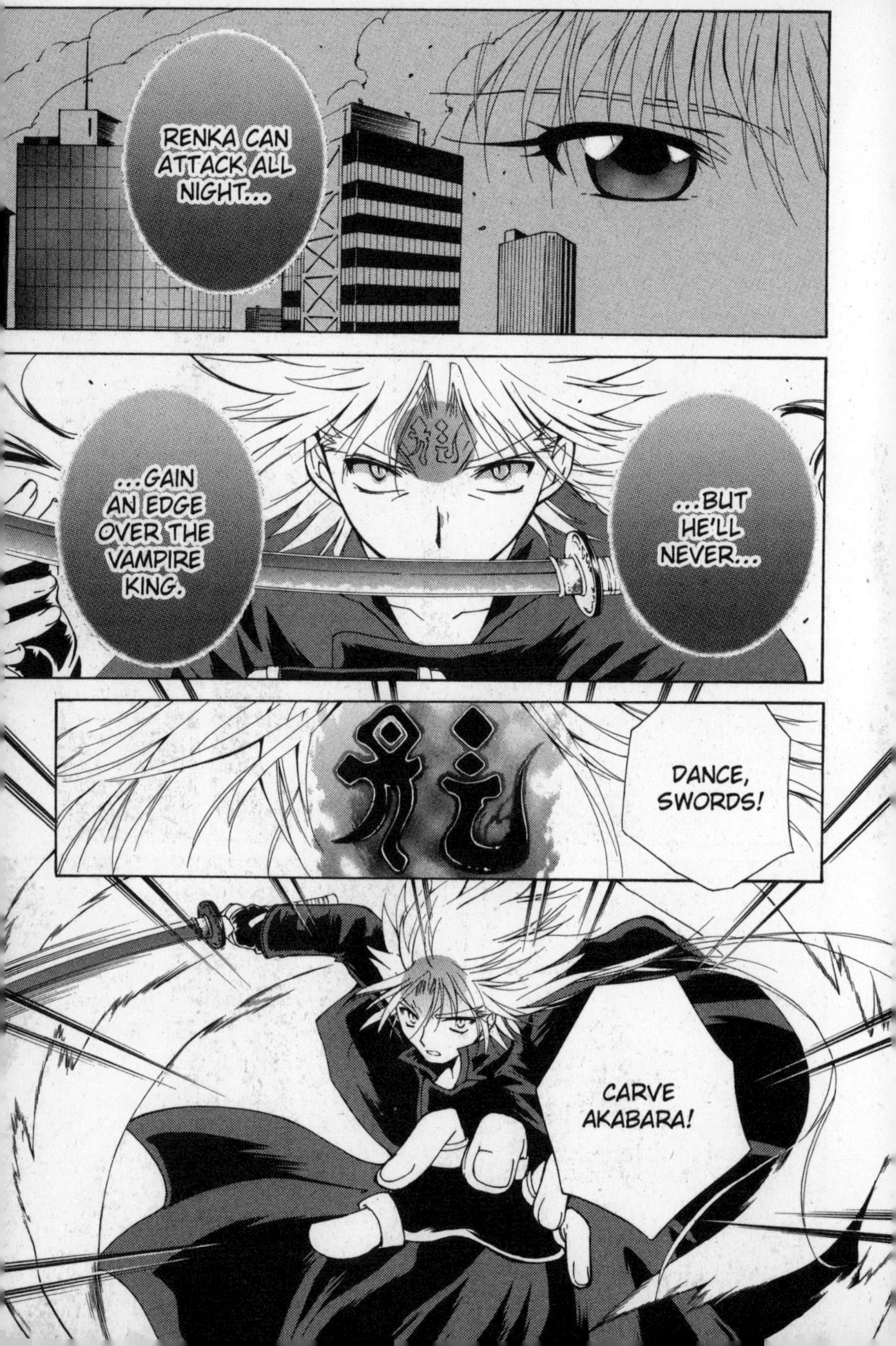
RENKA CAN ATTACK ALL NIGHT...
...BUT HE'LL NEVER...
...GAIN AN EDGE OVER THE VAMPIRE KING.
DANCE, SWORDS!
CARVE AKABARA!

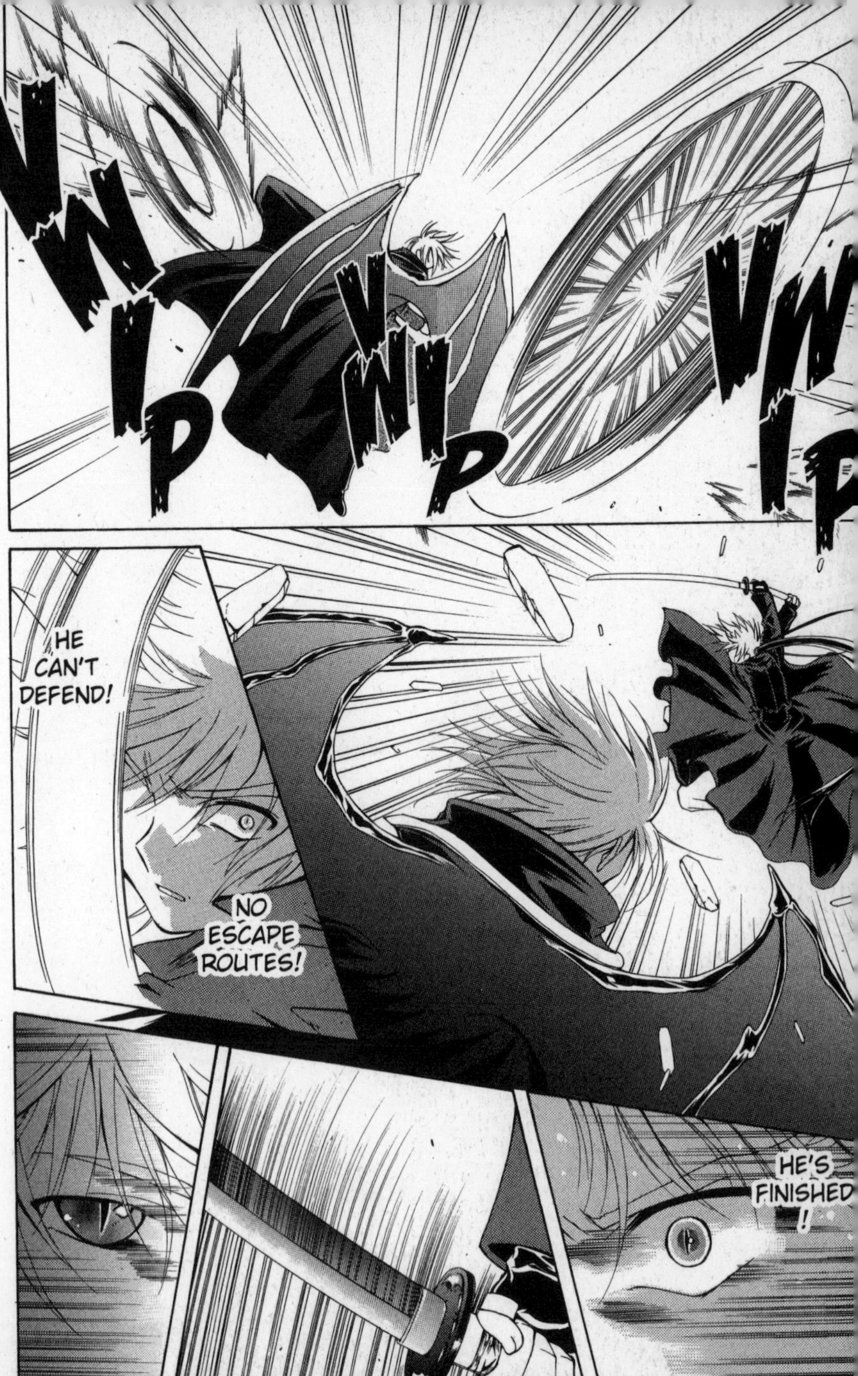
VWIP
VWIP
VWIP
HE CAN'T DEFEND!
NO ESCAPE ROUTES!
HE'S FINISHED!

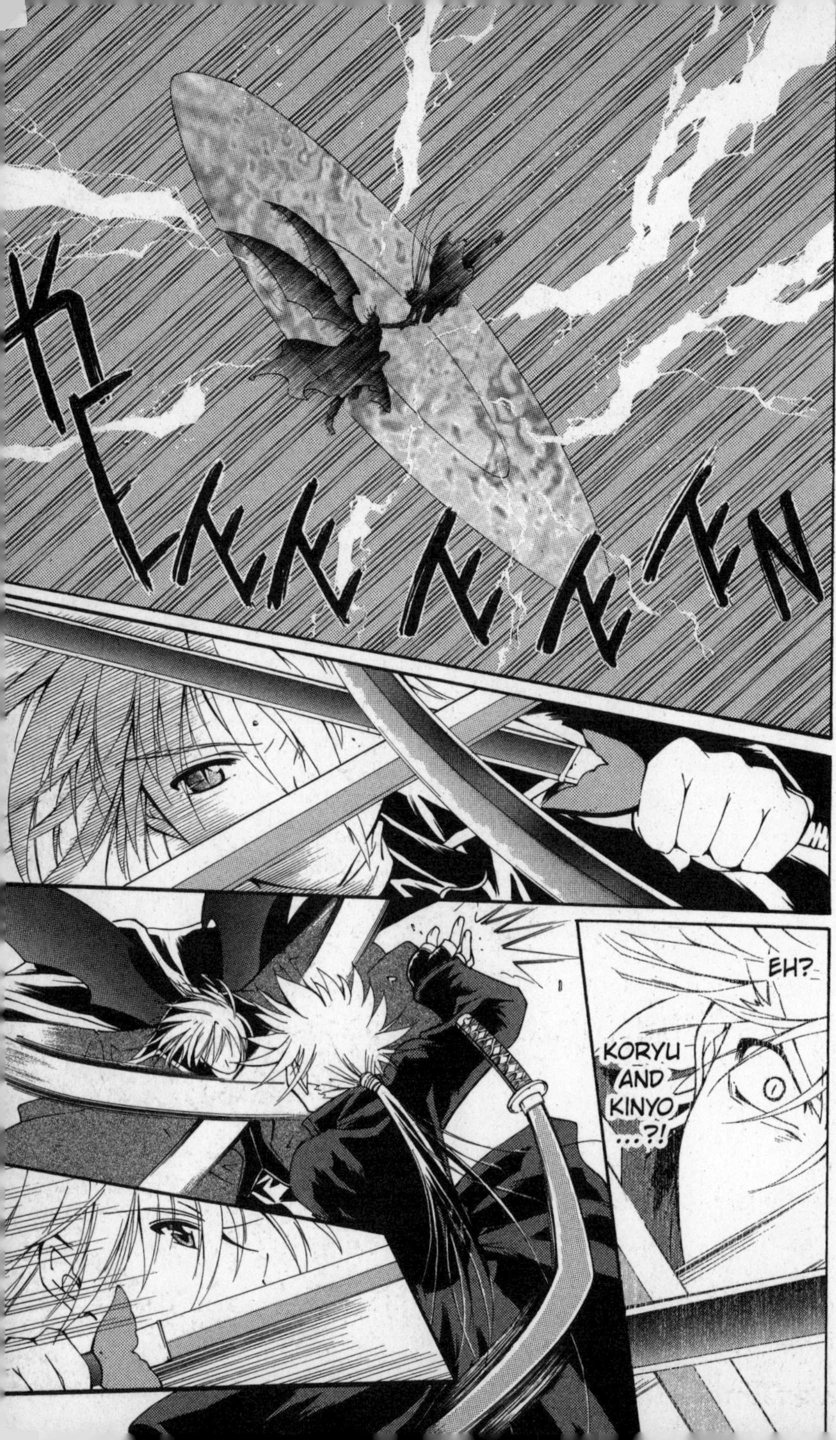
EH?
KORYU AND KINYO...?!

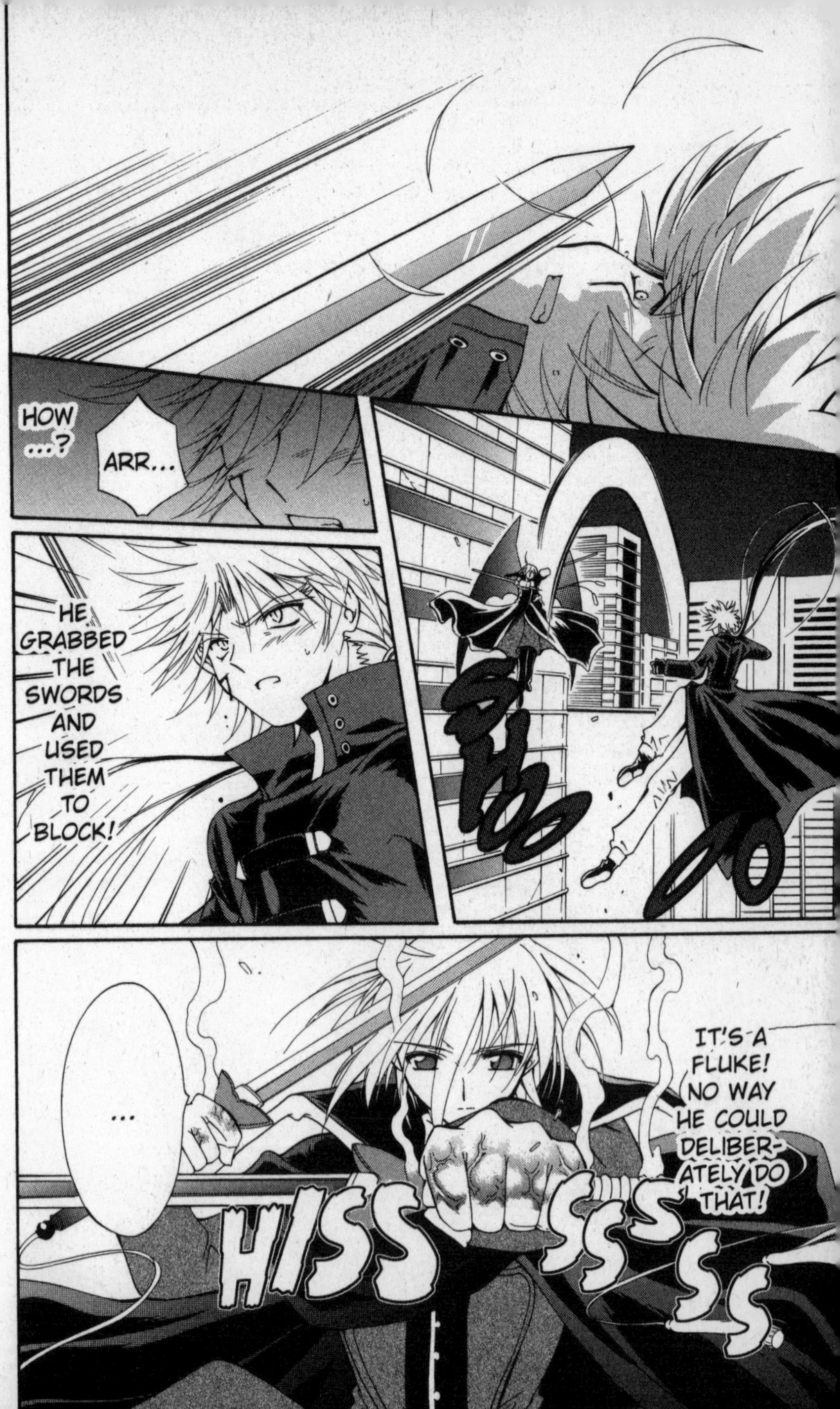
SHOOO
HOW...?
ARR...
HE GRABBED THE SWORDS AND USED THEM TO BLOCK!
IT'S A FLUKE! NO WAY HE COULD DELIBER-ATELY DO THAT!
...
HISSSSSSS

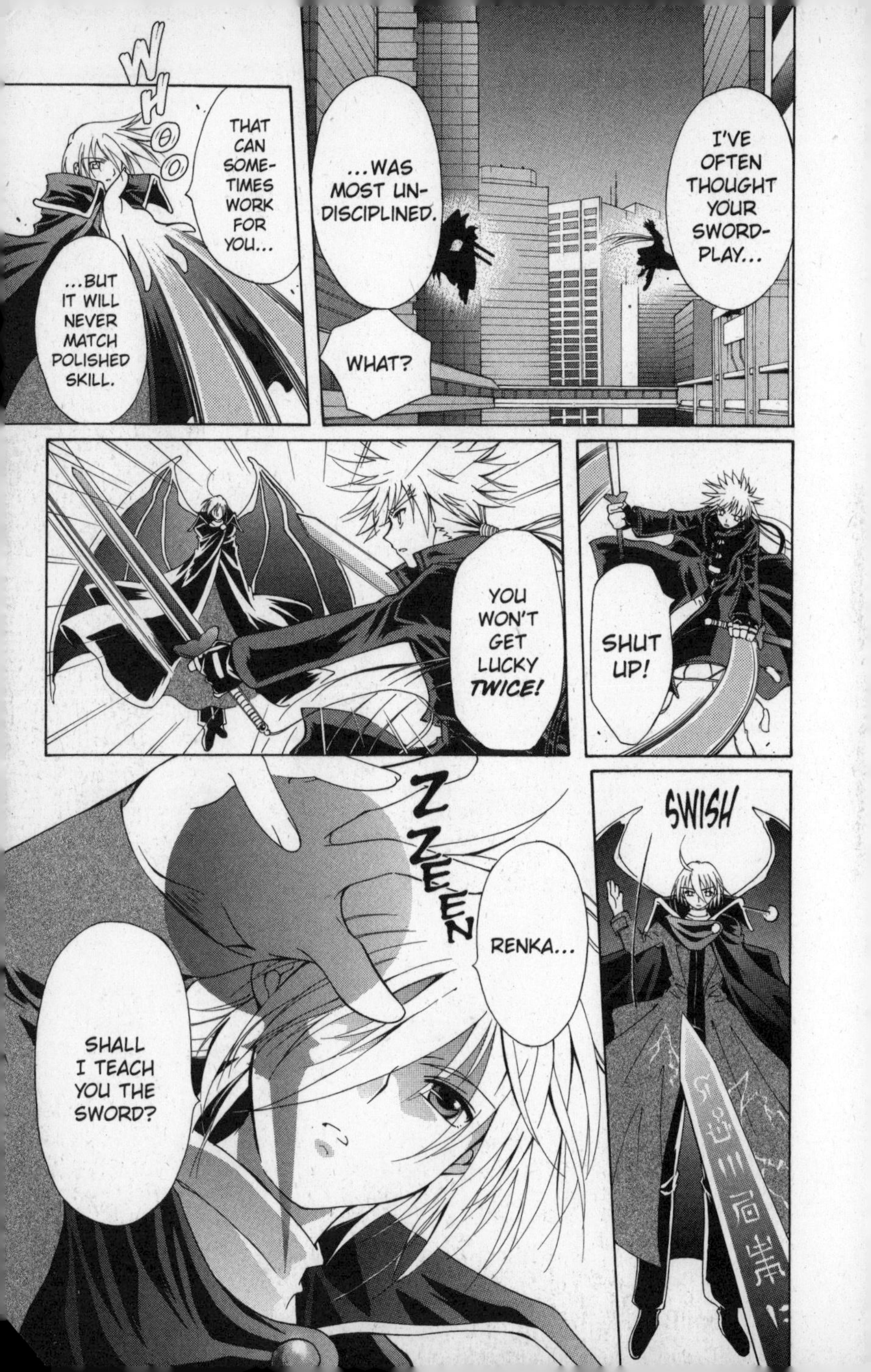
I'VE OFTEN THOUGHT YOUR SWORD-PLAY...
...WAS MOST UN-DISCIPLINED.
WHAT?
WHOO
THAT CAN SOME-TIMES WORK FOR YOU...
...BUT IT WILL NEVER MATCH POLISHED SKILL.
SHUT UP!
YOU WON'T GET LUCKY *TWICE!*
SWISH
ZZEEN
RENKA...
SHALL I TEACH YOU THE SWORD?

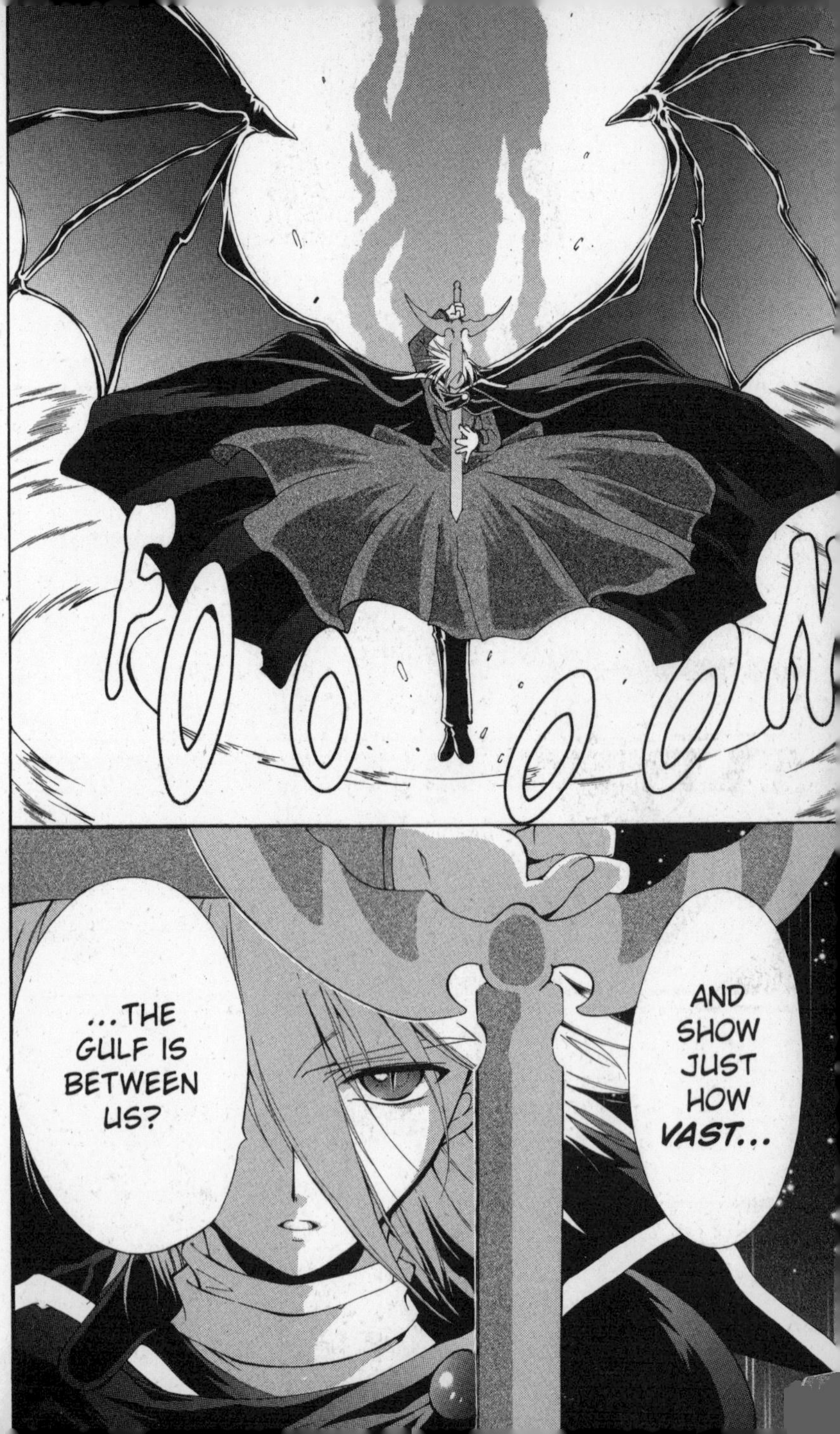
FOOOON
AND SHOW JUST HOW *VAST*...
...THE GULF IS BETWEEN US?

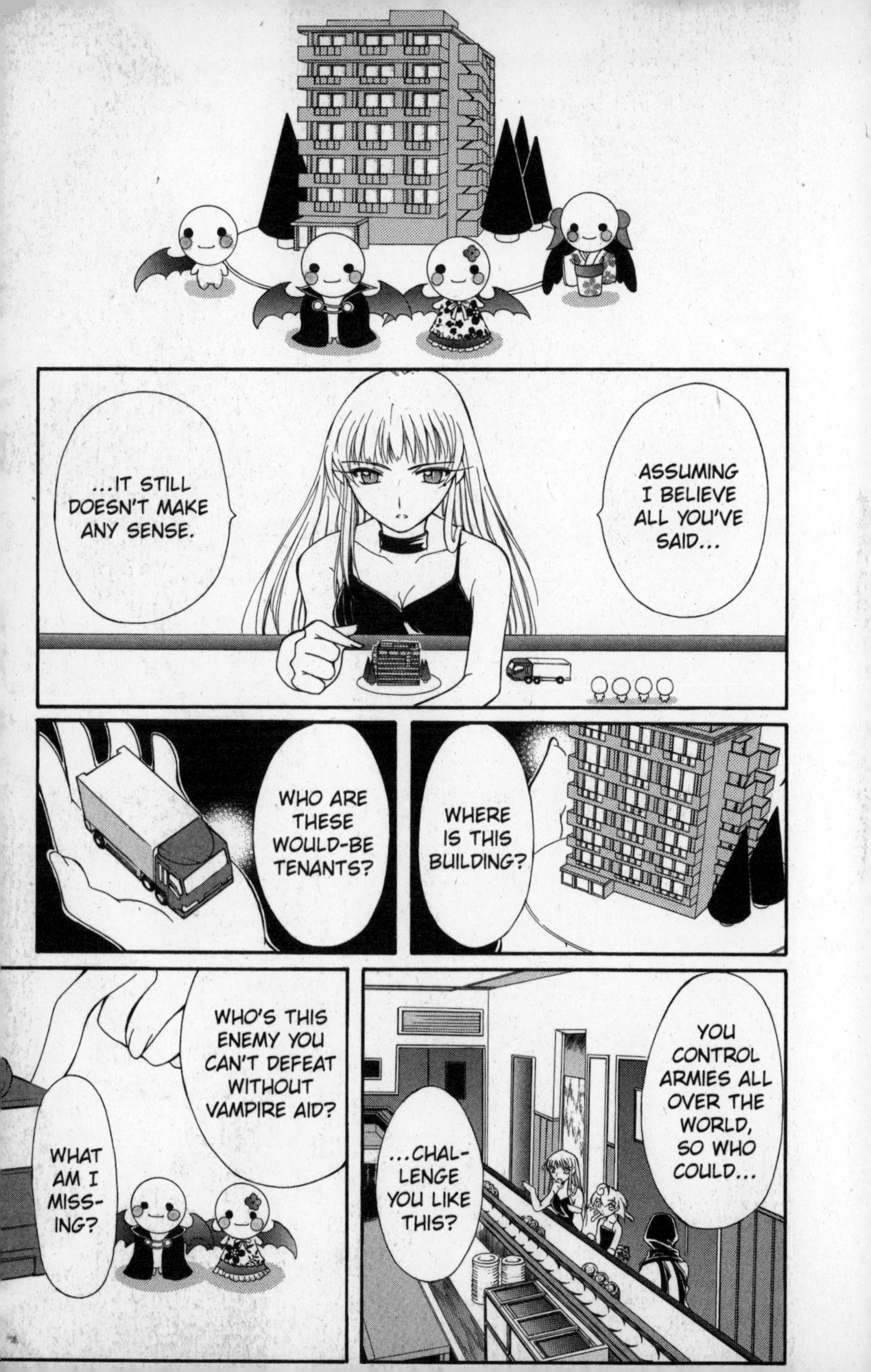
ASSUMING I BELIEVE ALL YOU'VE SAID...
...IT STILL DOESN'T MAKE ANY SENSE.
WHERE IS THIS BUILDING?
WHO ARE THESE WOULD-BE TENANTS?
YOU CONTROL ARMIES ALL OVER THE WORLD, SO WHO COULD...
...CHAL-LENGE YOU LIKE THIS?
WHO'S THIS ENEMY YOU CAN'T DEFEAT WITHOUT VAMPIRE AID?
WHAT AM I MISS-ING?

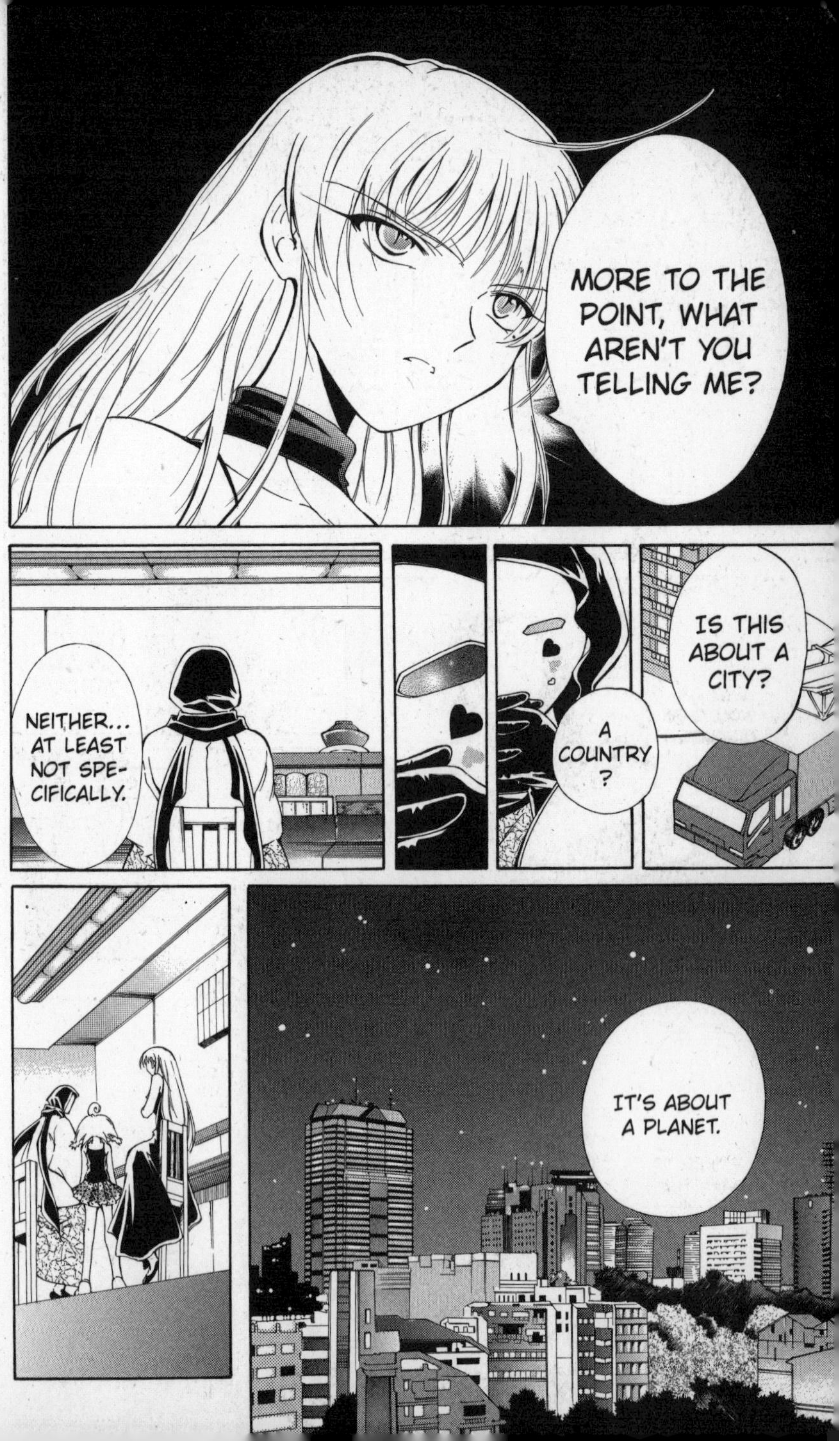
MORE TO THE POINT, WHAT AREN'T YOU TELLING ME?
IS THIS ABOUT A CITY?
A COUNTRY?
NEITHER... AT LEAST NOT SPE-CIFICALLY.
IT'S ABOUT A PLANET.

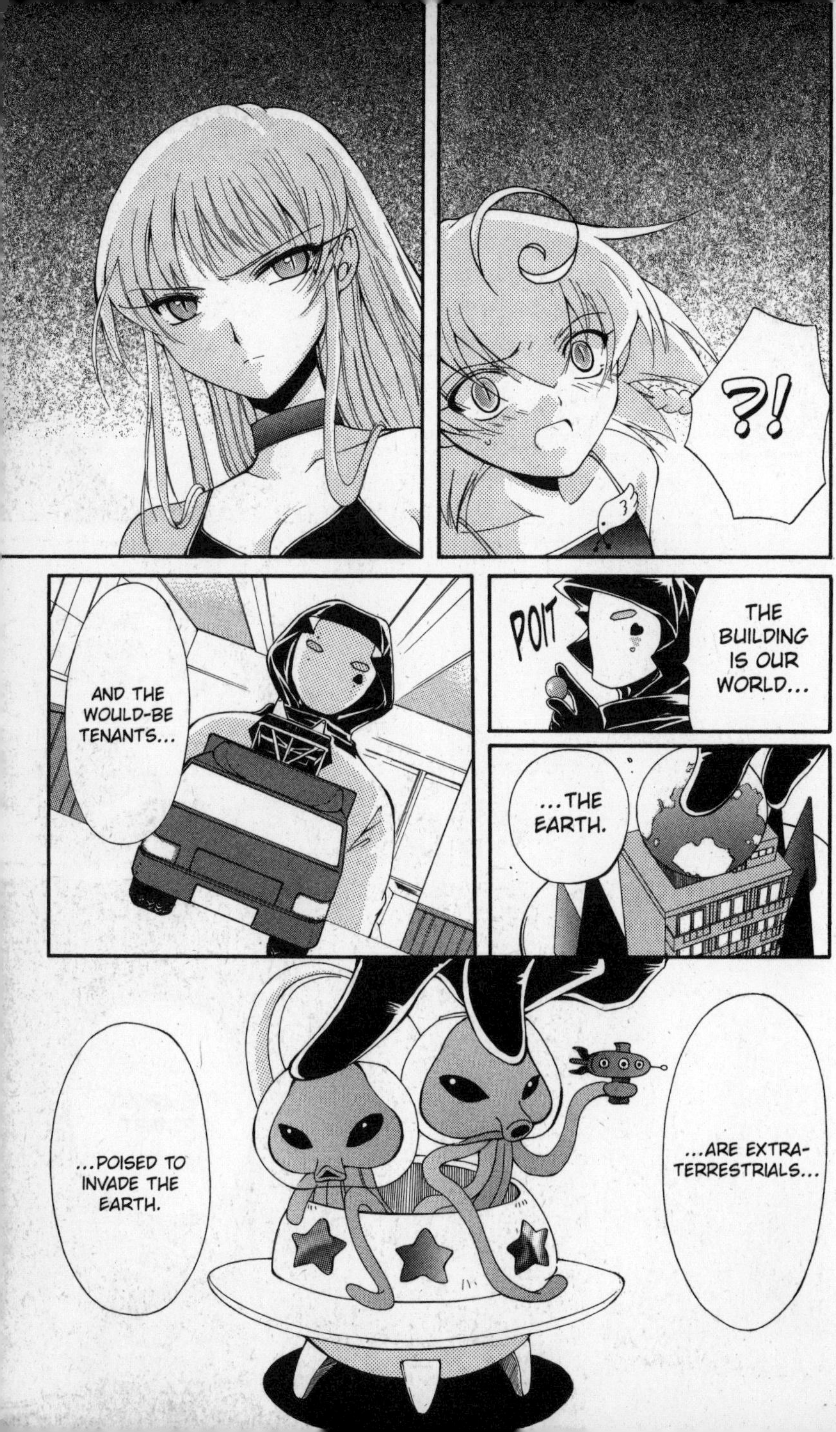
?!
THE BUILDING IS OUR WORLD...
POIT
...THE EARTH.
AND THE WOULD-BE TENANTS...
...ARE EXTRA-TERRESTRIALS...
...POISED TO INVADE THE EARTH.

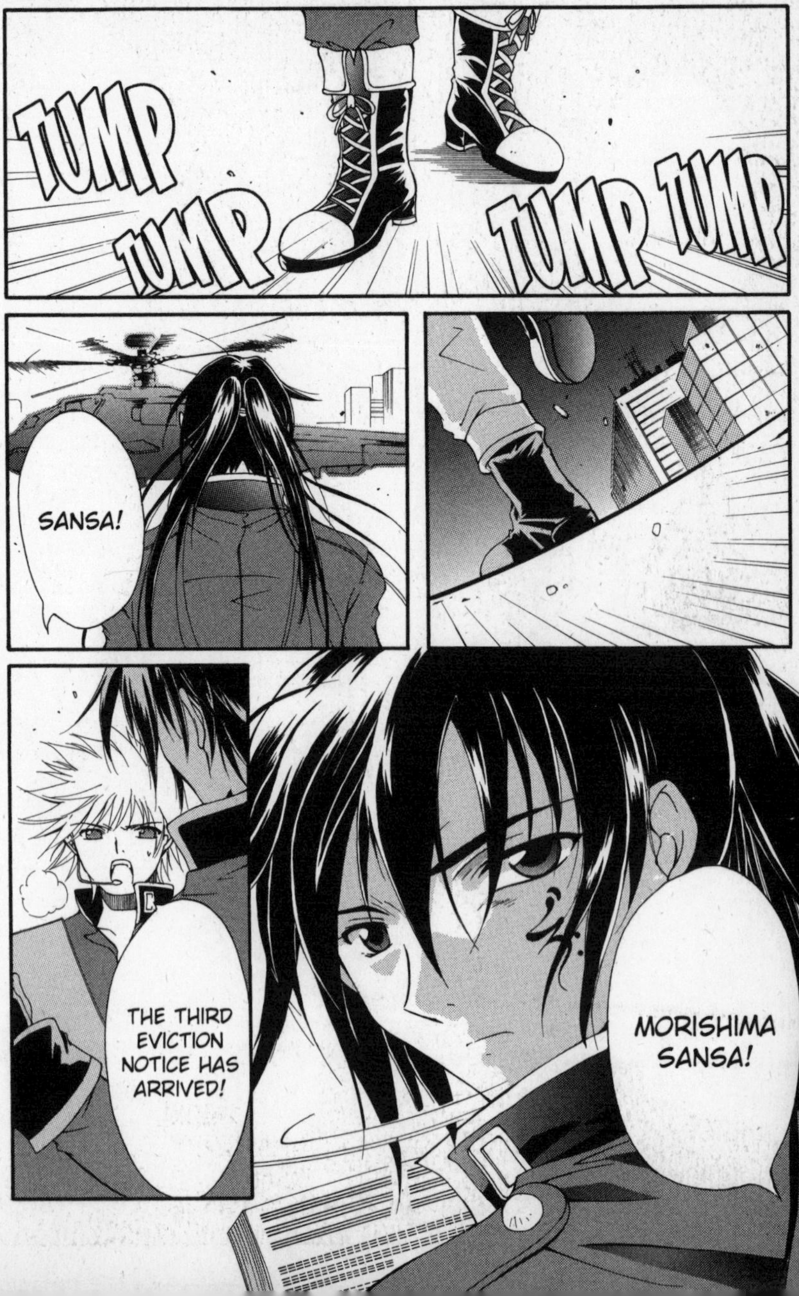
TUMP TUMP
TUMP
TUMP
SANSA!
MORISHIMA SANSA!
THE THIRD EVICTION NOTICE HAS ARRIVED!

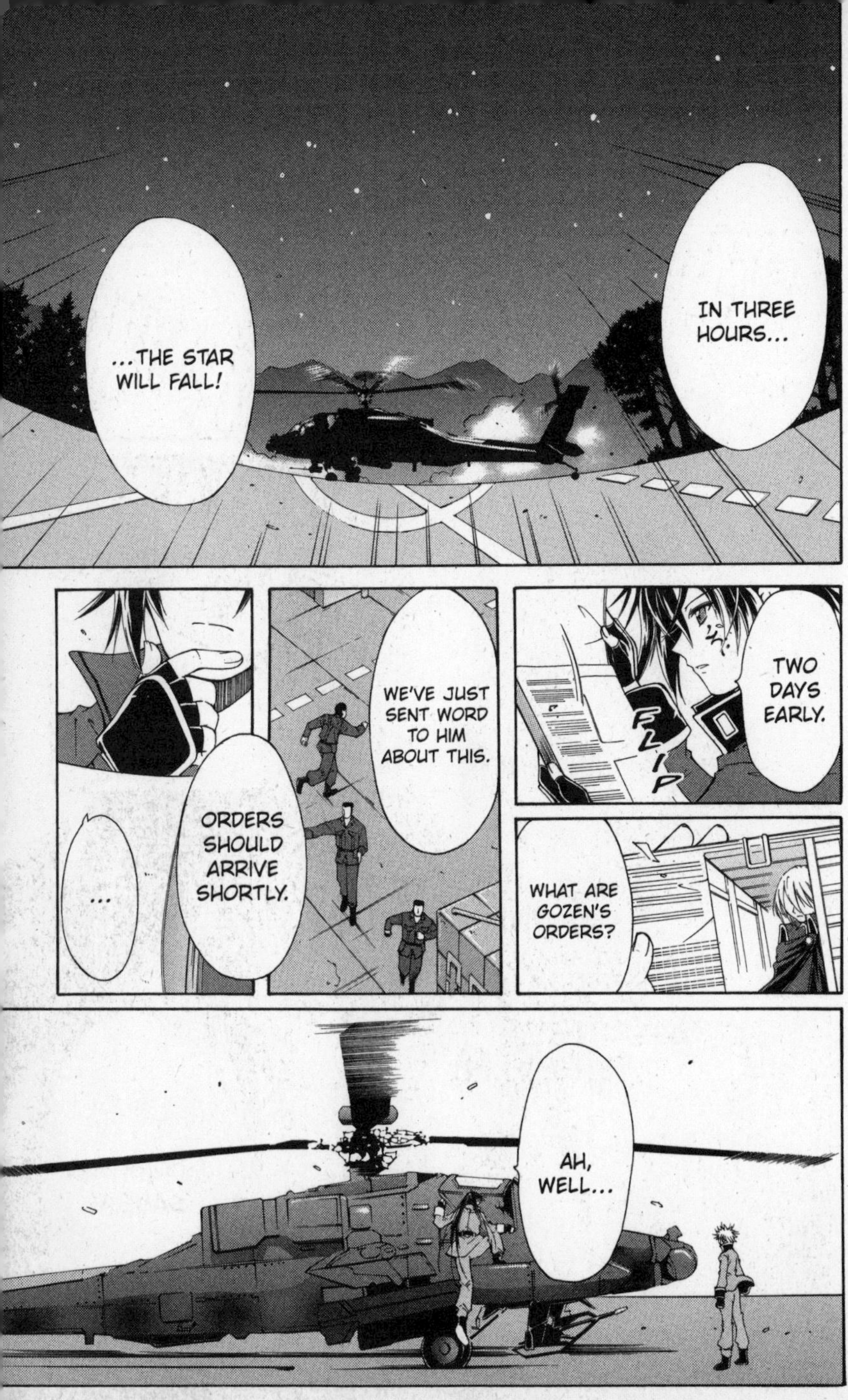

IN THREE HOURS...
...THE STAR WILL FALL!
TWO DAYS EARLY.
FLIP
WHAT ARE GOZEN'S ORDERS?
WE'VE JUST SENT WORD TO HIM ABOUT THIS.
ORDERS SHOULD ARRIVE SHORTLY.
...
AH, WELL...

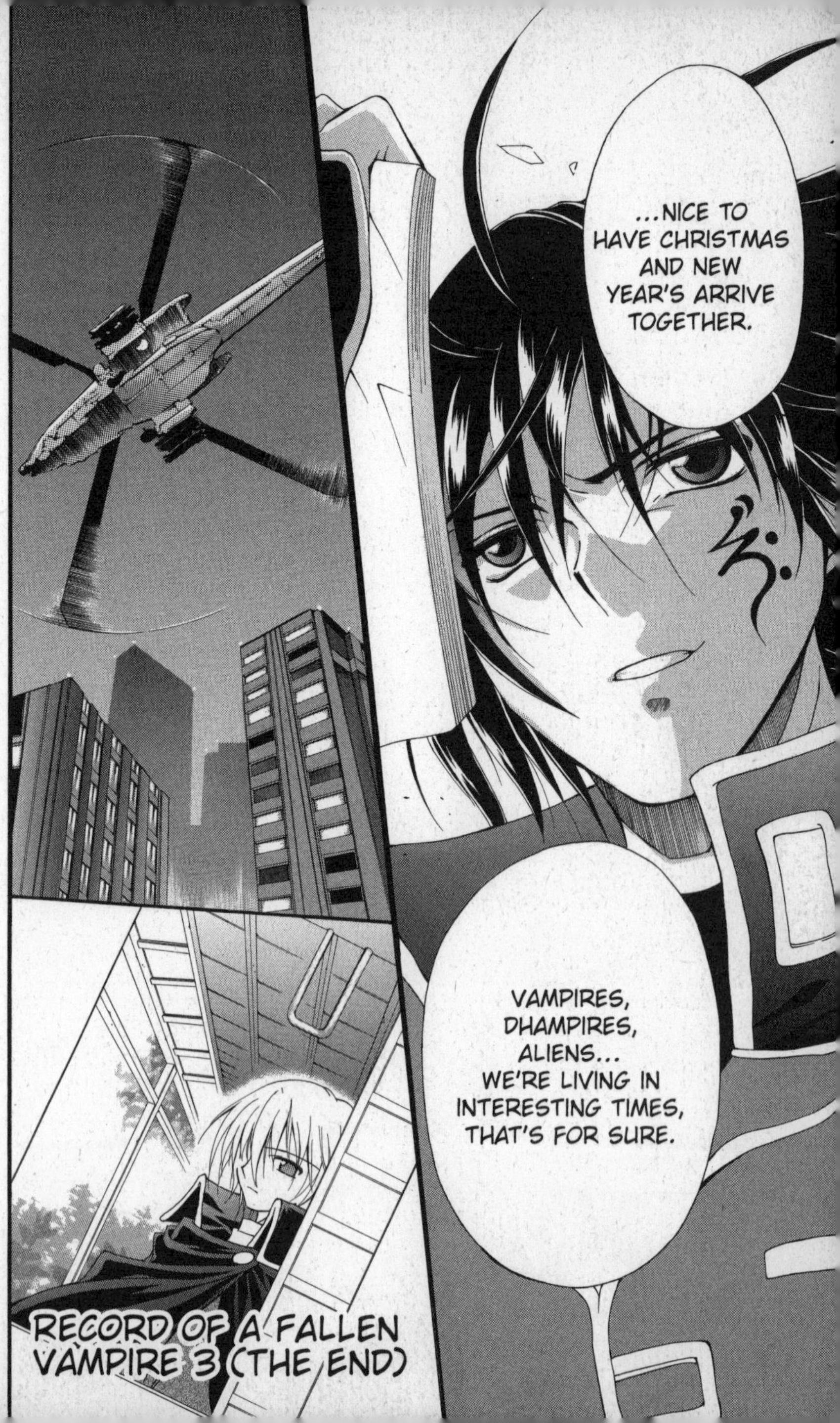
...NICE TO HAVE CHRISTMAS AND NEW YEAR'S ARRIVE TOGETHER.
VAMPIRES, DHAMPIRES, ALIENS... WE'RE LIVING IN INTERESTING TIMES, THAT'S FOR SURE.
RECORD OF A FALLEN VAMPIRE 3 (THE END)

THE RECORD OF A

FALLEN VAMPIRE

RECORD OF A FALLEN VAMPIRE 3!

FOR SOME REASON, THIS VOLUME INVOLVED LOTS OF FOOD, AND A SORT OF VAMPIRIC DINING GUIDE. NO ONE IN THE MAIN CAST SEEMS TO GO HUNGRY! I'M NOT TERRIBLY PICKY ABOUT WHAT I EAT, SO I RATHER ENJOY DRAWING JUST ABOUT ANY KIND OF FOOD.

FOOD IS IMPORTANT. MY MEALS HAVE BEEN VERY IRREGULAR OF LATE, TO MY SHAME. I'VE ONLY RECENTLY STARTED COOKING DINNER AGAIN. IT TASTES SO MUCH BETTER WHEN YOU MAKE IT YOURSELF. RELIEVED, I TRIED MY HAND AT A LUNCH BOX. I ADVISE KEEPING IT SIMPLE. IF I CAN, I'D LIKE TO START MAKING BREAKFAST AS WELL. IT SHOULD HELP KEEP ME HEALTHY.

...AS THE STORY GETS MORE AND MORE CONFUSING, I HOPE YOU'LL JOIN ME FOR VOLUME FOUR.
-YURI KIMURA

RECORD OF A FALLEN VAMPIRE 3

SPECIAL THANKS

MARUKO ASAGATANI

AIKO HIYAMA

•

KASUMI AKIRA

•

RESEARCH ASSISTANCE: K, Y

(THANK YOU SO MUCH)

•

EDITOR: NOBUAKI YUMURA

AND THANKS TO ALL MY READERS.

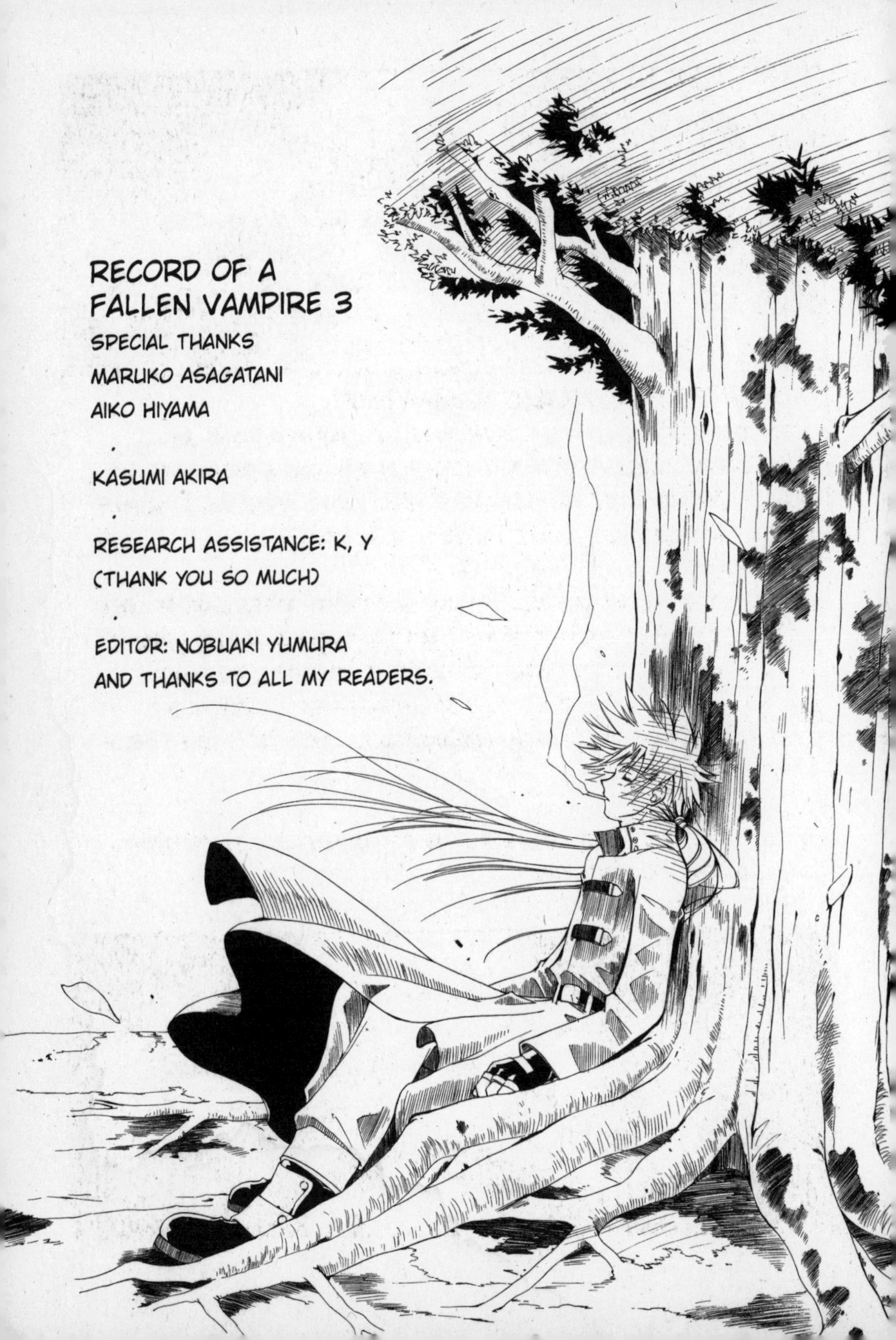

AUTHOR'S AFTERWORD

YOU'VE ALL SEEN OPTICAL ILLUSIONS, I'M SURE.

FOR INSTANCE, WHAT LOOKS LIKE A PICTURE OF A VASE CAN ALSO APPEAR TO BE TWO FACES LOOKING AT EACH OTHER, WHAT LOOKS LIKE A RABBIT CAN ALSO LOOK LIKE A DUCK, WHAT LOOKS LIKE A YOUNG WOMAN CAN ALSO BE SEEN AS AN OLD HAG. THEY'RE ALL IMAGES THAT CAN LOOK LIKE DIFFERENT THINGS DEPENDING ON HOW YOU VIEW THEM. THERE ARE MANY MORE EXAMPLES, AND THESE ARE NOT ONLY FASCINAT-ING, THEY ALSO POINT OUT JUST HOW STRANGE AND UNCERTAIN HUMAN PERCEPTION CAN BE.

THERE'S A BRITISH MYSTERY WRITER NAMED CHRISTIANNA BRAND. HER MOST FAMOUS BOOKS ARE *DEATH OF JEZEBEL, GREEN FOR DANGER, TOUR DE FORCE,* AND THE SHORT STORY "BUFFET FOR UNWELCOME GUESTS."

IN HER BOOKS THERE ARE ALMOST ALWAYS A NUMBER OF SUSPECTS, AND EACH IS IDENTIFIED AS THE KILLER AT LEAST ONCE, FOR THE SAME CRIME, FROM THE SAME CLUES, AND BY AN EXTREMELY LOGICAL SERIES OF DEDUCTIONS. THIS IS ESPECIALLY TRUE IN *DEATH OF JEZEBEL,* WHERE ALL THE SUSPECTS ABRUPTLY BEGIN TO CONFESS TO THE CRIME. (THIS IS ABOUT 70 PAGES FROM THE END OF THE BOOK AND HAPPENS OVER THE COURSE OF A FEW DOZEN PAGES. OF COURSE, THERE WAS ONLY ONE KILLER.)

THE SAME CLUES, THE SAME EVIDENCE, BUT EACH TIME SEEN FROM A SLIGHTLY DIFFERENT PERSPECTIVE. HER WORKS TAUGHT ME THAT THE SAME WITNESS TESTIMONIES, SEEN FROM SLIGHTLY DIFFERENT POINTS OF VIEW, CAN COMPLETELY CHANGE THE SHAPE OF THE CASE.

AT ANY RATE, I AM KYO SHIRODAIRA, AND THIS IS VOLUME 3.

IN THIS VOLUME WE GET TO SEE THE TRUTH OF THE PAST FROM BRIDGET'S POINT OF VIEW, BASED ON HER EXPERIENCE OF IT.

BUT THAT IS ONLY THE TRUTH AS SHE KNOWS IT. LIKE AN OPTICAL ILLUSION, LIKE BRAND'S WORKS, THE SAME FACTS (NAMELY, THAT THE VAMPIRE KING ABANDONED HIS KINGDOM AND PEOPLE, SEARCHING FOR THE SEAL AND HIS QUEEN) SHAPE UP INTO A VERY DIFFERENT STORY WHEN RELATED FROM A DIFFERENT PERSPECTIVE. WHAT DID THINGS LOOK LIKE TO THE OTHER PEOPLE INVOLVED BACK THEN—TO ADELHEID, STELLA, AND STRAUSS HIMSELF?

IN THE NEXT VOLUME, AS THE PROBLEM OF WHAT EXACTLY HAPPENED BACK IN THE DAY TAKES FORM, THE INVADERS FROM SPACE WILL SHOW THEMSELVES, ADDING A KEY FACTOR TO THE QUESTION OF WHAT WILL HAPPEN NEXT.

THE STORY IS BEGINNING TO SHIFT DRAMATICALLY. WHERE WILL IT END UP? REALLY, WHERE?

I PRAY WE WILL MEET AGAIN IN VOLUME 4.

- KYO SHIRODAIRA

THE RECORD OF A FALLEN VAMPIRE

VOL. 3
VIZ MEDIA EDITION

STORY BY: **KYO SHIRODAIRA**   ART BY: **YURI KIMURA**

Translation & Adaptation...**Andrew Cunningham**
Touch-up Art & Lettering...**John Hunt**
Cover Design...**Courtney Utt**
Interior Design...**Izumi Hirayama**
Editor...**Gary Leach**

Editor in Chief, Books...**Alvin Lu**
Editor in Chief, Magazines...**Marc Weidenbaum**
VP of Publishing Licensing...**Rika Inouye**
VP of Sales...**Gonzalo Ferreyra**
Sr. VP of Marketing...**Liza Coppola**
Publisher...**Hyoe Narita**

VAMPIRE JYUJIKAI vol.3 © 2004 Kyo Shirodaira, Yuri Kimura/
SQUARE ENIX. All rights reserved. First published in Japan in 2004
by SQUARE ENIX CO., LTD. English translation rights arranged with
SQUARE ENIX CO., LTD. and VIZ Media, LLC.

Printed in the U.S.A.

Published by VIZ Media, LLC
P.O. Box 77010
San Francisco, CA 94107

10 9 8 7 6 5 4 3 2 1
First printing, November 2008

store.viz.com